D1544671

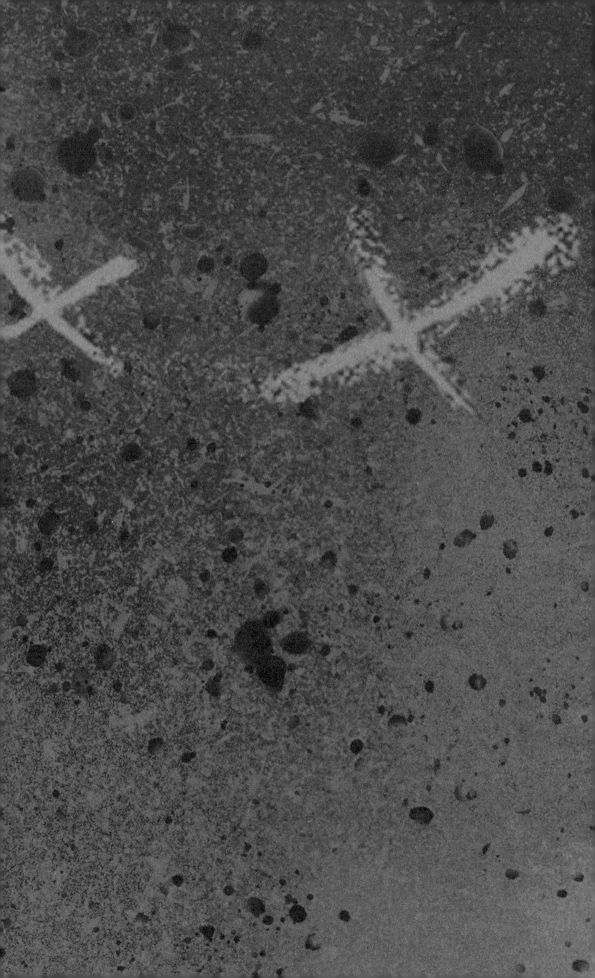

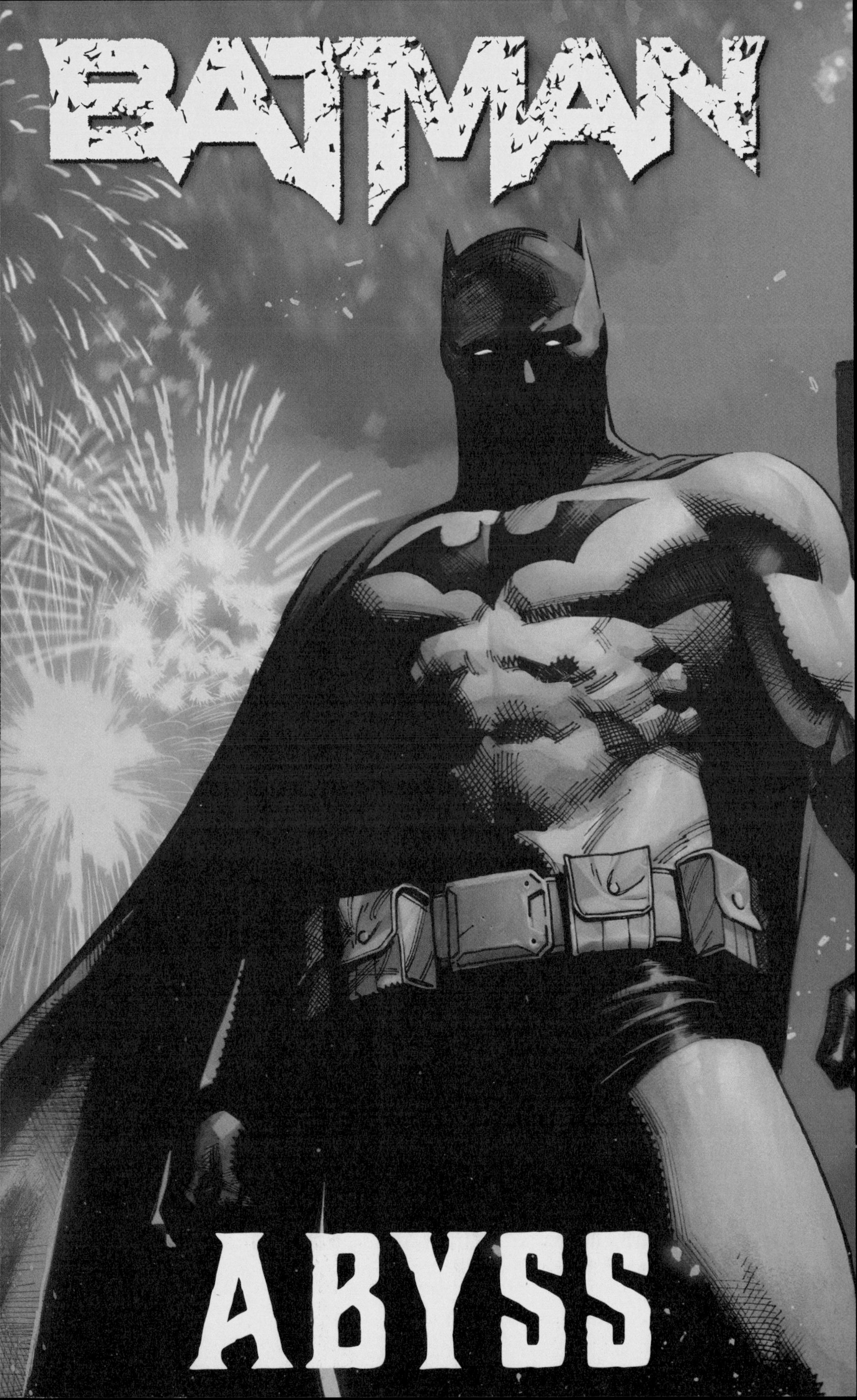
BATMAN
ABYSS

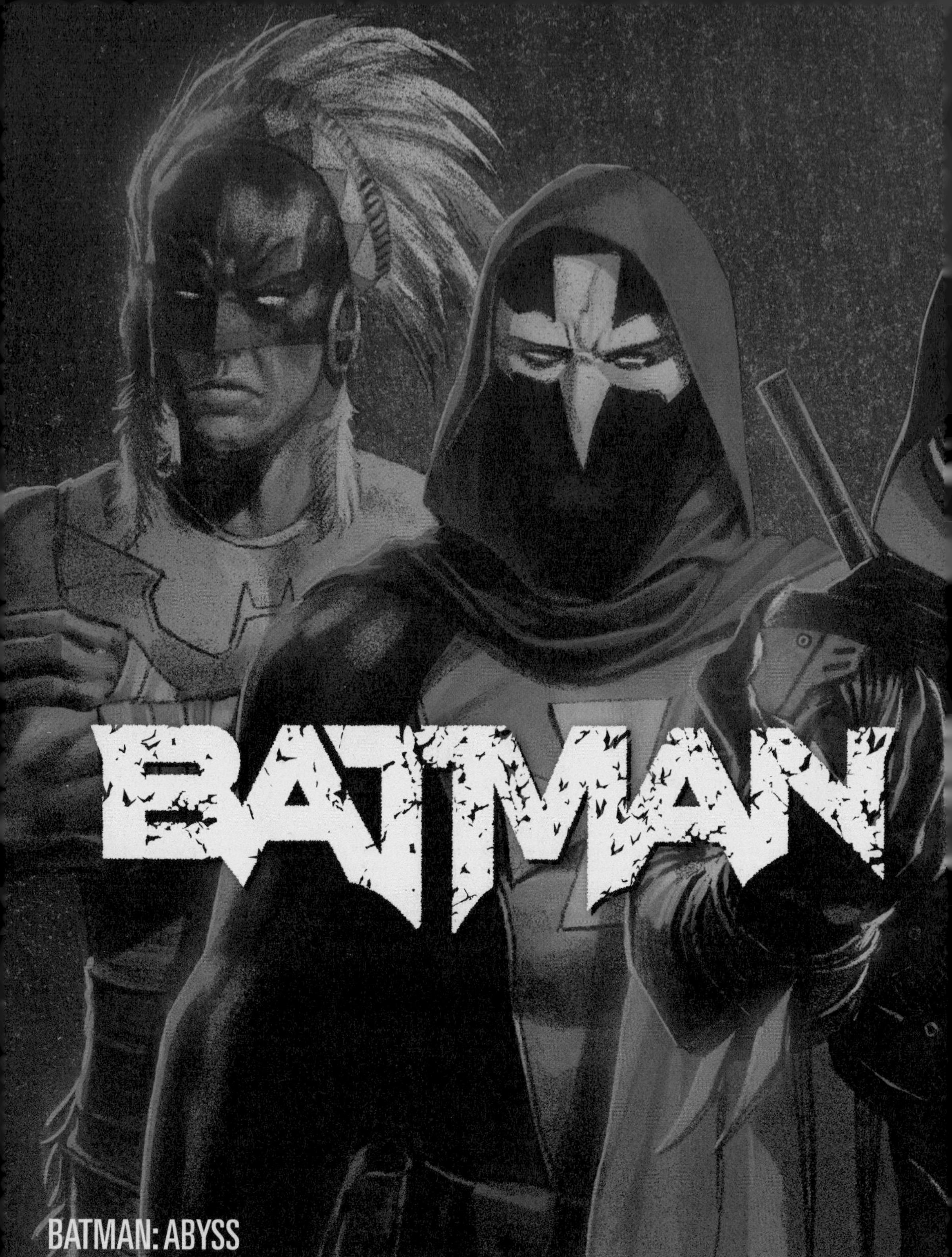
BATMAN

BATMAN: ABYSS

WRITER	ARTISTS	COLORIST	LETTERER
JOSHUA WILLIAMSON	JORGE MOLINA, MIKEL JANÍN & HOWARD PORTER, JORGE FORNÉS	TOMEU MOREY	CLAYTON COWLES

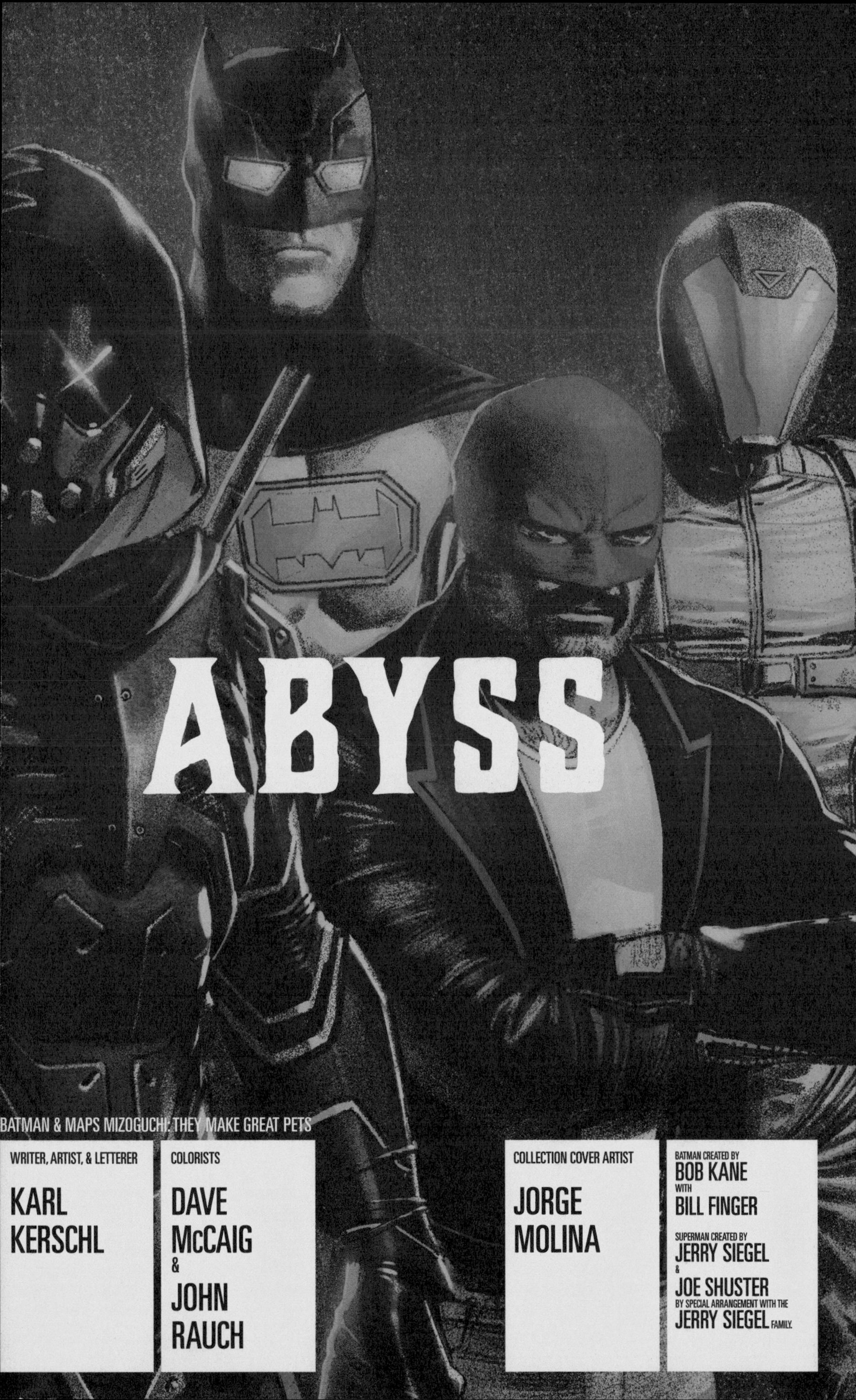

ABYSS

BATMAN & MAPS MIZOGUCHI: THEY MAKE GREAT PETS

WRITER, ARTIST, & LETTERER
KARL KERSCHL

COLORISTS
DAVE McCAIG
&
JOHN RAUCH

COLLECTION COVER ARTIST
JORGE MOLINA

BATMAN CREATED BY
BOB KANE
WITH
BILL FINGER

SUPERMAN CREATED BY
JERRY SIEGEL
&
JOE SHUSTER
BY SPECIAL ARRANGEMENT WITH THE
JERRY SIEGEL FAMILY.

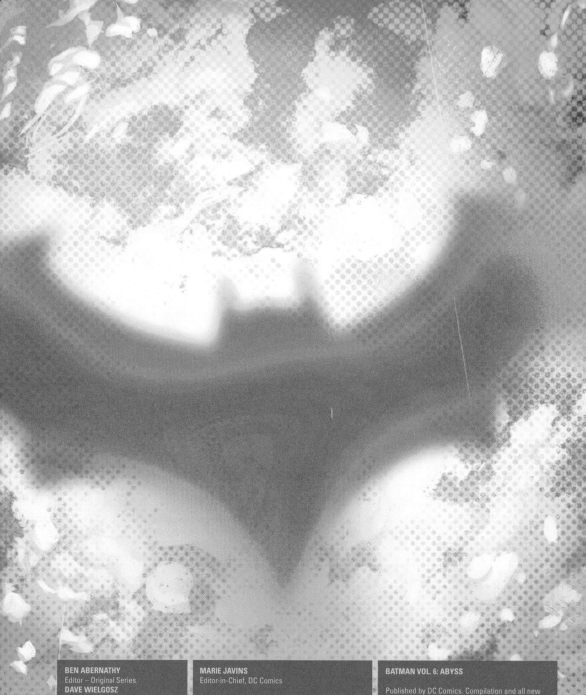

BEN ABERNATHY
Editor – Original Series
DAVE WIELGOSZ
Editor – Collected Edition &
Associate Editor – Original Series

STEVE COOK
Design Director – Books
AMIE BROCKWAY-METCALF
Publication Design
DANIELLE RAMONDELLI
Publication Production

MARIE JAVINS
Editor-in-Chief, DC Comics

ANNE DePIES
Senior VP – General Manager
JIM LEE
Publisher & Chief Creative Officer
DON FALLETTI
VP – Manufacturing Operations
& Workflow Management
LAWRENCE GANEM
VP – Talent Services
ALISON GILL
Senior VP – Manufacturing & Operations
JEFFREY KAUFMAN
VP – Editorial Strategy & Programming
NICK J. NAPOLITANO
VP – Manufacturing Administration & Design
NANCY SPEARS
VP – Revenue

BATMAN VOL. 6: ABYSS

Published by DC Comics. Compilation and all new
material Copyright © 2022 DC Comics. All Rights
Reserved. Originally published in single magazine
form in Batman 118-121, 124. Copyright © 2021, 2022
DC Comics. All Rights Reserved. All characters,
their distinctive likenesses, and related elements
featured in this publication are trademarks of DC
Comics. The stories, characters, and incidents
featured in this publication are entirely fictional.
DC Comics does not read or accept unsolicited
submissions of ideas, stories, or artwork.

DC Comics,
2900 West Alameda Ave., Burbank, CA 91505
Printed by Transcontinental Interglobe,
Beauceville, QC, Canada. 6/24/22. First Printing.
ISBN: 978-1-77951-656-5

Library of Congress Cataloging-in-Publication Data
is available.

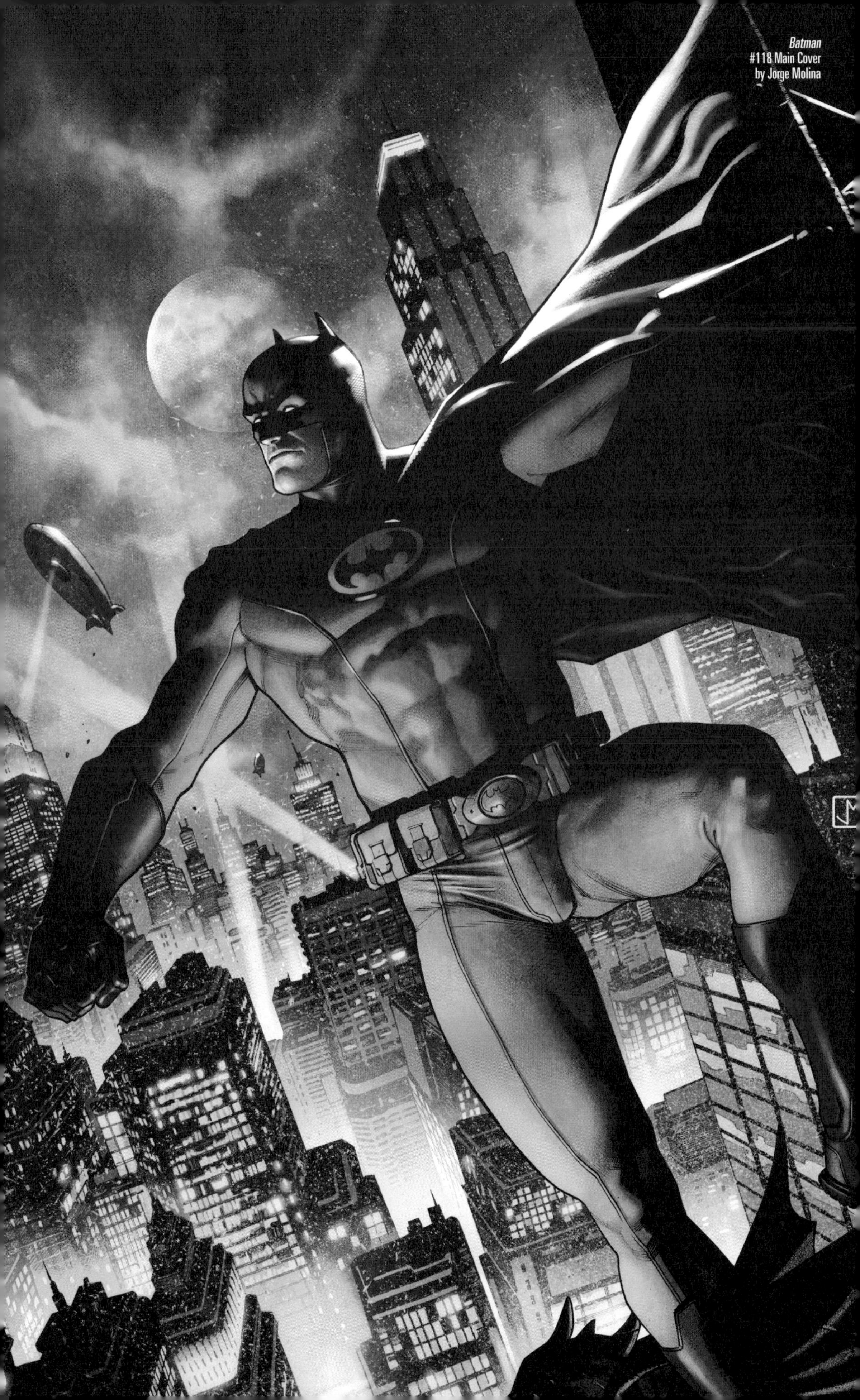

Batman
#118 Main Cover
by Jorge Molina

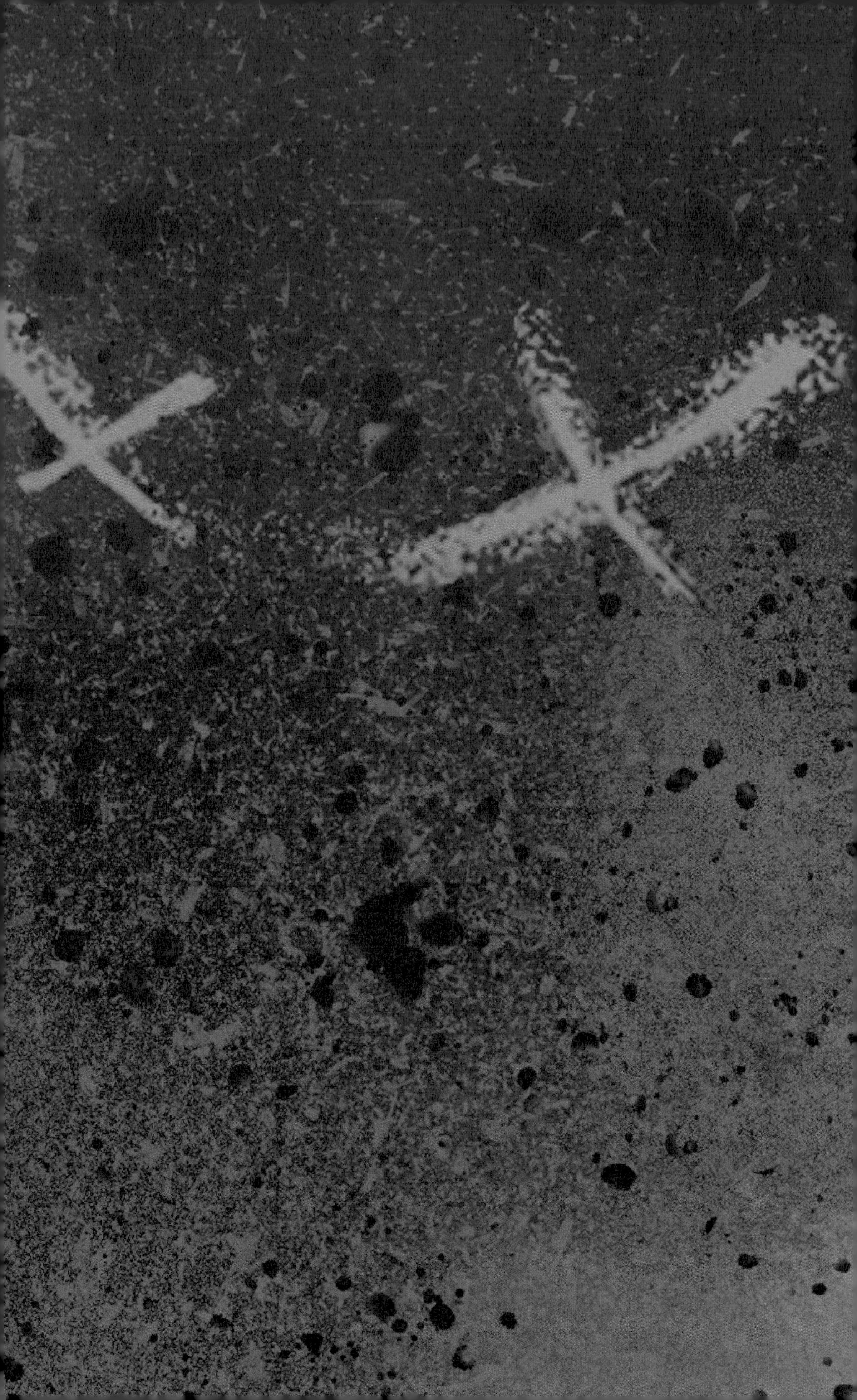

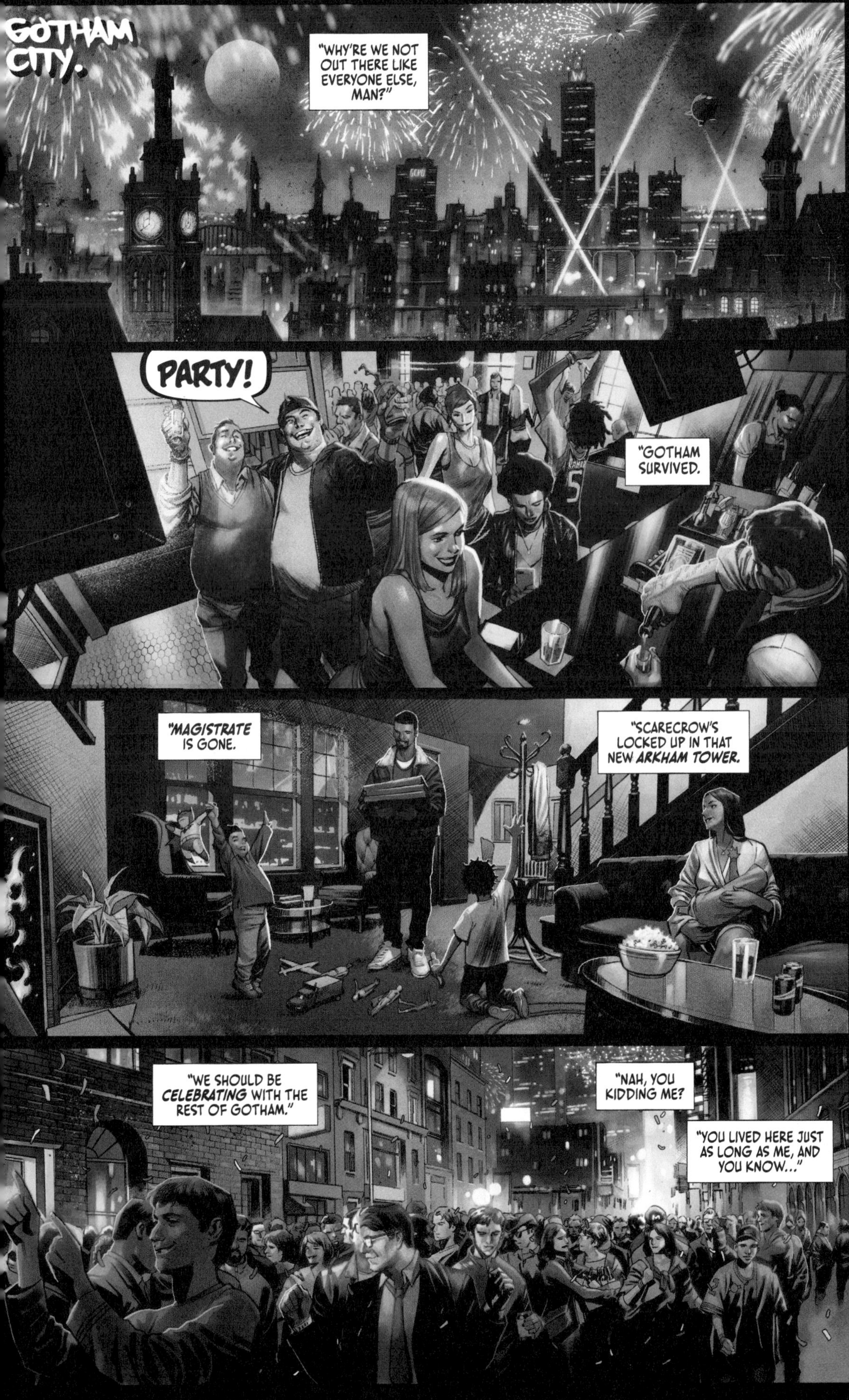
GOTHAM CITY.
"WHY'RE WE NOT OUT THERE LIKE EVERYONE ELSE, MAN?"
PARTY!
"GOTHAM SURVIVED.
"MAGISTRATE IS GONE.
"SCARECROW'S LOCKED UP IN THAT NEW ARKHAM TOWER.
"WE SHOULD BE CELEBRATING WITH THE REST OF GOTHAM."
"NAH, YOU KIDDING ME?
"YOU LIVED HERE JUST AS LONG AS ME, AND YOU KNOW..."

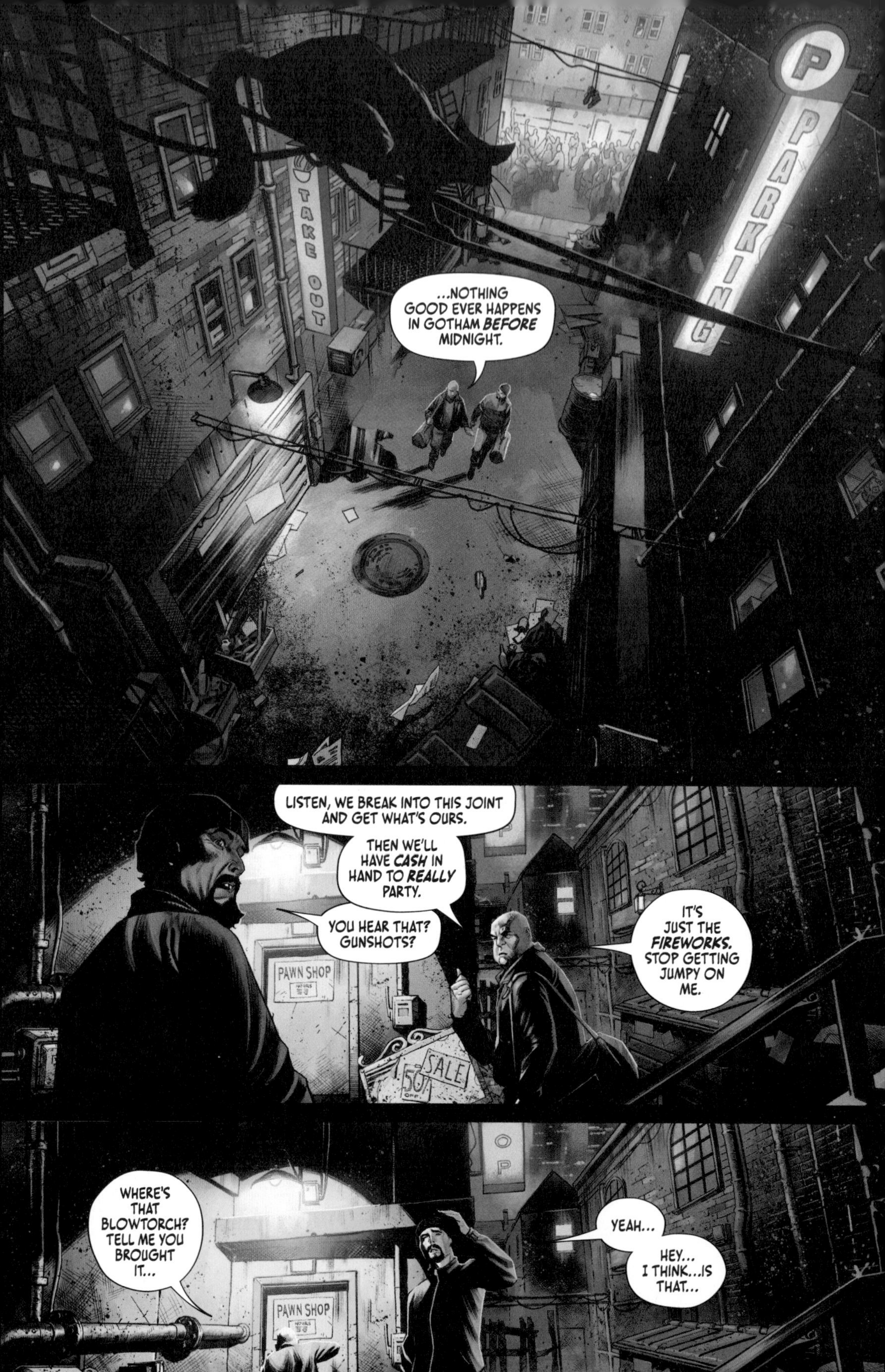

TAKE OUT
PARKING
...NOTHING GOOD EVER HAPPENS IN GOTHAM BEFORE MIDNIGHT.
LISTEN, WE BREAK INTO THIS JOINT AND GET WHAT'S OURS.
THEN WE'LL HAVE CASH IN HAND TO REALLY PARTY.
YOU HEAR THAT? GUNSHOTS?
PAWN SHOP
SALE
50% OFF
IT'S JUST THE FIREWORKS. STOP GETTING JUMPY ON ME.
WHERE'S THAT BLOWTORCH? TELL ME YOU BROUGHT IT...
PAWN SHOP
YEAH...
HEY... I THINK...IS THAT...

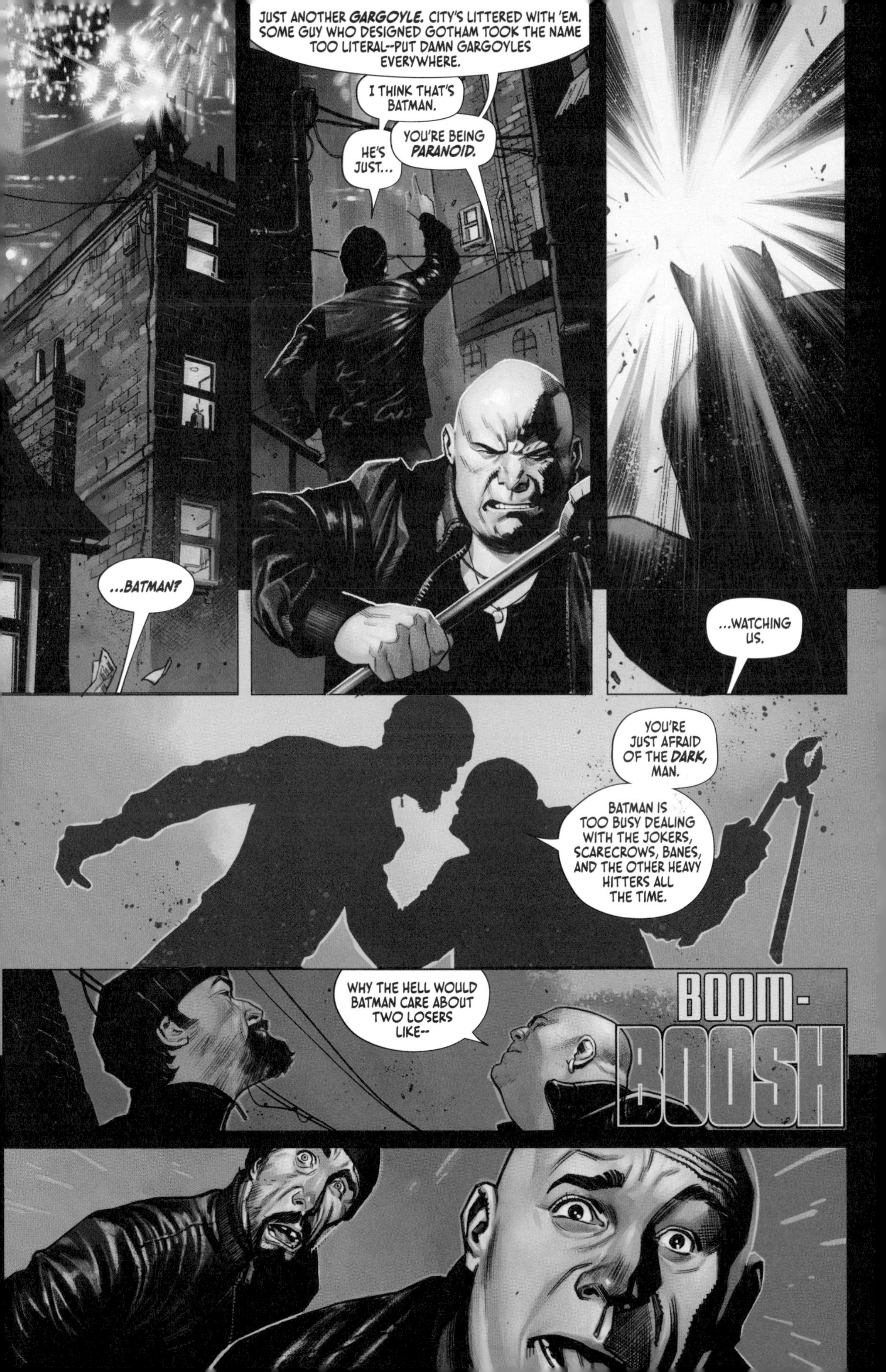
JUST ANOTHER GARGOYLE. CITY'S LITTERED WITH 'EM. SOME GUY WHO DESIGNED GOTHAM TOOK THE NAME TOO LITERAL--PUT DAMN GARGOYLES EVERYWHERE.
I THINK THAT'S BATMAN.
HE'S JUST...
YOU'RE BEING PARANOID.
...BATMAN?
...WATCHING US.
YOU'RE JUST AFRAID OF THE DARK, MAN.
BATMAN IS TOO BUSY DEALING WITH THE JOKERS, SCARECROWS, BANES, AND THE OTHER HEAVY HITTERS ALL THE TIME.
WHY THE HELL WOULD BATMAN CARE ABOUT TWO LOSERS LIKE--
BOOM-
BOOSH

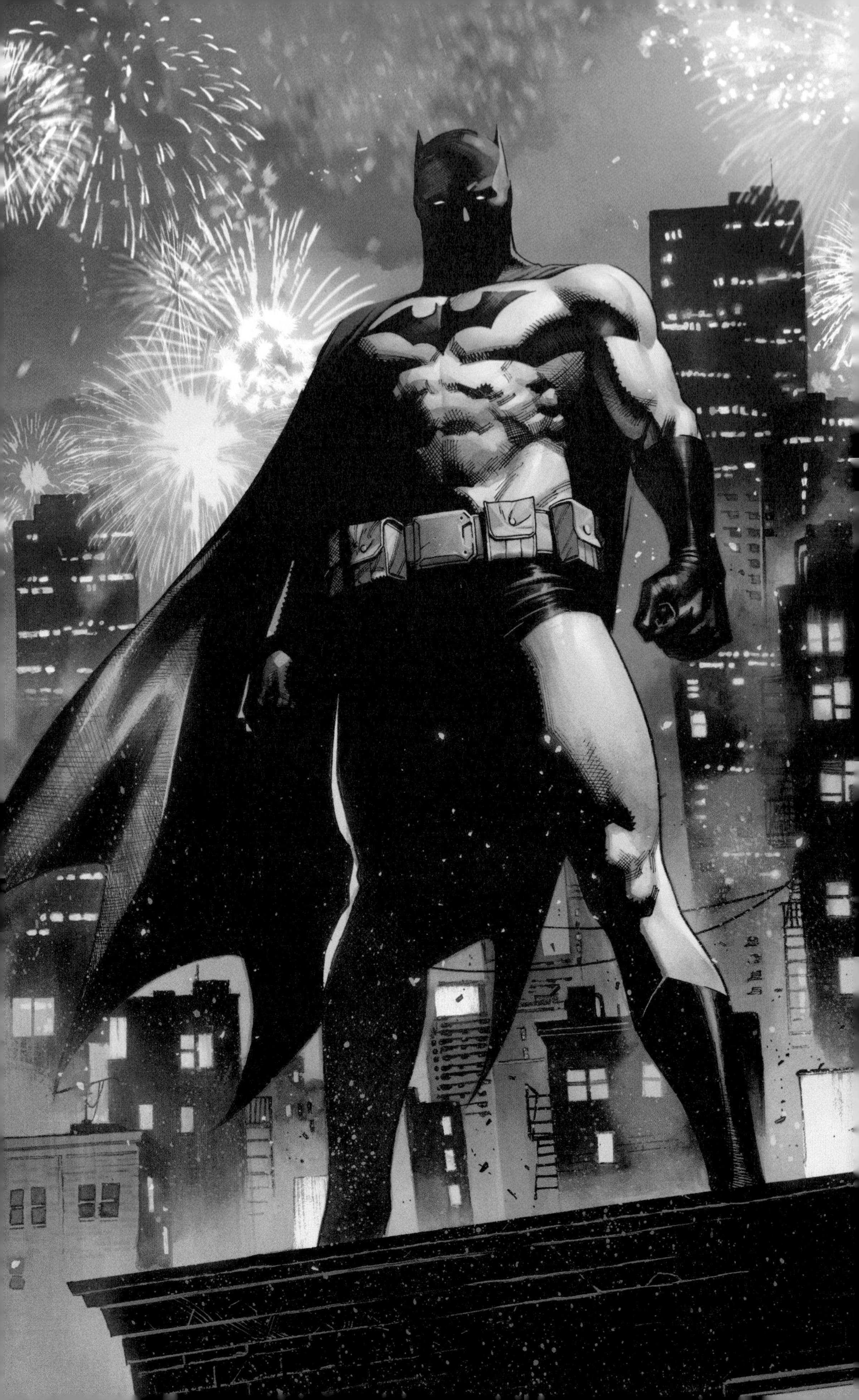

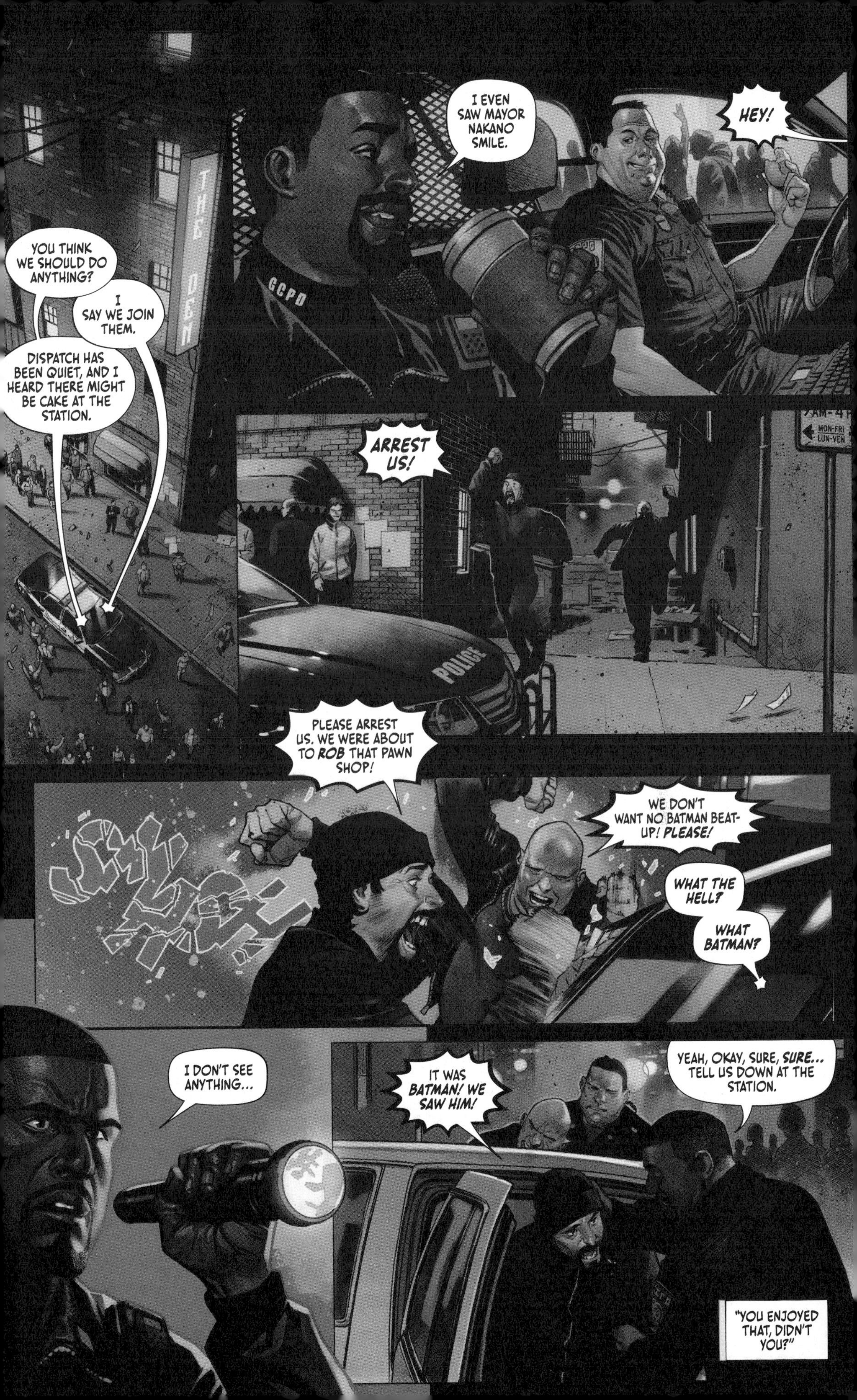
I EVEN SAW MAYOR NAKANO SMILE.
HEY!
GCPD
THE DEN
YOU THINK WE SHOULD DO ANYTHING?
I SAY WE JOIN THEM.
DISPATCH HAS BEEN QUIET, AND I HEARD THERE MIGHT BE CAKE AT THE STATION.
ARREST US!
MON-FRI LUN-VEN
POLICE
PLEASE ARREST US. WE WERE ABOUT TO ROB THAT PAWN SHOP!
WE DON'T WANT NO BATMAN BEAT-UP! PLEASE!
WHAT THE HELL?
WHAT BATMAN?
I DON'T SEE ANYTHING...
IT WAS BATMAN! WE SAW HIM!
YEAH, OKAY, SURE, SURE... TELL US DOWN AT THE STATION.
"YOU ENJOYED THAT, DIDN'T YOU?"

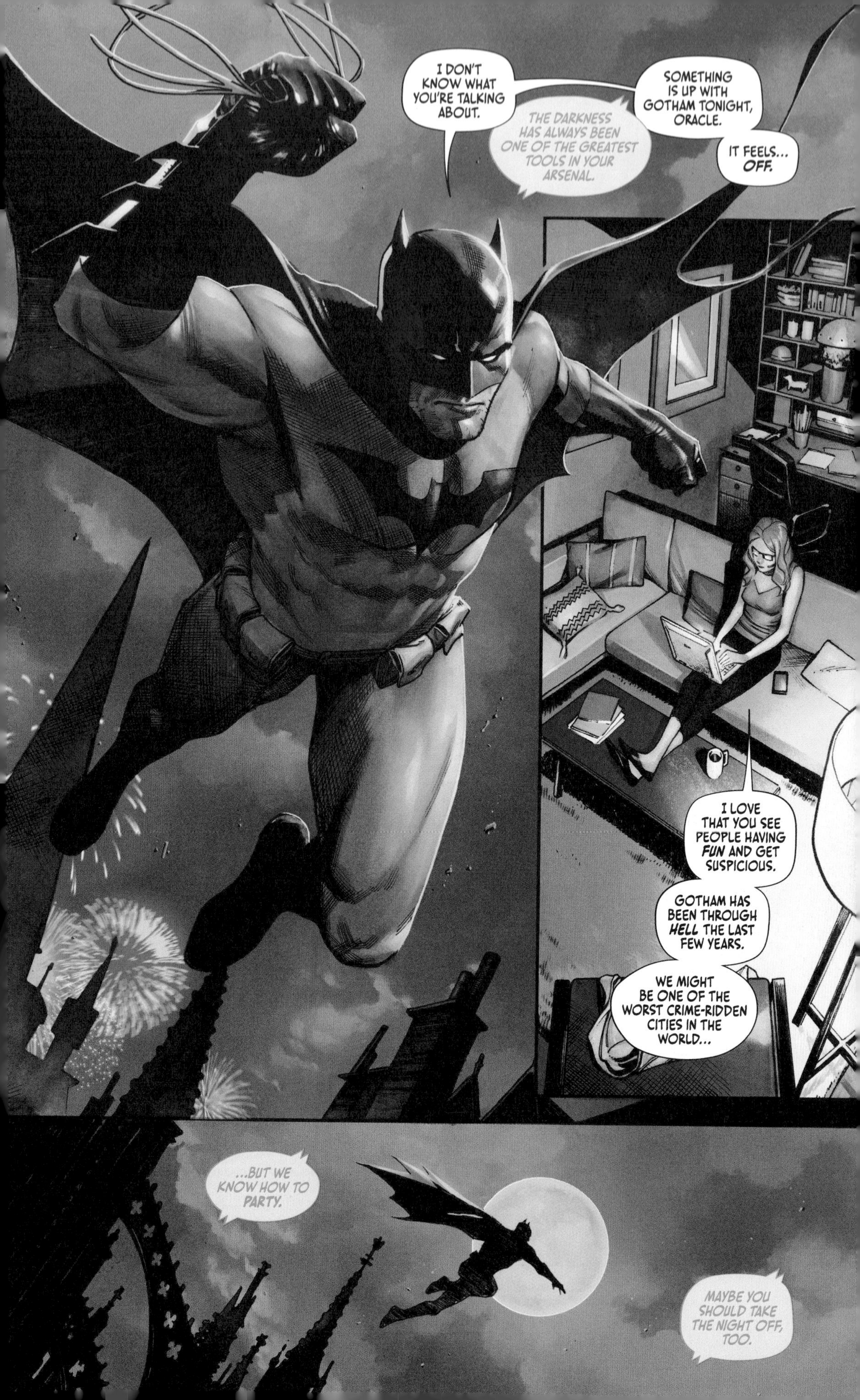

SOMETHING IS UP WITH GOTHAM TONIGHT, ORACLE.
IT FEELS... OFF.
I DON'T KNOW WHAT YOU'RE TALKING ABOUT.
THE DARKNESS HAS ALWAYS BEEN ONE OF THE GREATEST TOOLS IN YOUR ARSENAL.
I LOVE THAT YOU SEE PEOPLE HAVING FUN AND GET SUSPICIOUS.
GOTHAM HAS BEEN THROUGH HELL THE LAST FEW YEARS.
WE MIGHT BE ONE OF THE WORST CRIME-RIDDEN CITIES IN THE WORLD...
...BUT WE KNOW HOW TO PARTY.
MAYBE YOU SHOULD TAKE THE NIGHT OFF, TOO.

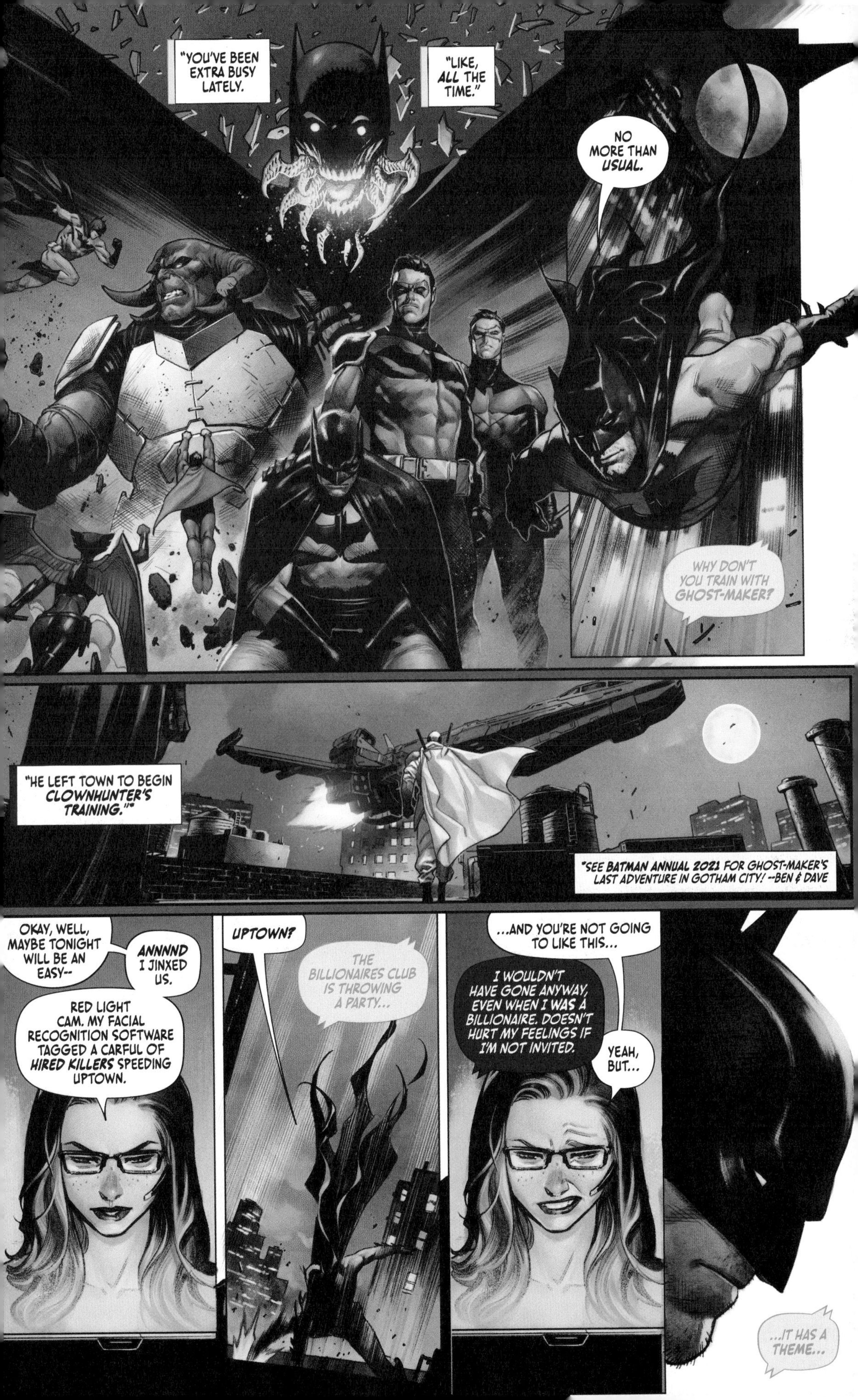
"YOU'VE BEEN EXTRA BUSY LATELY.
"LIKE, ALL THE TIME."
NO MORE THAN USUAL.
WHY DON'T YOU TRAIN WITH GHOST-MAKER?
"HE LEFT TOWN TO BEGIN CLOWNHUNTER'S TRAINING."*
*SEE BATMAN ANNUAL 2021 FOR GHOST-MAKER'S LAST ADVENTURE IN GOTHAM CITY! --BEN & DAVE
OKAY, WELL, MAYBE TONIGHT WILL BE AN EASY--
ANNNND I JINXED US.
RED LIGHT CAM. MY FACIAL RECOGNITION SOFTWARE TAGGED A CARFUL OF HIRED KILLERS SPEEDING UPTOWN.
UPTOWN?
THE BILLIONAIRES CLUB IS THROWING A PARTY...
...AND YOU'RE NOT GOING TO LIKE THIS...
I WOULDN'T HAVE GONE ANYWAY, EVEN WHEN I WAS A BILLIONAIRE. DOESN'T HURT MY FEELINGS IF I'M NOT INVITED.
YEAH, BUT...
...IT HAS A THEME...

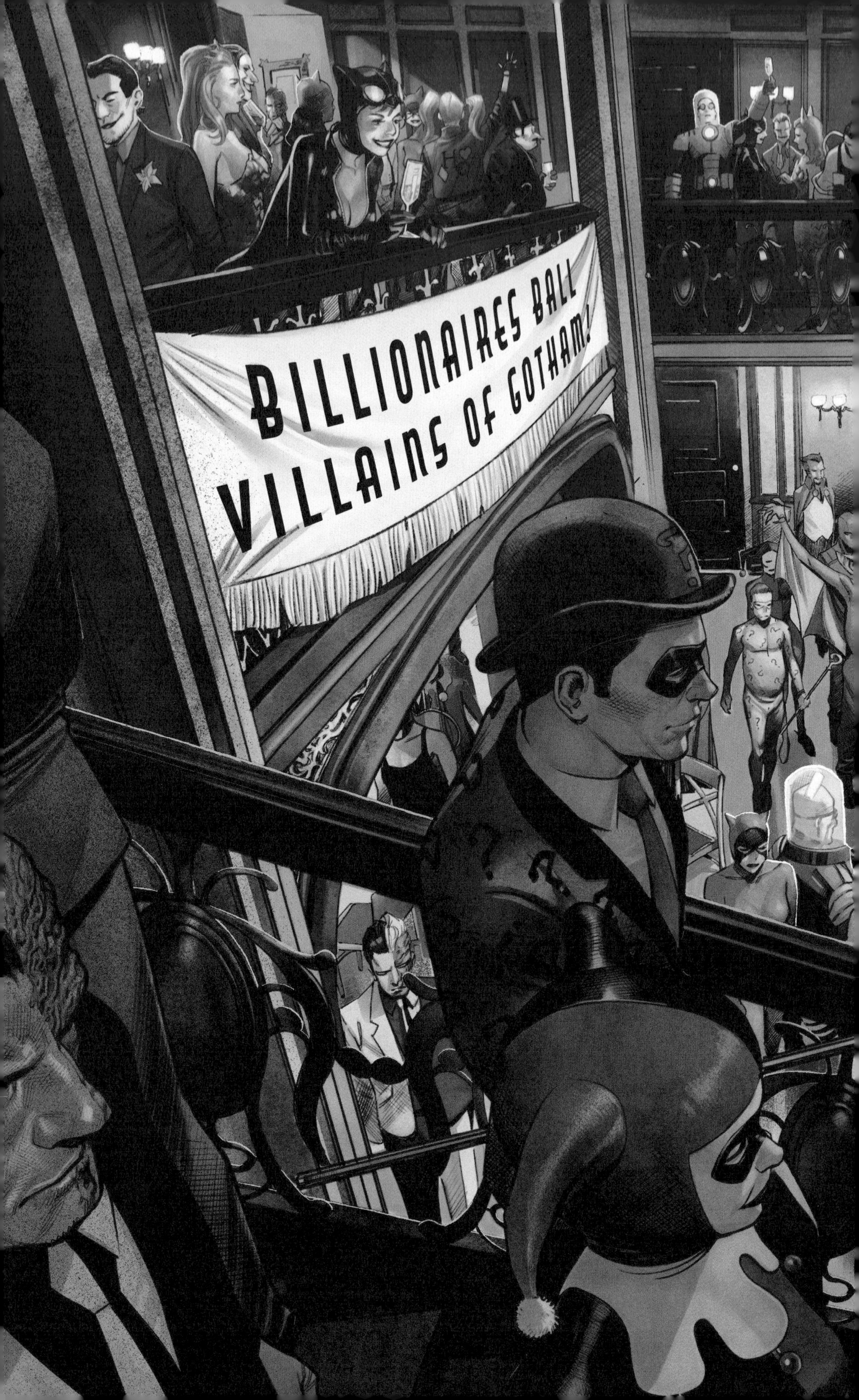
BILLIONAIRES BALL
VILLAINS OF GOTHAM!

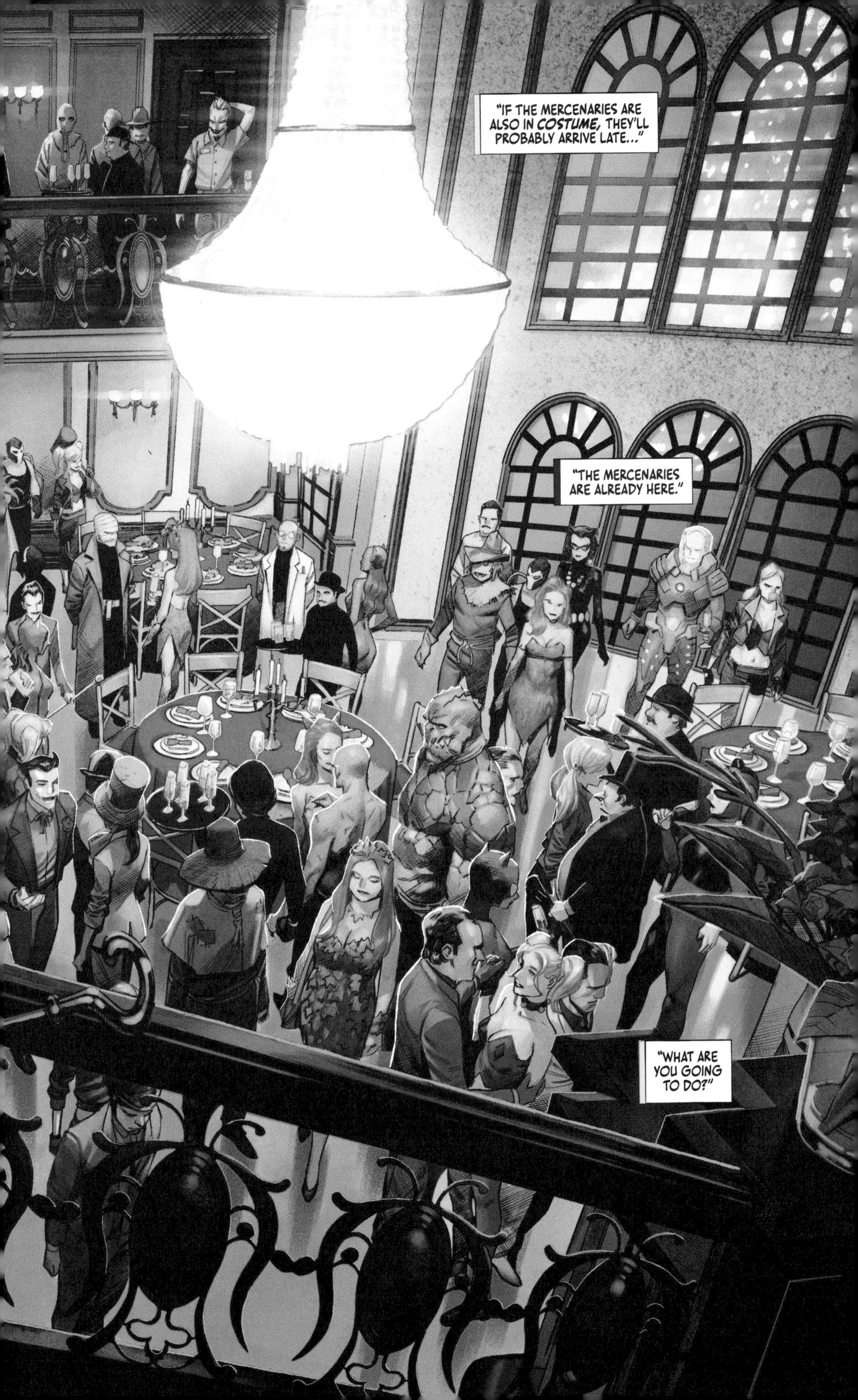
"IF THE MERCENARIES ARE ALSO IN *COSTUME,* THEY'LL PROBABLY ARRIVE LATE..."
"THE MERCENARIES ARE ALREADY HERE."
"WHAT ARE YOU GOING TO DO?"

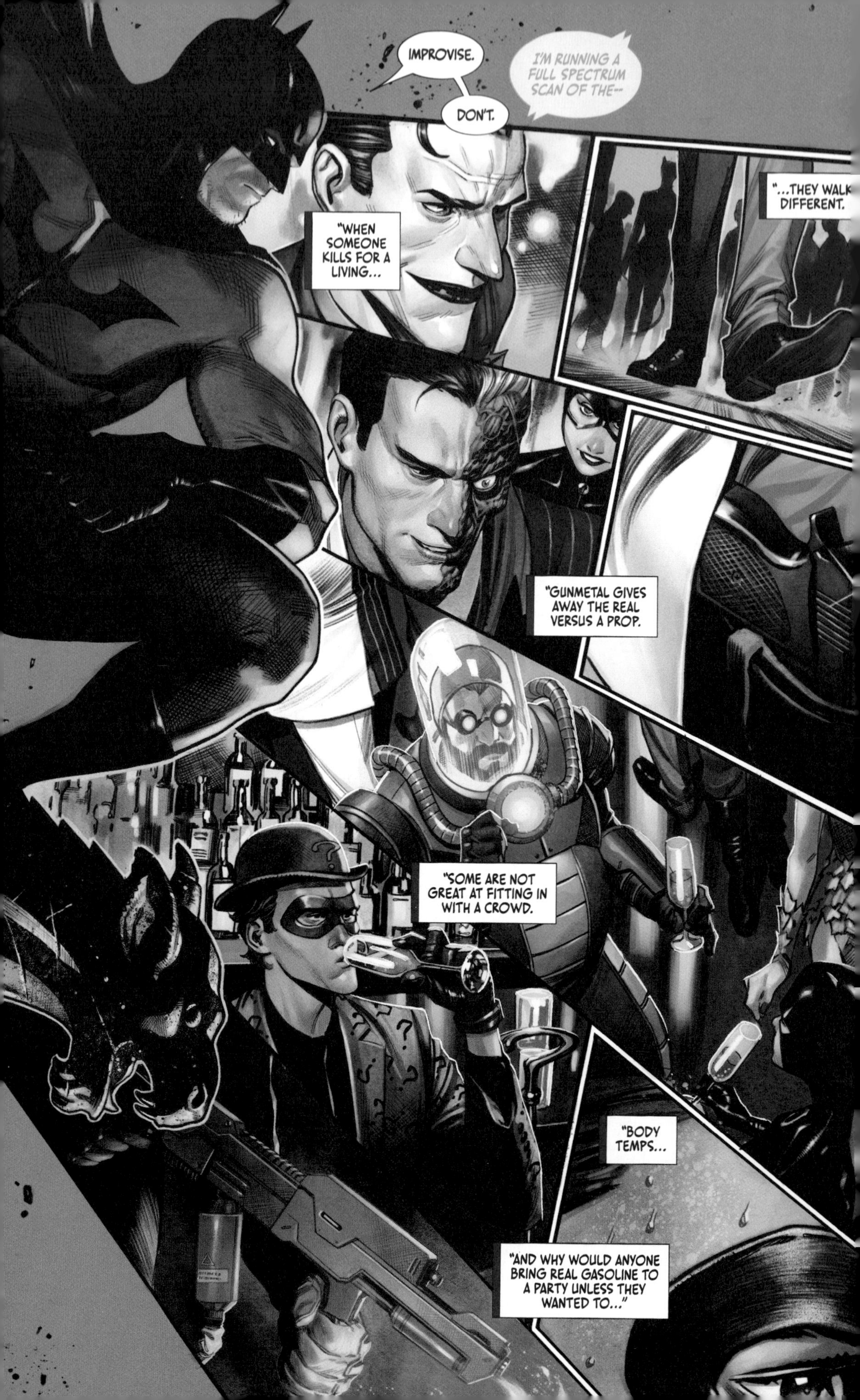
IMPROVISE.
I'M RUNNING A FULL SPECTRUM SCAN OF THE--
DON'T.
"WHEN SOMEONE KILLS FOR A LIVING...
"...THEY WALK DIFFERENT.
"GUNMETAL GIVES AWAY THE REAL VERSUS A PROP.
"SOME ARE NOT GREAT AT FITTING IN WITH A CROWD.
"BODY TEMPS...
"AND WHY WOULD ANYONE BRING REAL GASOLINE TO A PARTY UNLESS THEY WANTED TO..."

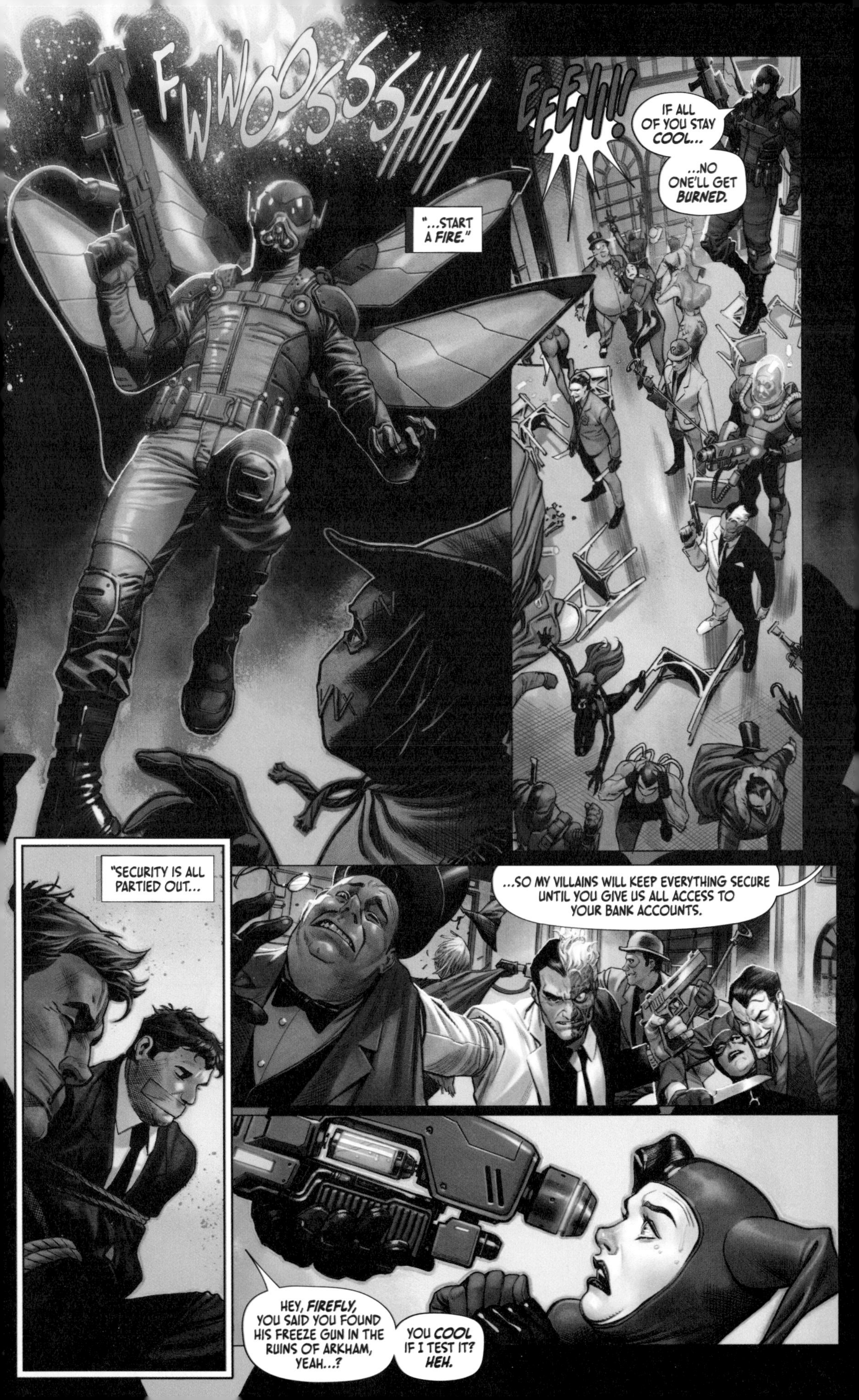
FWWOOSSSHHH
"...START A FIRE."
EEEIIII!!
IF ALL OF YOU STAY COOL...
...NO ONE'LL GET BURNED.
"SECURITY IS ALL PARTIED OUT...
...SO MY VILLAINS WILL KEEP EVERYTHING SECURE UNTIL YOU GIVE US ALL ACCESS TO YOUR BANK ACCOUNTS.
HEY, FIREFLY, YOU SAID YOU FOUND HIS FREEZE GUN IN THE RUINS OF ARKHAM, YEAH...?
YOU COOL IF I TEST IT? HEH.

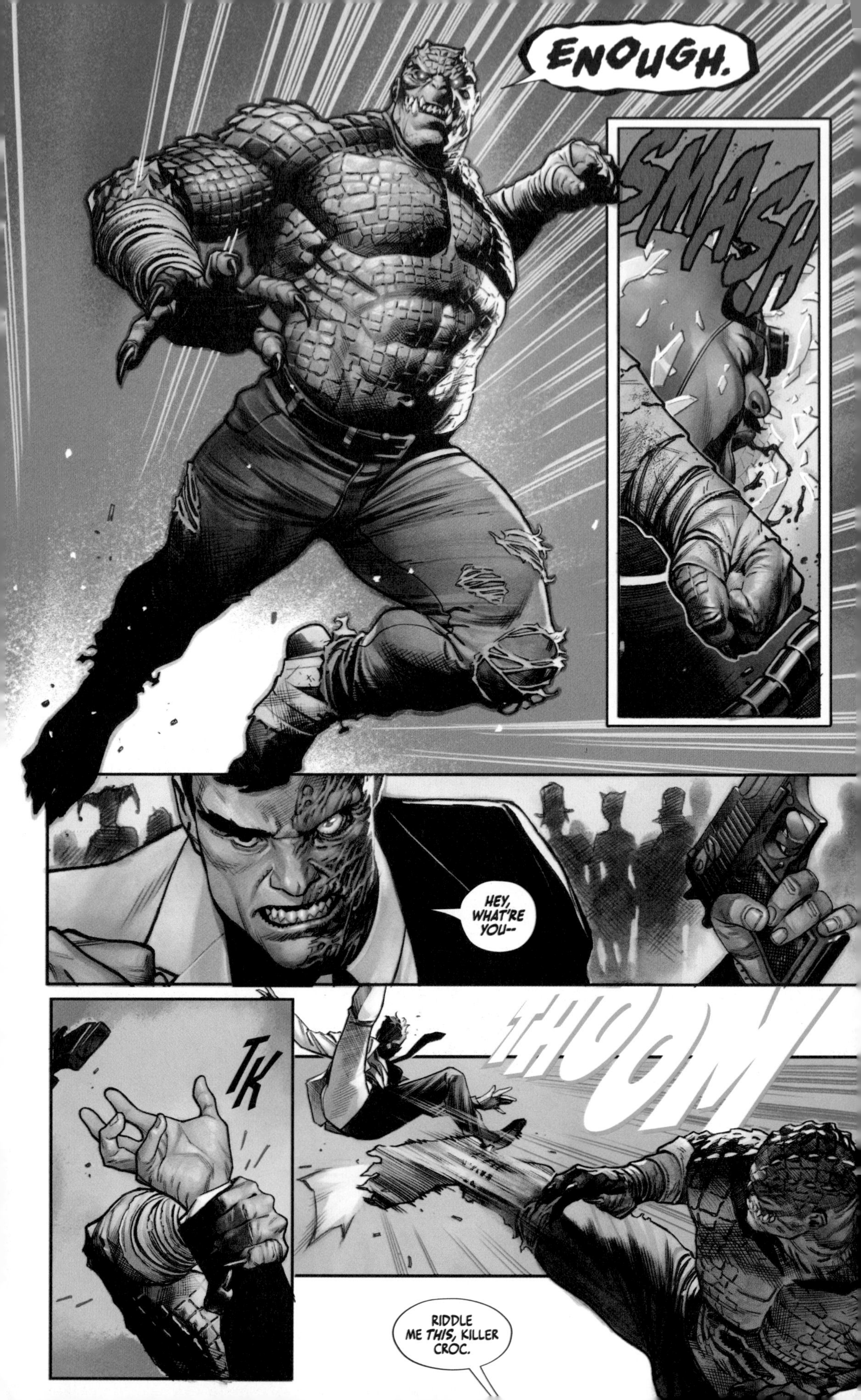
ENOUGH.
SMASH
HEY, WHAT'RE YOU--
TK
THOOOM
RIDDLE ME THIS, KILLER CROC.

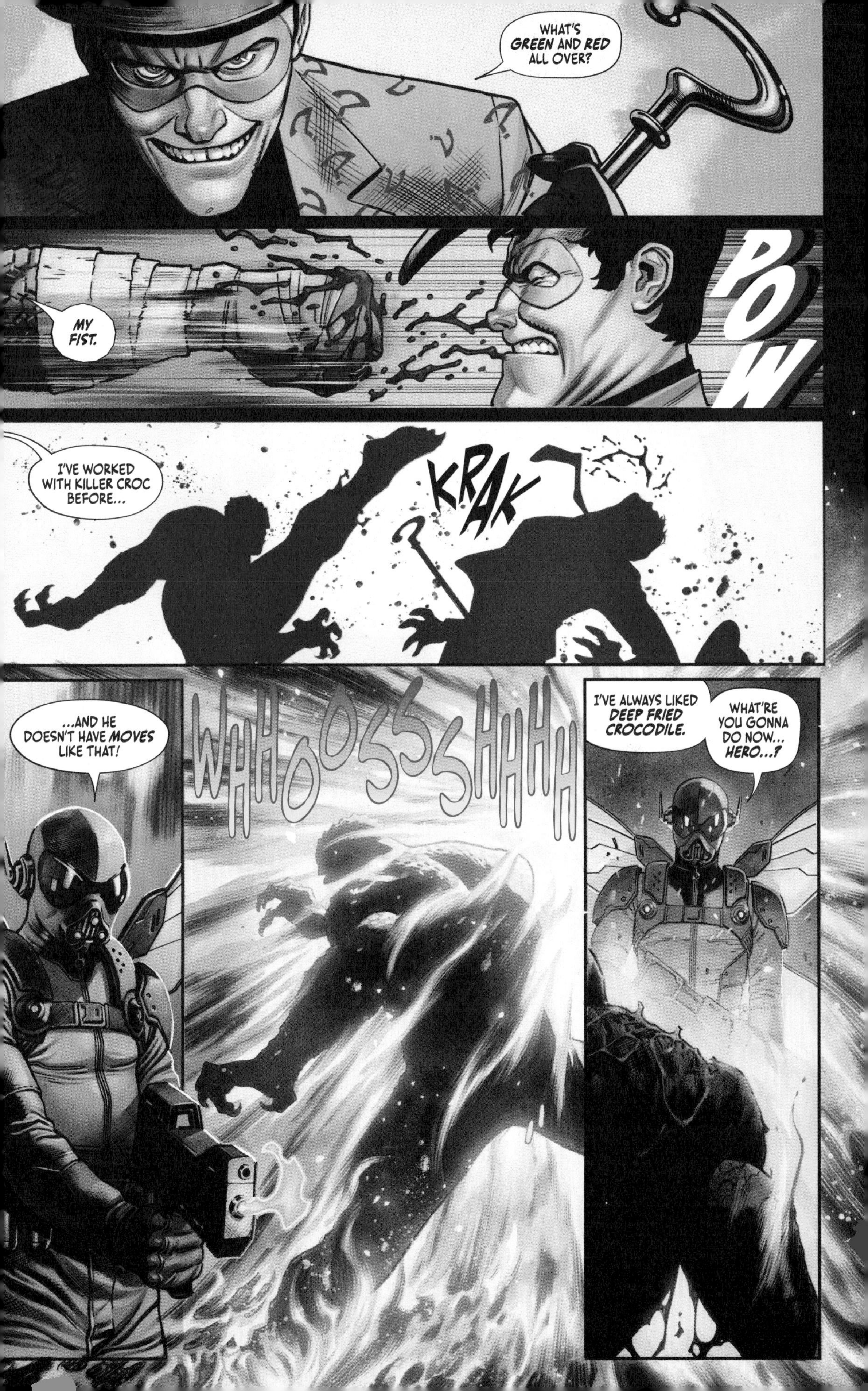
WHAT'S GREEN AND RED ALL OVER?
MY FIST.
POW
I'VE WORKED WITH KILLER CROC BEFORE...
KRAK
...AND HE DOESN'T HAVE MOVES LIKE THAT!
WHHOOSSSHHHH
I'VE ALWAYS LIKED DEEP FRIED CROCODILE.
WHAT'RE YOU GONNA DO NOW... HERO...?

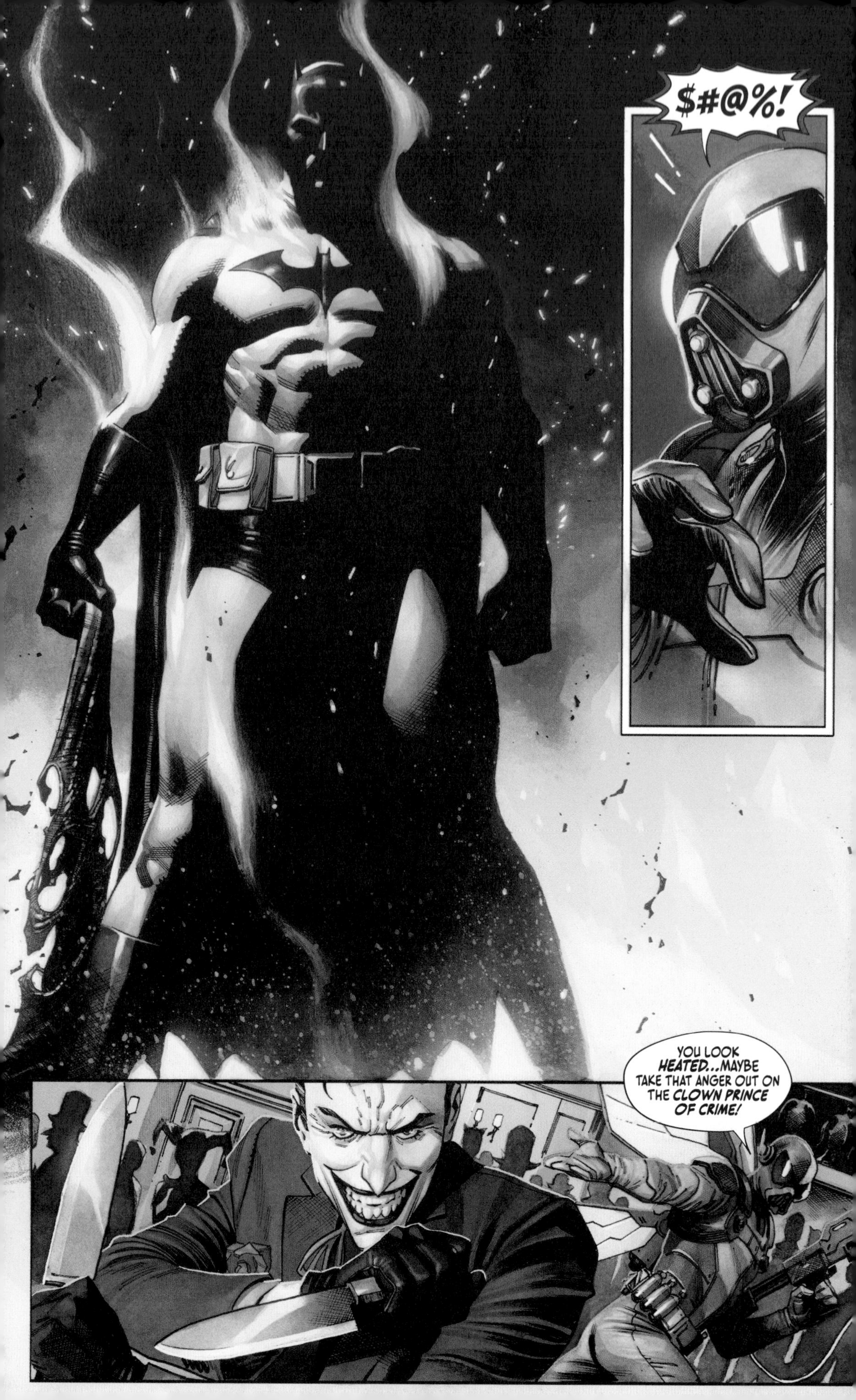
$#@%!
YOU LOOK HEATED...MAYBE TAKE THAT ANGER OUT ON THE CLOWN PRINCE OF CRIME!

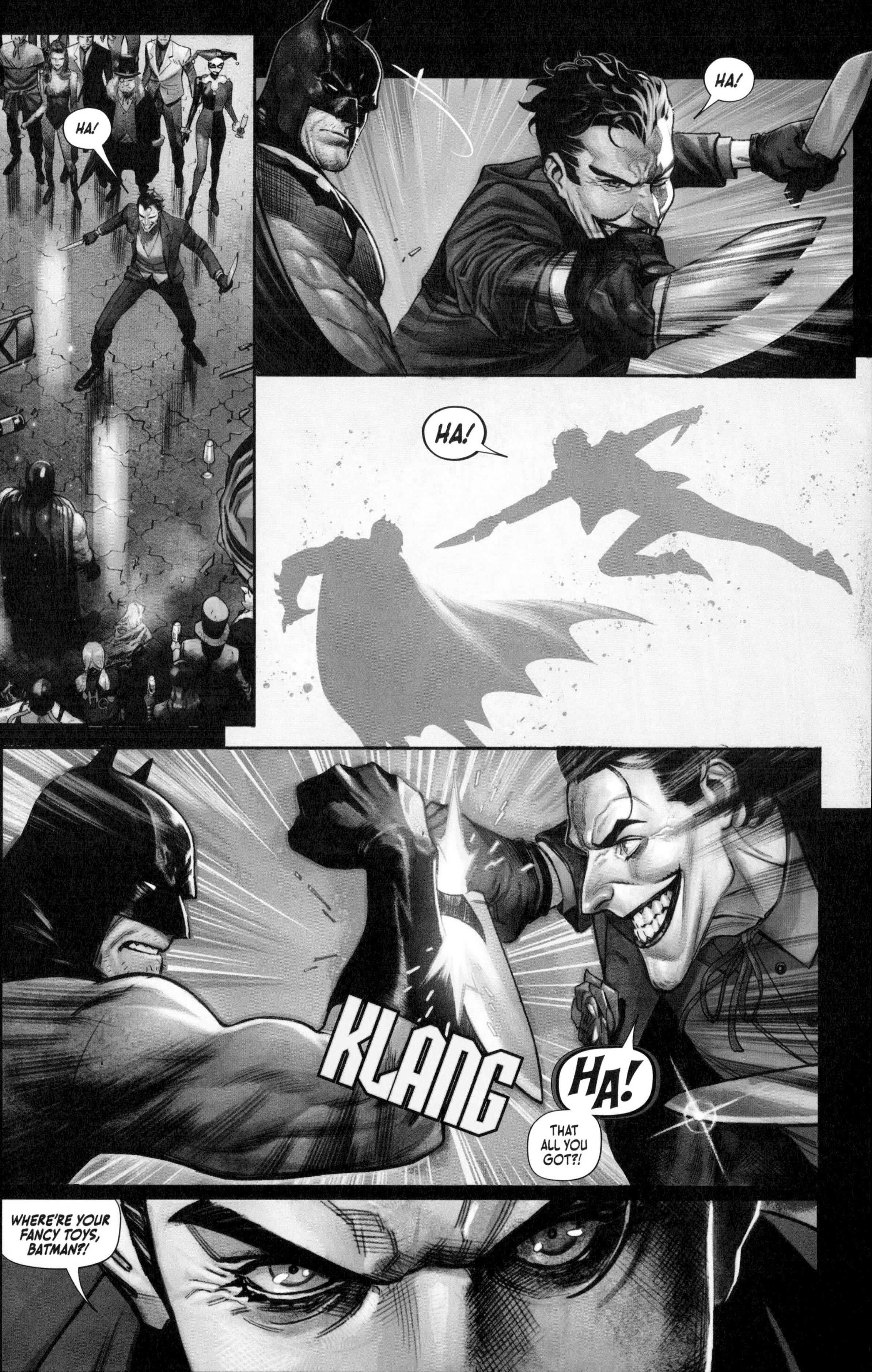
HA!
HA!
HA!
KLANG
HA!
THAT ALL YOU GOT?!
WHERE'RE YOUR FANCY TOYS, BATMAN?!

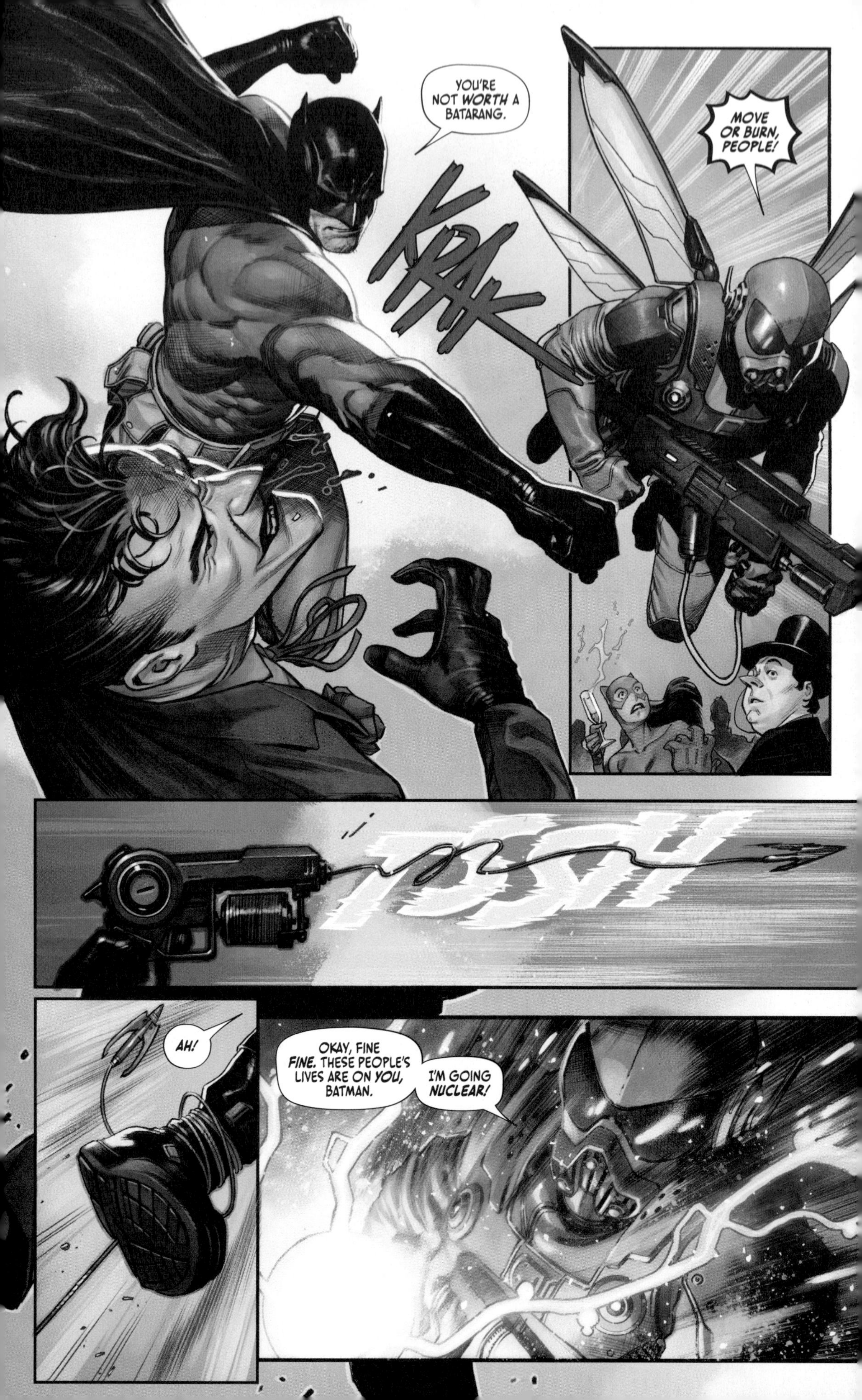
YOU'RE NOT WORTH A BATARANG.
KRAK
MOVE OR BURN, PEOPLE!
AH!
OKAY, FINE FINE. THESE PEOPLE'S LIVES ARE ON YOU, BATMAN.
I'M GOING NUCLEAR!

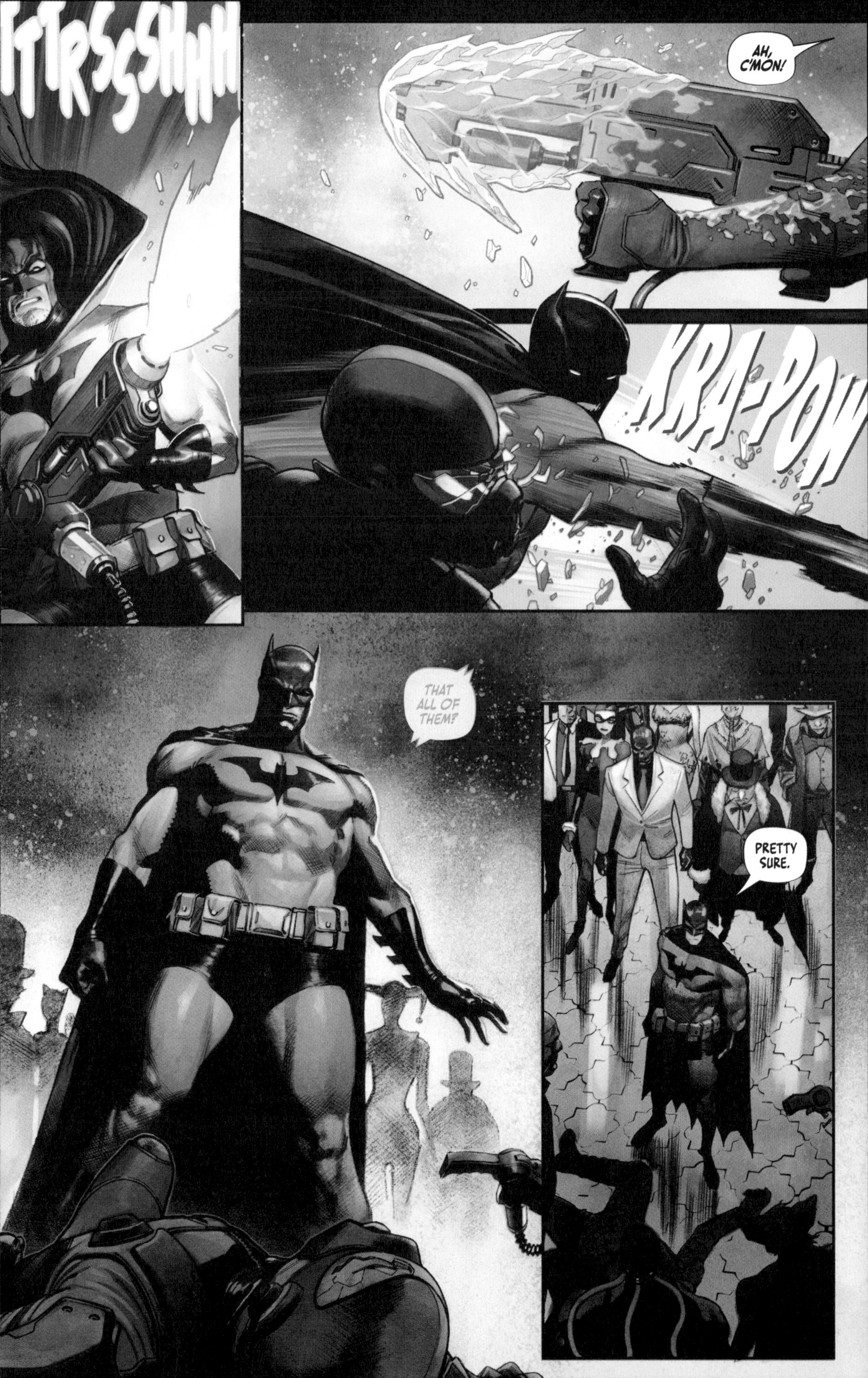
TTTRSSSHHH
AH, C'MON!
KRA-POW
THAT ALL OF THEM?
PRETTY SURE.

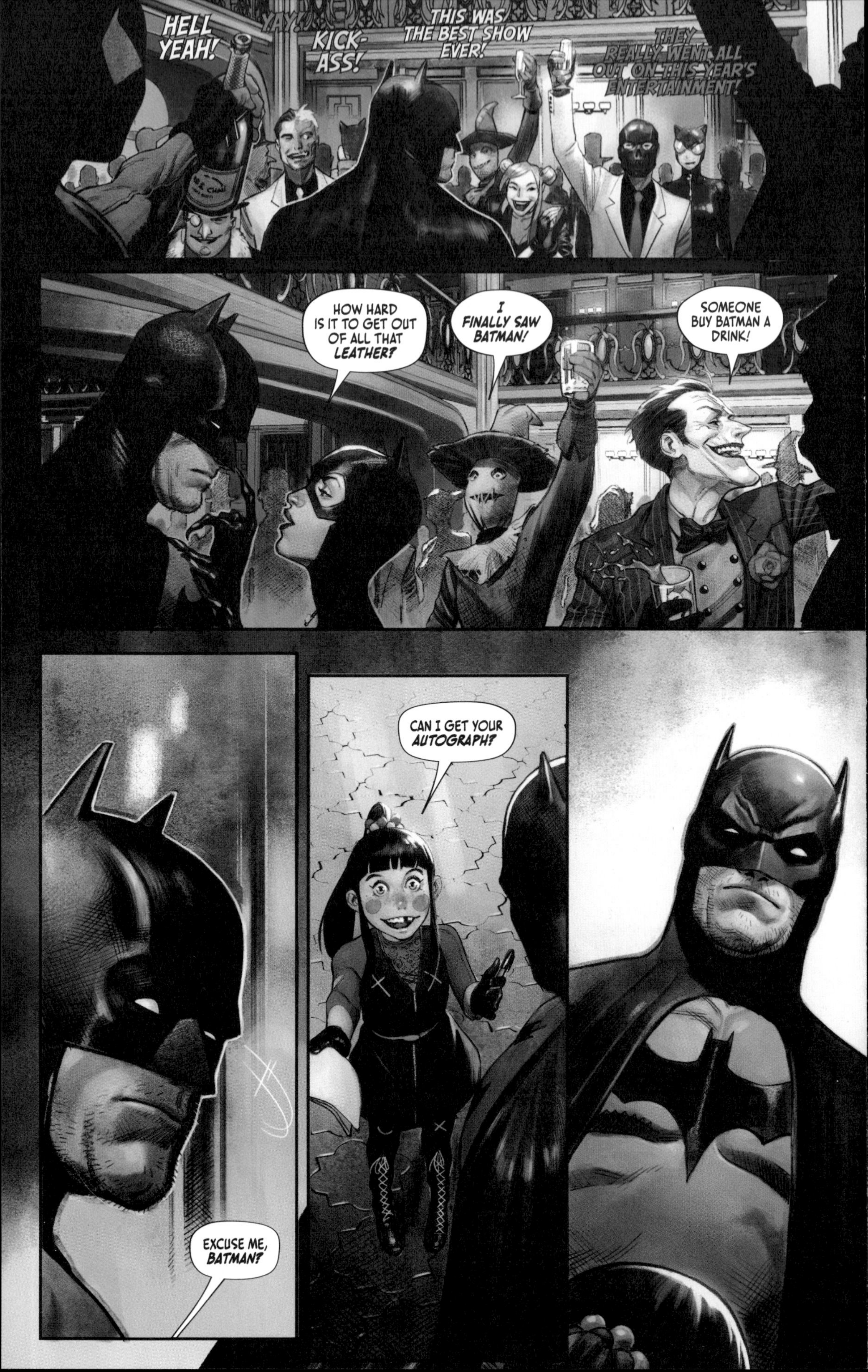
HELL YEAH!
YAY!
KICK-ASS!
THIS WAS THE BEST SHOW EVER!
THEY REALLY WENT ALL OUT ON THIS YEAR'S ENTERTAINMENT!
HOW HARD IS IT TO GET OUT OF ALL THAT LEATHER?
I FINALLY SAW BATMAN!
SOMEONE BUY BATMAN A DRINK!
EXCUSE ME, BATMAN?
CAN I GET YOUR AUTOGRAPH?

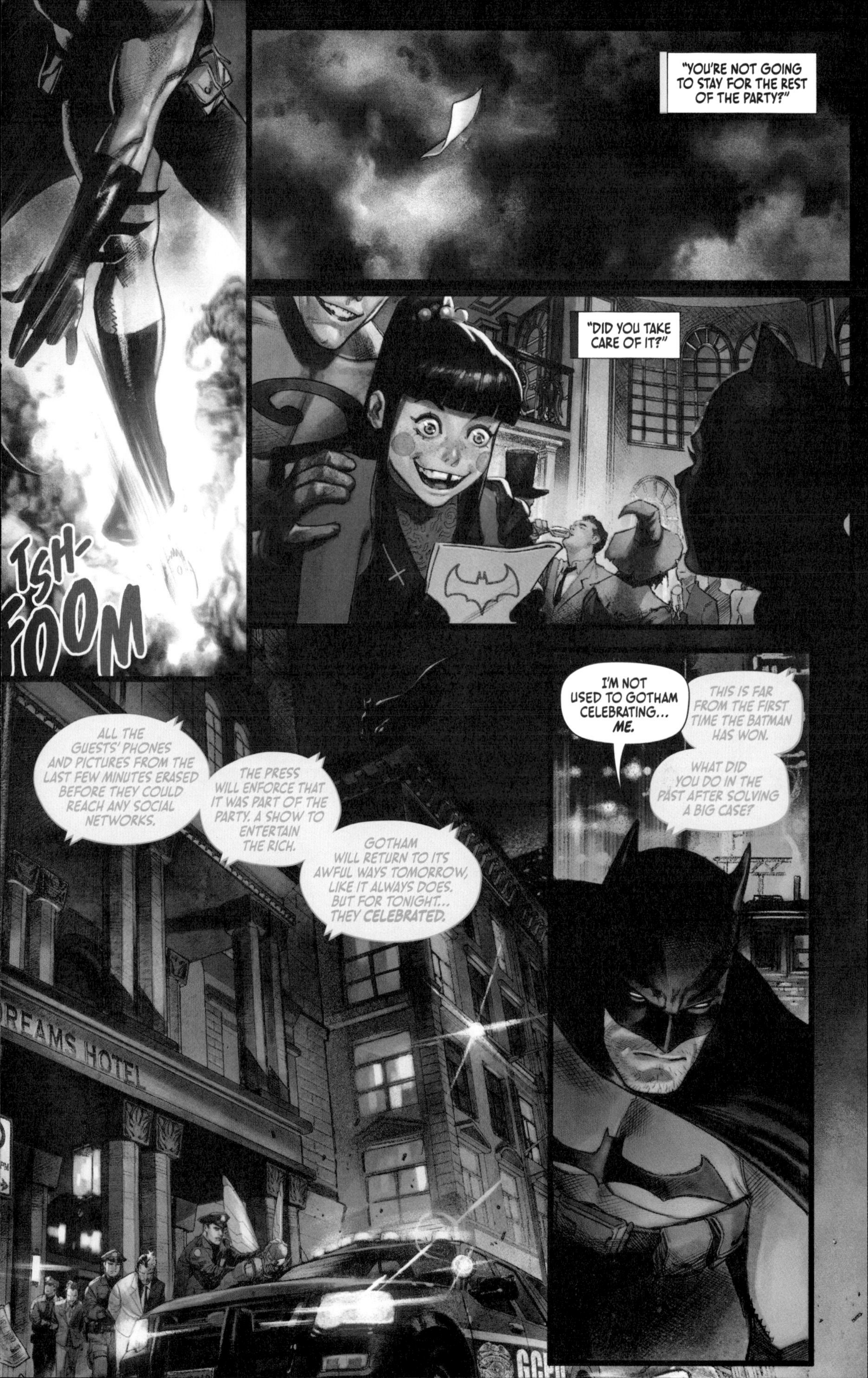
TSH-FOOM
"YOU'RE NOT GOING TO STAY FOR THE REST OF THE PARTY?"
"DID YOU TAKE CARE OF IT?"
ALL THE GUESTS' PHONES AND PICTURES FROM THE LAST FEW MINUTES ERASED BEFORE THEY COULD REACH ANY SOCIAL NETWORKS.
THE PRESS WILL ENFORCE THAT IT WAS PART OF THE PARTY. A SHOW TO ENTERTAIN THE RICH.
GOTHAM WILL RETURN TO ITS AWFUL WAYS TOMORROW, LIKE IT ALWAYS DOES. BUT FOR TONIGHT... THEY CELEBRATED.
I'M NOT USED TO GOTHAM CELEBRATING... ME.
THIS IS FAR FROM THE FIRST TIME THE BATMAN HAS WON.
WHAT DID YOU DO IN THE PAST AFTER SOLVING A BIG CASE?
DREAMS HOTEL

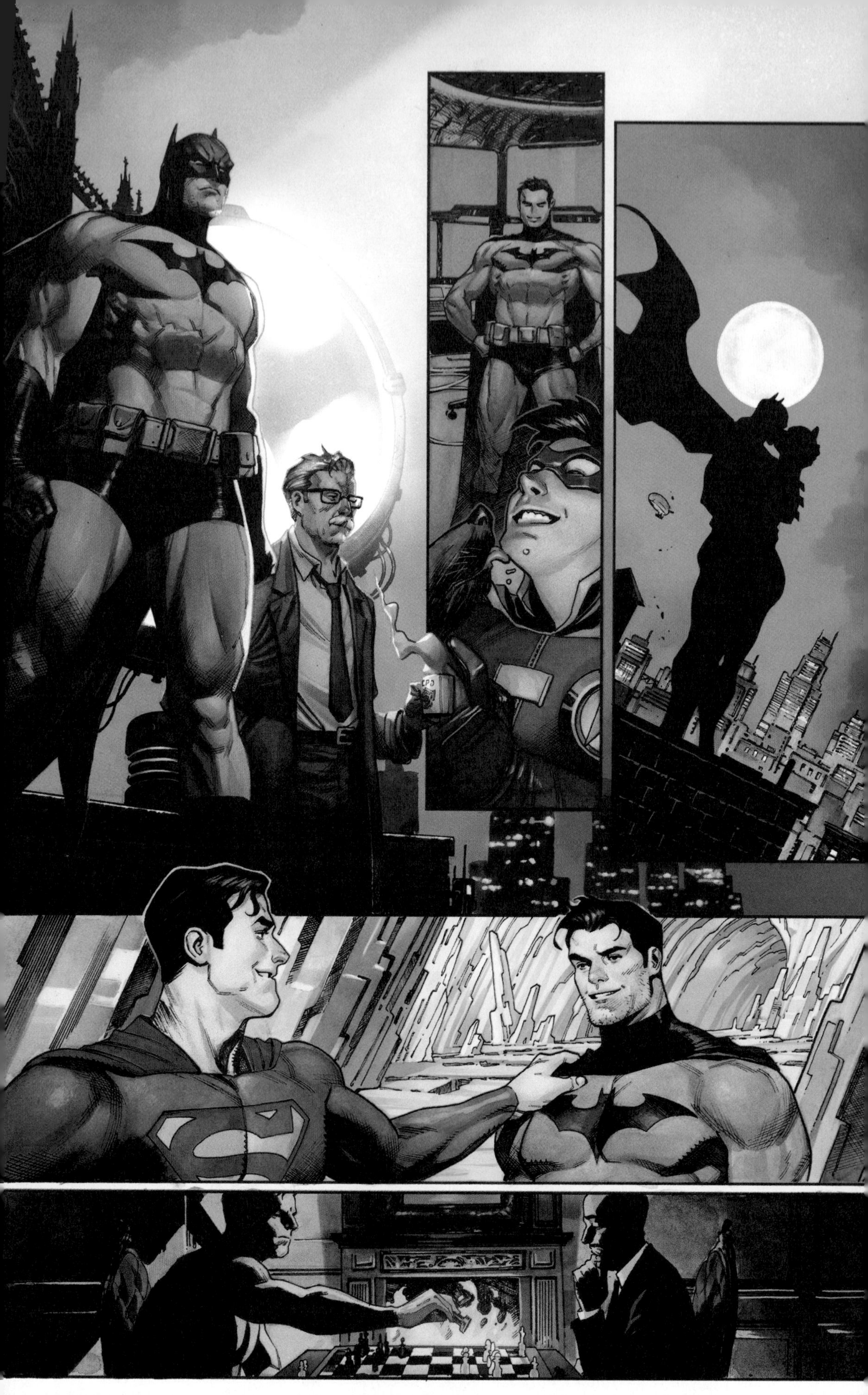

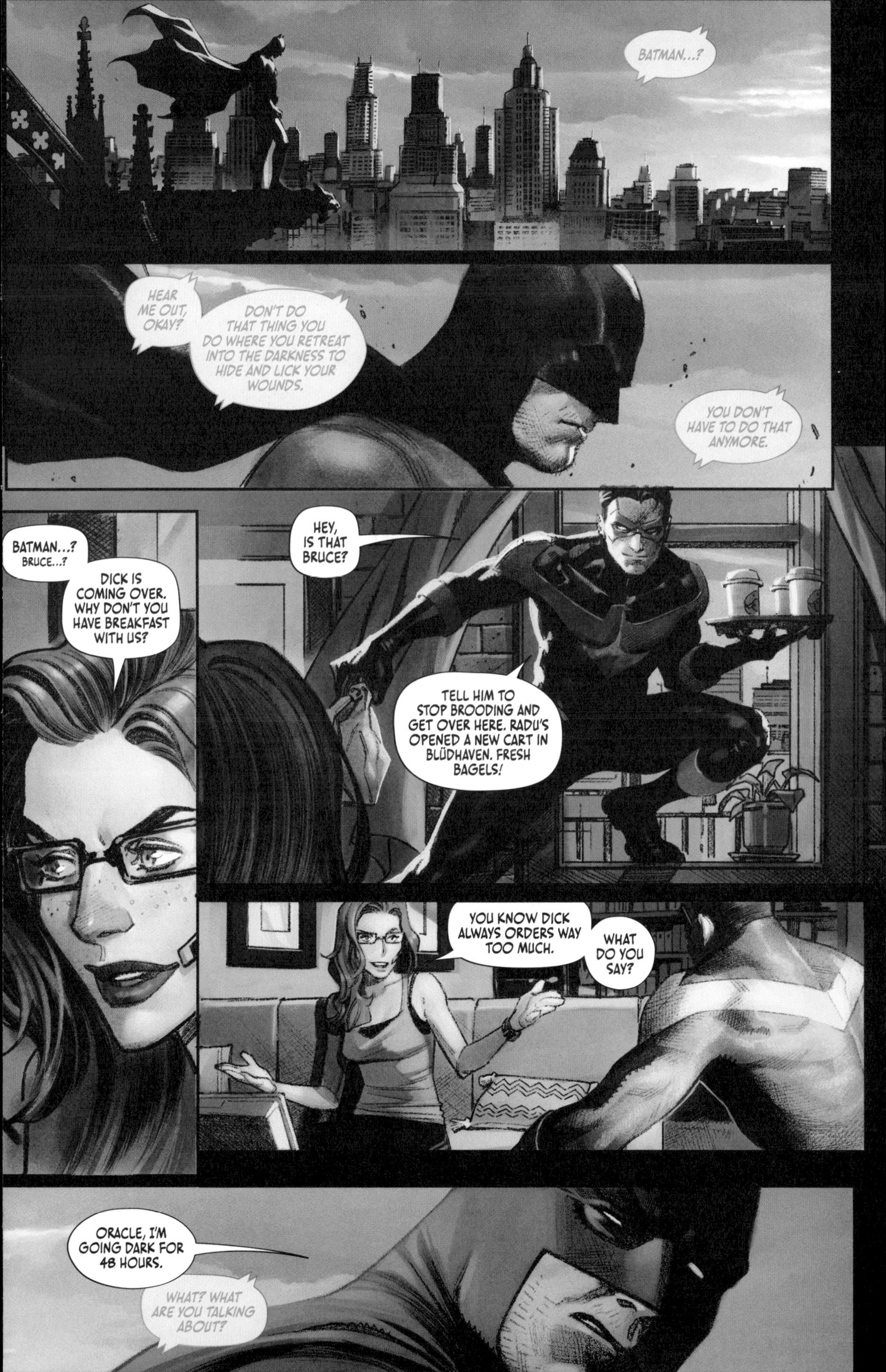
BATMAN...?
HEAR ME OUT, OKAY?
DON'T DO THAT THING YOU DO WHERE YOU RETREAT INTO THE DARKNESS TO HIDE AND LICK YOUR WOUNDS.
YOU DON'T HAVE TO DO THAT ANYMORE.
BATMAN...? BRUCE...?
DICK IS COMING OVER. WHY DON'T YOU HAVE BREAKFAST WITH US?
HEY, IS THAT BRUCE?
TELL HIM TO STOP BROODING AND GET OVER HERE. RADU'S OPENED A NEW CART IN BLÜDHAVEN. FRESH BAGELS!
YOU KNOW DICK ALWAYS ORDERS WAY TOO MUCH.
WHAT DO YOU SAY?
ORACLE, I'M GOING DARK FOR 48 HOURS.
WHAT? WHAT ARE YOU TALKING ABOUT?

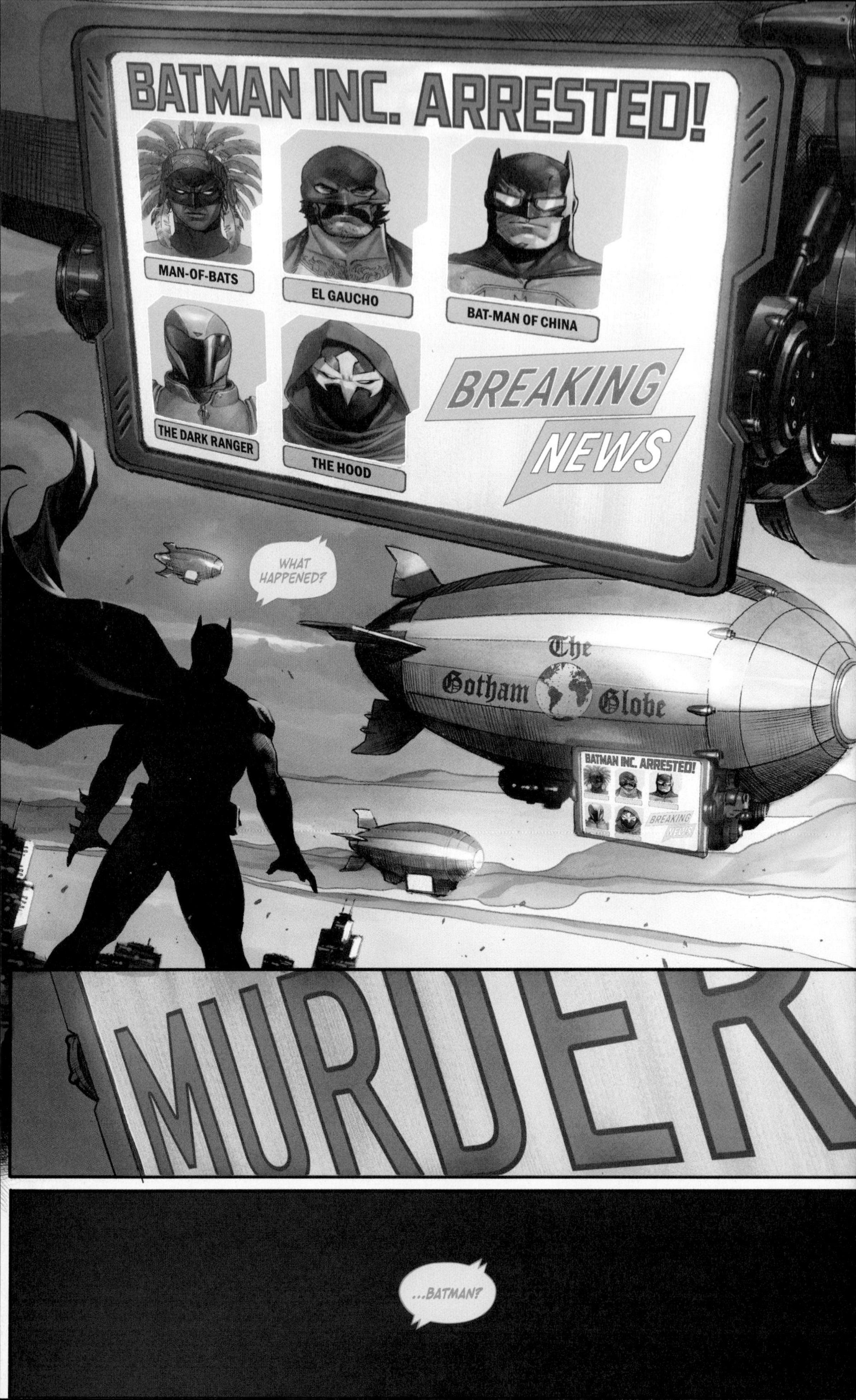

BATMAN INC. ARRESTED!
MAN-OF-BATS
EL GAUCHO
BAT-MAN OF CHINA
THE DARK RANGER
THE HOOD
BREAKING NEWS
WHAT HAPPENED?
The Gotham Globe
BATMAN INC. ARRESTED!
BREAKING NEWS
MURDER
...BATMAN?

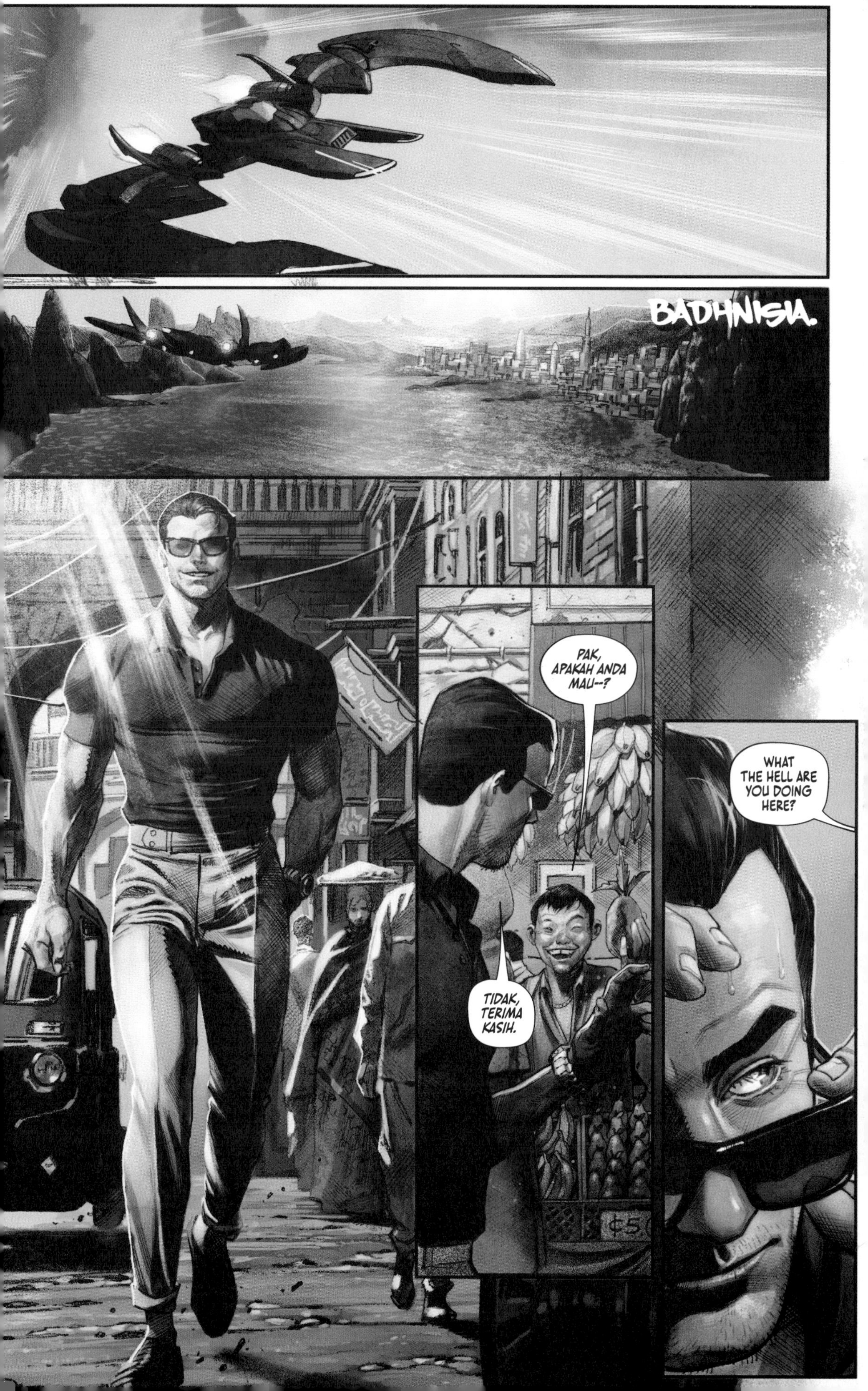
BADHNISIA.
PAK, APAKAH ANDA MAU--?
TIDAK, TERIMA KASIH.
WHAT THE HELL ARE YOU DOING HERE?

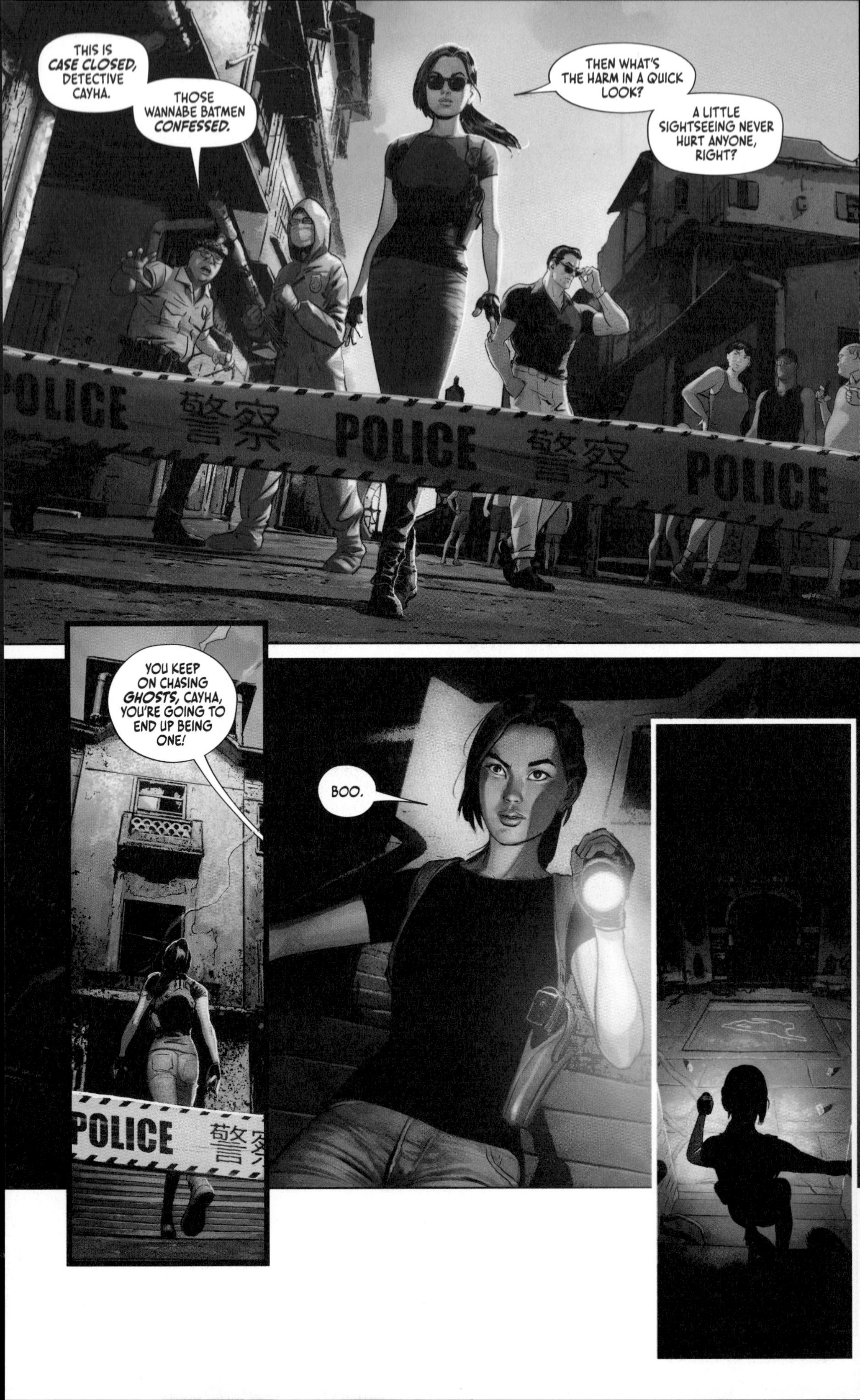

THIS IS CASE CLOSED, DETECTIVE CAYHA.
THOSE WANNABE BATMEN CONFESSED.
THEN WHAT'S THE HARM IN A QUICK LOOK?
A LITTLE SIGHTSEEING NEVER HURT ANYONE, RIGHT?
POLICE 警察 POLICE 警察 POLICE
YOU KEEP ON CHASING GHOSTS, CAYHA, YOU'RE GOING TO END UP BEING ONE!
POLICE
BOO.

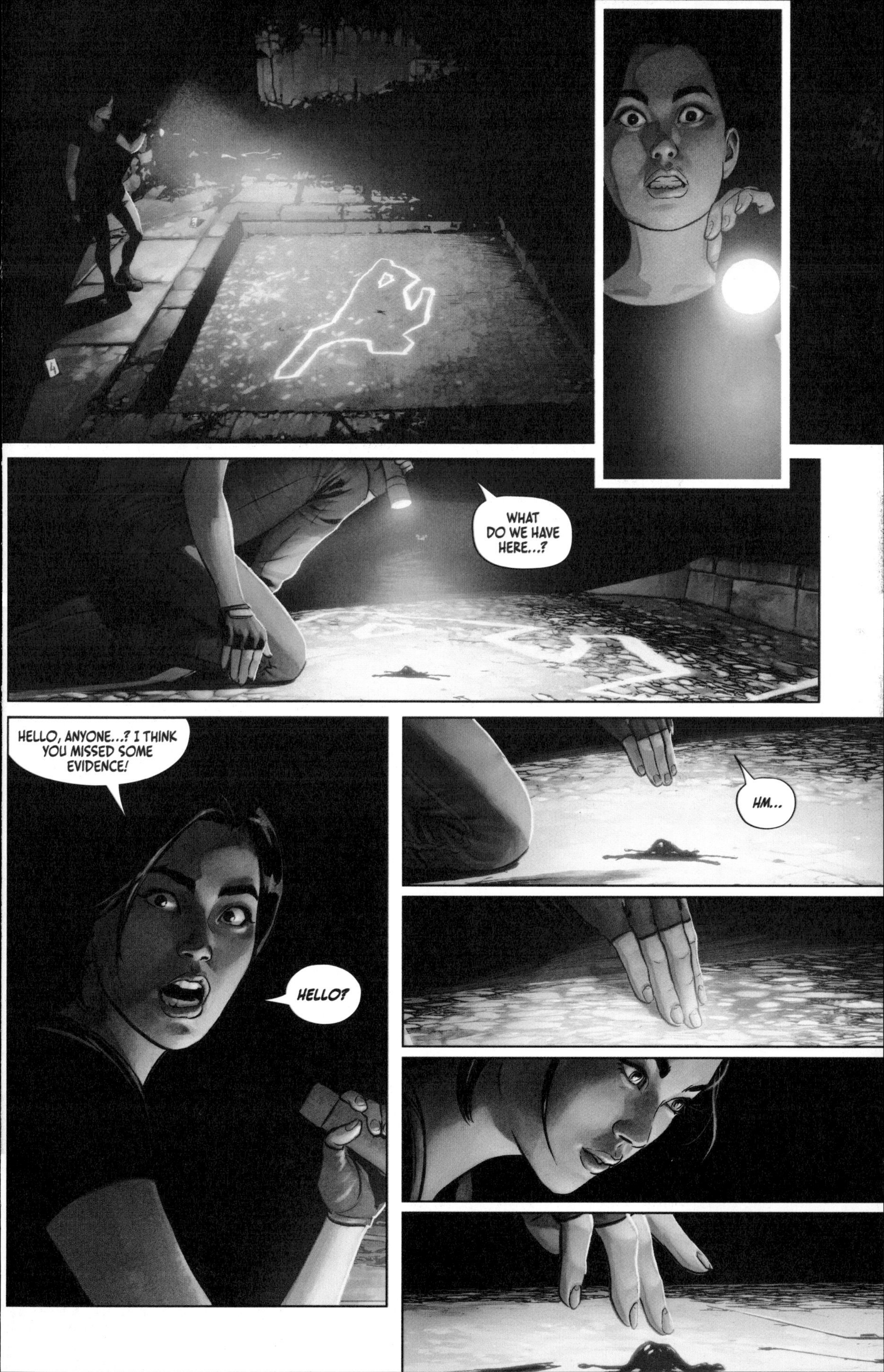
WHAT DO WE HAVE HERE...?
HELLO, ANYONE...? I THINK YOU MISSED SOME EVIDENCE!
HELLO?
HM...

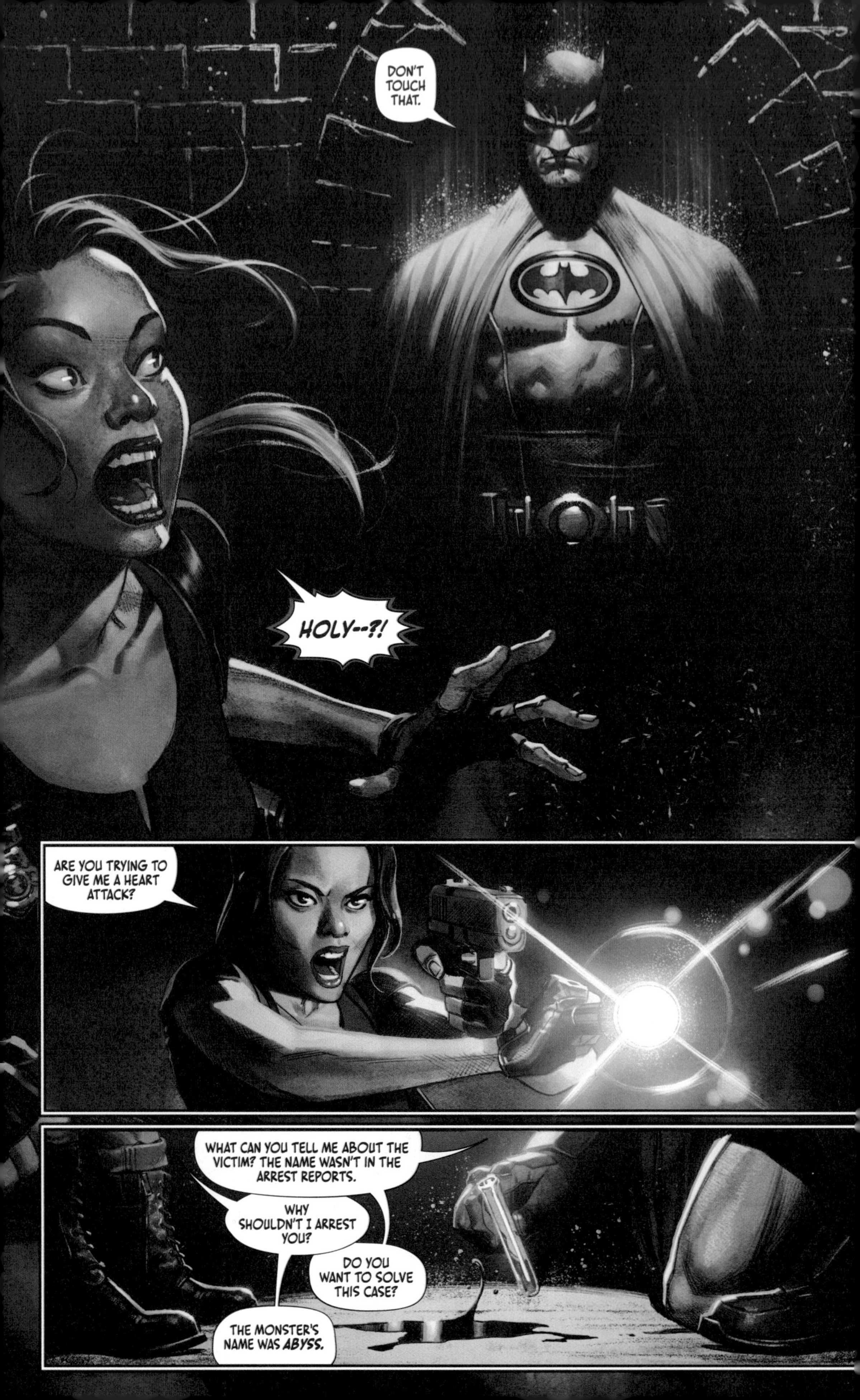
DON'T TOUCH THAT.
HOLY--?!
ARE YOU TRYING TO GIVE ME A HEART ATTACK?
WHAT CAN YOU TELL ME ABOUT THE VICTIM? THE NAME WASN'T IN THE ARREST REPORTS.
WHY SHOULDN'T I ARREST YOU?
DO YOU WANT TO SOLVE THIS CASE?
THE MONSTER'S NAME WAS *ABYSS.*

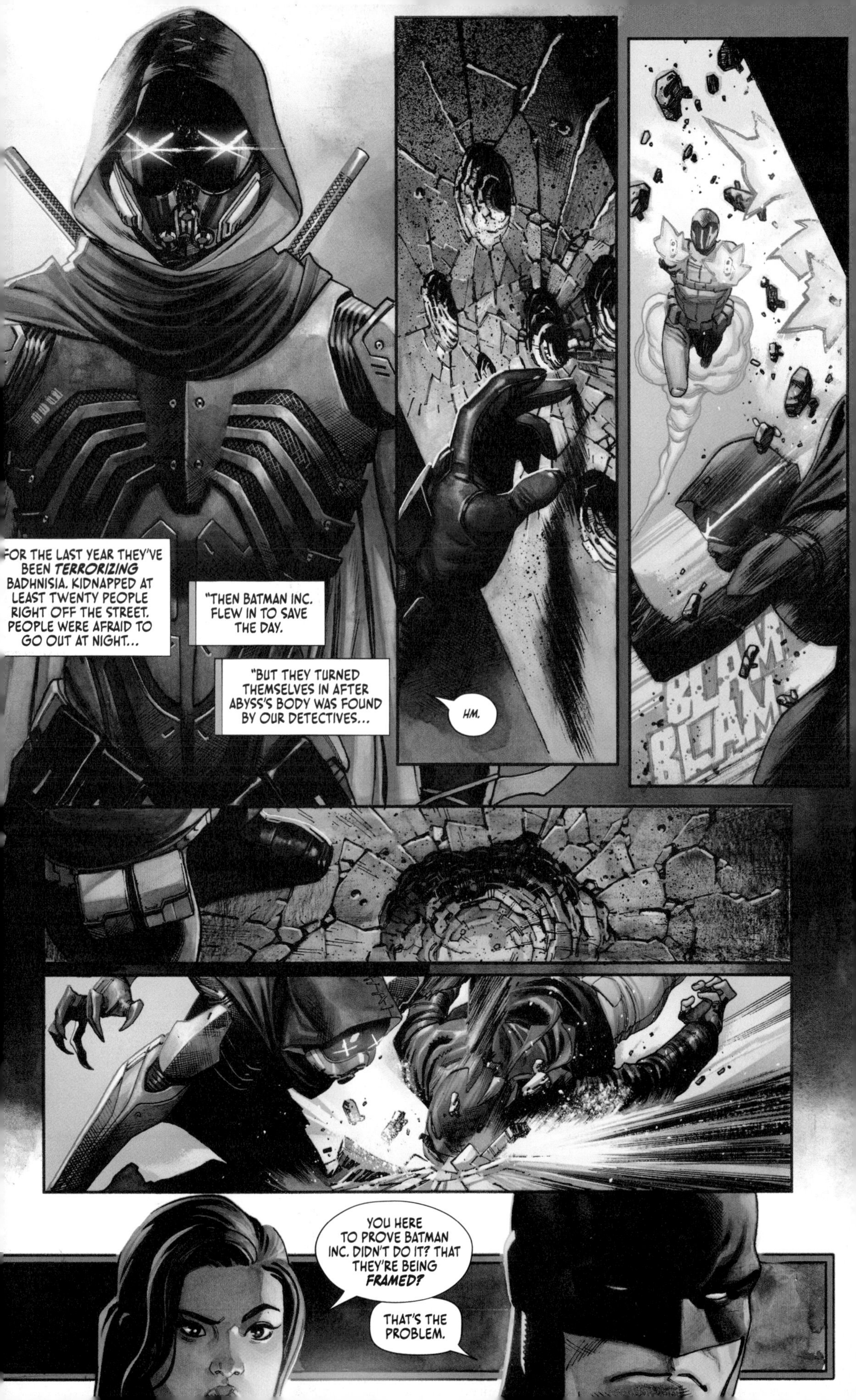

FOR THE LAST YEAR THEY'VE BEEN TERRORIZING BADHNISIA. KIDNAPPED AT LEAST TWENTY PEOPLE RIGHT OFF THE STREET. PEOPLE WERE AFRAID TO GO OUT AT NIGHT...
"THEN BATMAN INC. FLEW IN TO SAVE THE DAY.
"BUT THEY TURNED THEMSELVES IN AFTER ABYSS'S BODY WAS FOUND BY OUR DETECTIVES...
HM.
BLAM BLAM
YOU HERE TO PROVE BATMAN INC. DIDN'T DO IT? THAT THEY'RE BEING FRAMED?
THAT'S THE PROBLEM.

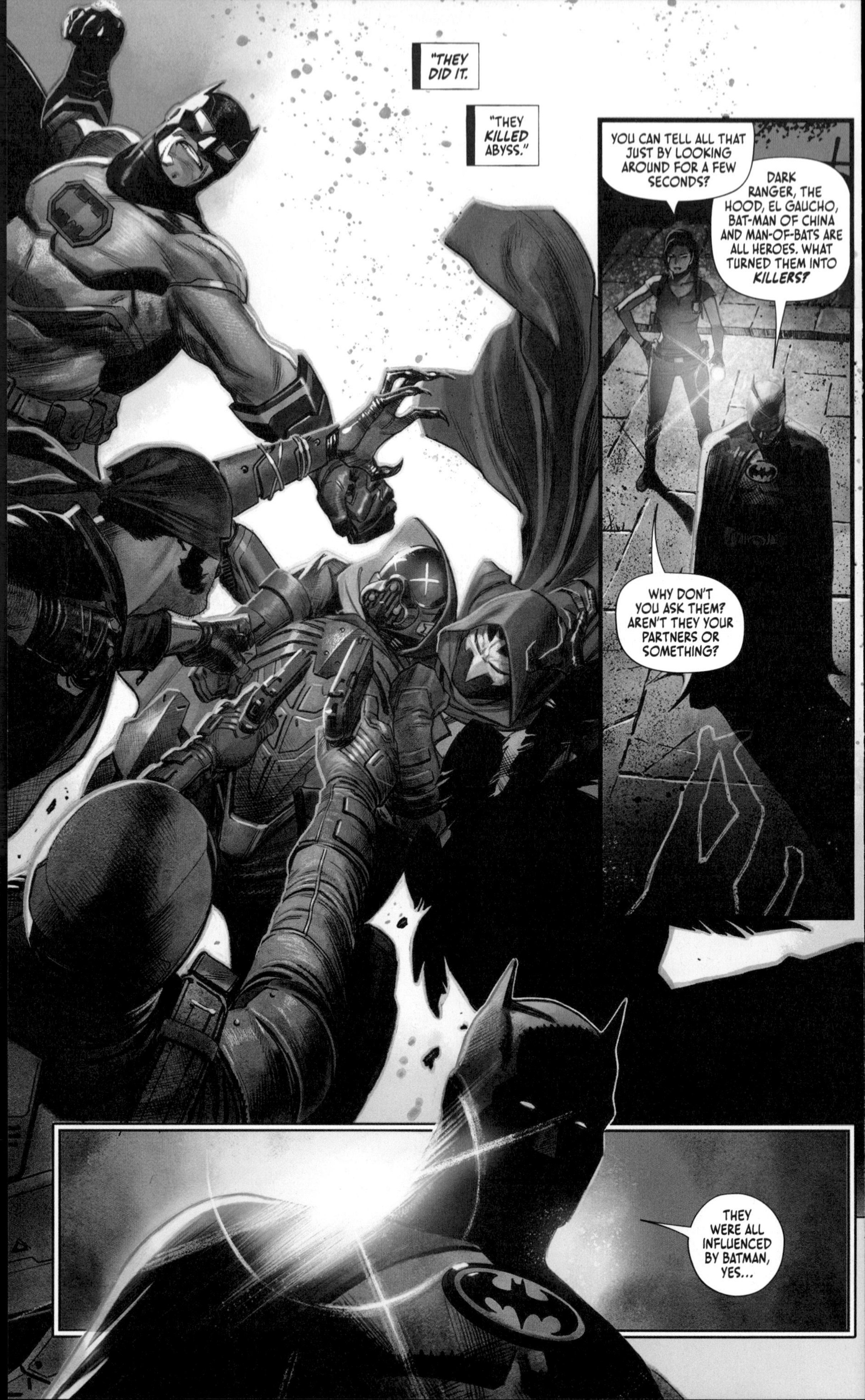
"THEY DID IT.
"THEY KILLED ABYSS."
YOU CAN TELL ALL THAT JUST BY LOOKING AROUND FOR A FEW SECONDS?
DARK RANGER, THE HOOD, EL GAUCHO, BAT-MAN OF CHINA AND MAN-OF-BATS ARE ALL HEROES. WHAT TURNED THEM INTO KILLERS?
WHY DON'T YOU ASK THEM? AREN'T THEY YOUR PARTNERS OR SOMETHING?
THEY WERE ALL INFLUENCED BY BATMAN, YES...

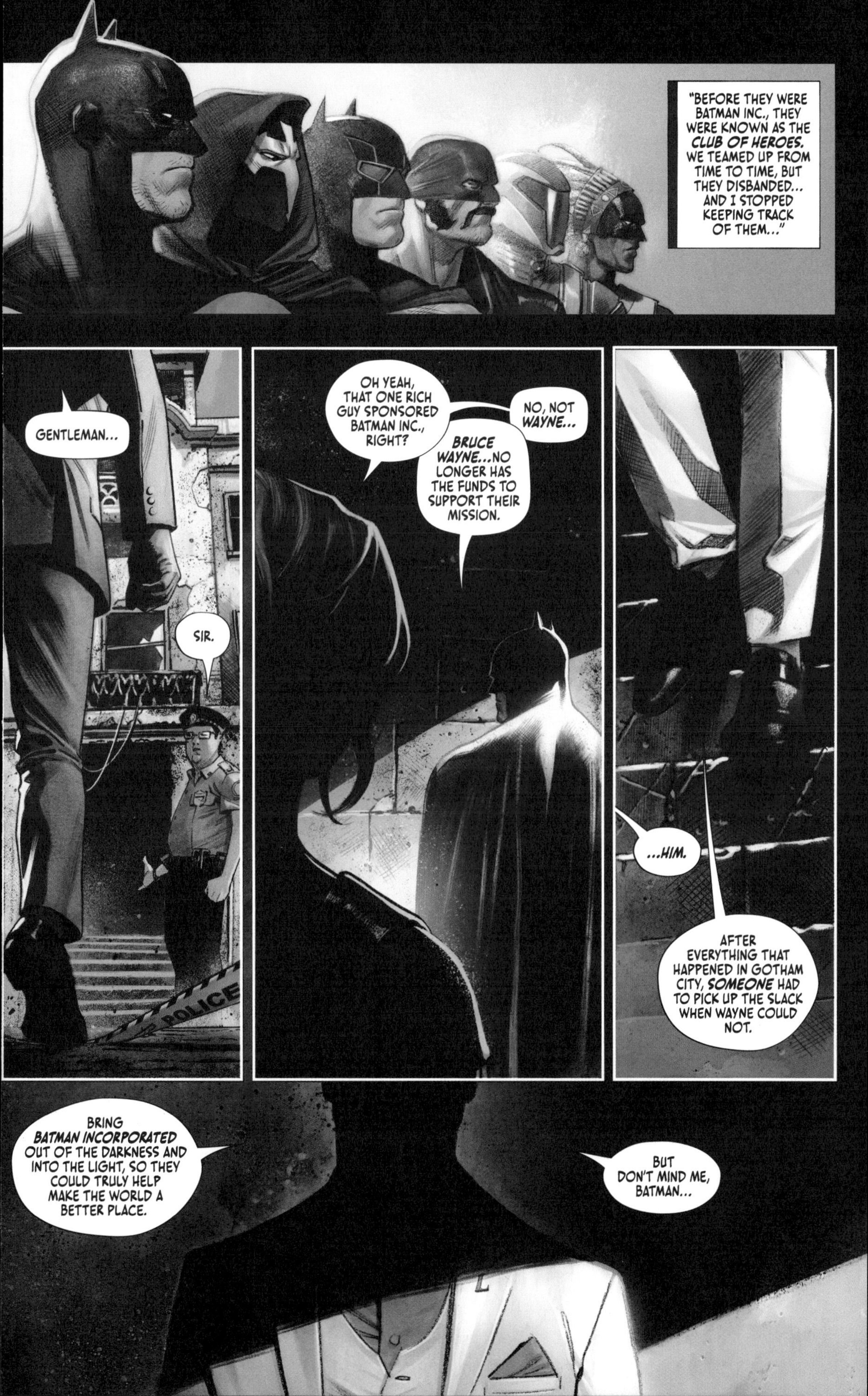
"BEFORE THEY WERE BATMAN INC., THEY WERE KNOWN AS THE *CLUB OF HEROES.* WE TEAMED UP FROM TIME TO TIME, BUT THEY DISBANDED... AND I STOPPED KEEPING TRACK OF THEM..."
GENTLEMAN...
SIR.
POLICE
OH YEAH, THAT ONE RICH GUY SPONSORED BATMAN INC., RIGHT?
NO, NOT *WAYNE...*
*BRUCE WAYNE...*NO LONGER HAS THE FUNDS TO SUPPORT THEIR MISSION.
...*HIM.*
AFTER EVERYTHING THAT HAPPENED IN GOTHAM CITY, *SOMEONE* HAD TO PICK UP THE SLACK WHEN WAYNE COULD NOT.
BRING *BATMAN INCORPORATED* OUT OF THE DARKNESS AND INTO THE LIGHT, SO THEY COULD TRULY HELP MAKE THE WORLD A BETTER PLACE.
BUT DON'T MIND ME, BATMAN...

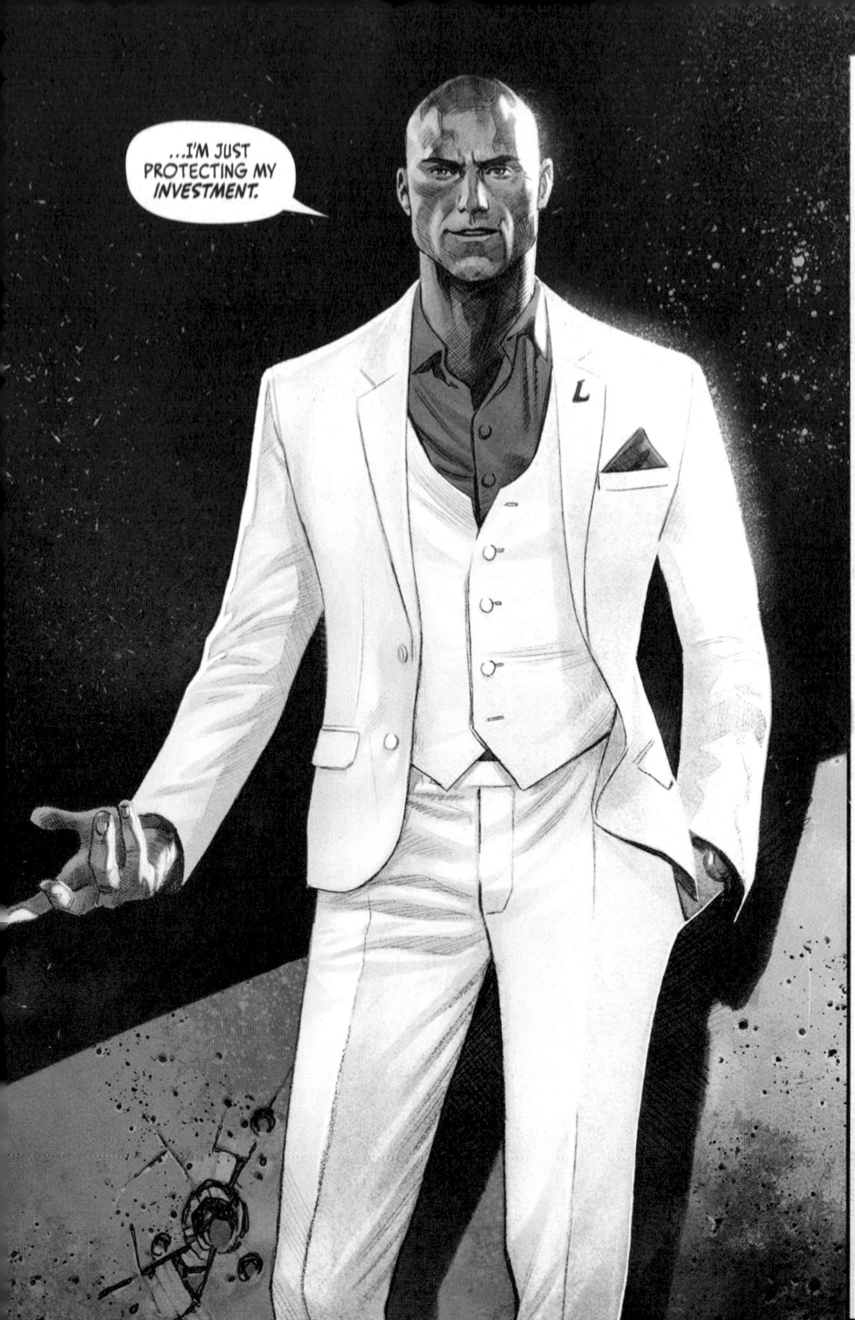
...I'M JUST PROTECTING MY *INVESTMENT.*

THE ABYSS
Part 1
"NOW IT'S A PARTY!"

JOSHUA WILLIAMSON writer
JORGE MOLINA
& MIKEL JANÍN artists
TOMEU MOREY colors
CLAYTON COWLES letters

JORGE MOLINA cover
FRANCESCO MATTINA, JOCK &
VIKTOR BOGDANOVIC variant covers

DAVE WIELGOSZ associate editor
BEN ABERNATHY editor

BATMAN created by
BOB KANE with BILL FINGER

SUPERMAN created by
JERRY SIEGEL & JOE SHUSTER
By Special Arrangement with the
JERRY SIEGEL FAMILY.

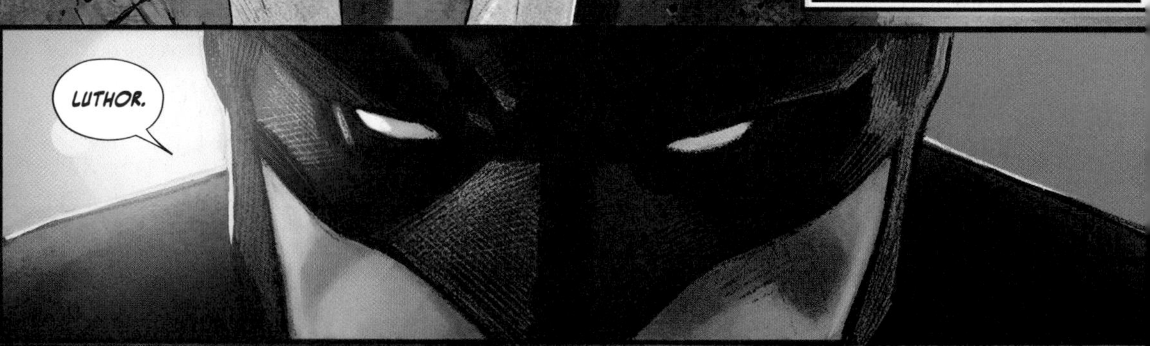
LUTHOR.

NEXT ISSUE: WHO WAS abyss?

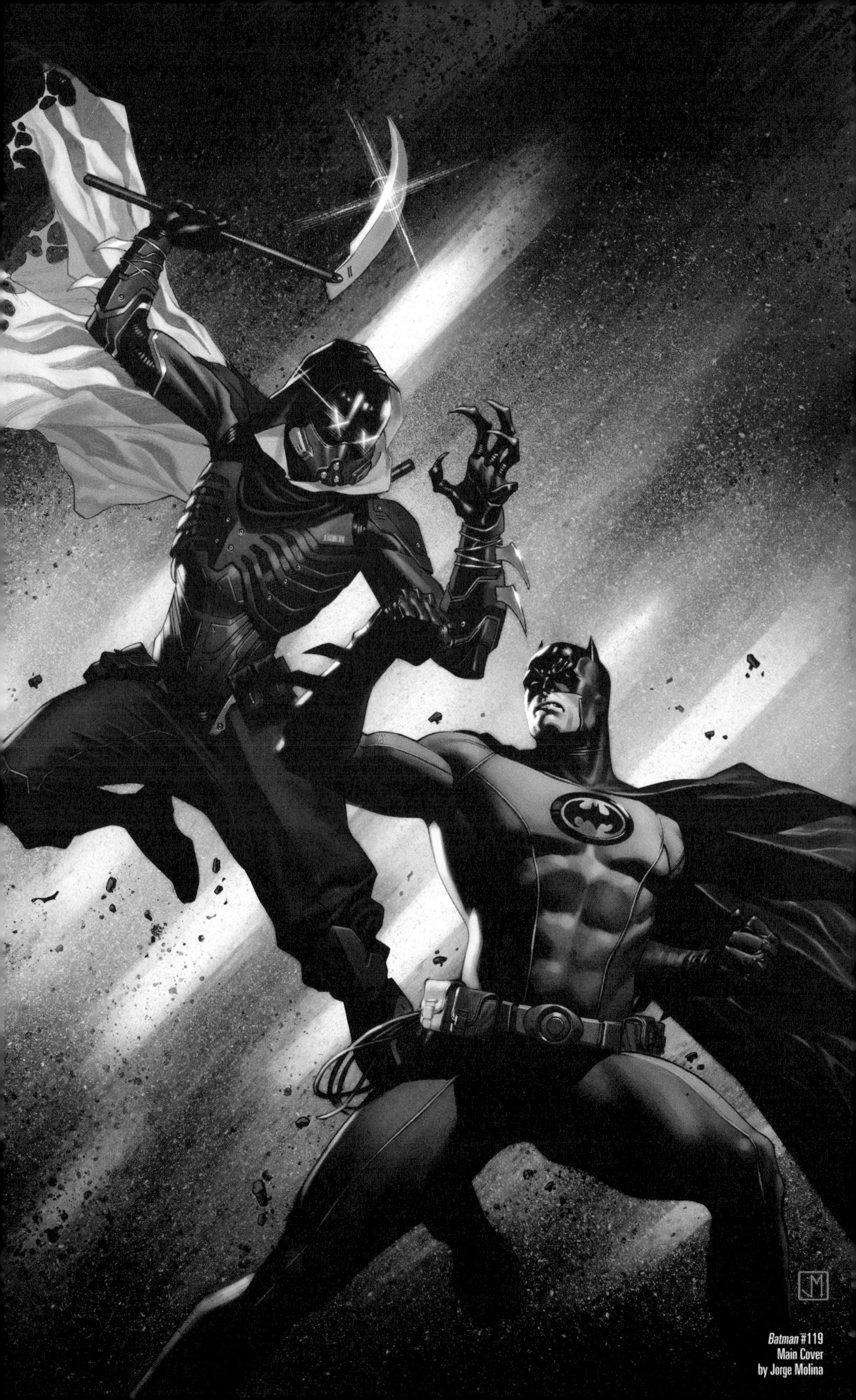

Batman #119
Main Cover
by Jorge Molina

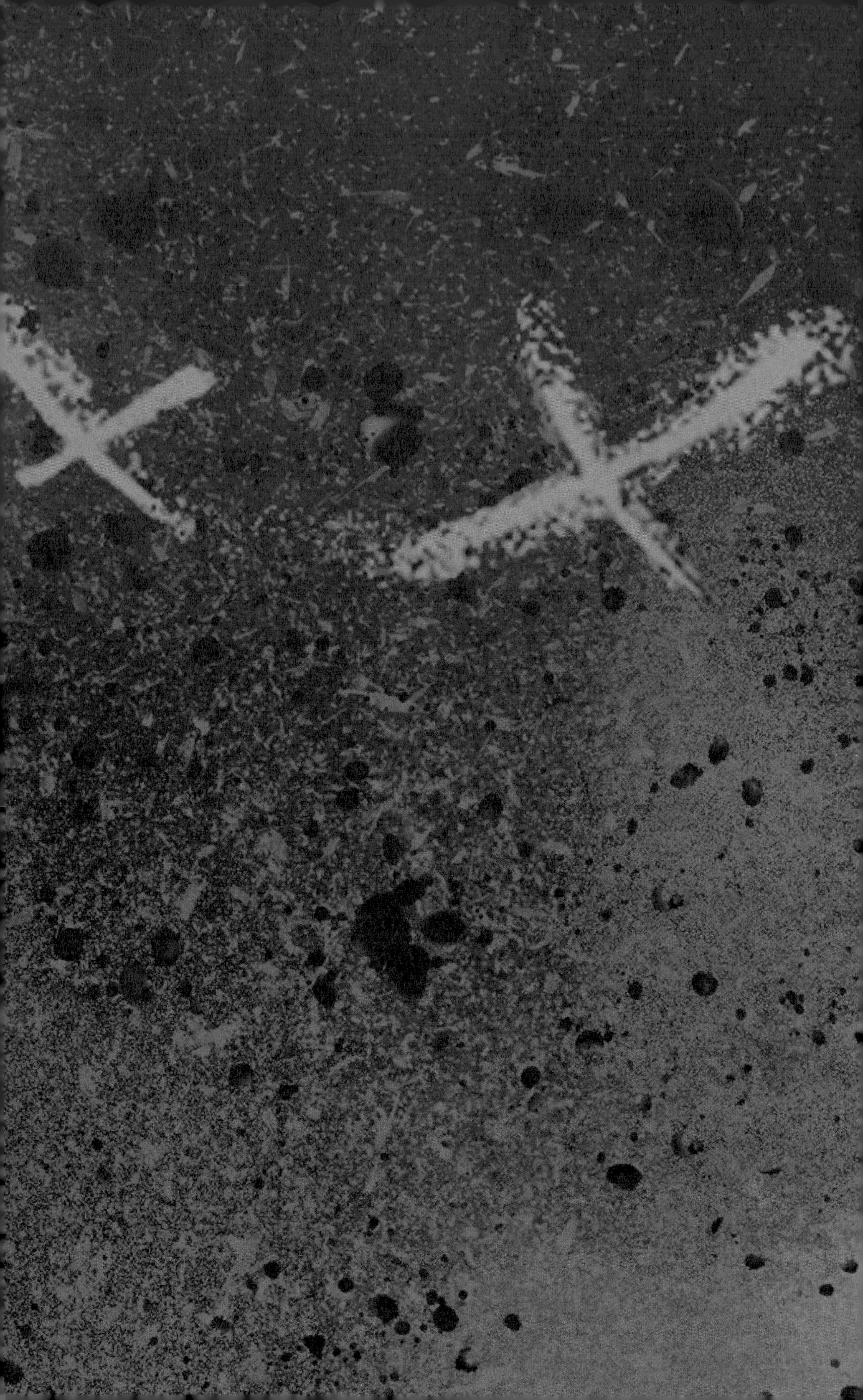

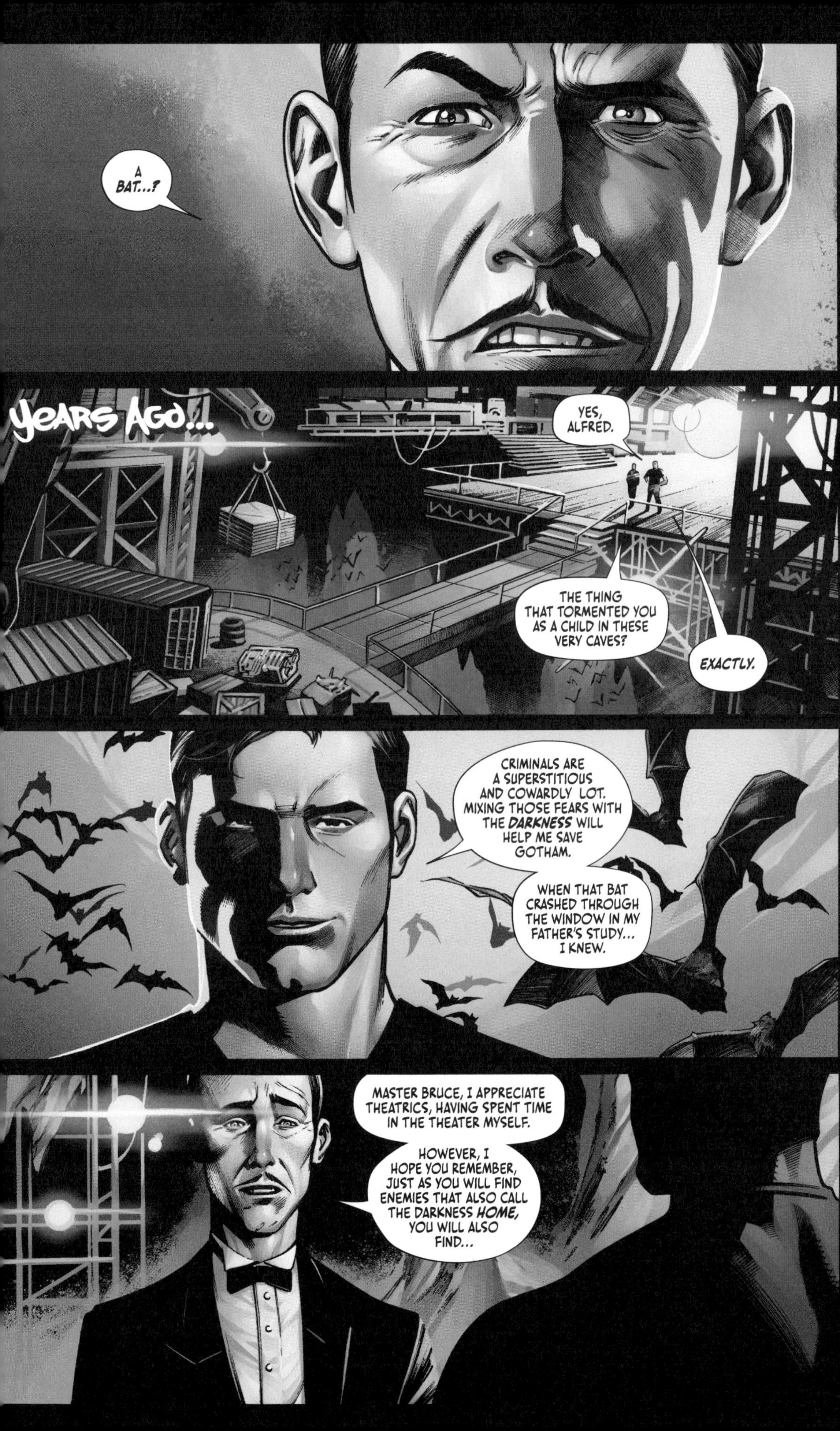
A BAT...?
YEARS AGO...
YES, ALFRED.
THE THING THAT TORMENTED YOU AS A CHILD IN THESE VERY CAVES?
EXACTLY.
CRIMINALS ARE A SUPERSTITIOUS AND COWARDLY LOT. MIXING THOSE FEARS WITH THE DARKNESS WILL HELP ME SAVE GOTHAM.
WHEN THAT BAT CRASHED THROUGH THE WINDOW IN MY FATHER'S STUDY... I KNEW.
MASTER BRUCE, I APPRECIATE THEATRICS, HAVING SPENT TIME IN THE THEATER MYSELF.
HOWEVER, I HOPE YOU REMEMBER, JUST AS YOU WILL FIND ENEMIES THAT ALSO CALL THE DARKNESS HOME, YOU WILL ALSO FIND...

THE ABYSS, PART 2 "OLD AND NEW ENEMIES"

JOSHUA WILLIAMSON *WRITER* JORGE MOLINA & ADRIANO DI BENEDETTO AND MIKEL JANÍN ARTISTS
TOMEU MOREY *COLORS* CLAYTON COWLES *LETTERS* JORGE MOLINA *COVER*
FRANCESCO MATTINA, JOCK, AND DAN HIPP *VARIANT COVERS* DAVE WIELGOSZ *ASSOC. EDITOR* BEN ABERNATHY *EDITOR*
BATMAN *CREATED BY* BOB KANE WITH BILL FINGER

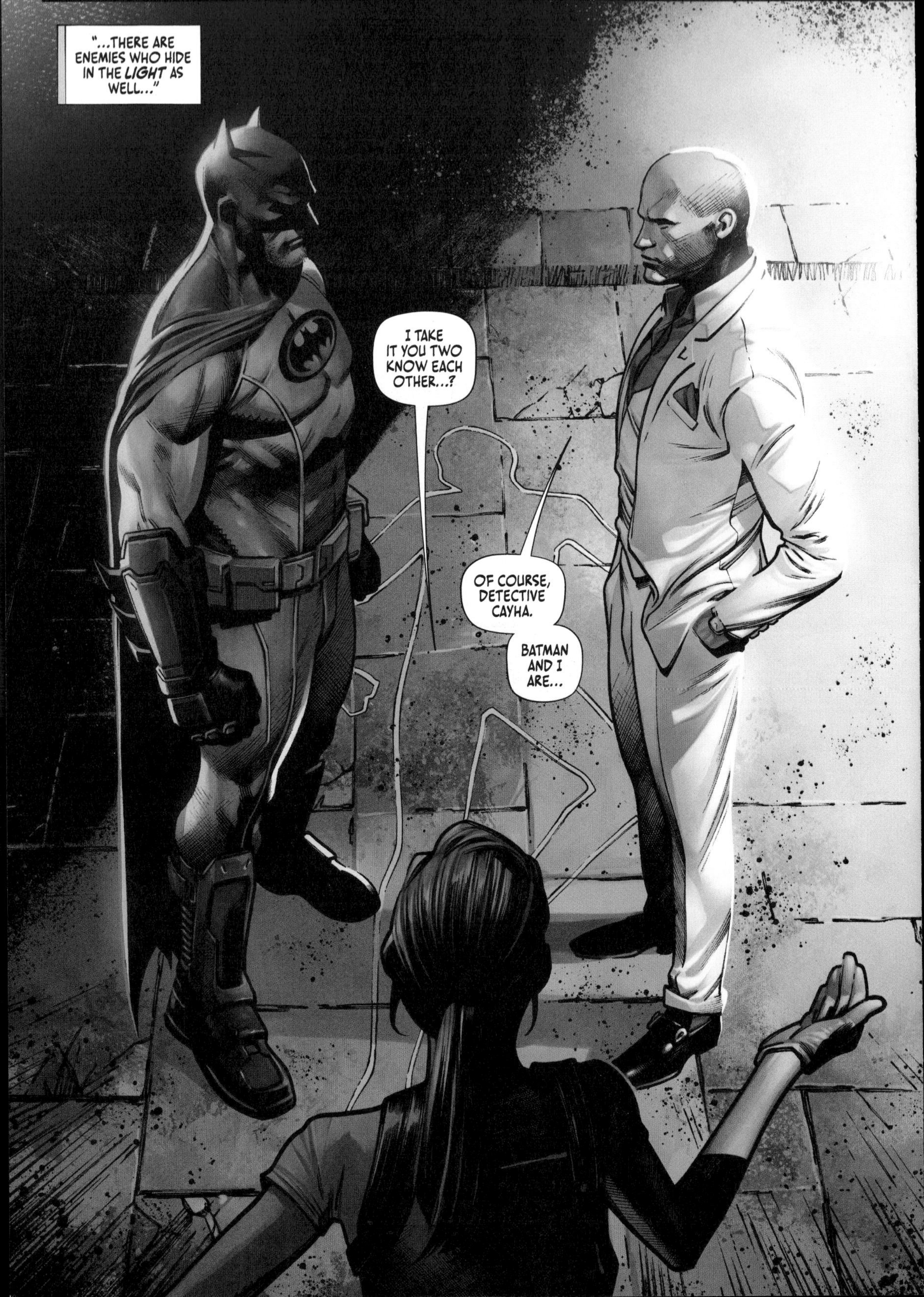
"...THERE ARE ENEMIES WHO HIDE IN THE *LIGHT* AS WELL..."
I TAKE IT YOU TWO KNOW EACH OTHER...?
OF COURSE, DETECTIVE CAYHA.
BATMAN AND I ARE...

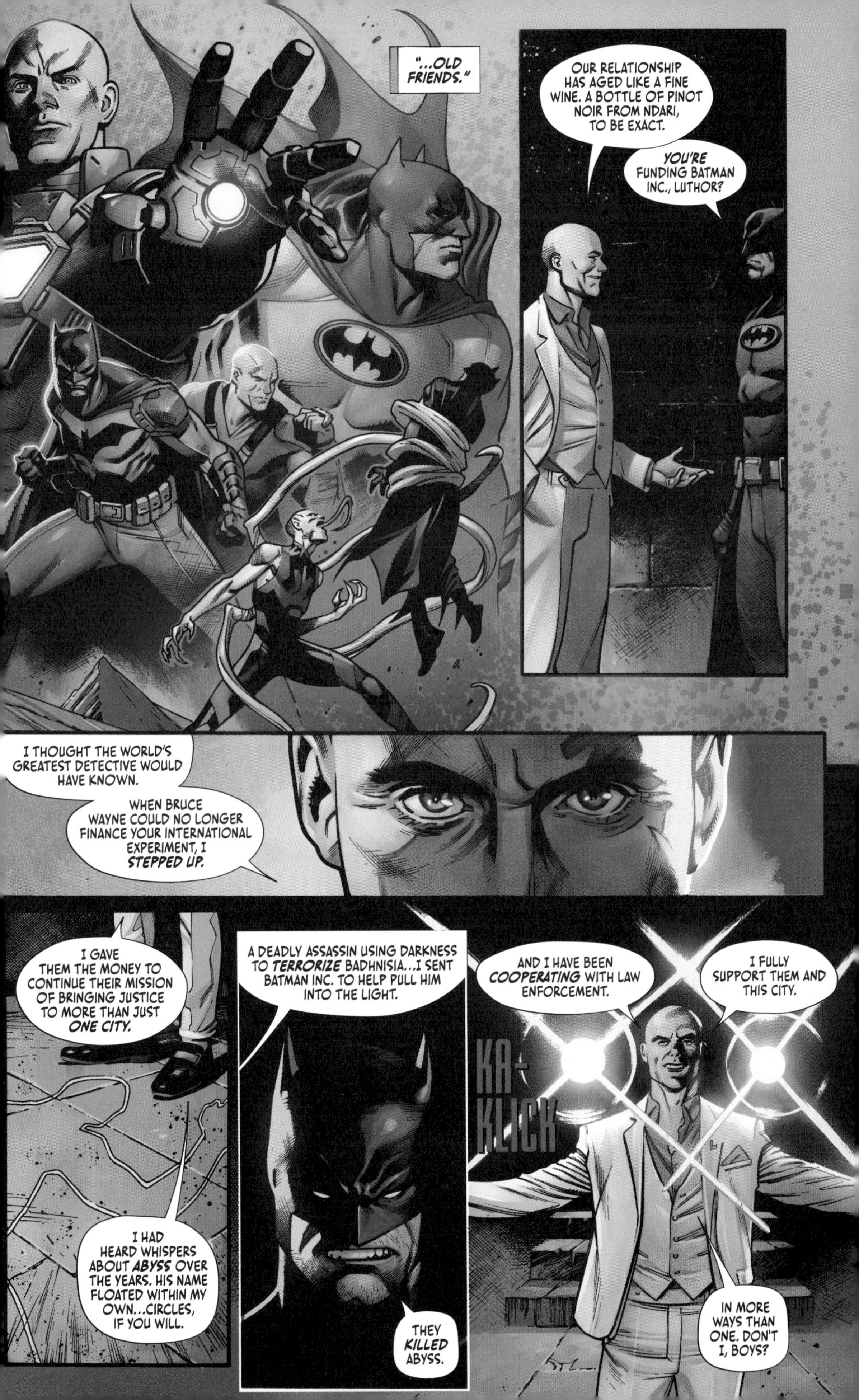
"...OLD FRIENDS."
OUR RELATIONSHIP HAS AGED LIKE A FINE WINE. A BOTTLE OF PINOT NOIR FROM NDARI, TO BE EXACT.
YOU'RE FUNDING BATMAN INC., LUTHOR?
I THOUGHT THE WORLD'S GREATEST DETECTIVE WOULD HAVE KNOWN.
WHEN BRUCE WAYNE COULD NO LONGER FINANCE YOUR INTERNATIONAL EXPERIMENT, I STEPPED UP.
I GAVE THEM THE MONEY TO CONTINUE THEIR MISSION OF BRINGING JUSTICE TO MORE THAN JUST ONE CITY.
I HAD HEARD WHISPERS ABOUT ABYSS OVER THE YEARS. HIS NAME FLOATED WITHIN MY OWN...CIRCLES, IF YOU WILL.
A DEADLY ASSASSIN USING DARKNESS TO TERRORIZE BADHNISIA...I SENT BATMAN INC. TO HELP PULL HIM INTO THE LIGHT.
THEY KILLED ABYSS.
KA-KLICK
AND I HAVE BEEN COOPERATING WITH LAW ENFORCEMENT.
I FULLY SUPPORT THEM AND THIS CITY.
IN MORE WAYS THAN ONE. DON'T I, BOYS?

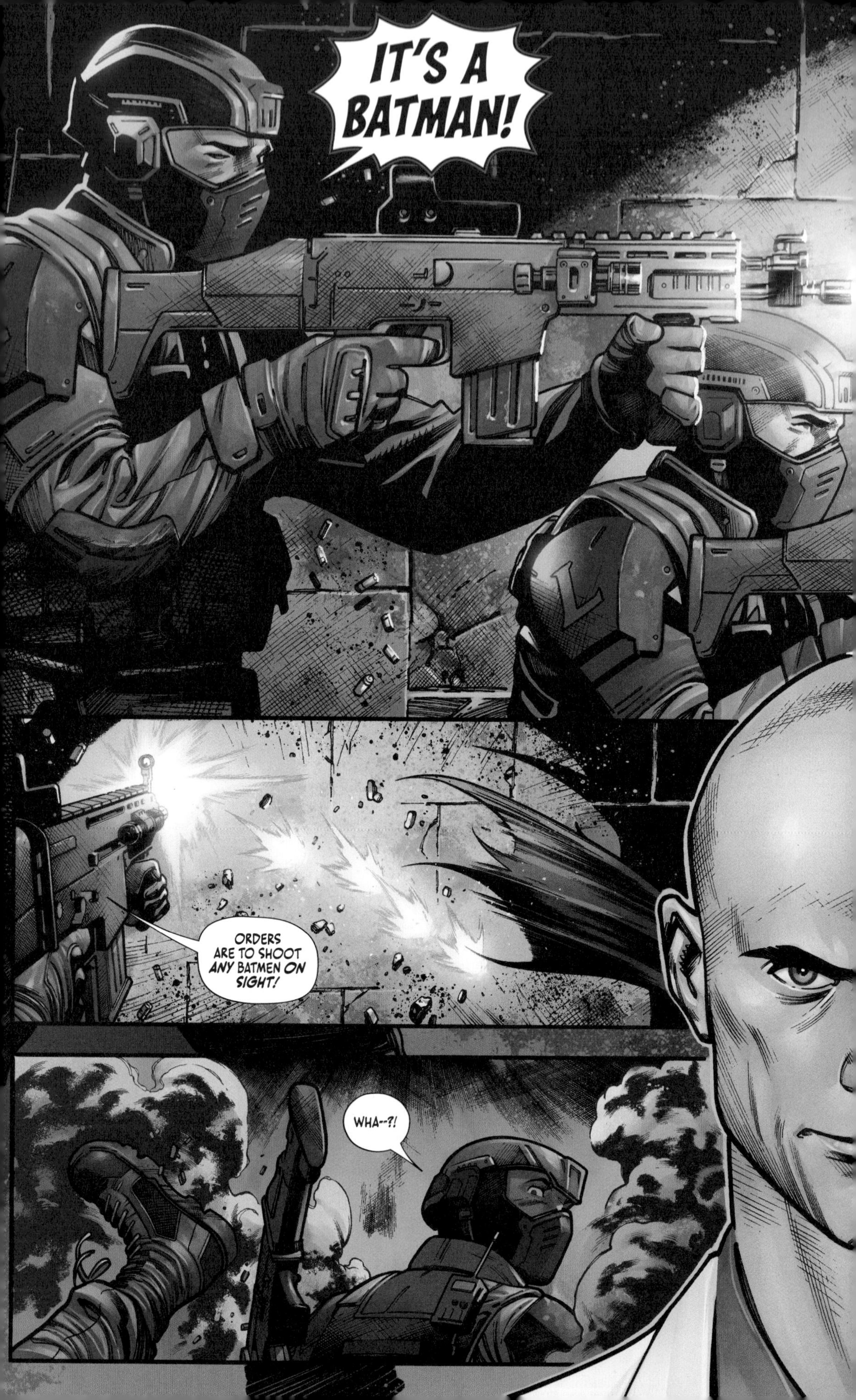
IT'S A BATMAN!
ORDERS ARE TO SHOOT ANY BATMEN ON SIGHT!
WHA--?!

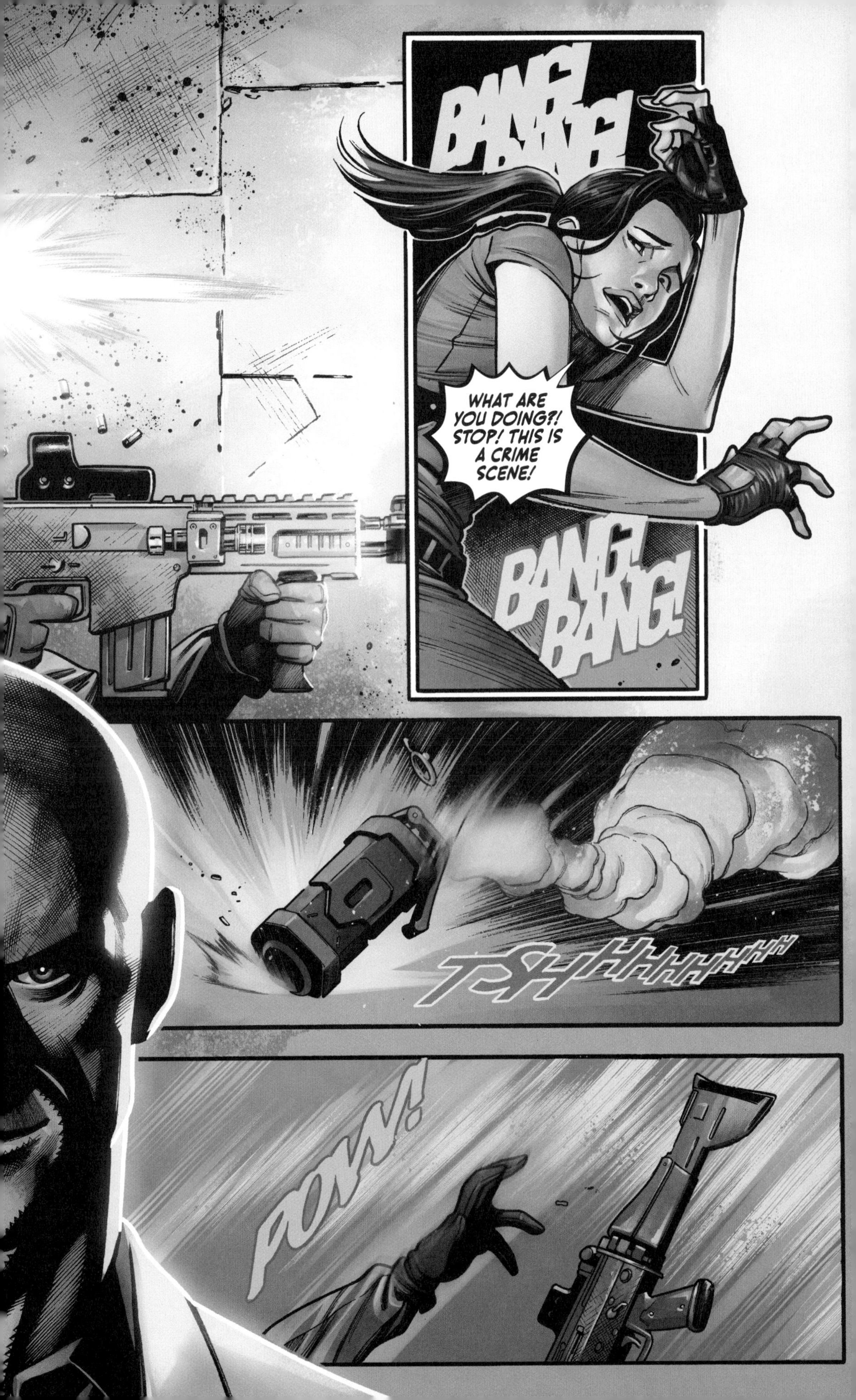
BANG! BANG!
WHAT ARE YOU DOING?! STOP! THIS IS A CRIME SCENE!
BANG! BANG!
TSHHHHHHHHH
POW!

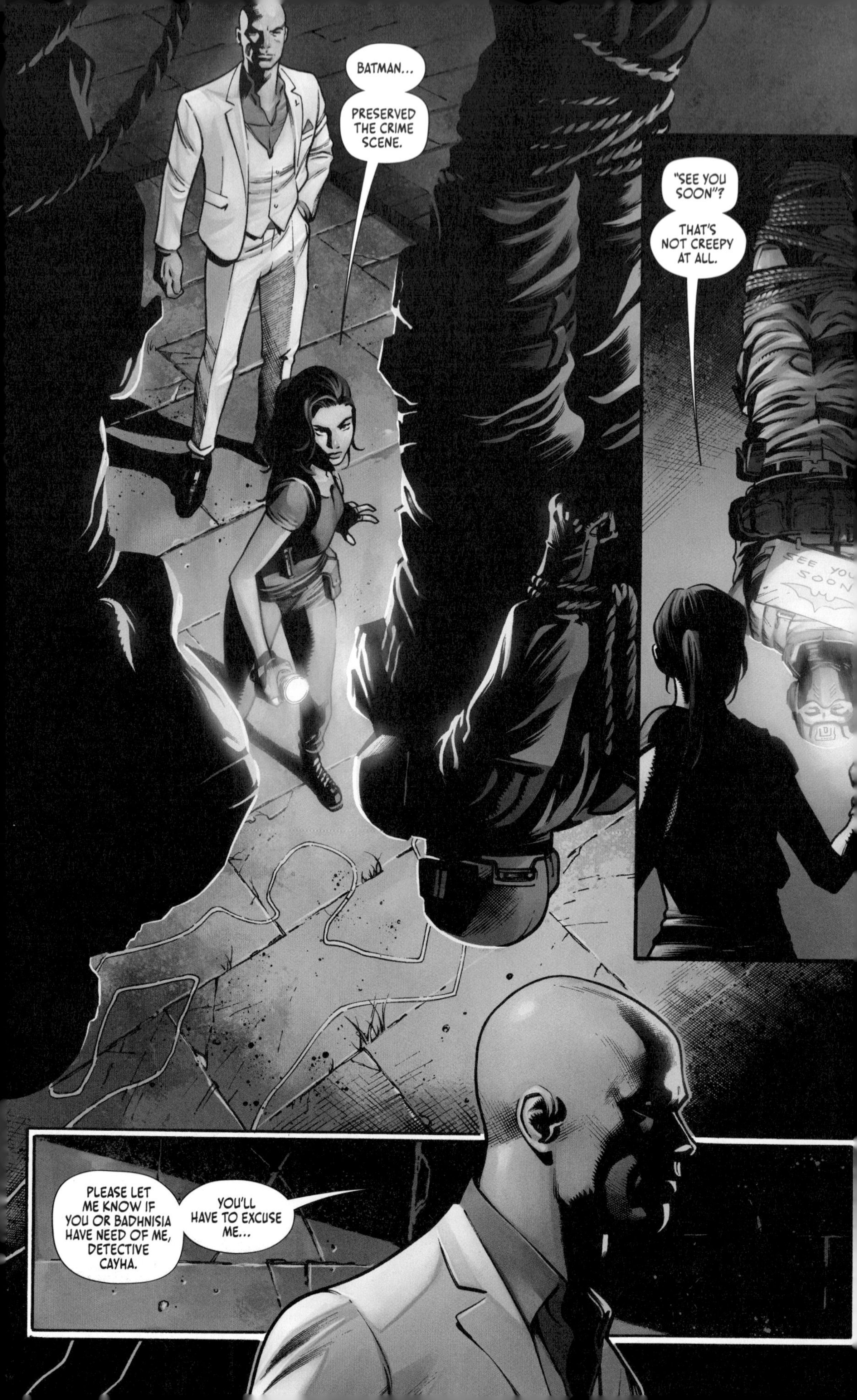
BATMAN...
PRESERVED THE CRIME SCENE.
"SEE YOU SOON"?
THAT'S NOT CREEPY AT ALL.
SEE YOU SOON
PLEASE LET ME KNOW IF YOU OR BADHNISIA HAVE NEED OF ME, DETECTIVE CAYHA.
YOU'LL HAVE TO EXCUSE ME...

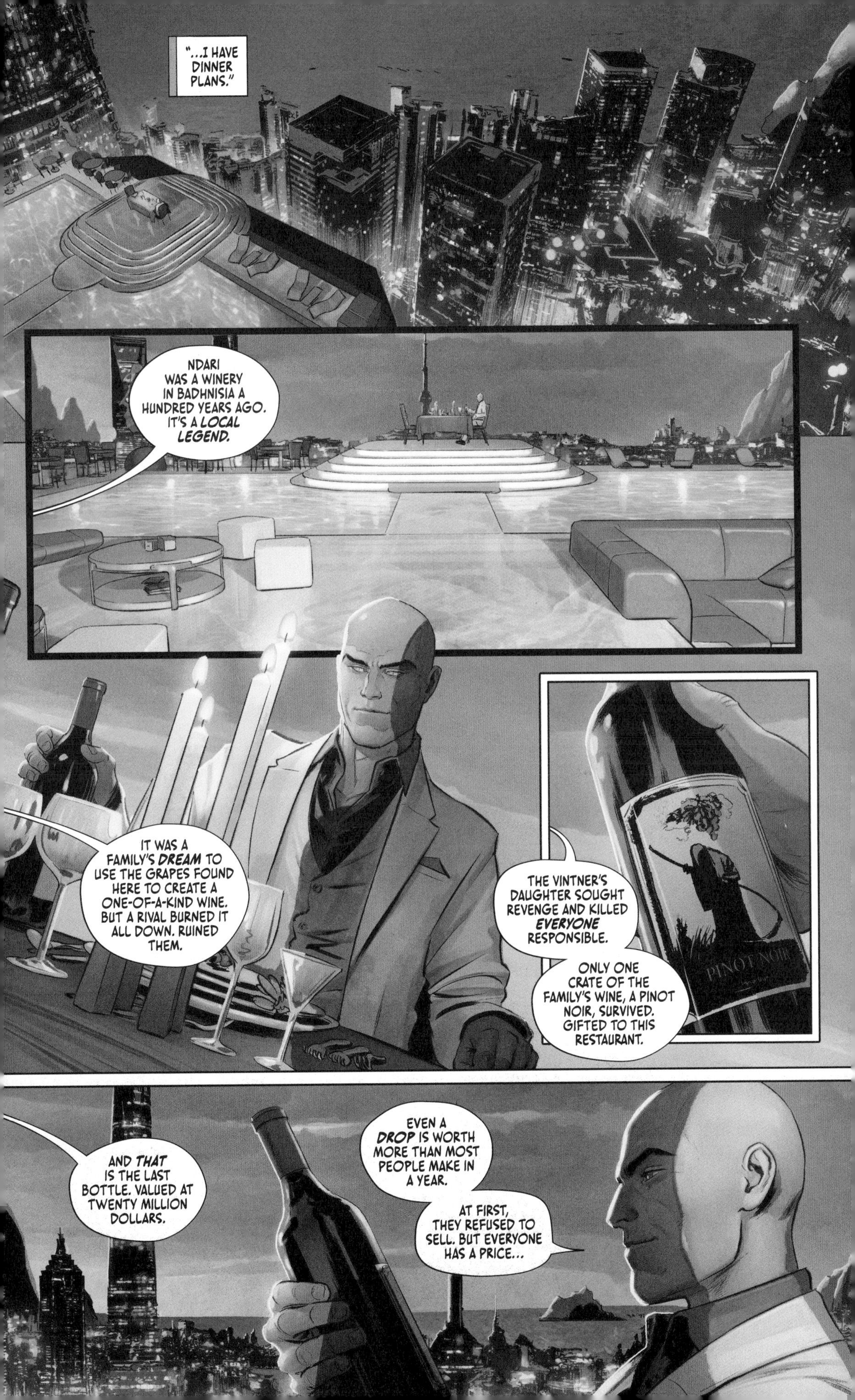
"...I HAVE DINNER PLANS."
NDARI WAS A WINERY IN BADHNISIA A HUNDRED YEARS AGO. IT'S A *LOCAL LEGEND.*
IT WAS A FAMILY'S *DREAM* TO USE THE GRAPES FOUND HERE TO CREATE A ONE-OF-A-KIND WINE. BUT A RIVAL BURNED IT ALL DOWN. RUINED THEM.
THE VINTNER'S DAUGHTER SOUGHT REVENGE AND KILLED *EVERYONE* RESPONSIBLE.
ONLY ONE CRATE OF THE FAMILY'S WINE, A PINOT NOIR, SURVIVED. GIFTED TO THIS RESTAURANT.
PINOT NOIR
AND *THAT* IS THE LAST BOTTLE. VALUED AT TWENTY MILLION DOLLARS.
EVEN A *DROP* IS WORTH MORE THAN MOST PEOPLE MAKE IN A YEAR.
AT FIRST, THEY REFUSED TO SELL. BUT EVERYONE HAS A PRICE...

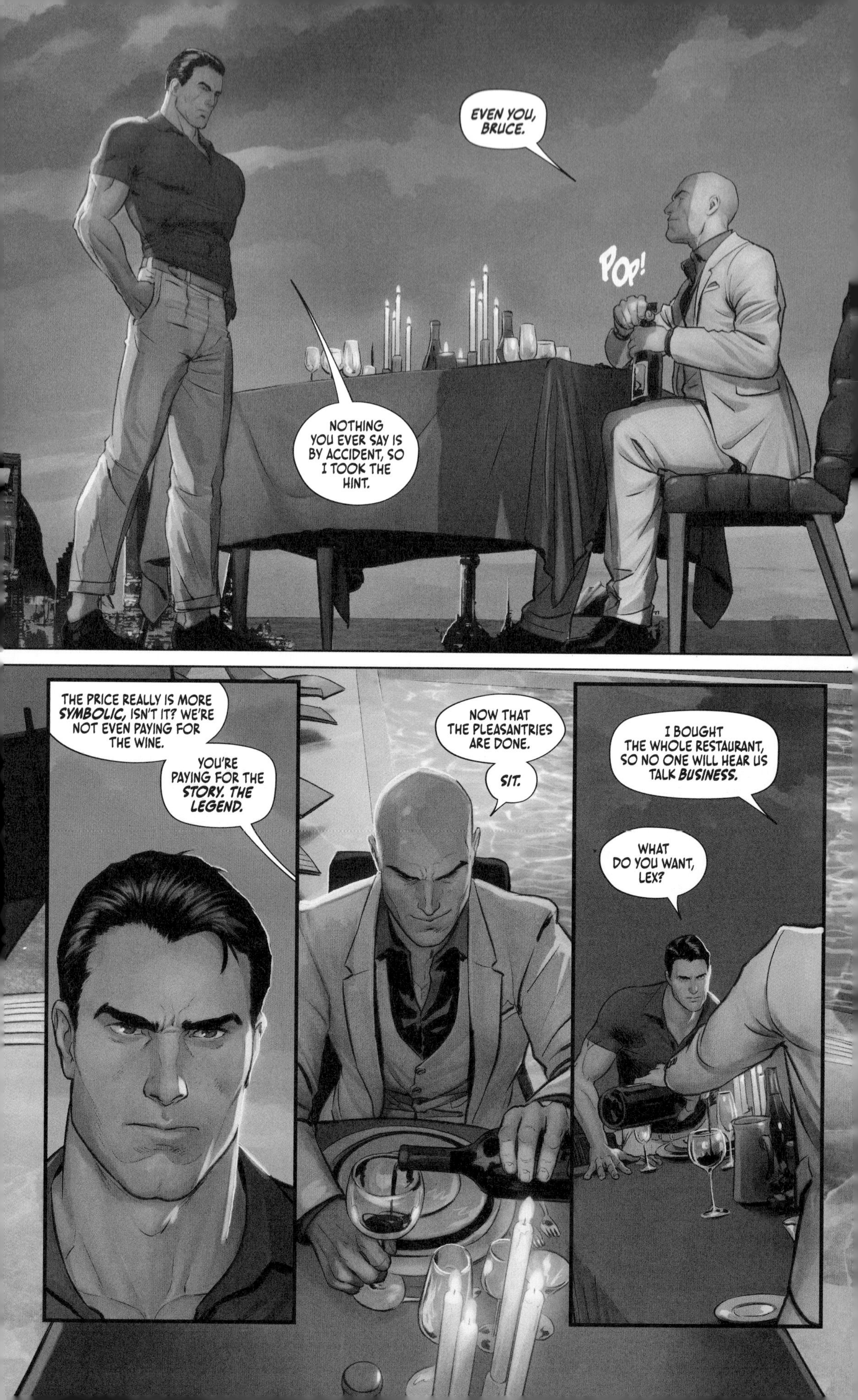
EVEN YOU, BRUCE.
POP!
NOTHING YOU EVER SAY IS BY ACCIDENT, SO I TOOK THE HINT.
THE PRICE REALLY IS MORE SYMBOLIC, ISN'T IT? WE'RE NOT EVEN PAYING FOR THE WINE.
YOU'RE PAYING FOR THE STORY. THE LEGEND.
NOW THAT THE PLEASANTRIES ARE DONE.
SIT.
I BOUGHT THE WHOLE RESTAURANT, SO NO ONE WILL HEAR US TALK BUSINESS.
WHAT DO YOU WANT, LEX?

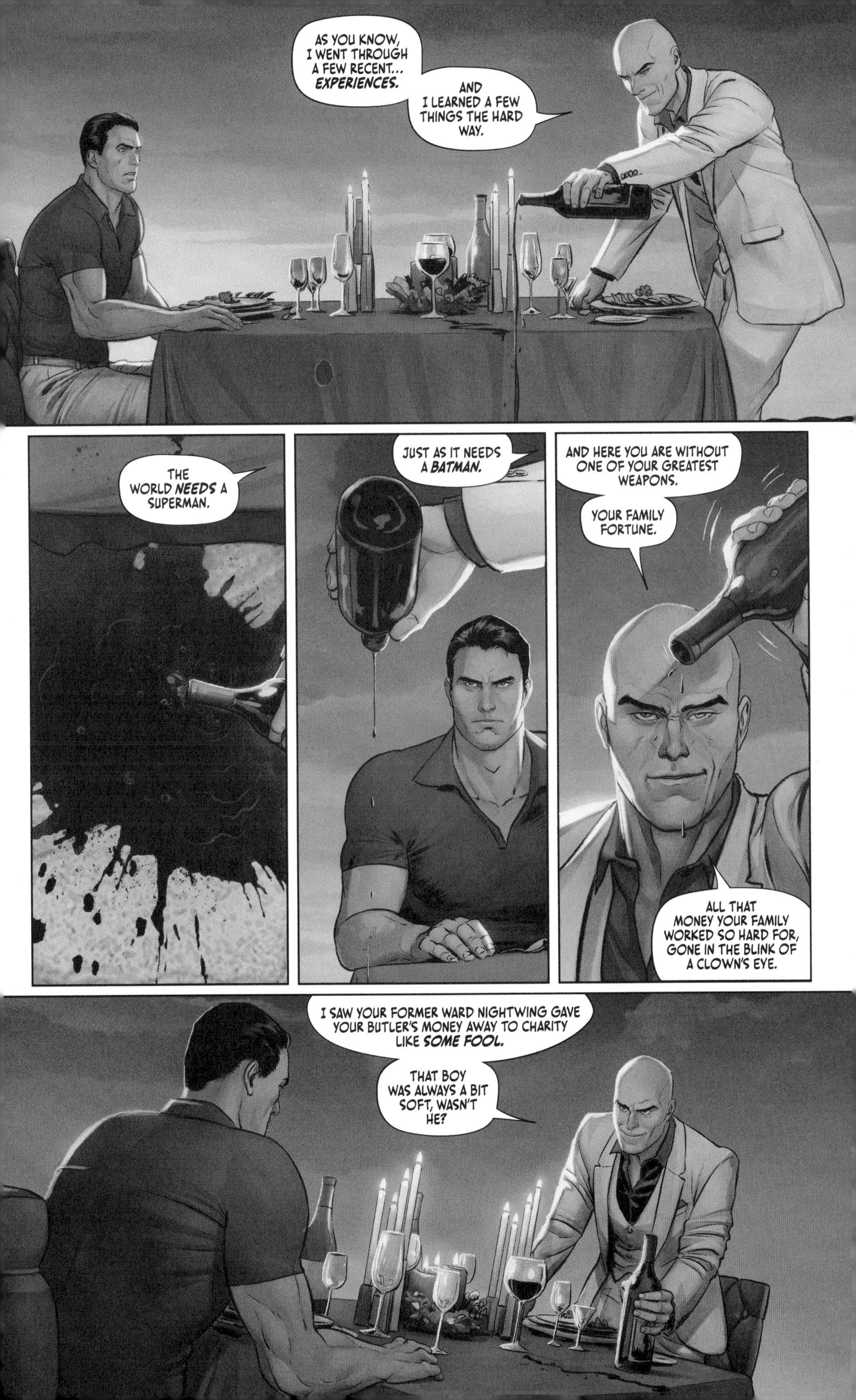
AS YOU KNOW, I WENT THROUGH A FEW RECENT... ***EXPERIENCES.***
AND I LEARNED A FEW THINGS THE HARD WAY.
THE WORLD ***NEEDS*** A SUPERMAN.
JUST AS IT NEEDS A ***BATMAN.***
AND HERE YOU ARE WITHOUT ONE OF YOUR GREATEST WEAPONS.
YOUR FAMILY FORTUNE.
ALL THAT MONEY YOUR FAMILY WORKED SO HARD FOR, GONE IN THE BLINK OF A CLOWN'S EYE.
I SAW YOUR FORMER WARD NIGHTWING GAVE YOUR BUTLER'S MONEY AWAY TO CHARITY LIKE ***SOME FOOL.***
THAT BOY WAS ALWAYS A BIT SOFT, WASN'T HE?

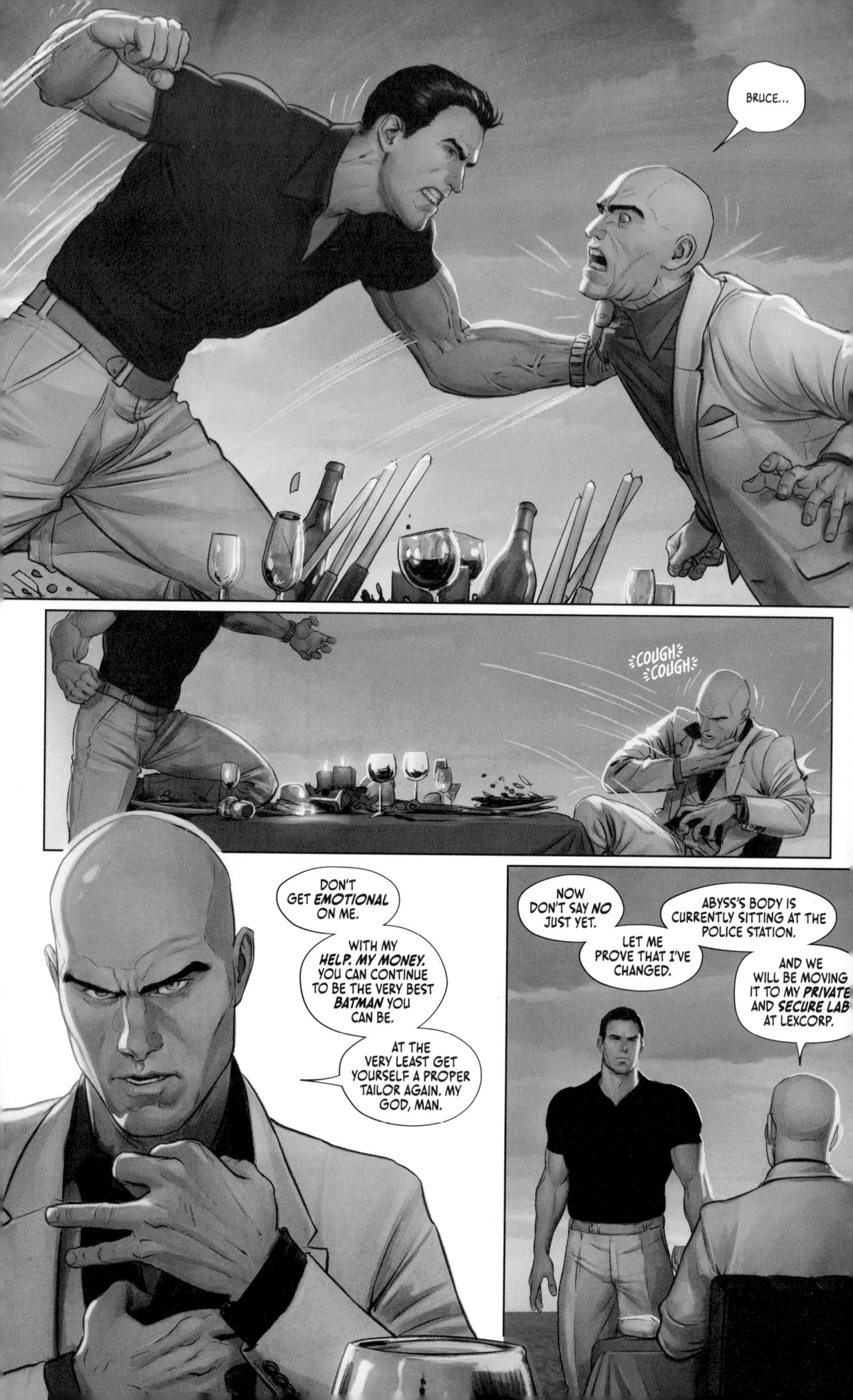
BRUCE...
COUGH COUGH
DON'T GET EMOTIONAL ON ME.
WITH MY HELP. MY MONEY. YOU CAN CONTINUE TO BE THE VERY BEST BATMAN YOU CAN BE.
AT THE VERY LEAST GET YOURSELF A PROPER TAILOR AGAIN. MY GOD, MAN.
NOW DON'T SAY NO JUST YET.
LET ME PROVE THAT I'VE CHANGED.
ABYSS'S BODY IS CURRENTLY SITTING AT THE POLICE STATION.
AND WE WILL BE MOVING IT TO MY PRIVATE AND SECURE LAB AT LEXCORP.

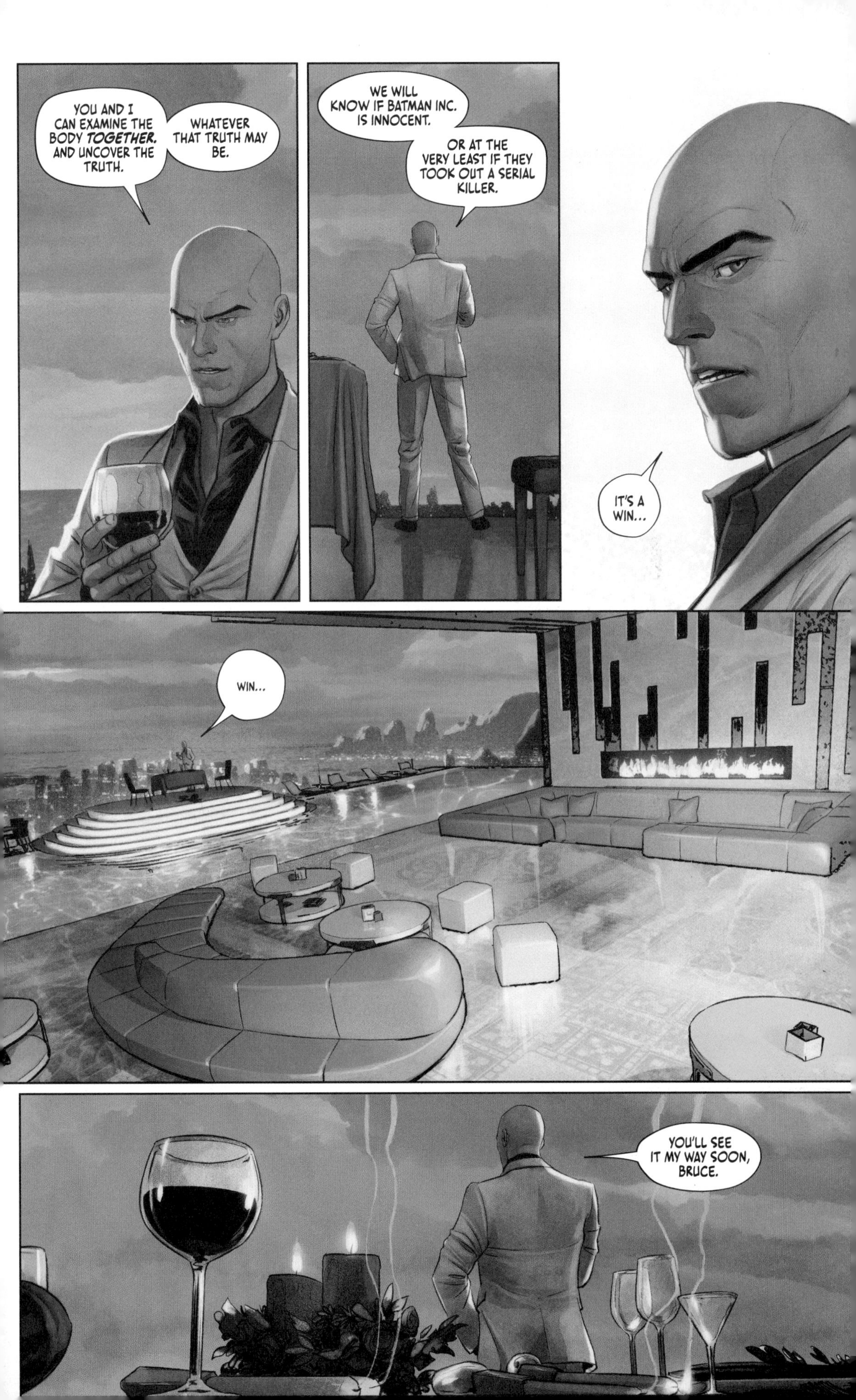
YOU AND I CAN EXAMINE THE BODY *TOGETHER.* AND UNCOVER THE TRUTH.
WHATEVER THAT TRUTH MAY BE.
WE WILL KNOW IF BATMAN INC. IS INNOCENT.
OR AT THE VERY LEAST IF THEY TOOK OUT A SERIAL KILLER.
IT'S A WIN...
WIN...
YOU'LL SEE IT MY WAY SOON, BRUCE.

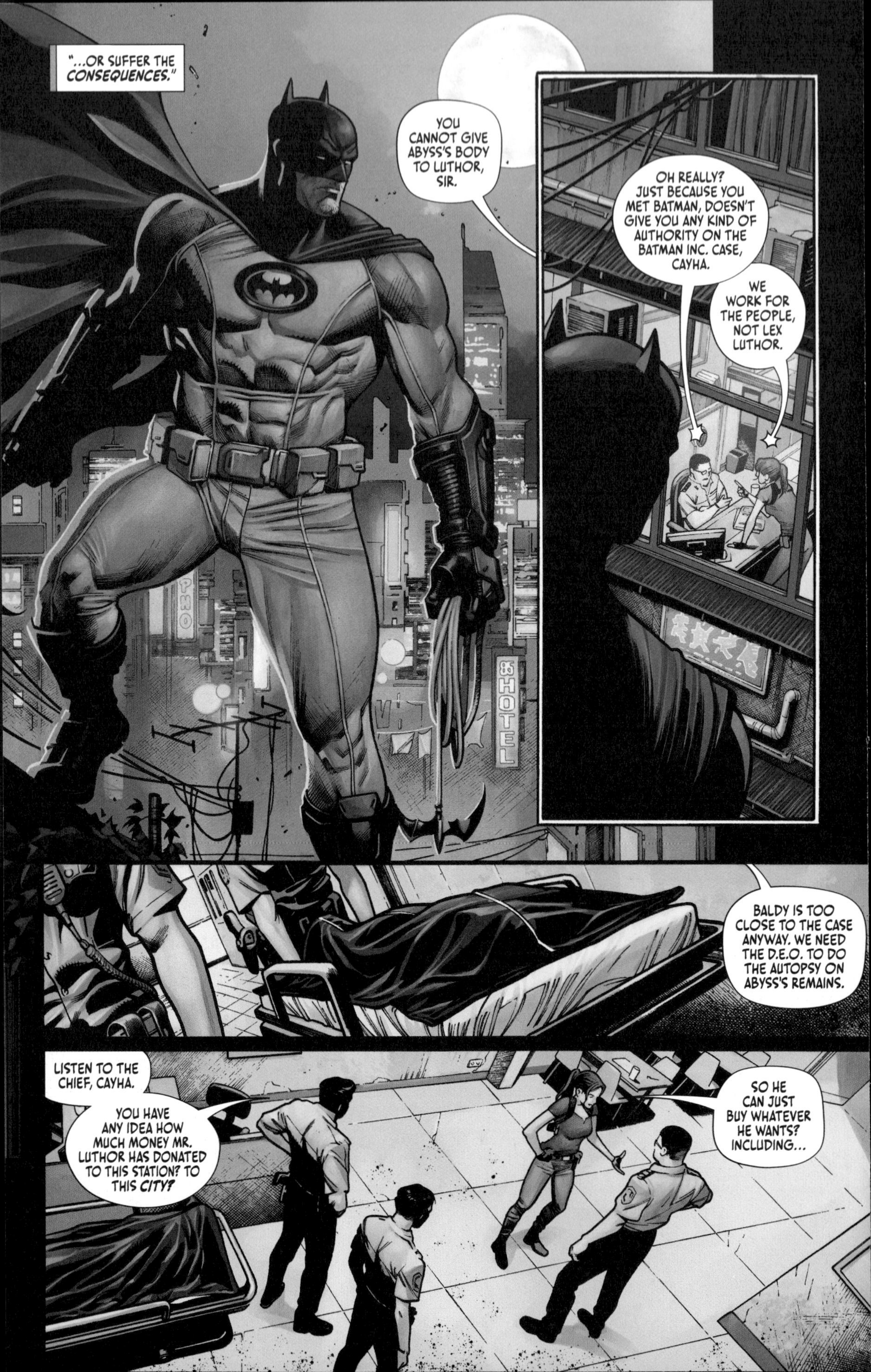
"...OR SUFFER THE CONSEQUENCES."
YOU CANNOT GIVE ABYSS'S BODY TO LUTHOR, SIR.
OH REALLY? JUST BECAUSE YOU MET BATMAN, DOESN'T GIVE YOU ANY KIND OF AUTHORITY ON THE BATMAN INC. CASE, CAYHA.
WE WORK FOR THE PEOPLE, NOT LEX LUTHOR.
HOTEL
BALDY IS TOO CLOSE TO THE CASE ANYWAY. WE NEED THE D.E.O. TO DO THE AUTOPSY ON ABYSS'S REMAINS.
LISTEN TO THE CHIEF, CAYHA.
YOU HAVE ANY IDEA HOW MUCH MONEY MR. LUTHOR HAS DONATED TO THIS STATION? TO THIS CITY?
SO HE CAN JUST BUY WHATEVER HE WANTS? INCLUDING...

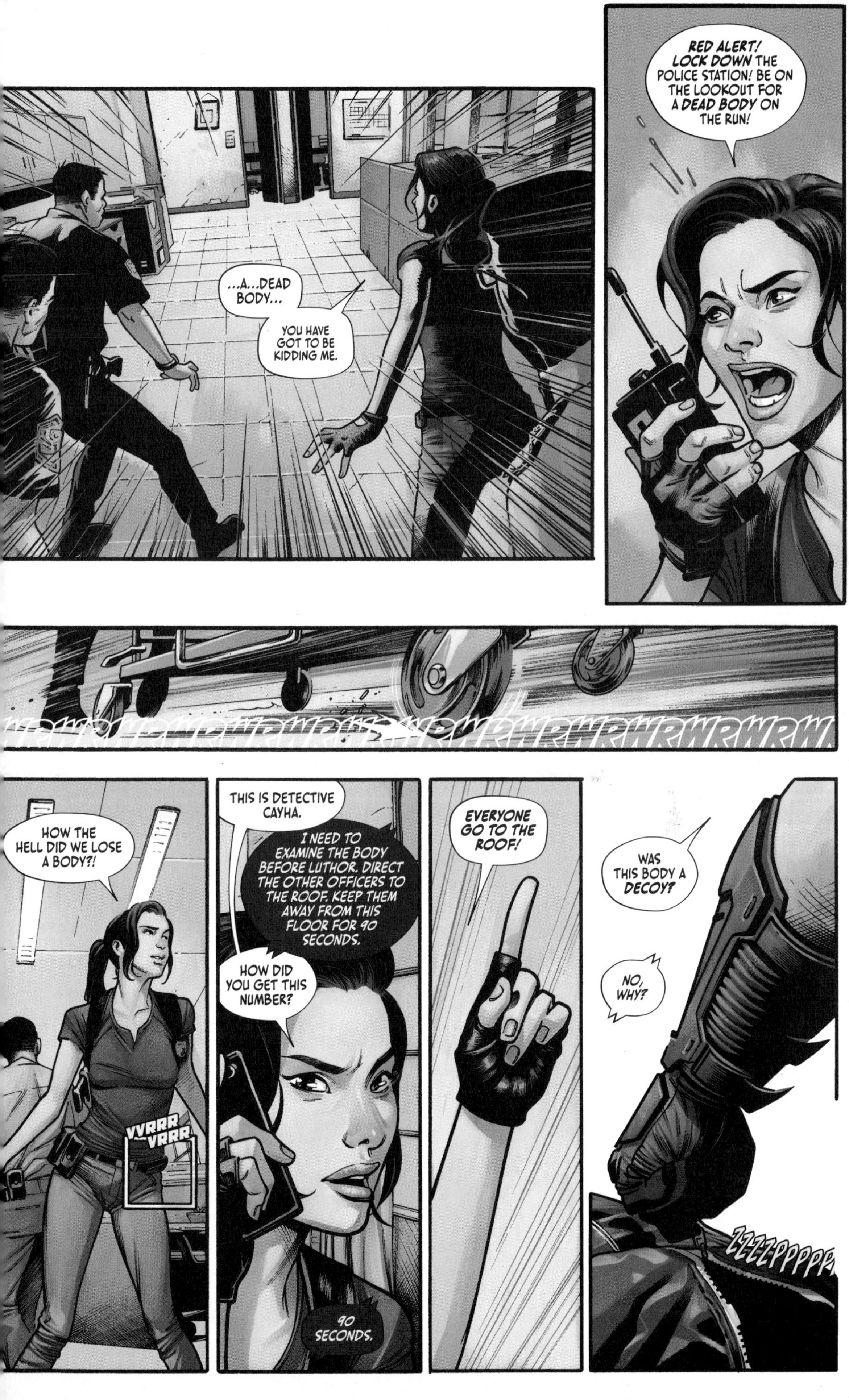

...A...DEAD BODY...
YOU HAVE GOT TO BE KIDDING ME.
RED ALERT! LOCK DOWN THE POLICE STATION! BE ON THE LOOKOUT FOR A DEAD BODY ON THE RUN!
RWRWRWRWRWRWRWRWRWRWRW
HOW THE HELL DID WE LOSE A BODY?!
VVRRR VRRR
THIS IS DETECTIVE CAYHA.
I NEED TO EXAMINE THE BODY BEFORE LUTHOR. DIRECT THE OTHER OFFICERS TO THE ROOF. KEEP THEM AWAY FROM THIS FLOOR FOR 90 SECONDS.
HOW DID YOU GET THIS NUMBER?
90 SECONDS.
EVERYONE GO TO THE ROOF!
WAS THIS BODY A DECOY?
NO, WHY?
ZZZZPPPPP

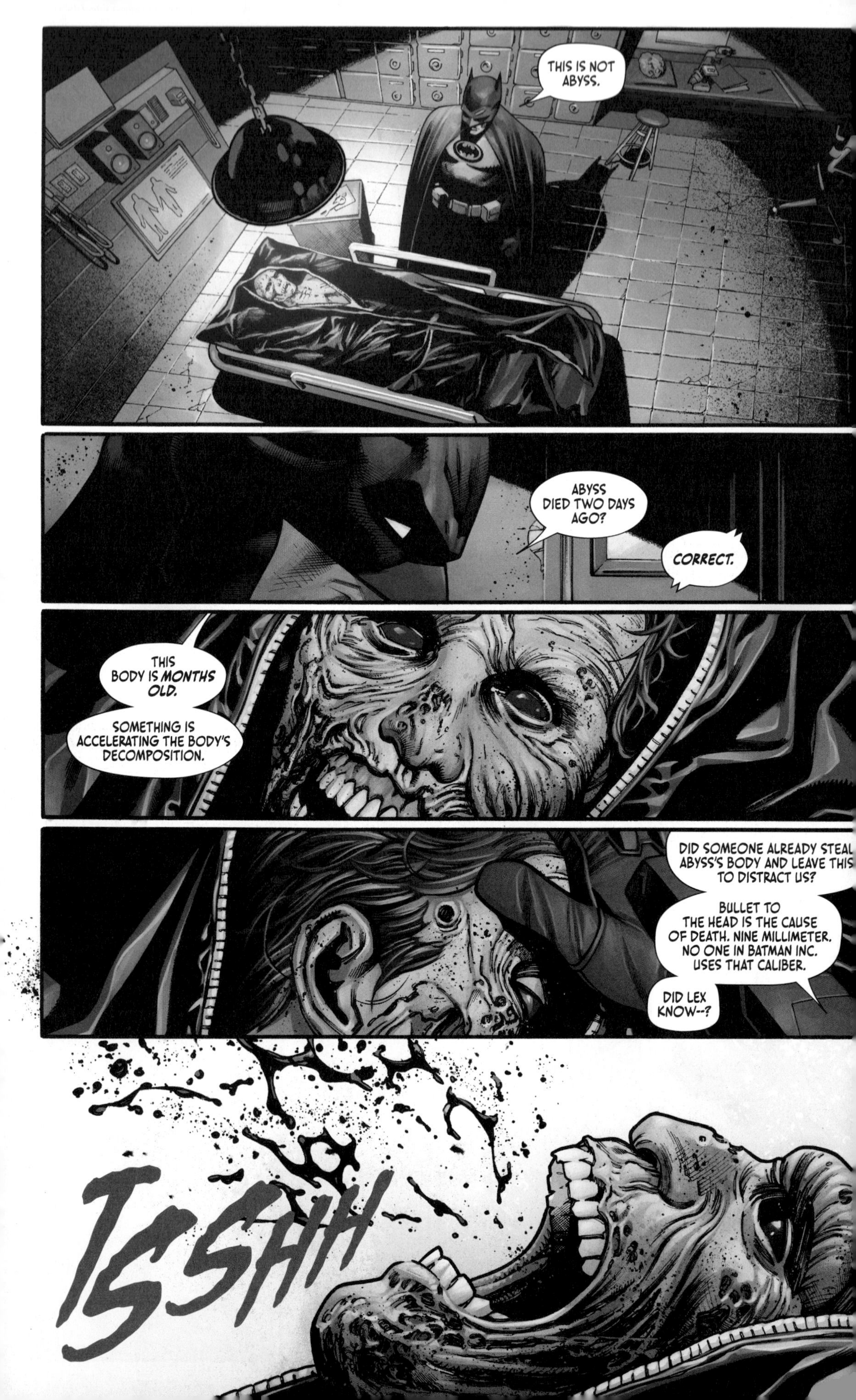
THIS IS NOT ABYSS.
ABYSS DIED TWO DAYS AGO?
CORRECT.
THIS BODY IS MONTHS OLD.
SOMETHING IS ACCELERATING THE BODY'S DECOMPOSITION.
DID SOMEONE ALREADY STEAL ABYSS'S BODY AND LEAVE THIS TO DISTRACT US?
BULLET TO THE HEAD IS THE CAUSE OF DEATH. NINE MILLIMETER. NO ONE IN BATMAN INC. USES THAT CALIBER.
DID LEX KNOW--?
TSSHH

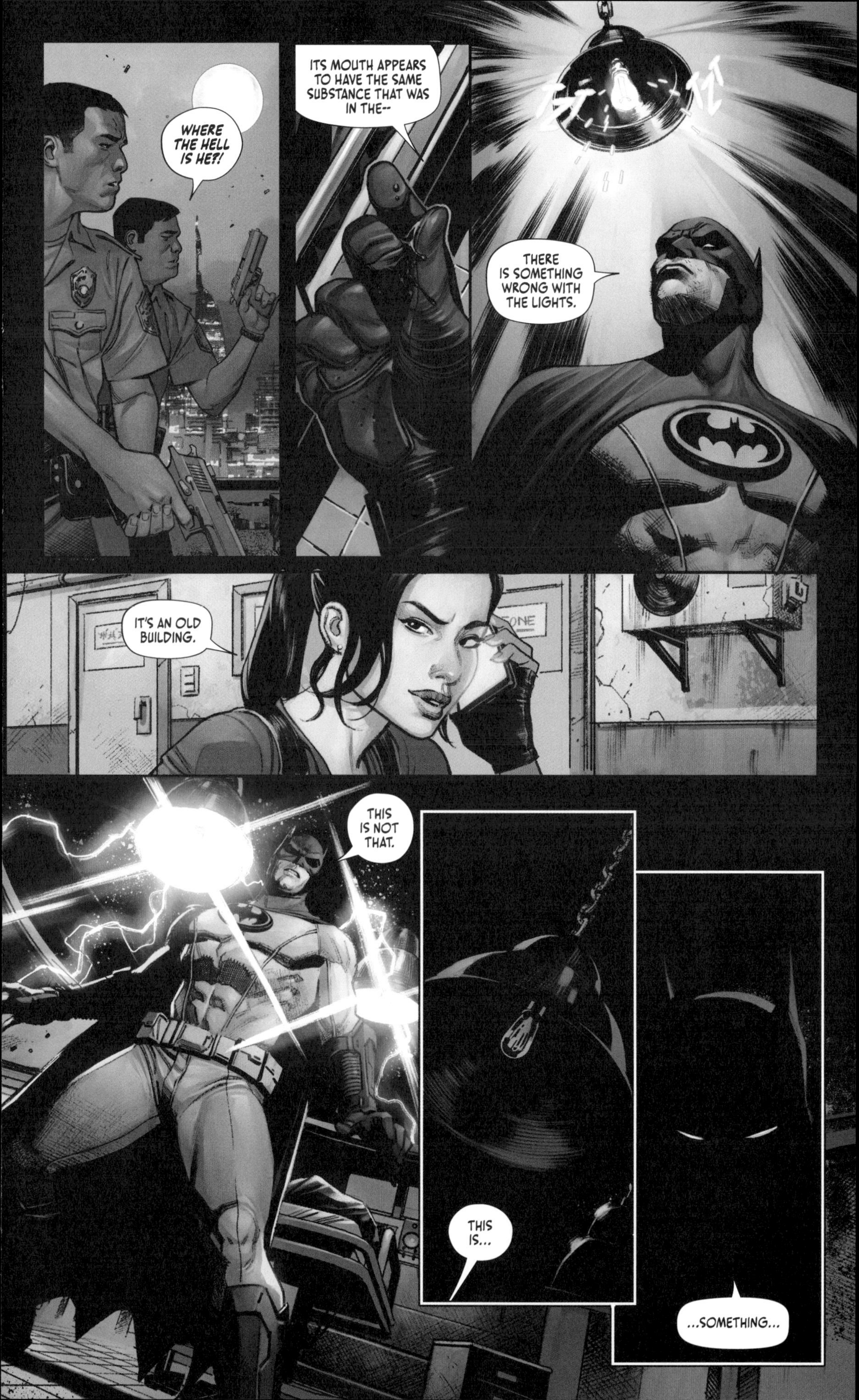
WHERE THE HELL IS HE?!
ITS MOUTH APPEARS TO HAVE THE SAME SUBSTANCE THAT WAS IN THE--
TZT TZT
THERE IS SOMETHING WRONG WITH THE LIGHTS.
IT'S AN OLD BUILDING.
THIS IS NOT THAT.
THIS IS...
...SOMETHING...

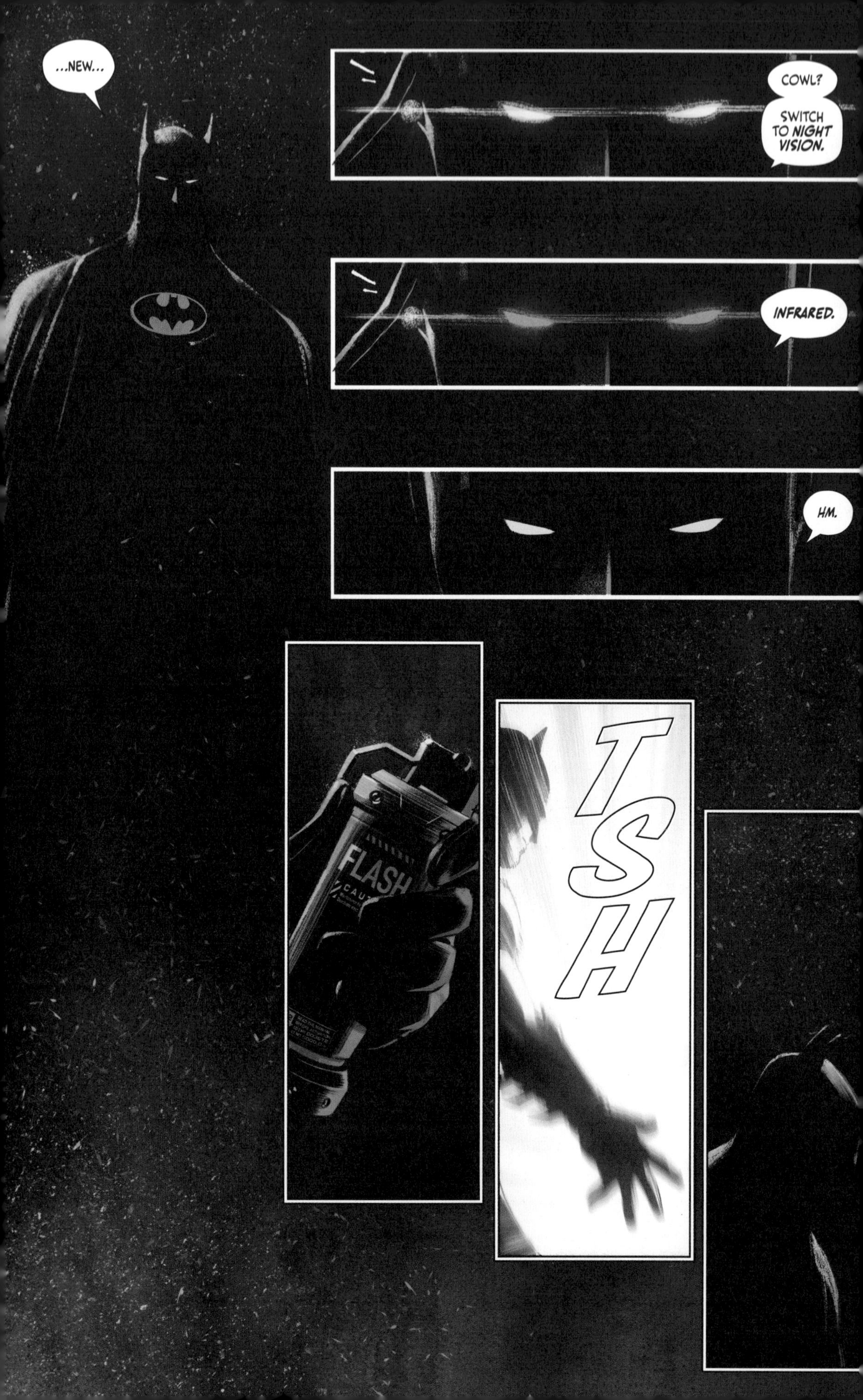
...NEW...
COWL?
SWITCH TO NIGHT VISION.
INFRARED.
HM.
FLASH
TSH

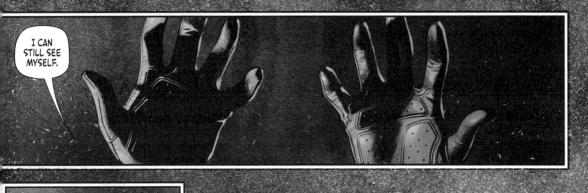

I CAN STILL SEE MYSELF.

I'M STILL IN THE POLICE STATION.

THE SMELLS OF THE CLEANER ON THE FLOOR.

NICE TRICK.

BUT I'M USED TO FIGHTING IN THE DARK.

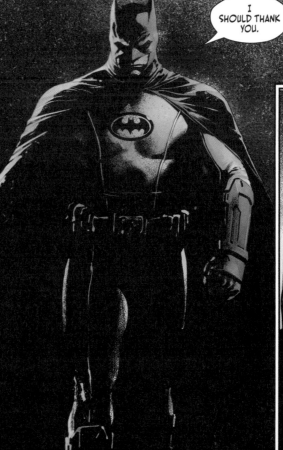

I SHOULD THANK YOU.

FOR HELPING ME PROVE BATMAN'S INNOCENCE IN THE DEATH OF ABYSS...

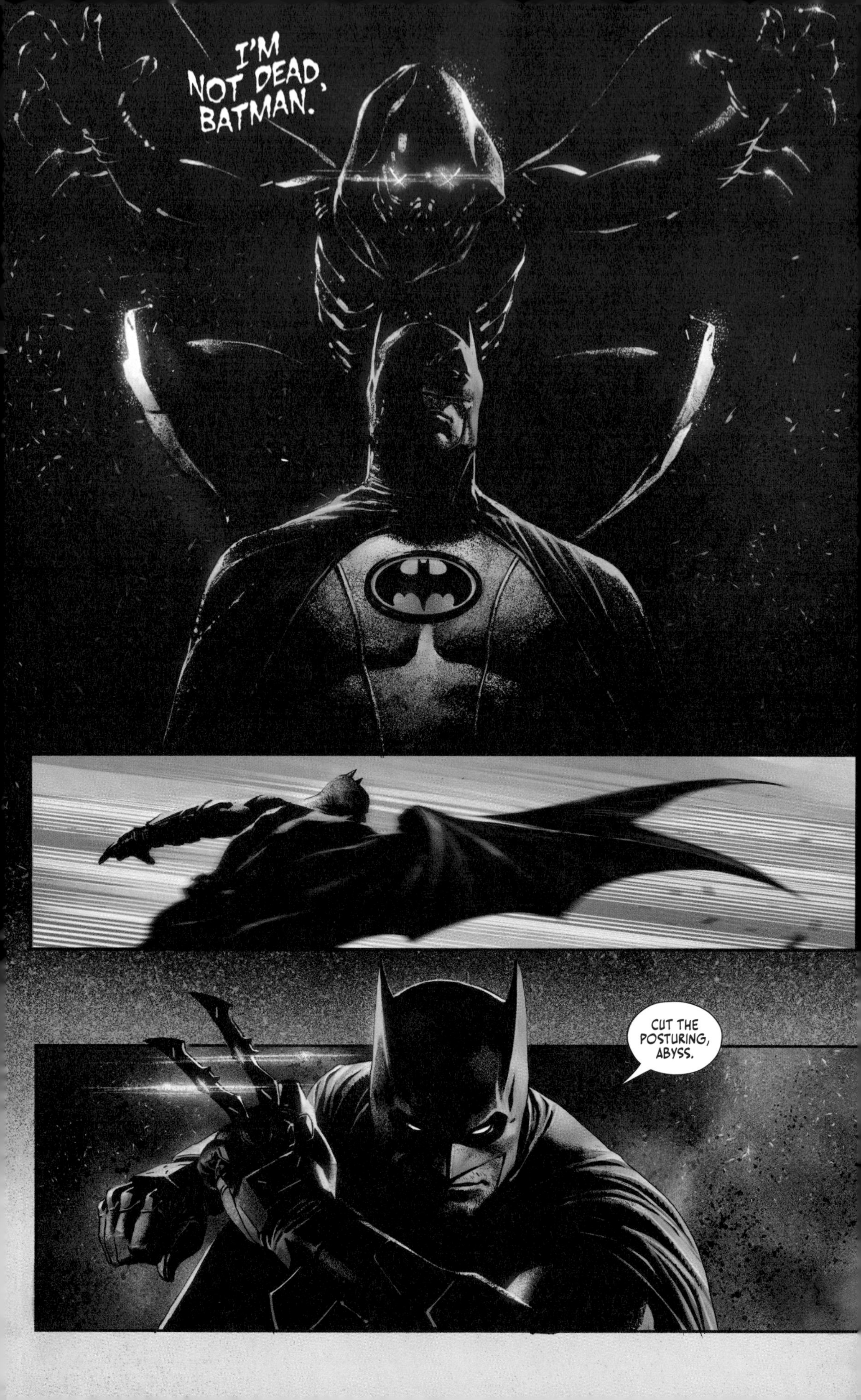
I'M NOT DEAD, BATMAN.
CUT THE POSTURING, ABYSS.

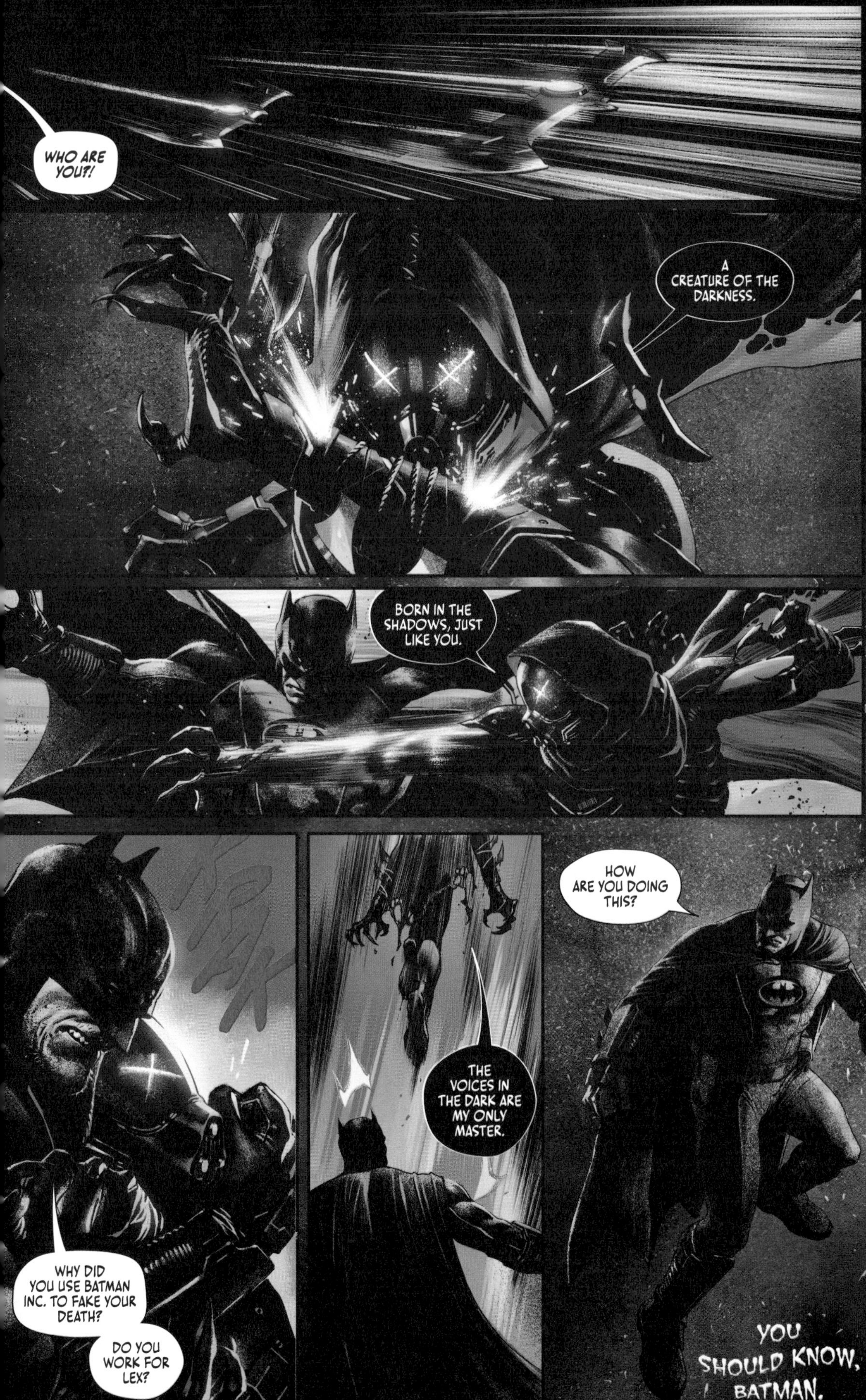
WHO ARE YOU?!
A CREATURE OF THE DARKNESS.
BORN IN THE SHADOWS, JUST LIKE YOU.
WHY DID YOU USE BATMAN INC. TO FAKE YOUR DEATH?
DO YOU WORK FOR LEX?
THE VOICES IN THE DARK ARE MY ONLY MASTER.
HOW ARE YOU DOING THIS?
YOU SHOULD KNOW, BATMAN.

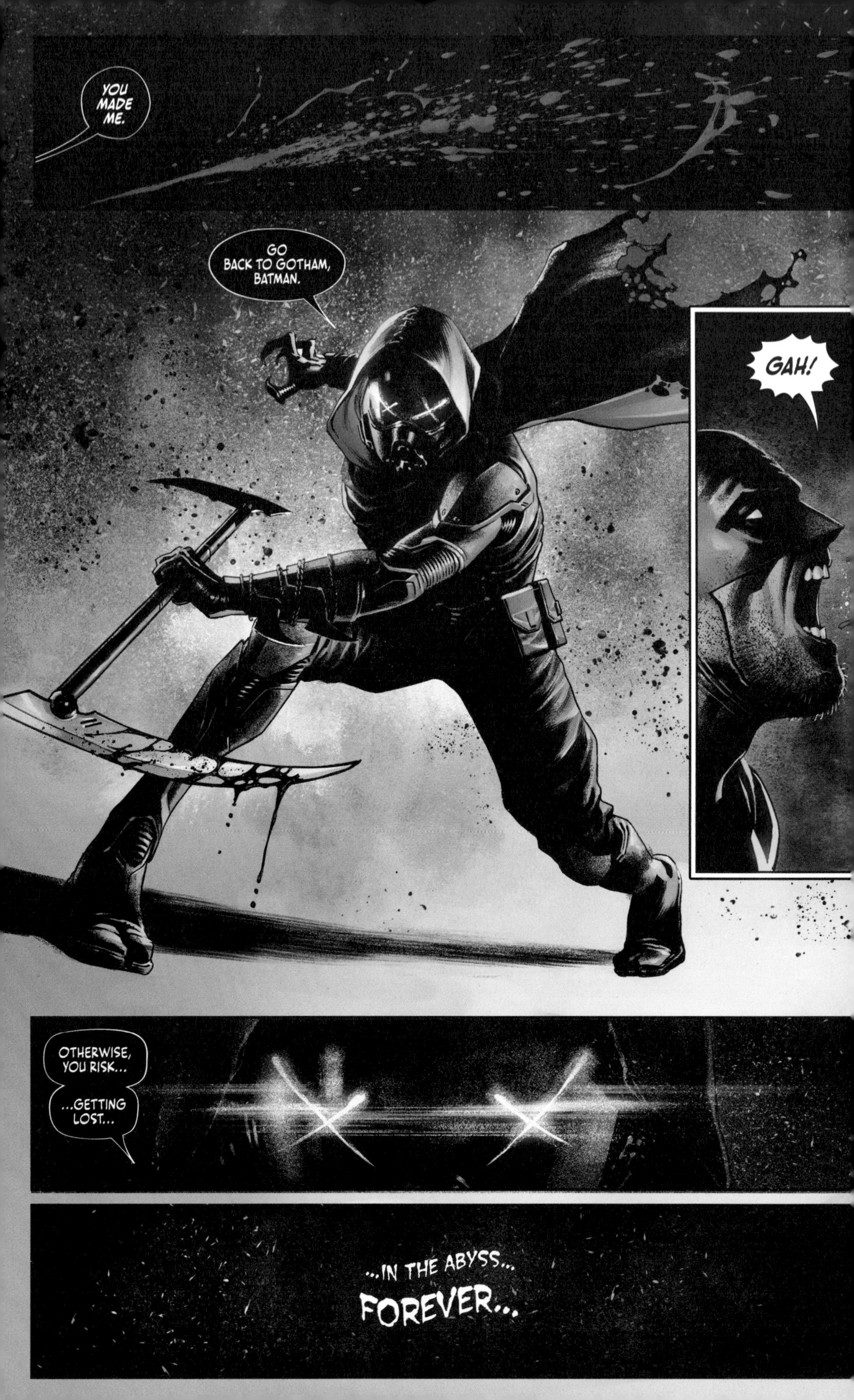
YOU MADE ME.
GO BACK TO GOTHAM, BATMAN.
GAH!
OTHERWISE, YOU RISK...
...GETTING LOST...
...IN THE ABYSS...
FOREVER...

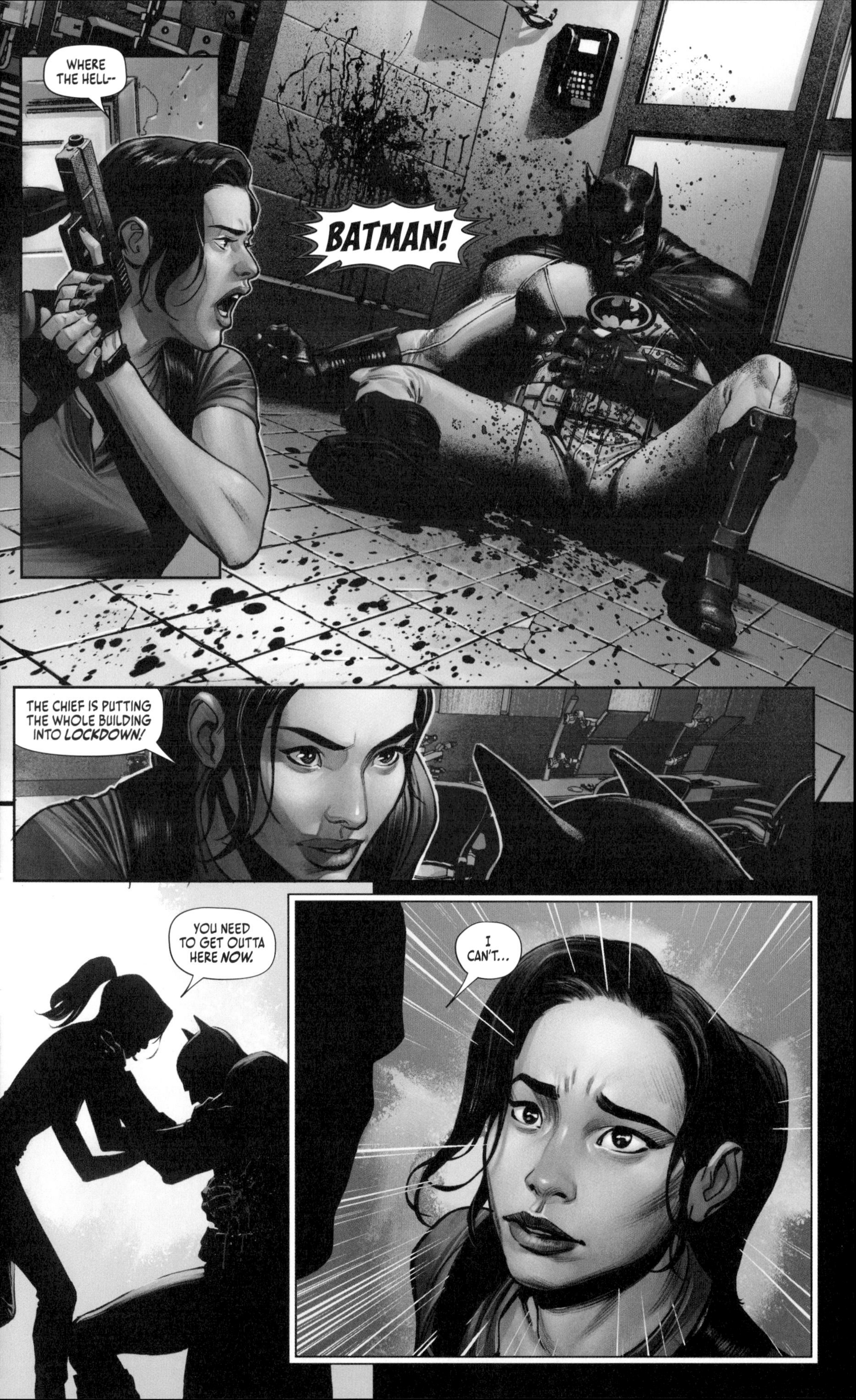
WHERE THE HELL--
BATMAN!
THE CHIEF IS PUTTING THE WHOLE BUILDING INTO LOCKDOWN!
YOU NEED TO GET OUTTA HERE NOW.
I CAN'T...

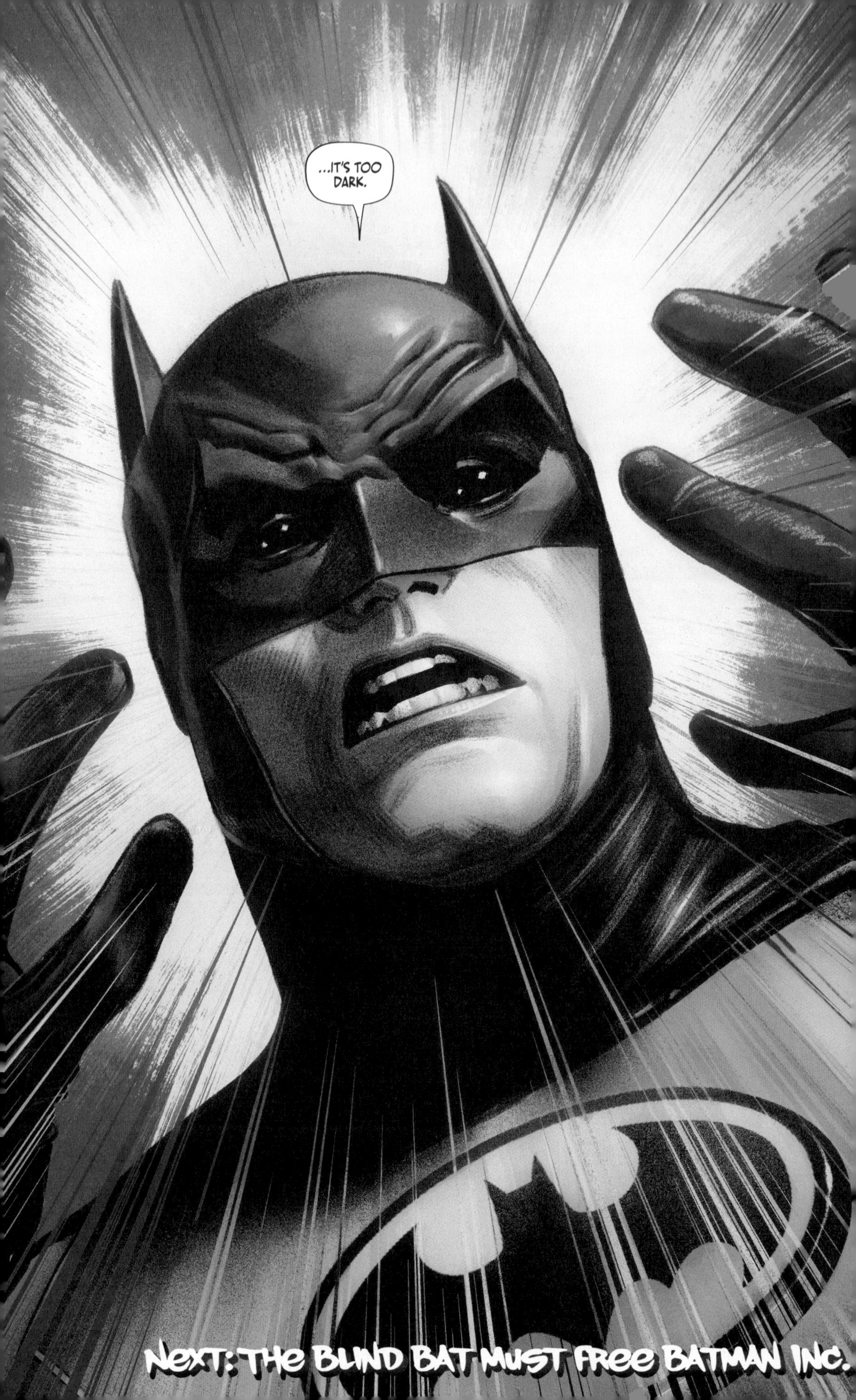
...IT'S TOO DARK.
NEXT: THE BLIND BAT MUST FREE BATMAN INC.

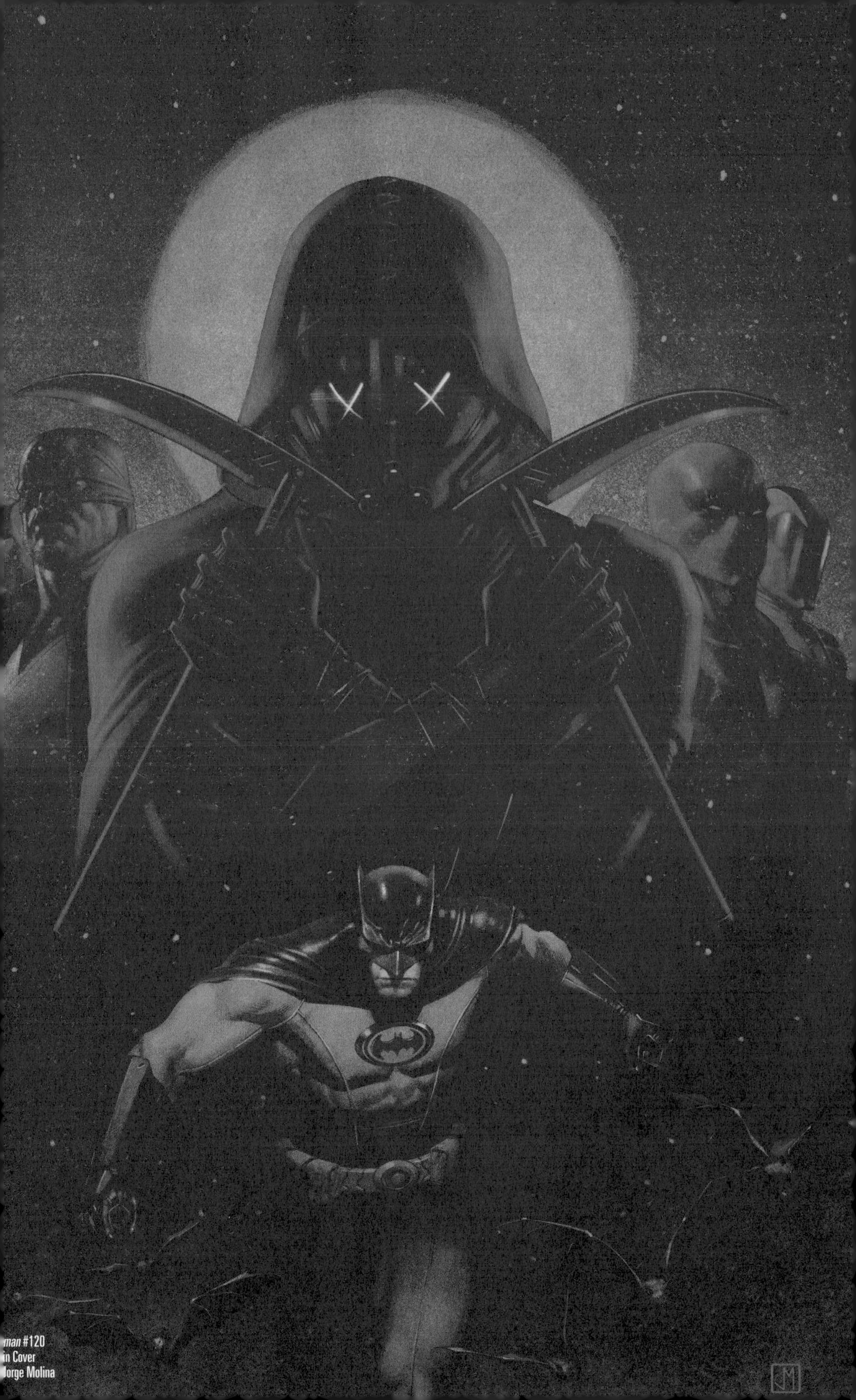

man #120
in Cover
Jorge Molina

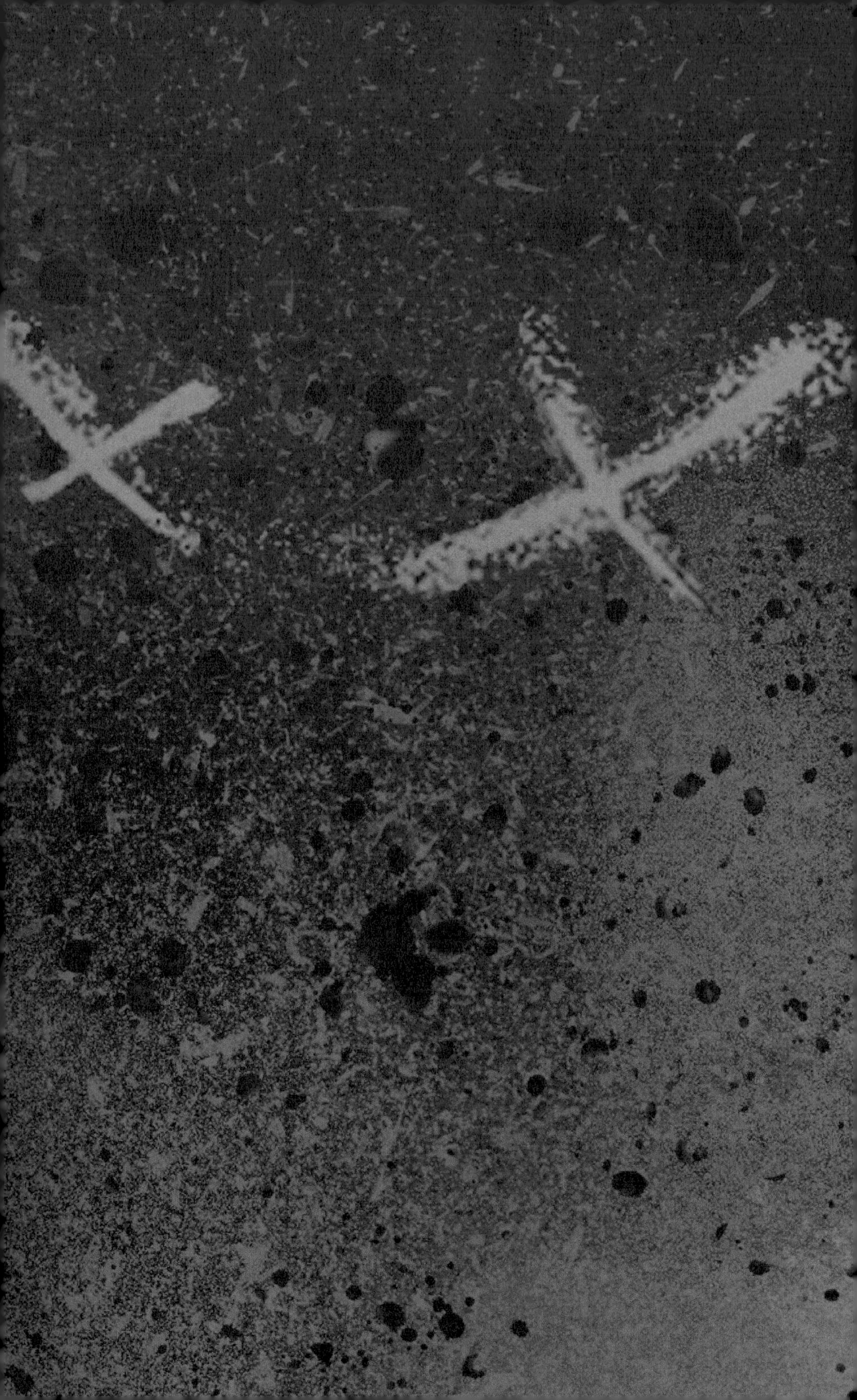

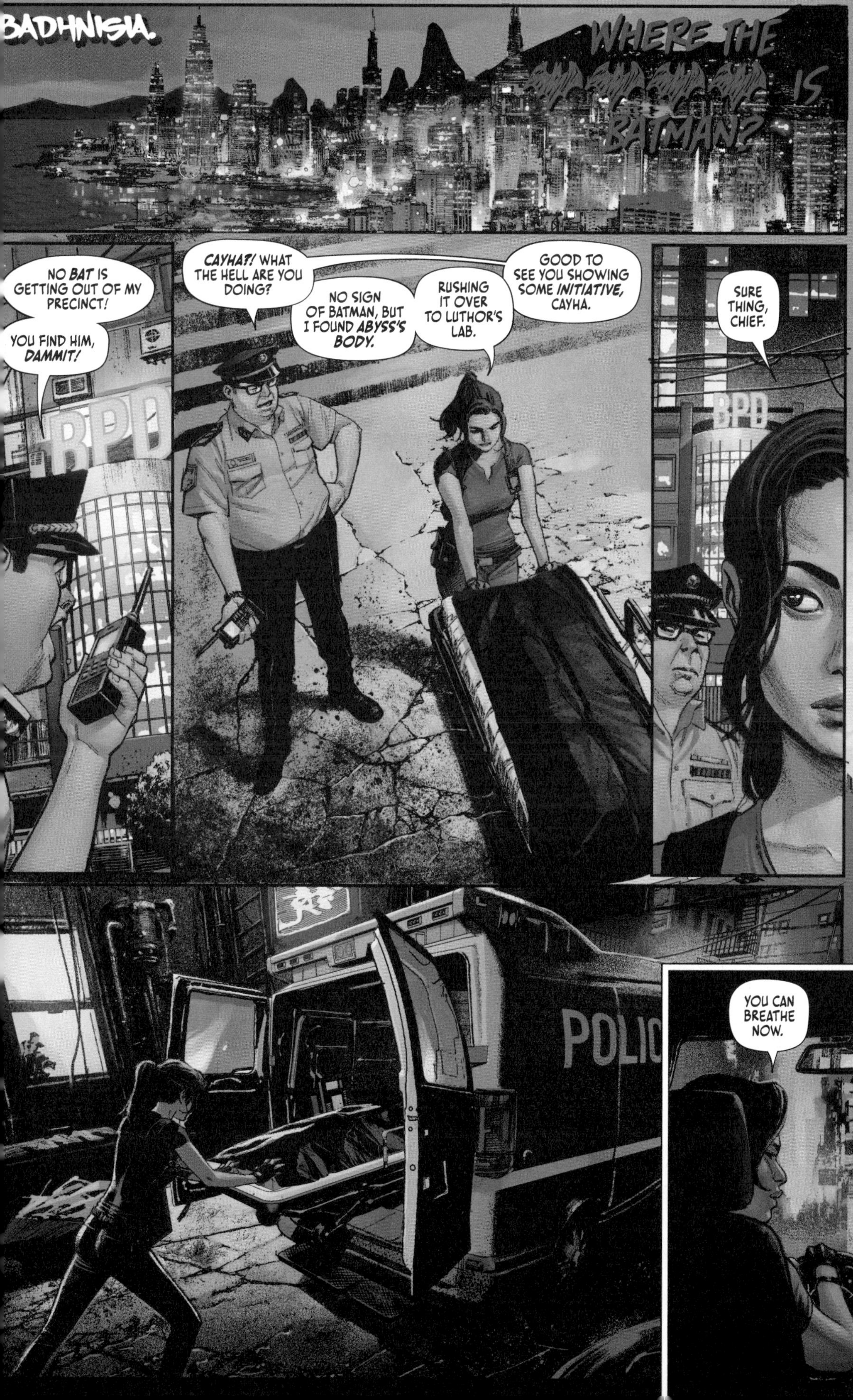
BADHNISIA.
WHERE THE IS BATMAN?
NO BAT IS GETTING OUT OF MY PRECINCT!
YOU FIND HIM, DAMMIT!
BPD
CAYHA?! WHAT THE HELL ARE YOU DOING?
NO SIGN OF BATMAN, BUT I FOUND ABYSS'S BODY.
RUSHING IT OVER TO LUTHOR'S LAB.
GOOD TO SEE YOU SHOWING SOME INITIATIVE, CAYHA.
SURE THING, CHIEF.
BPD
POLIC
YOU CAN BREATHE NOW.

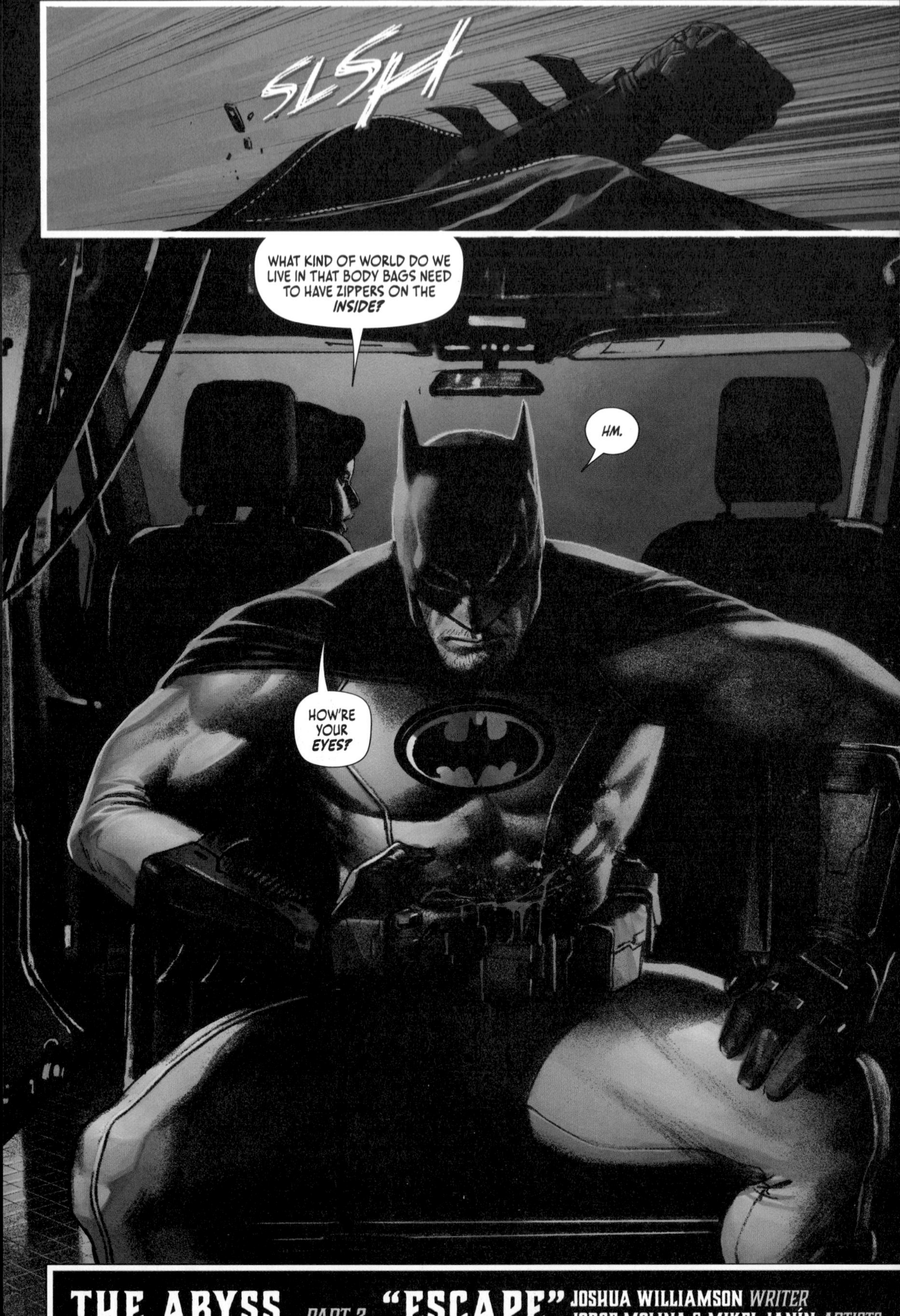
SLSH
WHAT KIND OF WORLD DO WE LIVE IN THAT BODY BAGS NEED TO HAVE ZIPPERS ON THE *INSIDE?*
HM.
HOW'RE YOUR *EYES?*

THE ABYSS, *PART 3* **"ESCAPE"** **JOSHUA WILLIAMSON** *WRITER*
JORGE MOLINA & MIKEL JANÍN *ARTISTS*

TOMEU MOREY *COLORS* **CLAYTON COWLES** *LETTERS* **JORGE MOLINA** *COVER*

FRANCESCO MATTINA, JOCK, AND DAN HIPP *VARIANT COVERS* **DAVE WIELGOSZ** *ASSOC. EDITOR* **BEN ABERNATHY** *EDITOR*

BATMAN *CREATED BY* **BOB KANE WITH BILL FINGER**

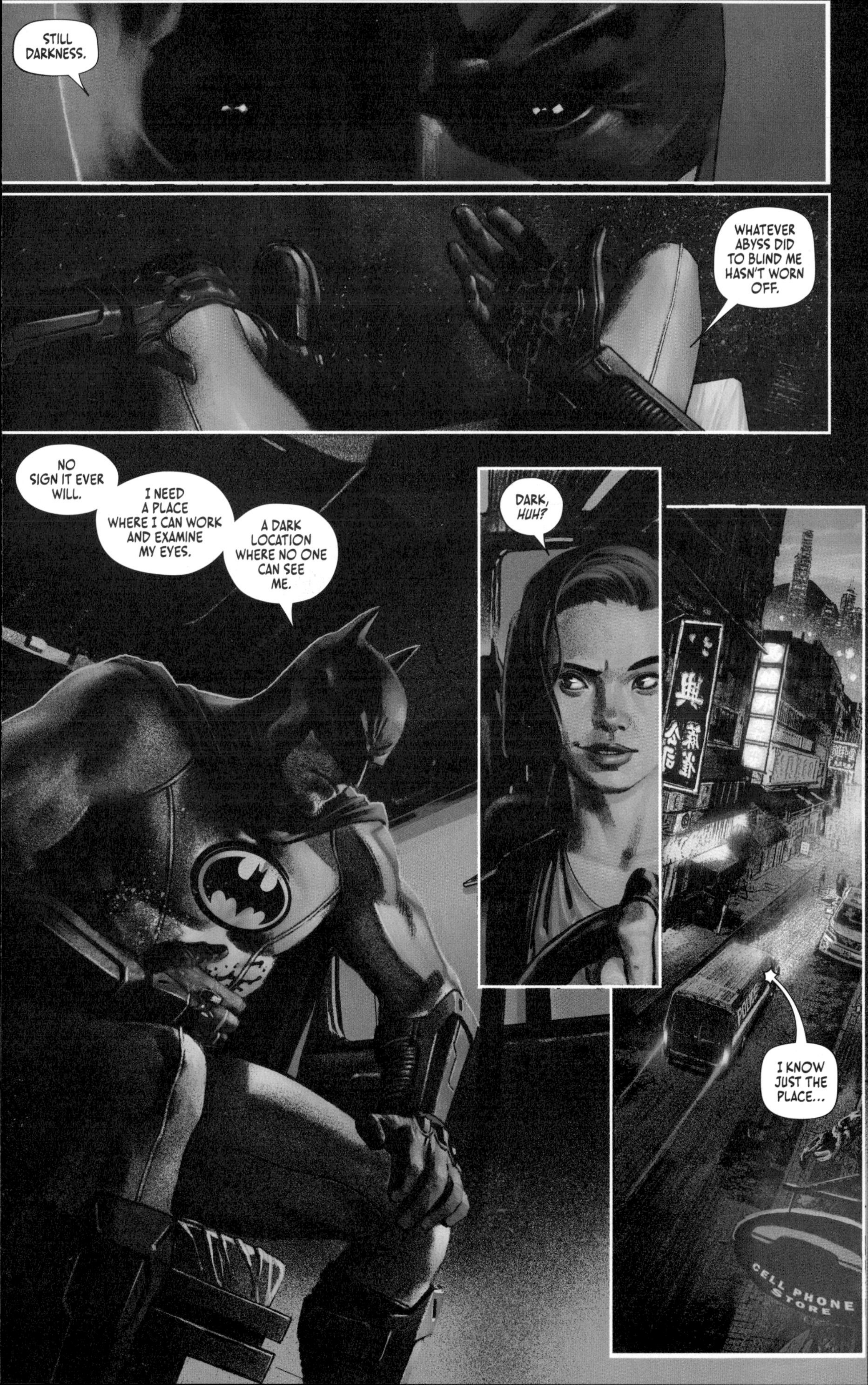
STILL DARKNESS.
WHATEVER ABYSS DID TO BLIND ME HASN'T WORN OFF.
NO SIGN IT EVER WILL.
I NEED A PLACE WHERE I CAN WORK AND EXAMINE MY EYES.
A DARK LOCATION WHERE NO ONE CAN SEE ME.
DARK, HUH?
I KNOW JUST THE PLACE...
CELL PHONE STORE

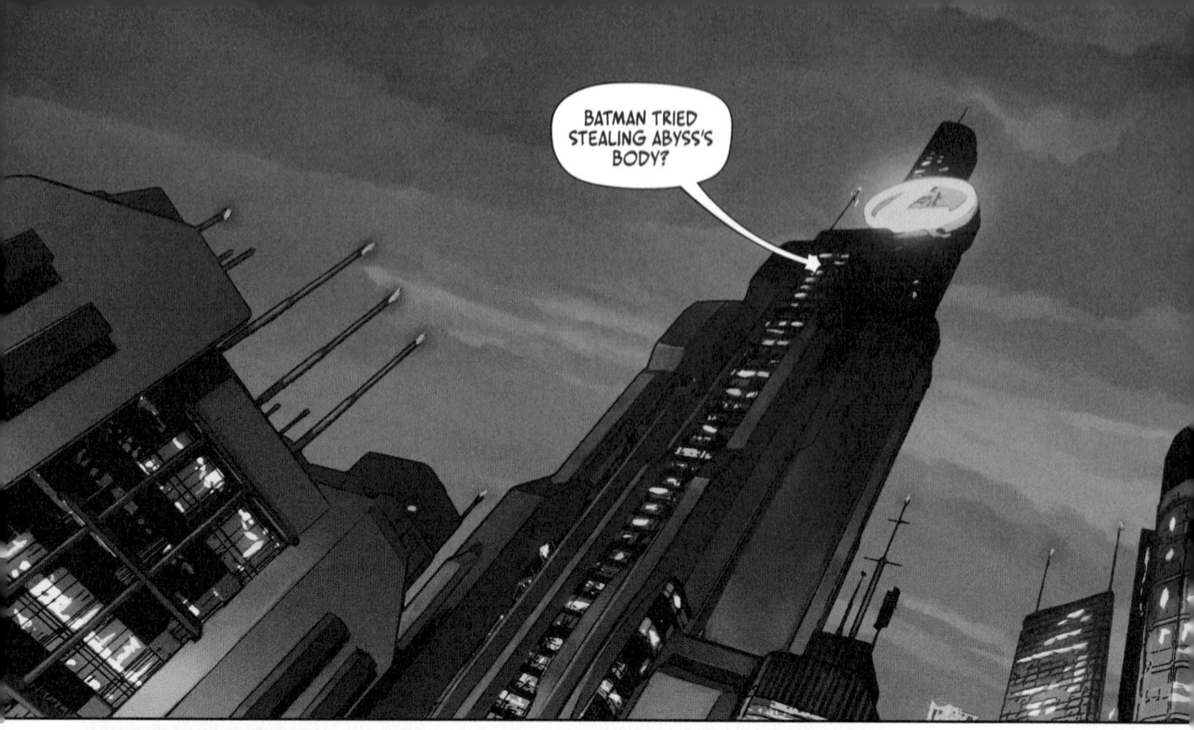
BATMAN TRIED STEALING ABYSS'S BODY?

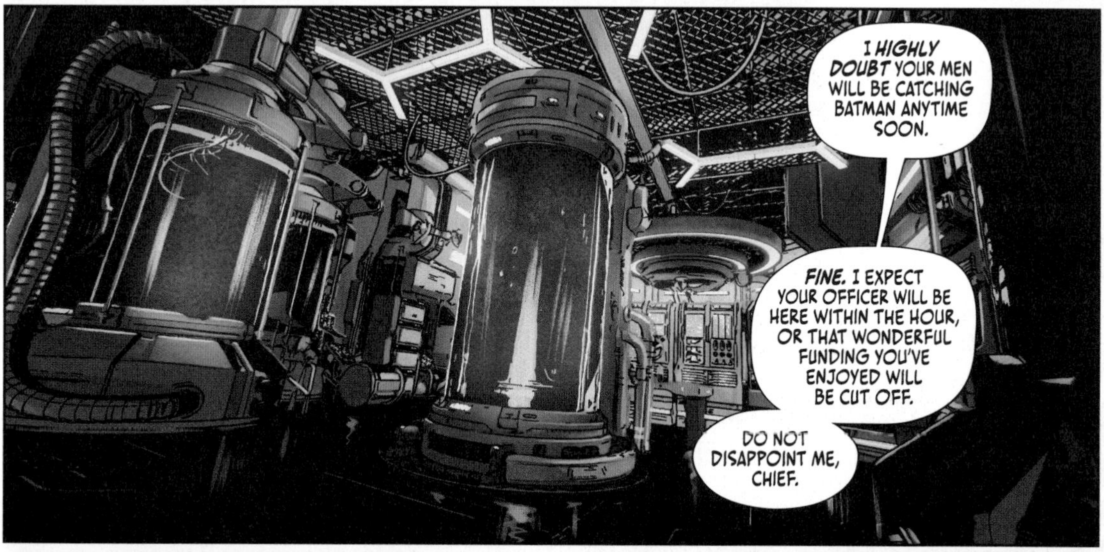
I *HIGHLY DOUBT* YOUR MEN WILL BE CATCHING BATMAN ANYTIME SOON.
FINE. I EXPECT YOUR OFFICER WILL BE HERE WITHIN THE HOUR, OR THAT WONDERFUL FUNDING YOU'VE ENJOYED WILL BE CUT OFF.
DO NOT DISAPPOINT ME, CHIEF.

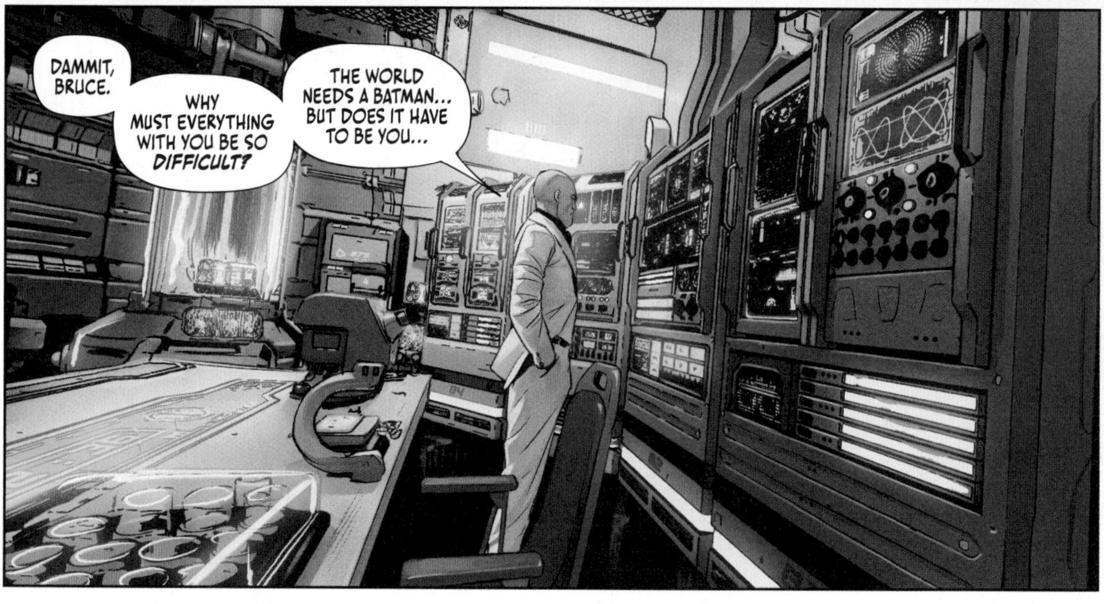
DAMMIT, BRUCE.
WHY MUST EVERYTHING WITH YOU BE SO *DIFFICULT?*
THE WORLD NEEDS A BATMAN... BUT DOES IT HAVE TO BE YOU...

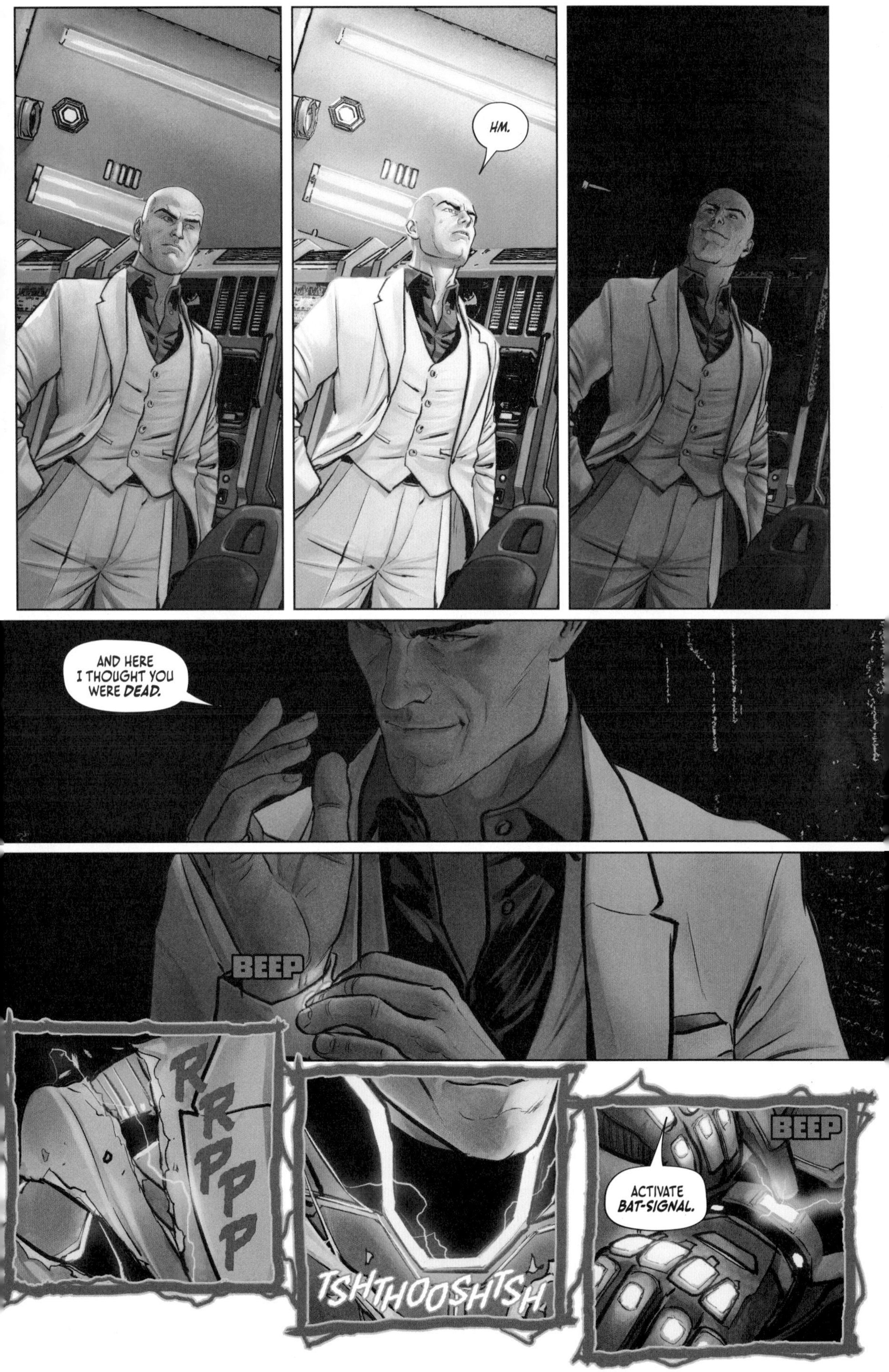
HM.
AND HERE I THOUGHT YOU WERE *DEAD.*
BEEP
RRPPP
TSHTHOOSHTSH
BEEP
ACTIVATE *BAT-SIGNAL.*

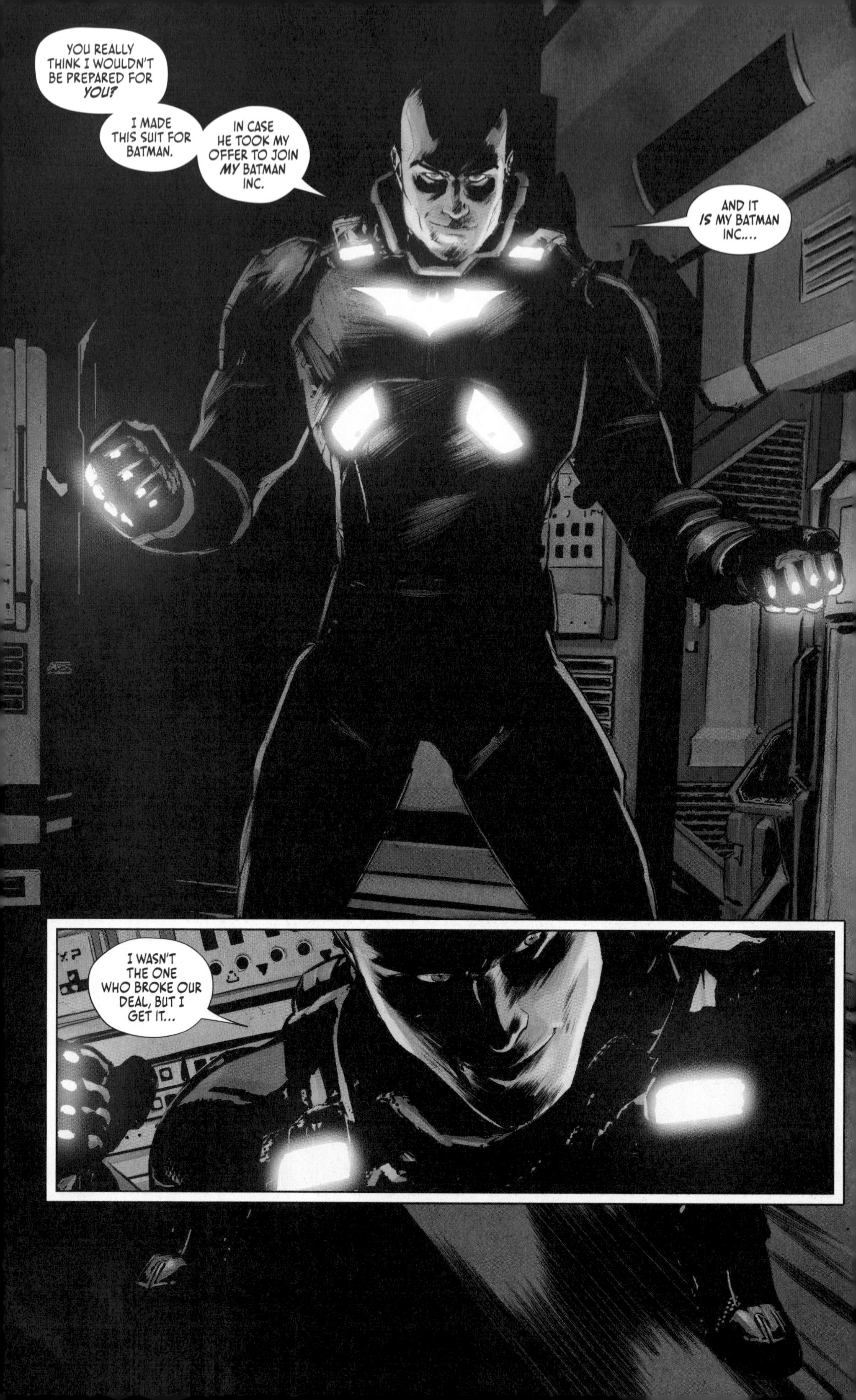
YOU REALLY THINK I WOULDN'T BE PREPARED FOR *YOU?*
I MADE THIS SUIT FOR BATMAN.
IN CASE HE TOOK MY OFFER TO JOIN *MY* BATMAN INC.
AND IT *IS* MY BATMAN INC....
I WASN'T THE ONE WHO BROKE OUR DEAL, BUT I GET IT...

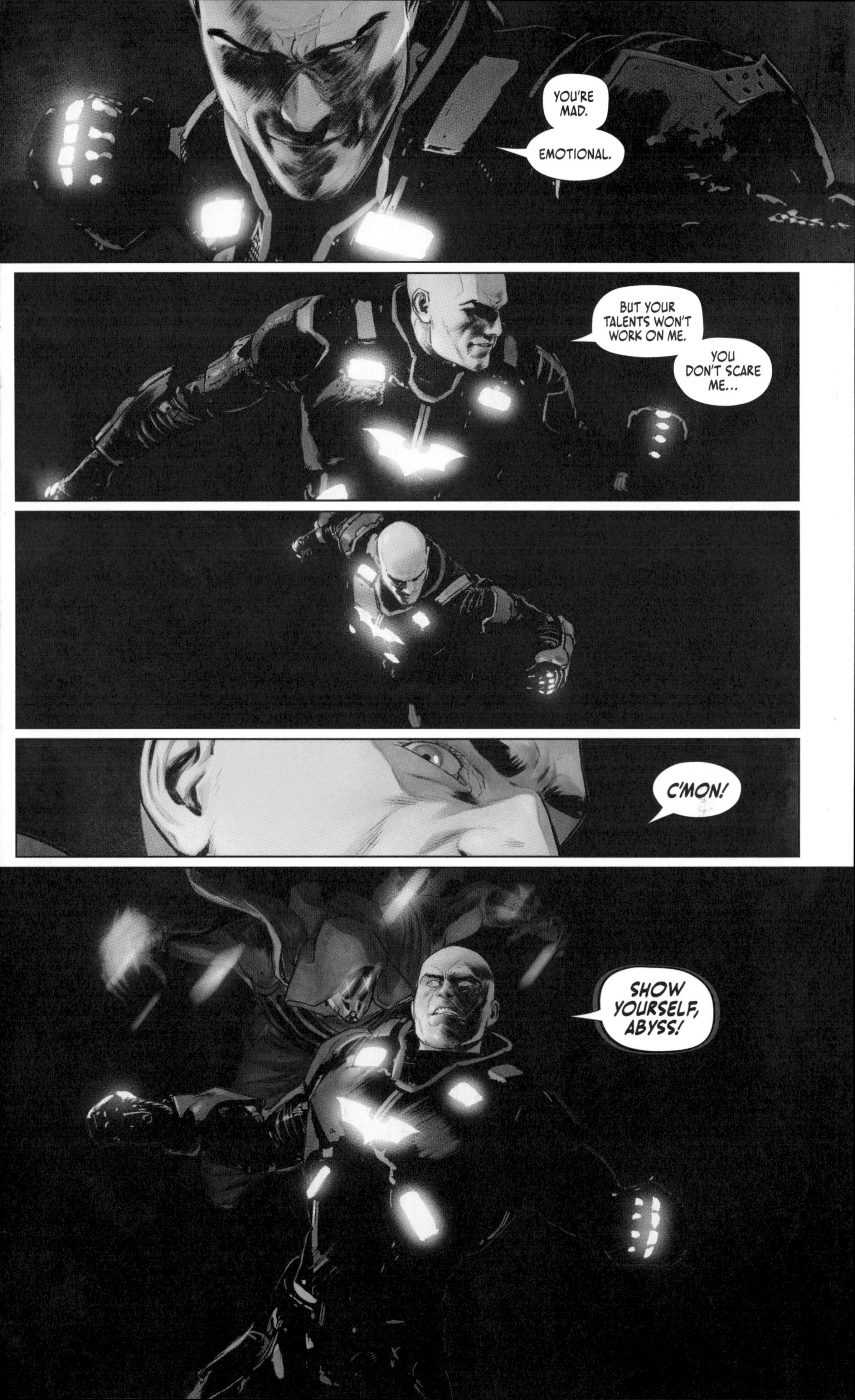
YOU'RE MAD.
EMOTIONAL.
BUT YOUR TALENTS WON'T WORK ON ME.
YOU DON'T SCARE ME...
C'MON!
SHOW YOURSELF, ABYSS!

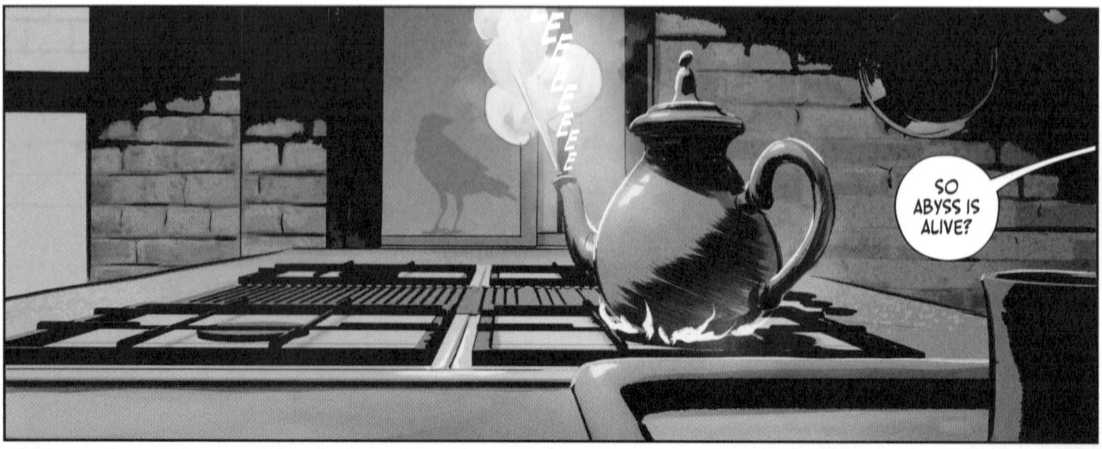
SO ABYSS IS ALIVE?

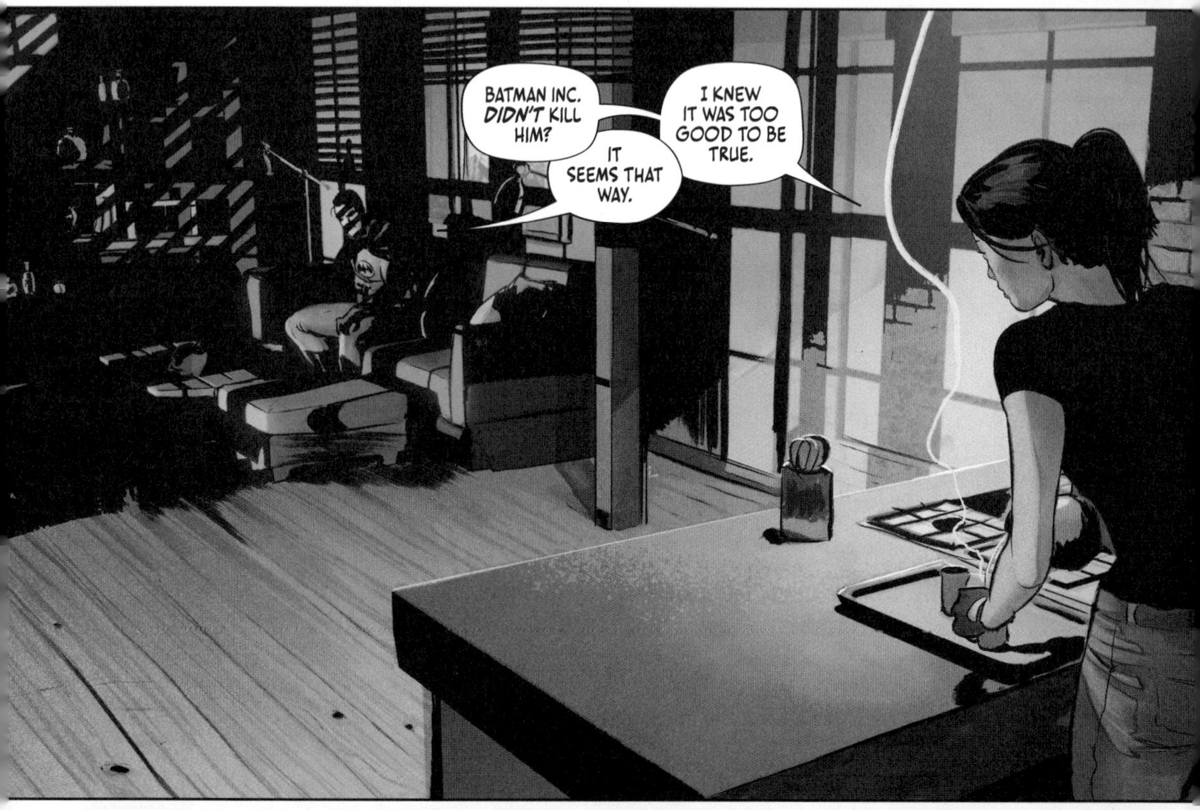
BATMAN INC. DIDN'T KILL HIM?
I KNEW IT WAS TOO GOOD TO BE TRUE.
IT SEEMS THAT WAY.

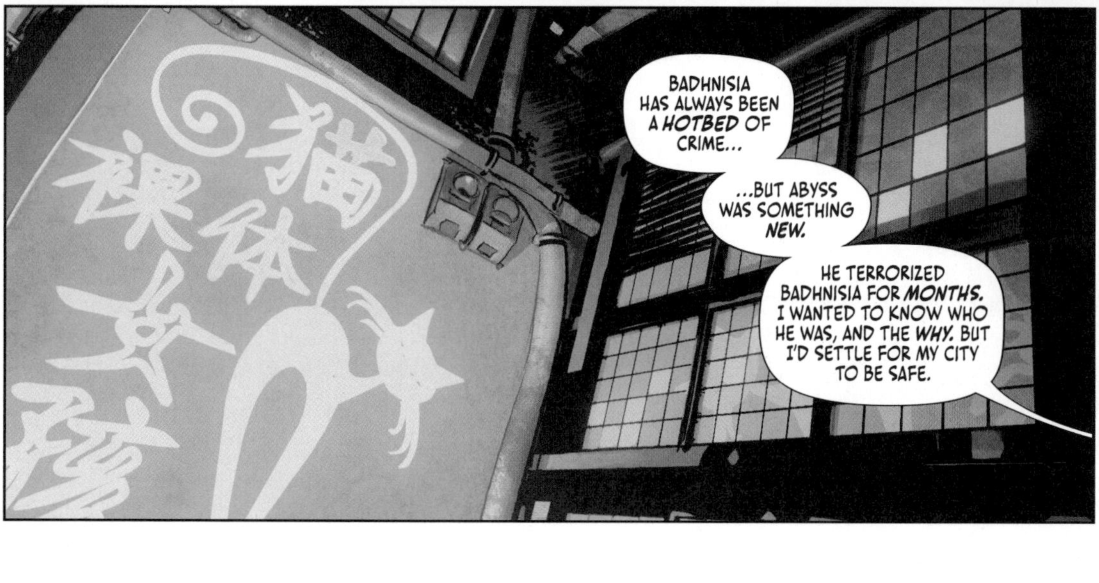
BADHNISIA HAS ALWAYS BEEN A HOTBED OF CRIME...
...BUT ABYSS WAS SOMETHING NEW.
HE TERRORIZED BADHNISIA FOR MONTHS. I WANTED TO KNOW WHO HE WAS, AND THE WHY. BUT I'D SETTLE FOR MY CITY TO BE SAFE.

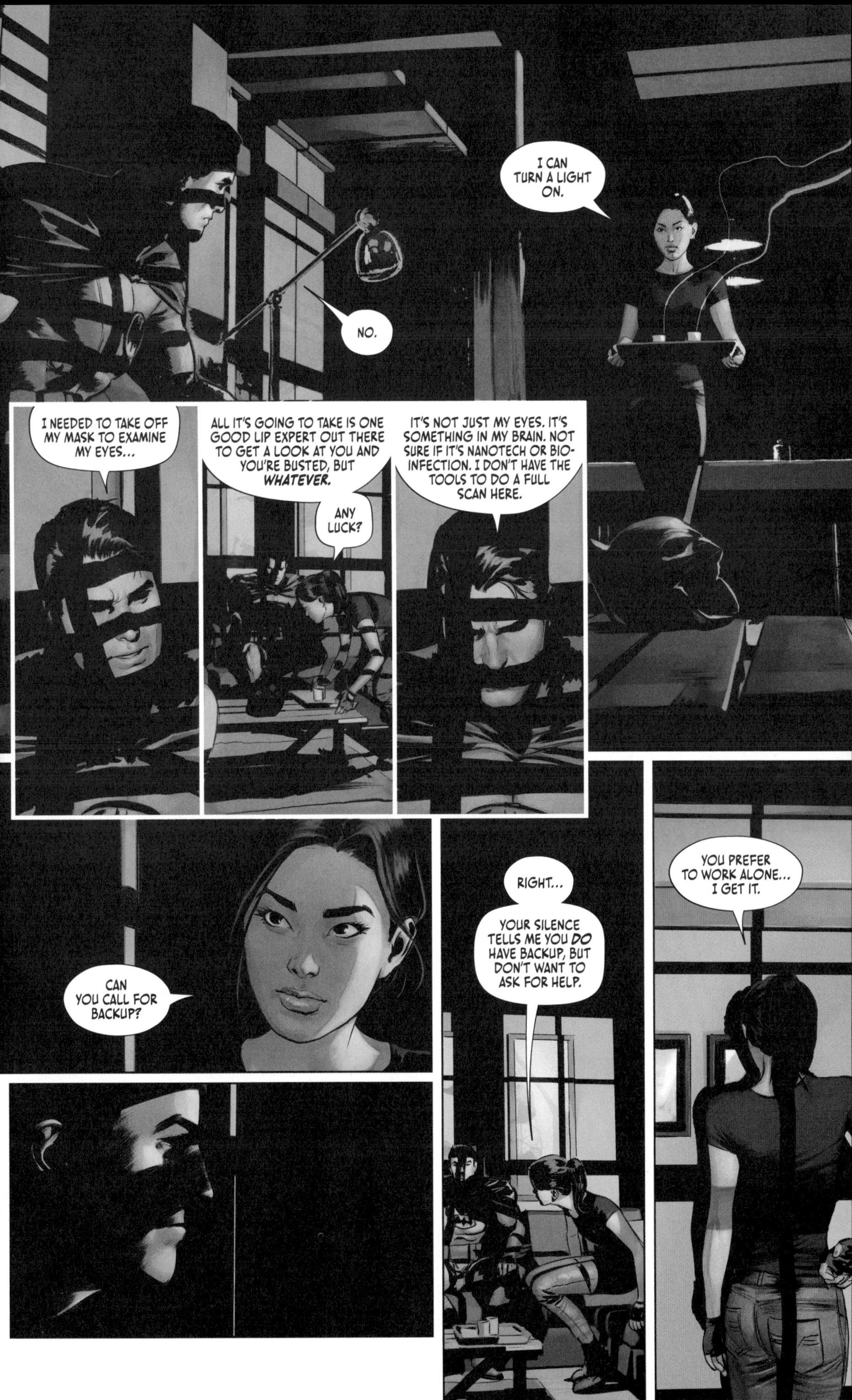

I CAN TURN A LIGHT ON.
NO.
I NEEDED TO TAKE OFF MY MASK TO EXAMINE MY EYES...
ALL IT'S GOING TO TAKE IS ONE GOOD LIP EXPERT OUT THERE TO GET A LOOK AT YOU AND YOU'RE BUSTED, BUT *WHATEVER.*
ANY LUCK?
IT'S NOT JUST MY EYES. IT'S SOMETHING IN MY BRAIN. NOT SURE IF IT'S NANOTECH OR BIO-INFECTION. I DON'T HAVE THE TOOLS TO DO A FULL SCAN HERE.
CAN YOU CALL FOR BACKUP?
RIGHT...
YOUR SILENCE TELLS ME YOU *DO* HAVE BACKUP, BUT DON'T WANT TO ASK FOR HELP.
YOU PREFER TO WORK ALONE... I GET IT.

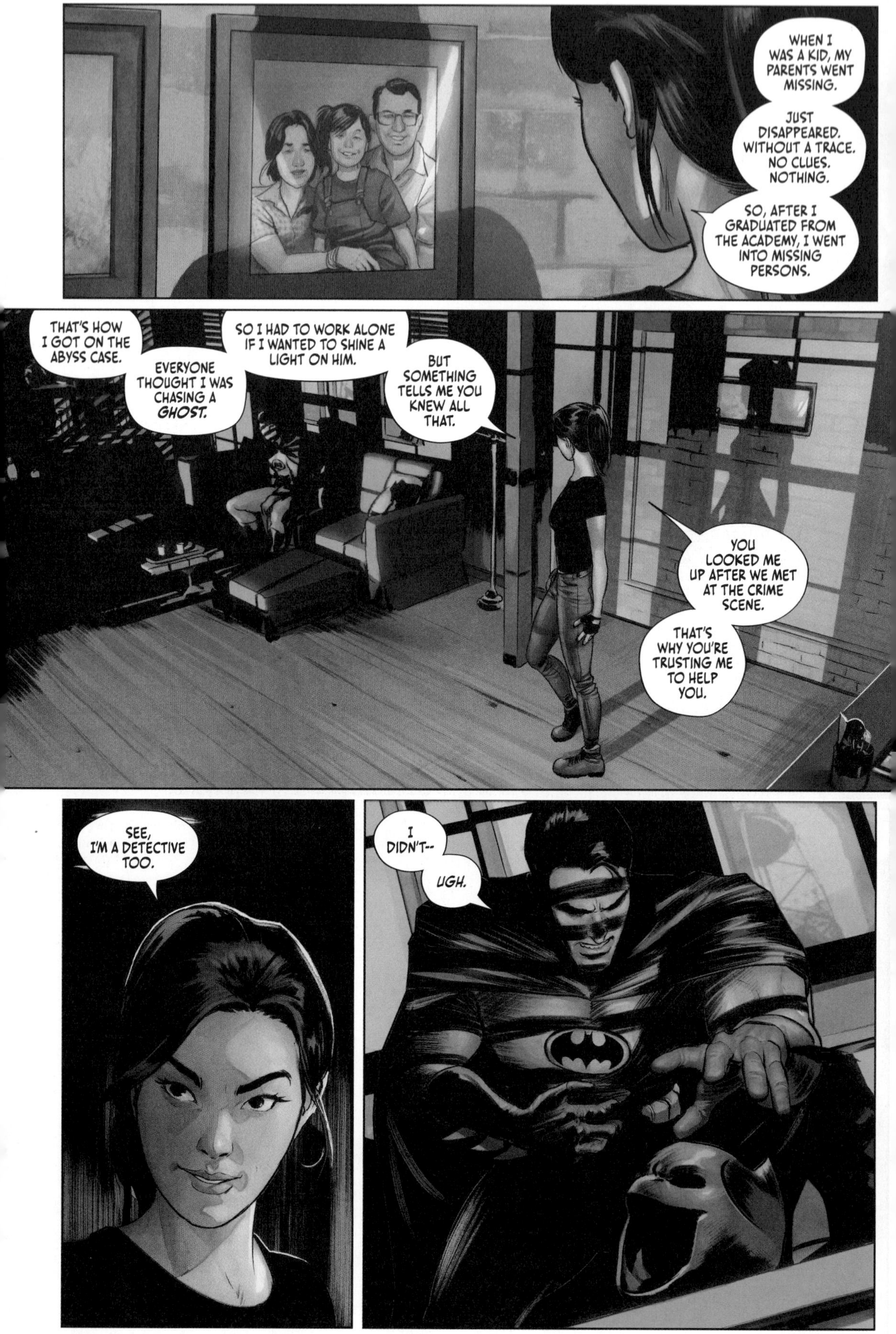
WHEN I WAS A KID, MY PARENTS WENT MISSING.
JUST DISAPPEARED. WITHOUT A TRACE. NO CLUES. NOTHING.
SO, AFTER I GRADUATED FROM THE ACADEMY, I WENT INTO MISSING PERSONS.
THAT'S HOW I GOT ON THE ABYSS CASE.
EVERYONE THOUGHT I WAS CHASING A *GHOST.*
SO I HAD TO WORK ALONE IF I WANTED TO SHINE A LIGHT ON HIM.
BUT SOMETHING TELLS ME YOU KNEW ALL THAT.
YOU LOOKED ME UP AFTER WE MET AT THE CRIME SCENE.
THAT'S WHY YOU'RE TRUSTING ME TO HELP YOU.
SEE, I'M A DETECTIVE TOO.
I DIDN'T--
UGH.

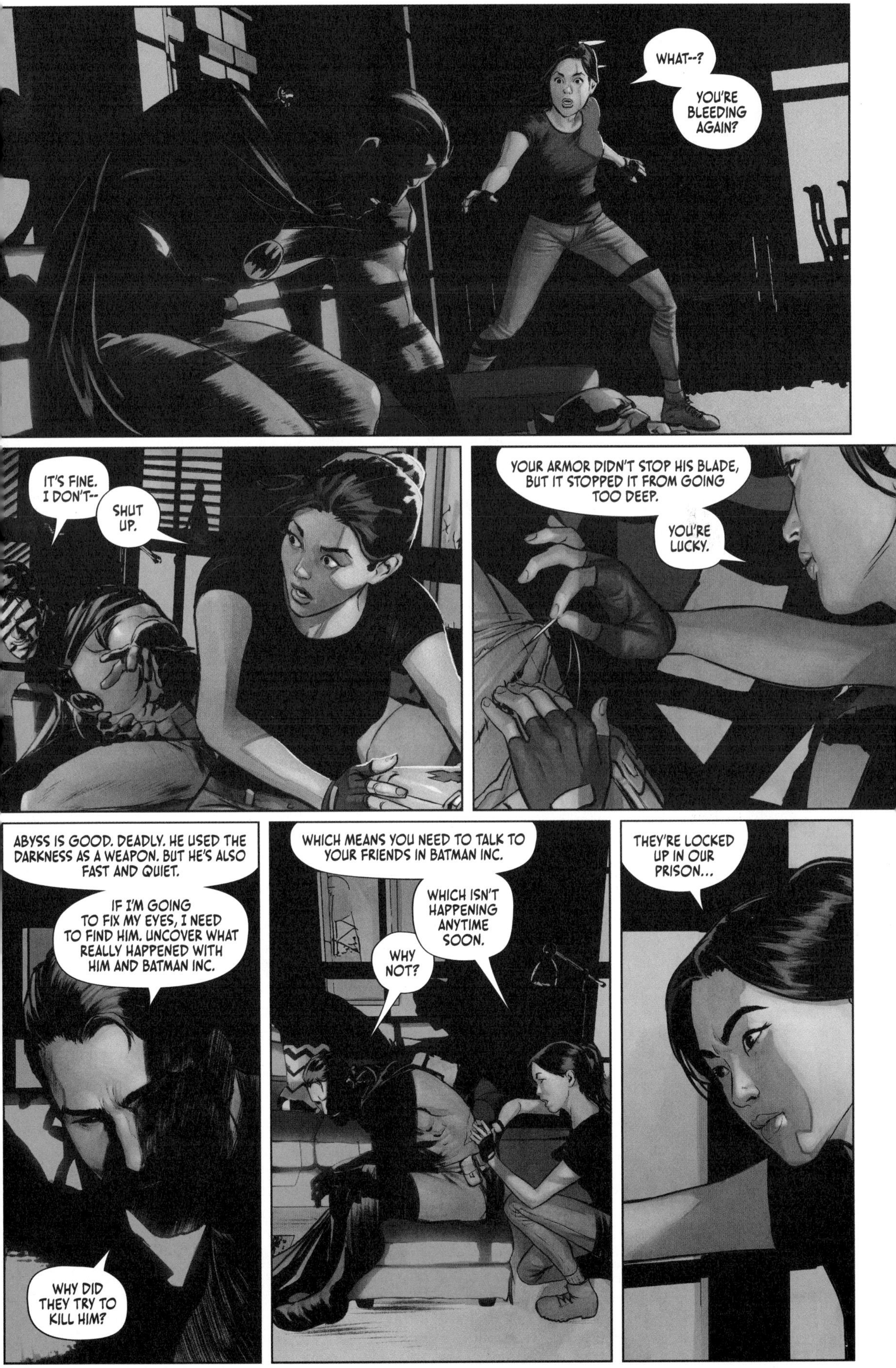
WHAT--?
YOU'RE BLEEDING AGAIN?
IT'S FINE. I DON'T--
SHUT UP.
YOUR ARMOR DIDN'T STOP HIS BLADE, BUT IT STOPPED IT FROM GOING TOO DEEP.
YOU'RE LUCKY.
ABYSS IS GOOD. DEADLY. HE USED THE DARKNESS AS A WEAPON. BUT HE'S ALSO FAST AND QUIET.
IF I'M GOING TO FIX MY EYES, I NEED TO FIND HIM. UNCOVER WHAT REALLY HAPPENED WITH HIM AND BATMAN INC.
WHY DID THEY TRY TO KILL HIM?
WHICH MEANS YOU NEED TO TALK TO YOUR FRIENDS IN BATMAN INC.
WHICH ISN'T HAPPENING ANYTIME SOON.
WHY NOT?
THEY'RE LOCKED UP IN OUR PRISON...

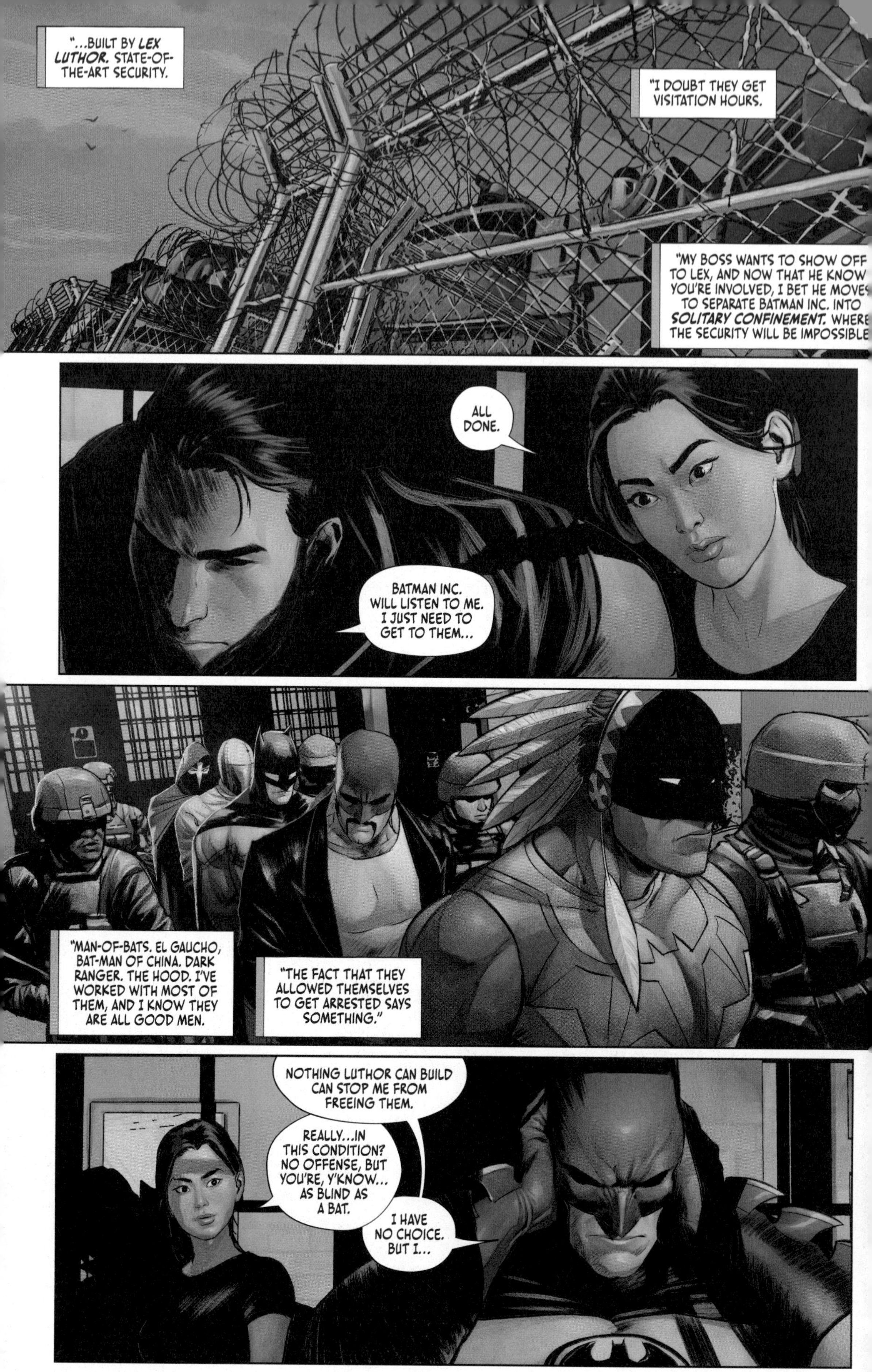
"...BUILT BY LEX LUTHOR. STATE-OF-THE-ART SECURITY.
"I DOUBT THEY GET VISITATION HOURS.
"MY BOSS WANTS TO SHOW OFF TO LEX, AND NOW THAT HE KNOW YOU'RE INVOLVED, I BET HE MOVES TO SEPARATE BATMAN INC. INTO SOLITARY CONFINEMENT. WHERE THE SECURITY WILL BE IMPOSSIBLE
ALL DONE.
BATMAN INC. WILL LISTEN TO ME. I JUST NEED TO GET TO THEM...
"MAN-OF-BATS. EL GAUCHO, BAT-MAN OF CHINA. DARK RANGER. THE HOOD. I'VE WORKED WITH MOST OF THEM, AND I KNOW THEY ARE ALL GOOD MEN.
"THE FACT THAT THEY ALLOWED THEMSELVES TO GET ARRESTED SAYS SOMETHING."
NOTHING LUTHOR CAN BUILD CAN STOP ME FROM FREEING THEM.
REALLY...IN THIS CONDITION? NO OFFENSE, BUT YOU'RE, Y'KNOW... AS BLIND AS A BAT.
I HAVE NO CHOICE. BUT I...

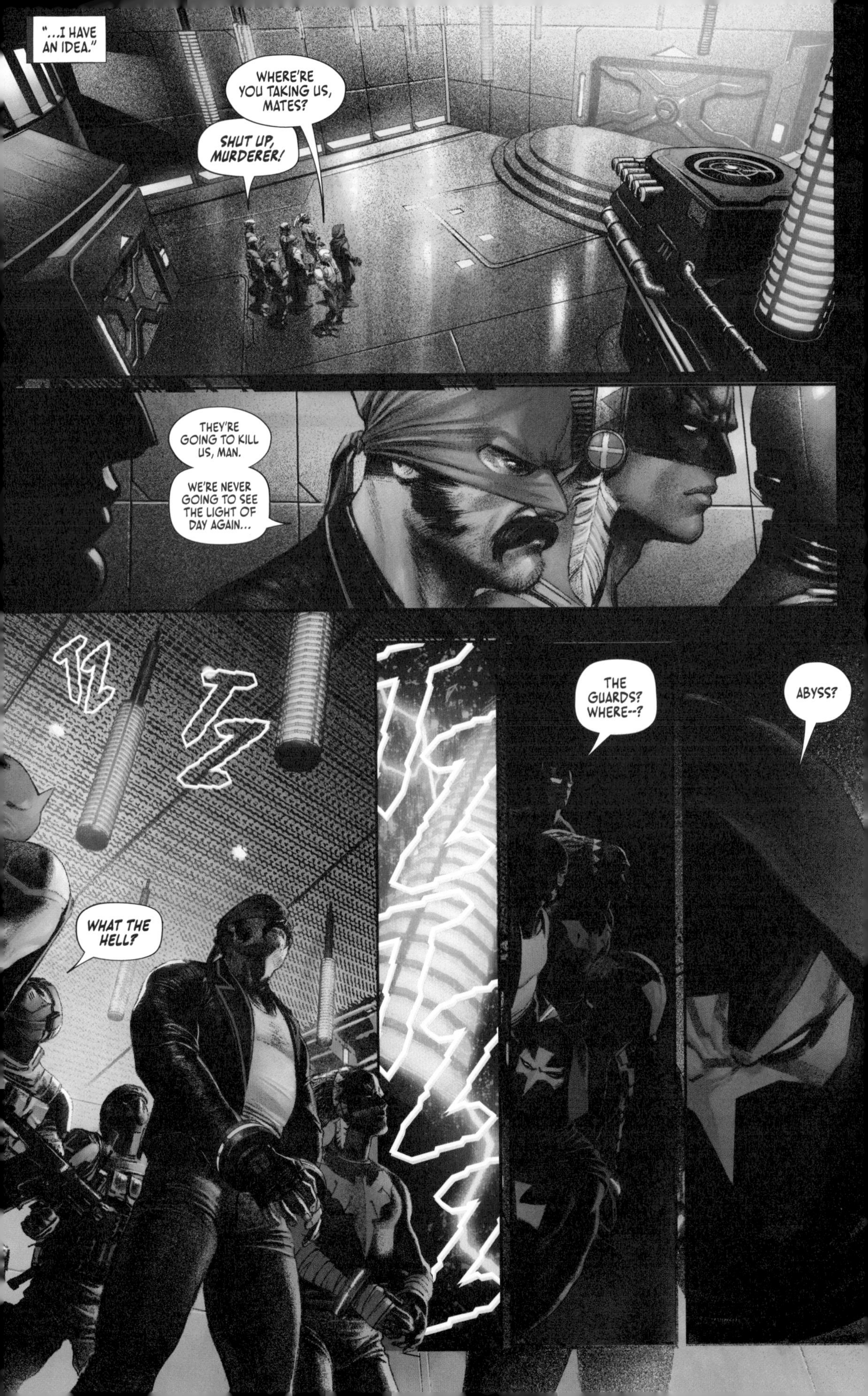
"...I HAVE AN IDEA."
WHERE'RE YOU TAKING US, MATES?
SHUT UP, MURDERER!
THEY'RE GOING TO KILL US, MAN.
WE'RE NEVER GOING TO SEE THE LIGHT OF DAY AGAIN...
WHAT THE HELL?
THE GUARDS? WHERE--?
ABYSS?

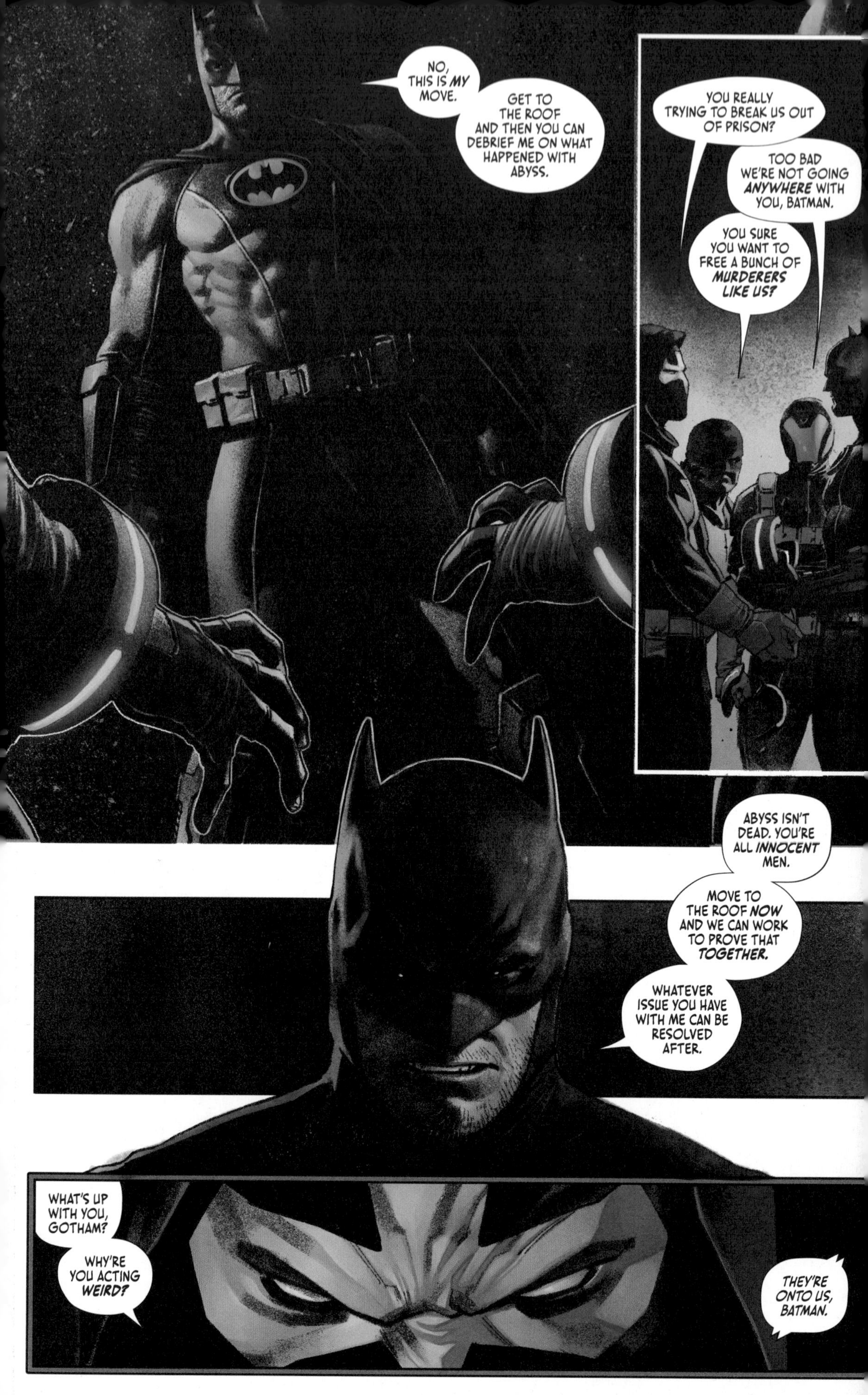
NO, THIS IS MY MOVE.
GET TO THE ROOF AND THEN YOU CAN DEBRIEF ME ON WHAT HAPPENED WITH ABYSS.
YOU REALLY TRYING TO BREAK US OUT OF PRISON?
TOO BAD WE'RE NOT GOING ANYWHERE WITH YOU, BATMAN.
YOU SURE YOU WANT TO FREE A BUNCH OF MURDERERS LIKE US?
ABYSS ISN'T DEAD. YOU'RE ALL INNOCENT MEN.
MOVE TO THE ROOF NOW AND WE CAN WORK TO PROVE THAT TOGETHER.
WHATEVER ISSUE YOU HAVE WITH ME CAN BE RESOLVED AFTER.
WHAT'S UP WITH YOU, GOTHAM?
WHY'RE YOU ACTING WEIRD?
THEY'RE ONTO US, BATMAN.

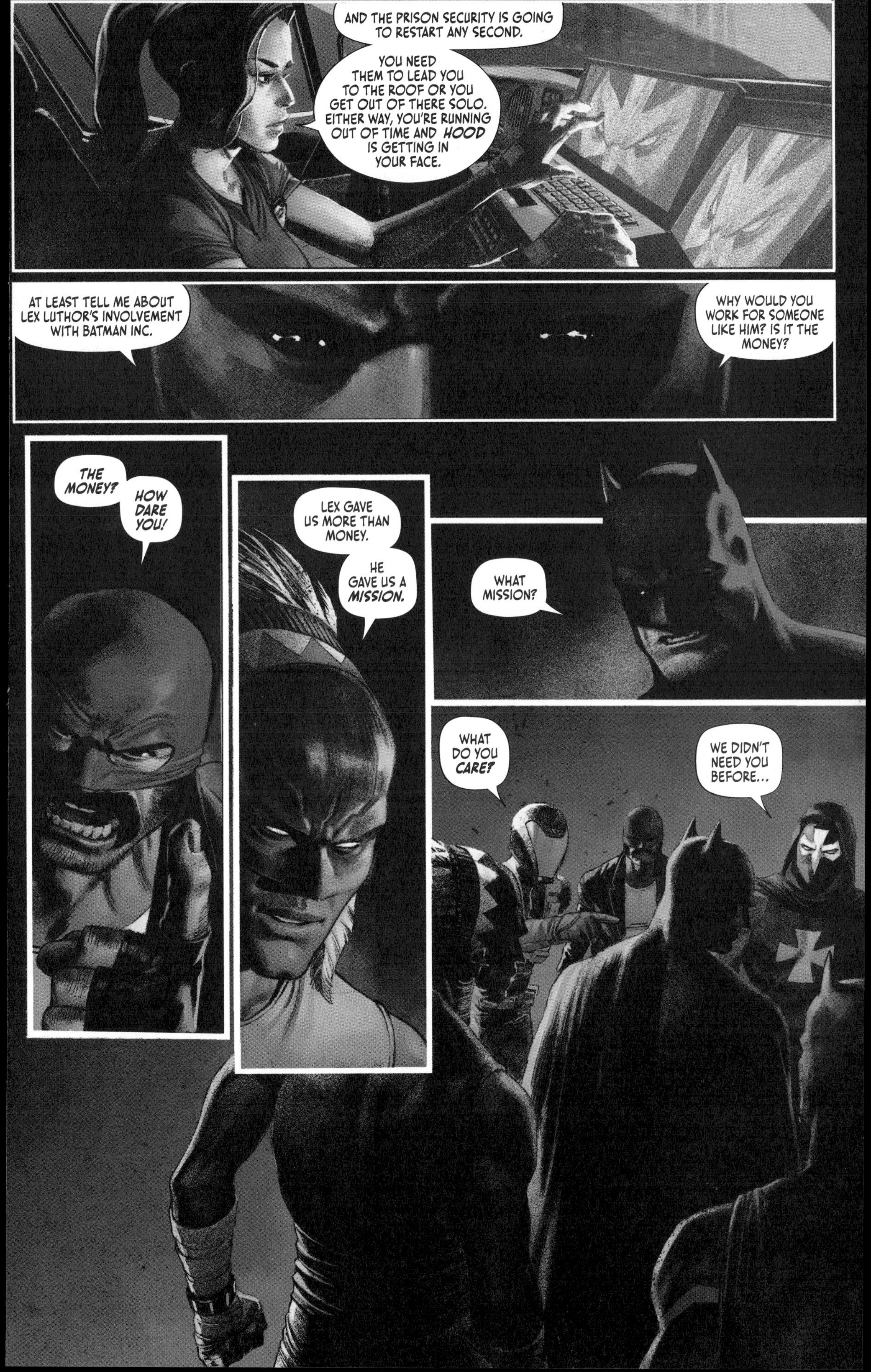

AND THE PRISON SECURITY IS GOING TO RESTART ANY SECOND.
YOU NEED THEM TO LEAD YOU TO THE ROOF OR YOU GET OUT OF THERE SOLO. EITHER WAY, YOU'RE RUNNING OUT OF TIME AND *HOOD* IS GETTING IN YOUR FACE.
AT LEAST TELL ME ABOUT LEX LUTHOR'S INVOLVEMENT WITH BATMAN INC.
WHY WOULD YOU WORK FOR SOMEONE LIKE HIM? IS IT THE MONEY?
THE MONEY?
HOW DARE YOU!
LEX GAVE US MORE THAN MONEY.
HE GAVE US A *MISSION.*
WHAT MISSION?
WHAT DO YOU *CARE?*
WE DIDN'T NEED YOU BEFORE...

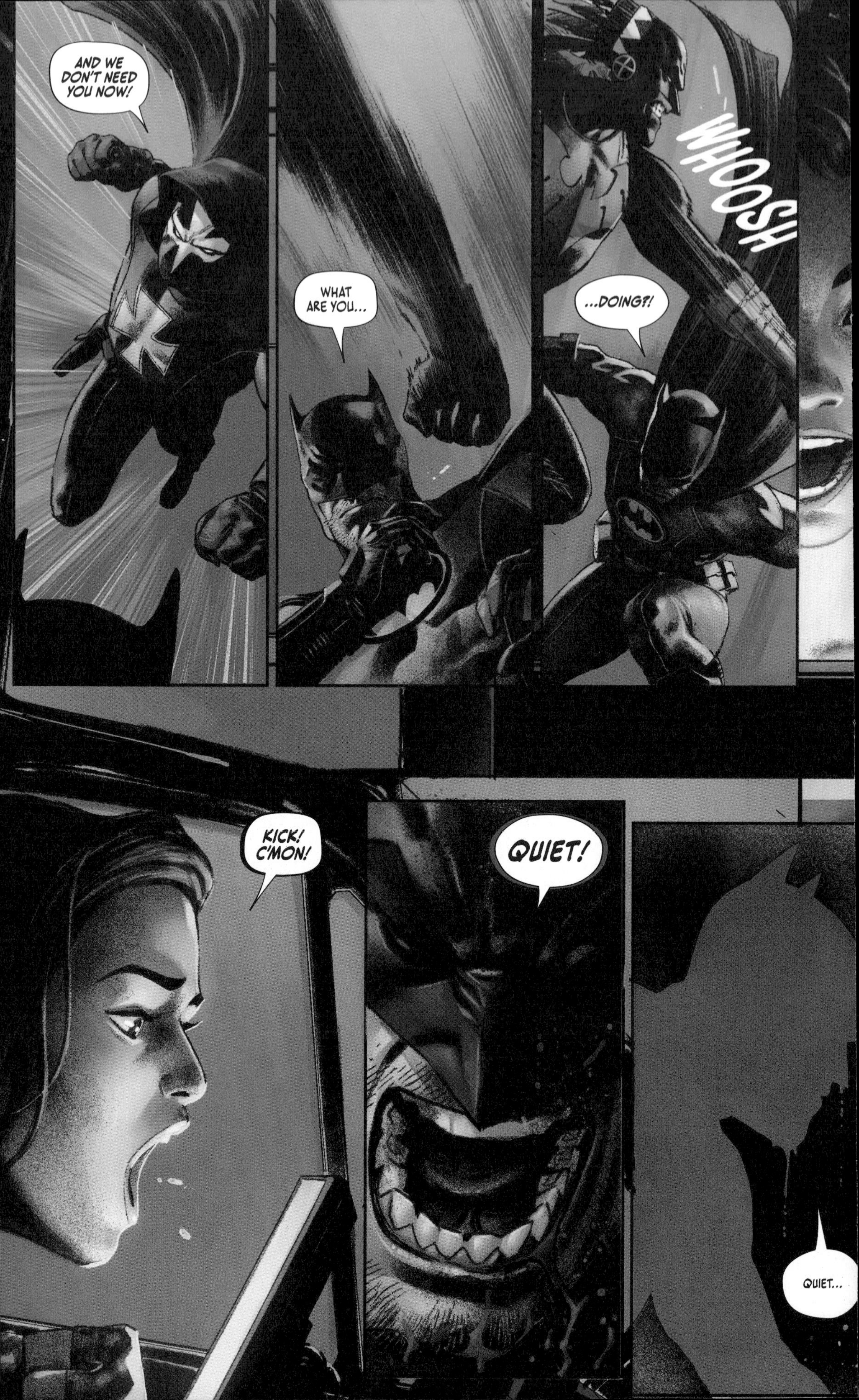
AND WE DON'T NEED YOU NOW!
WHAT ARE YOU...
...DOING?!
WHOOSH
KICK! C'MON!
QUIET!
QUIET...

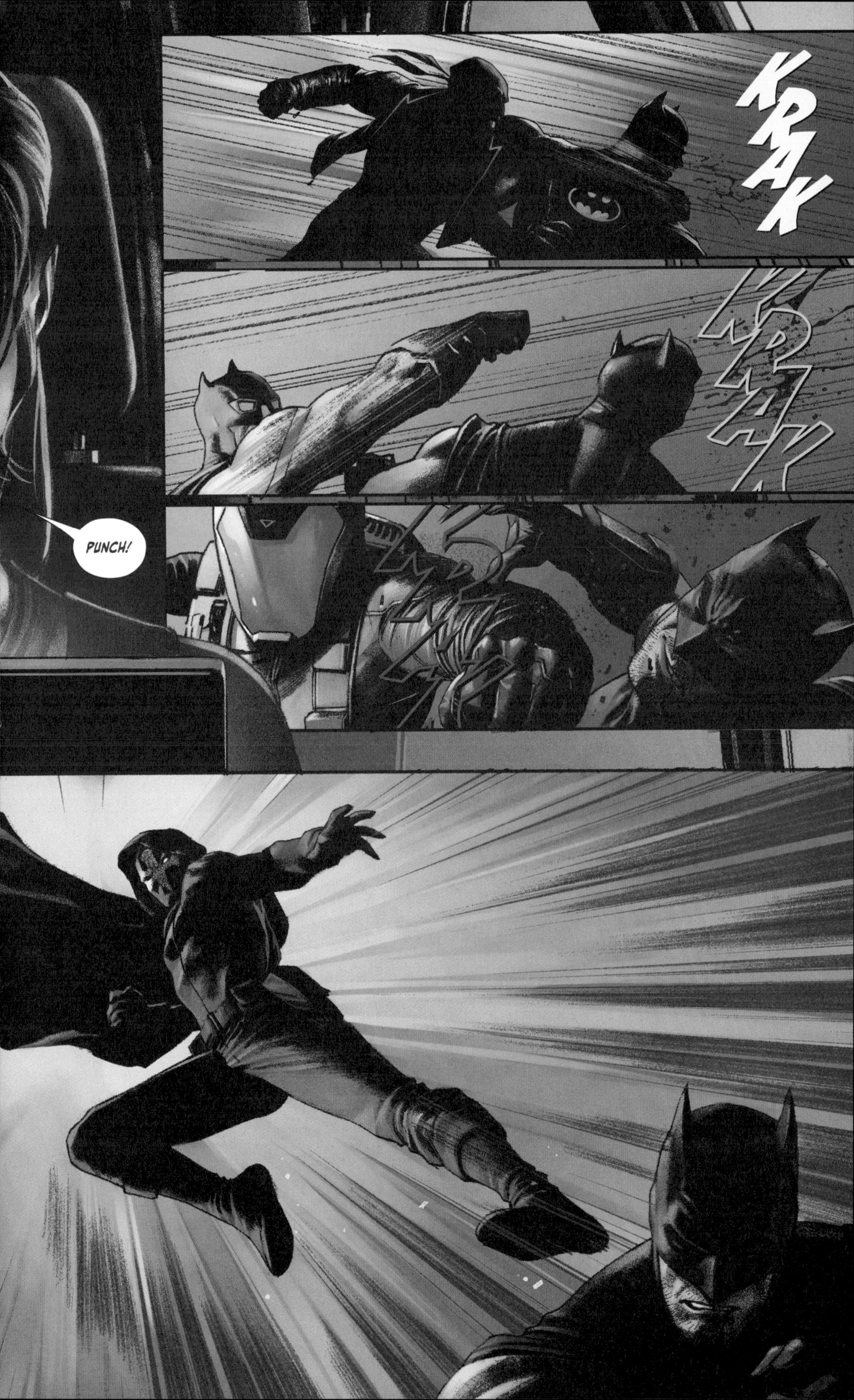
KRAK
PUNCH!

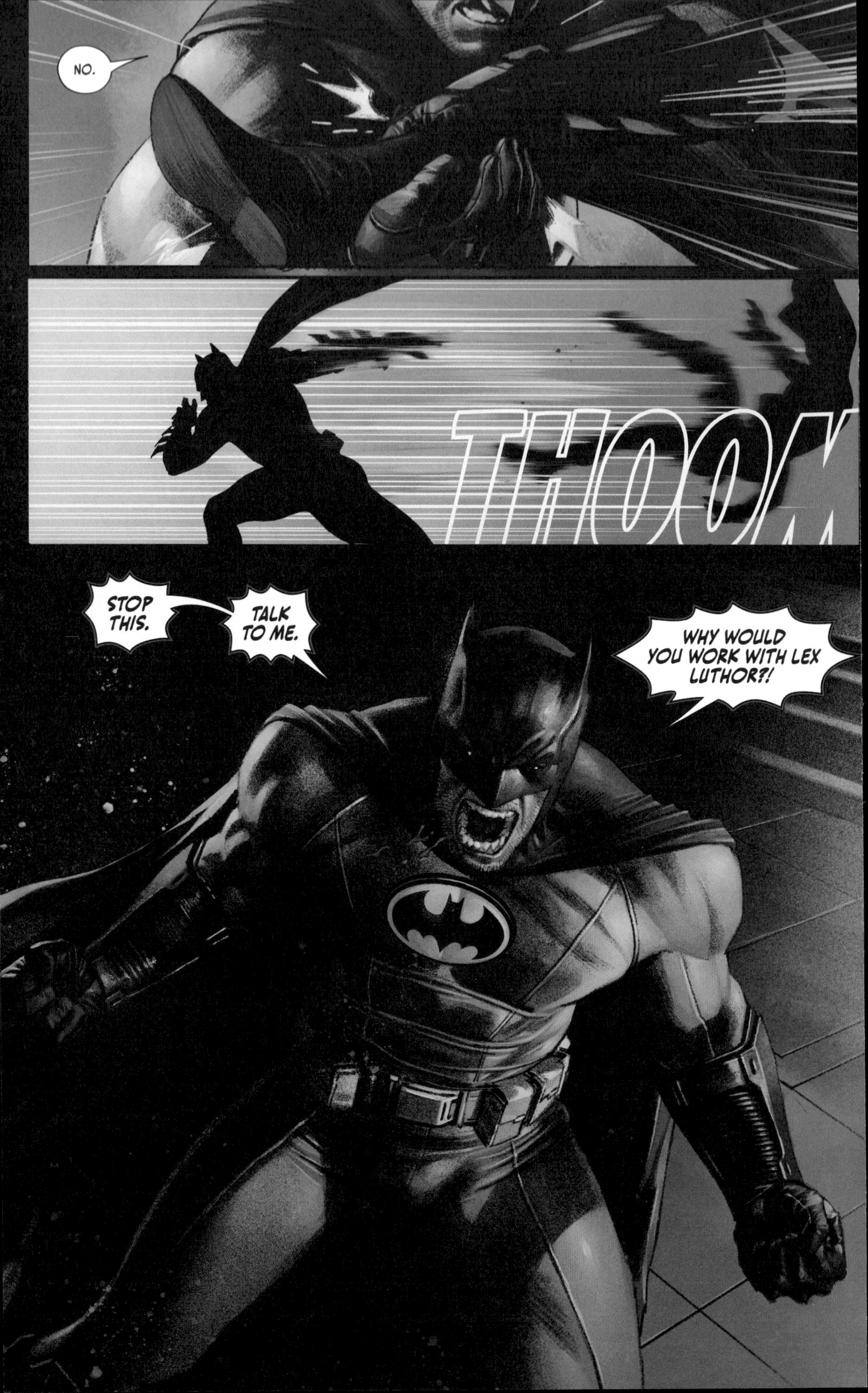
NO.
THOOM
STOP THIS.
TALK TO ME.
WHY WOULD YOU WORK WITH LEX LUTHOR?!

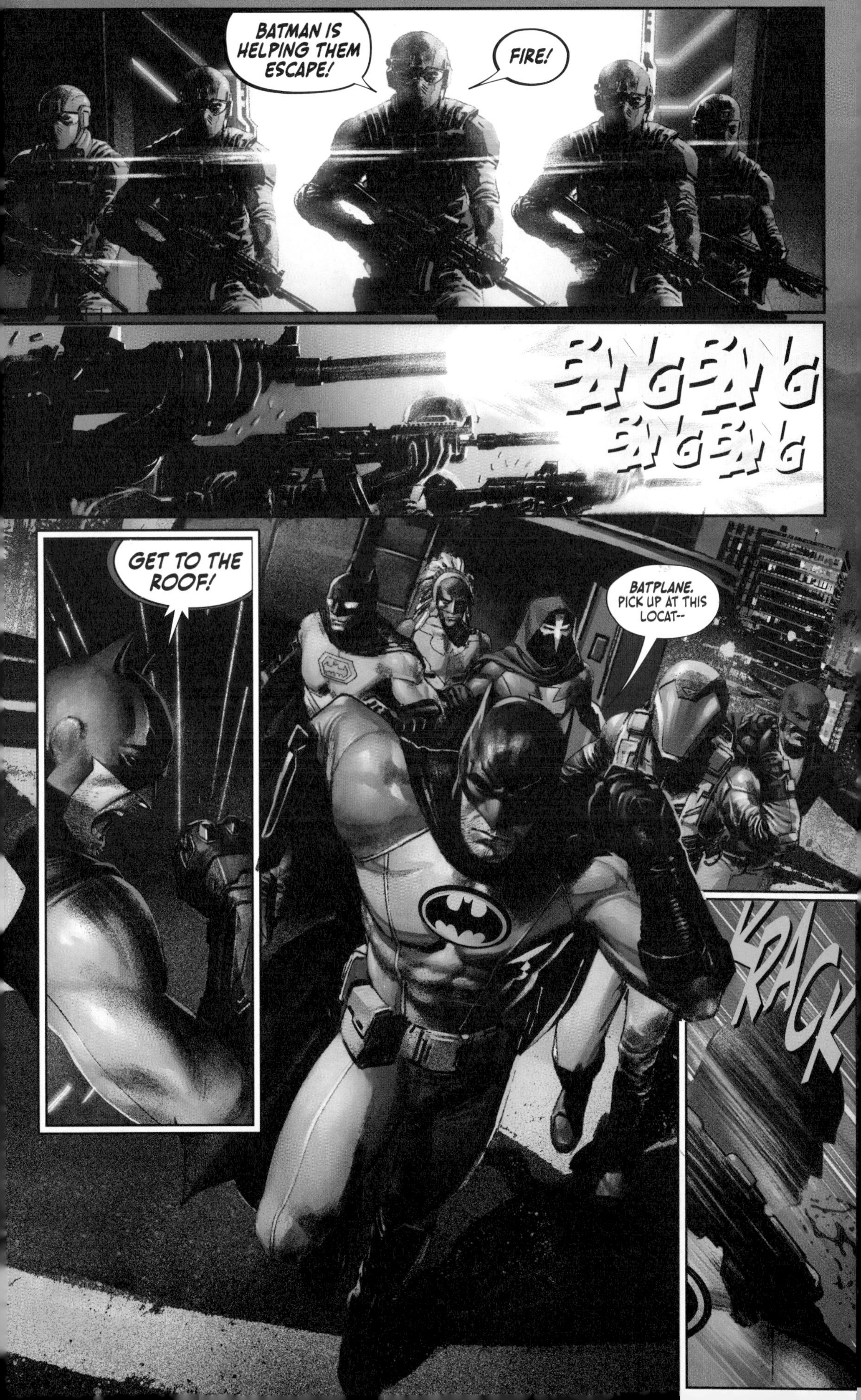
BATMAN IS HELPING THEM ESCAPE!
FIRE!
BANG BANG
BANG BANG
GET TO THE ROOF!
BATPLANE. PICK UP AT THIS LOCAT--
KRACK

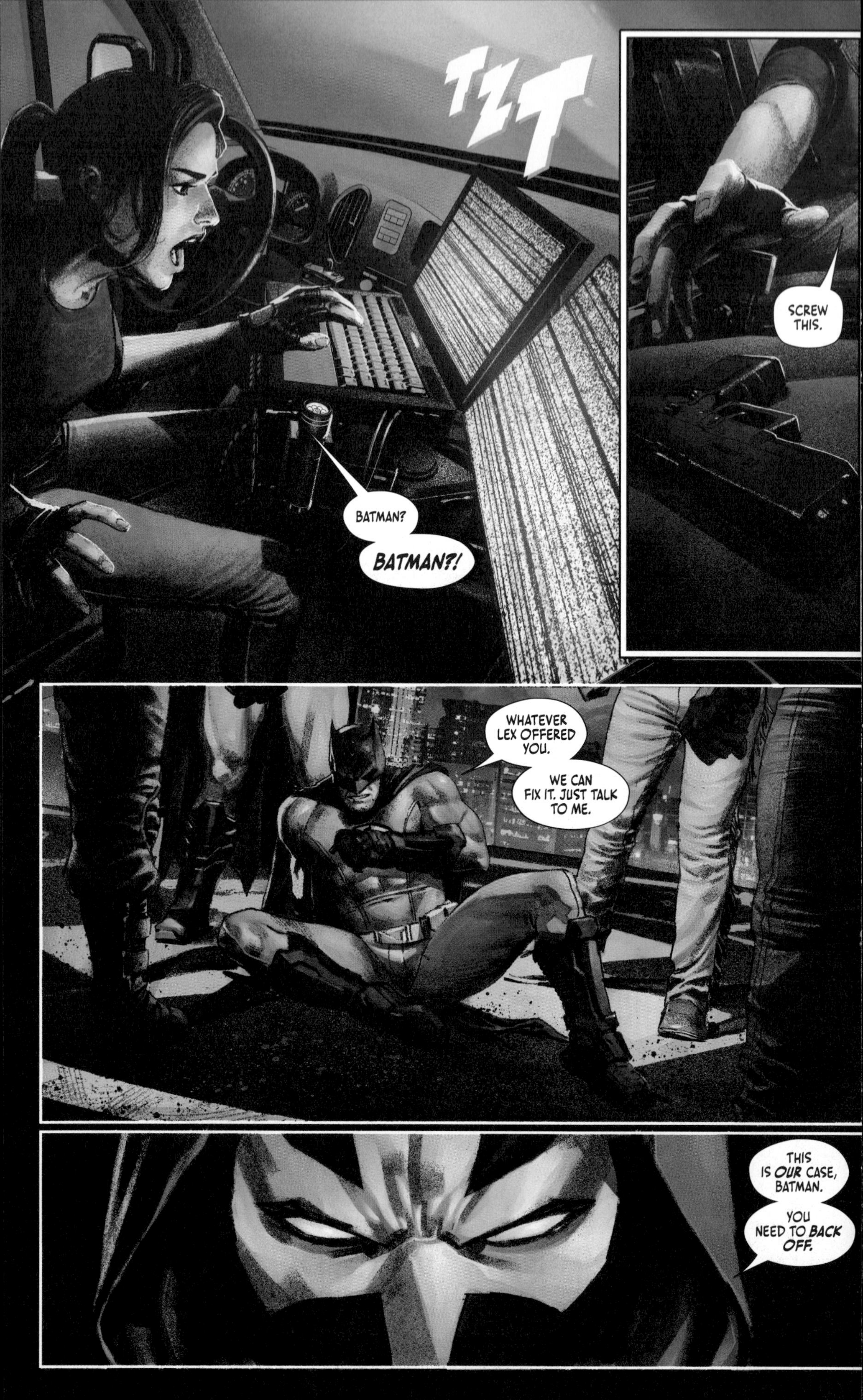
TZZT
BATMAN?
BATMAN?!
SCREW THIS.
WHATEVER LEX OFFERED YOU.
WE CAN FIX IT. JUST TALK TO ME.
THIS IS OUR CASE, BATMAN.
YOU NEED TO BACK OFF.

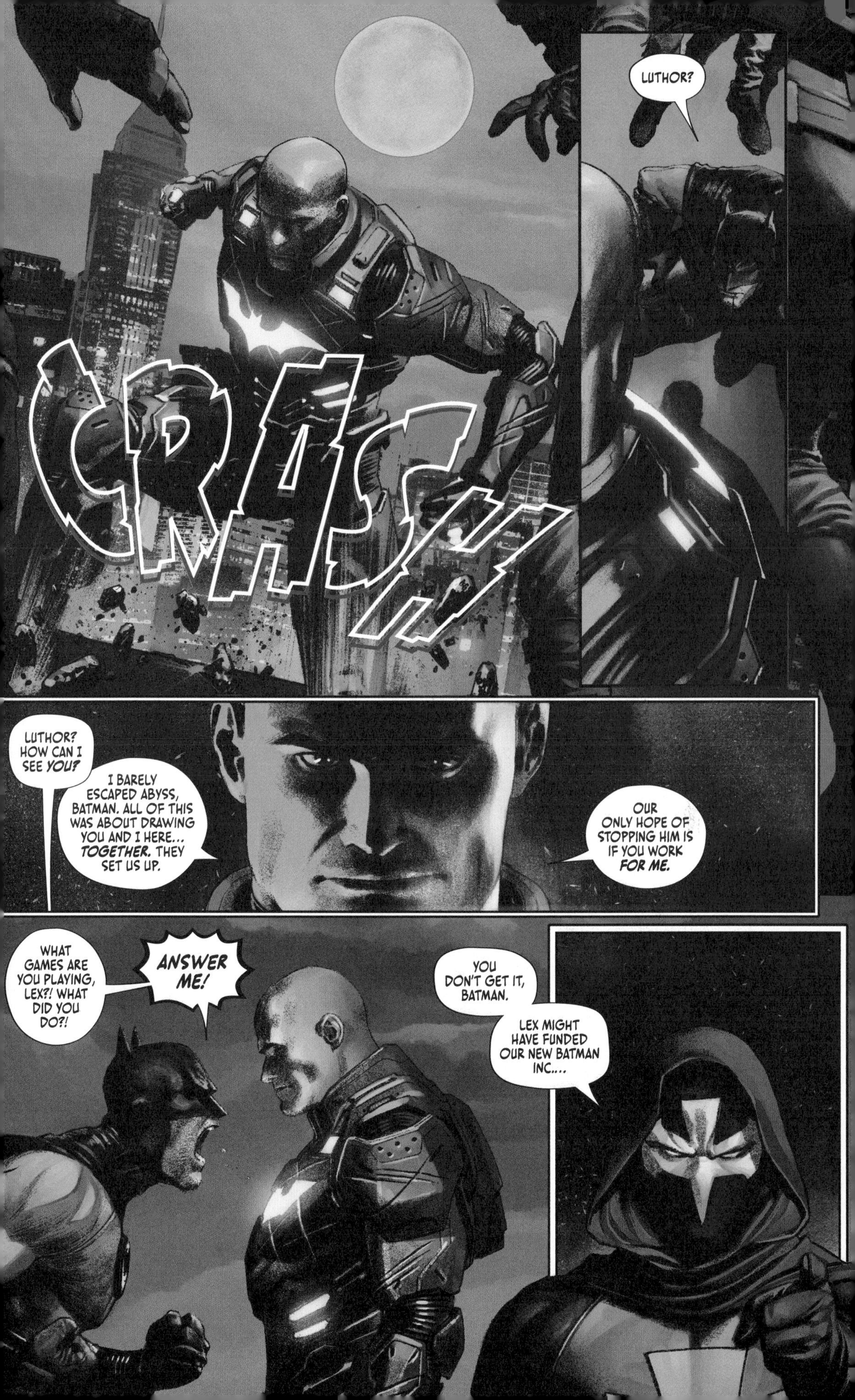

LUTHOR?
CRASH
LUTHOR? HOW CAN I SEE *YOU?*
I BARELY ESCAPED ABYSS, BATMAN. ALL OF THIS WAS ABOUT DRAWING YOU AND I HERE... *TOGETHER.* THEY SET US UP.
OUR ONLY HOPE OF STOPPING HIM IS IF YOU WORK *FOR ME.*
WHAT GAMES ARE YOU PLAYING, LEX?! WHAT DID YOU DO?!
ANSWER ME!
YOU DON'T GET IT, BATMAN.
LEX MIGHT HAVE FUNDED OUR NEW BATMAN INC....

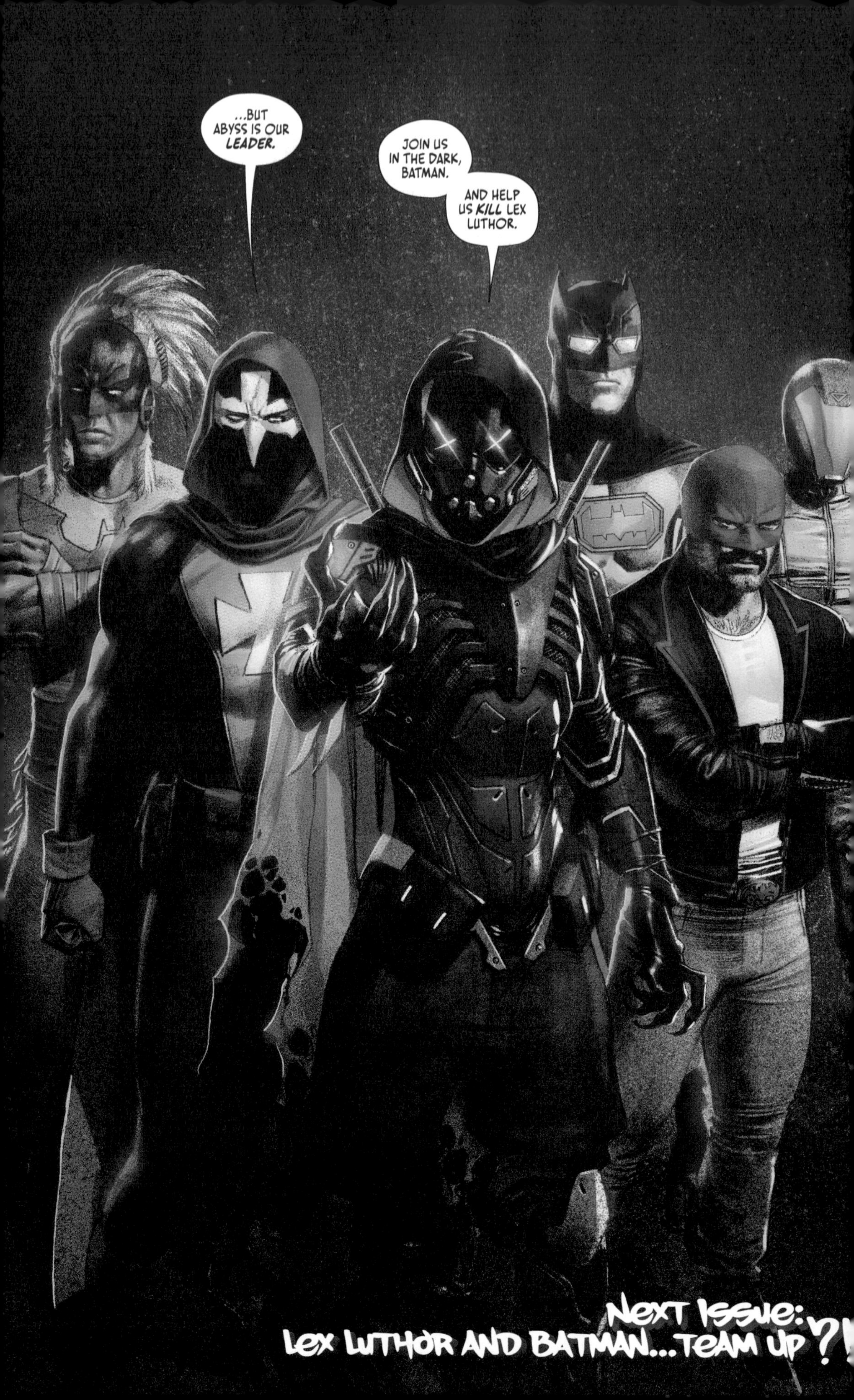
...BUT ABYSS IS OUR LEADER.
JOIN US IN THE DARK, BATMAN.
AND HELP US KILL LEX LUTHOR.
Next Issue: Lex Luthor and Batman...Team up?!

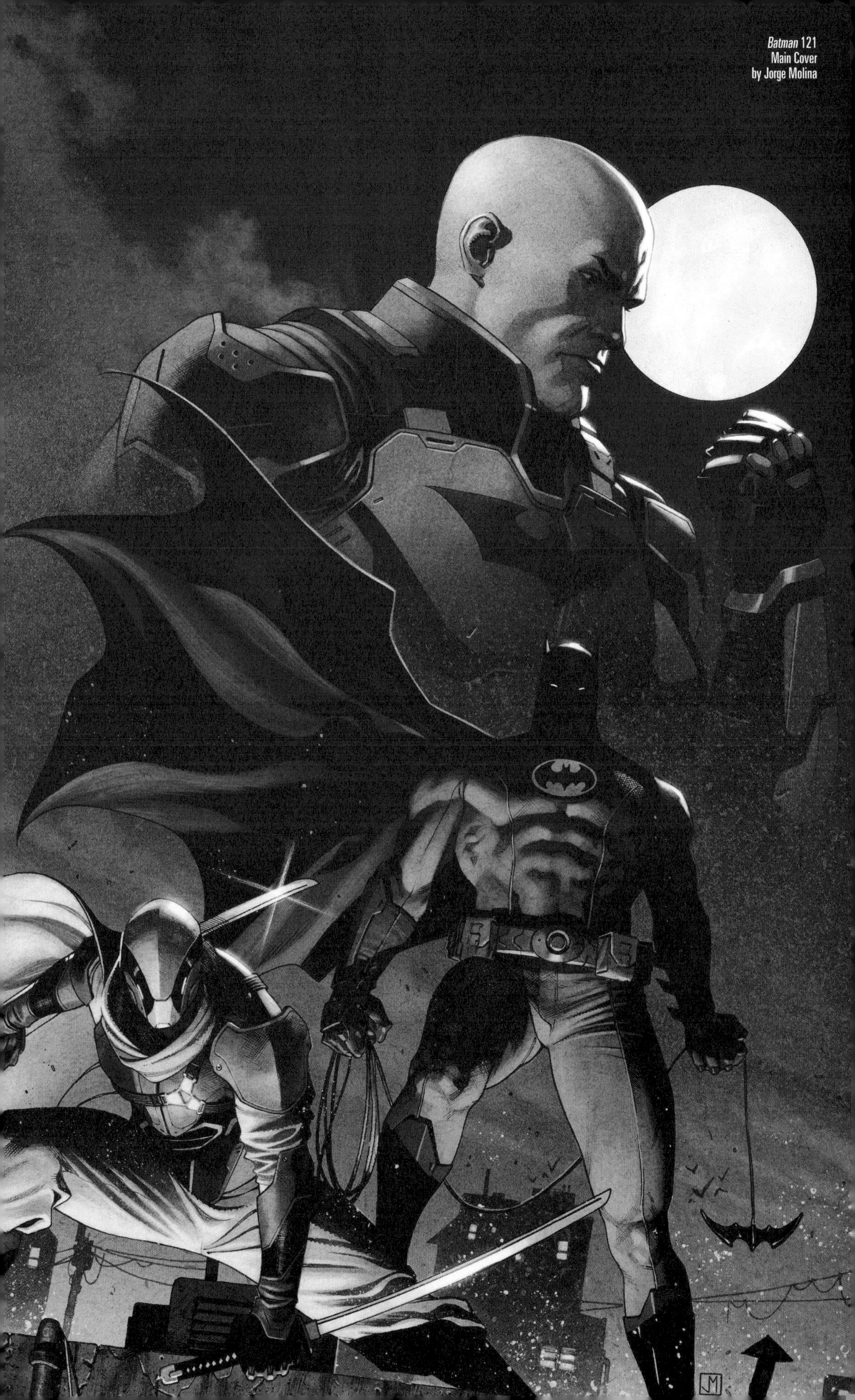

Batman 121
Main Cover
by Jorge Molina

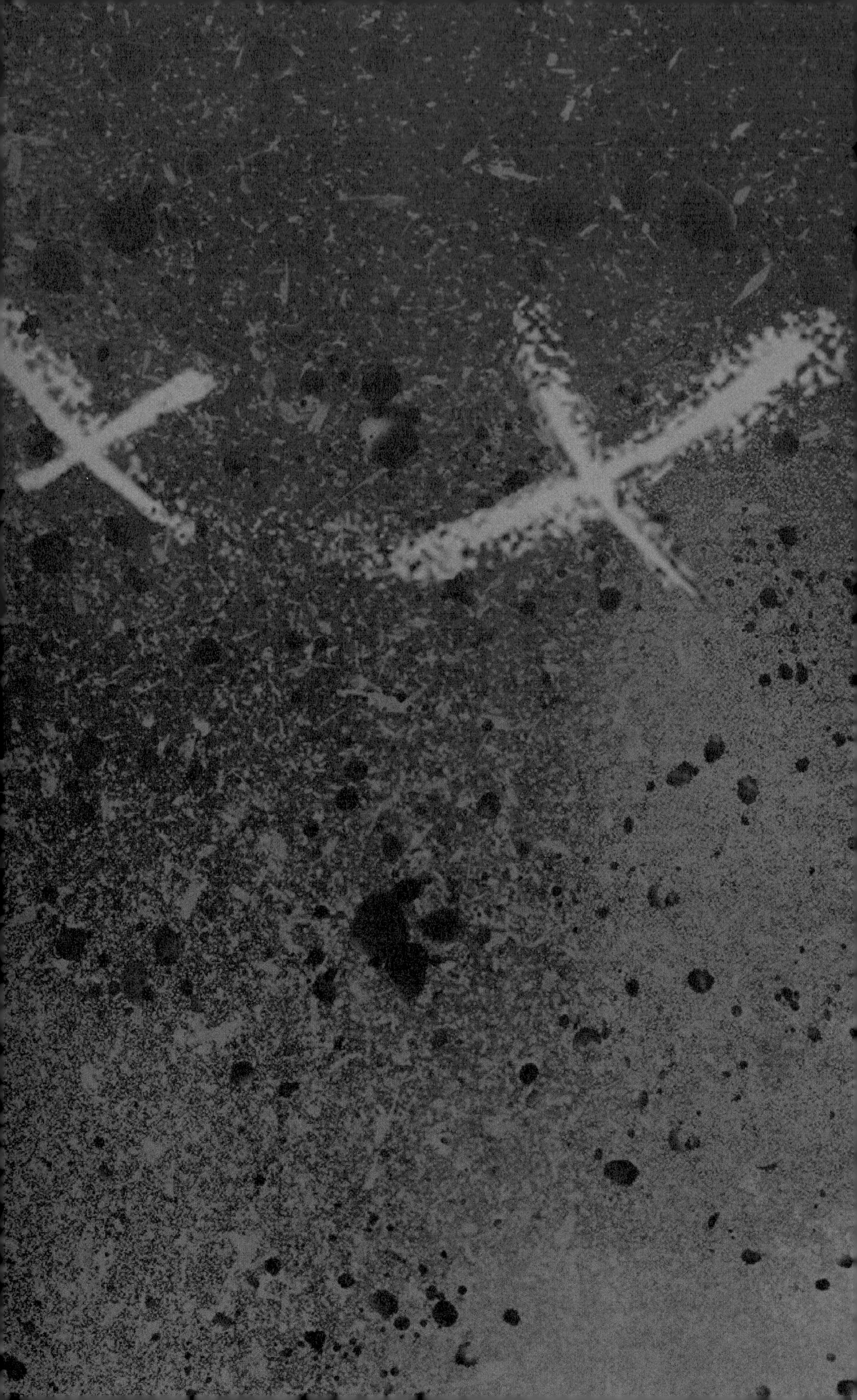

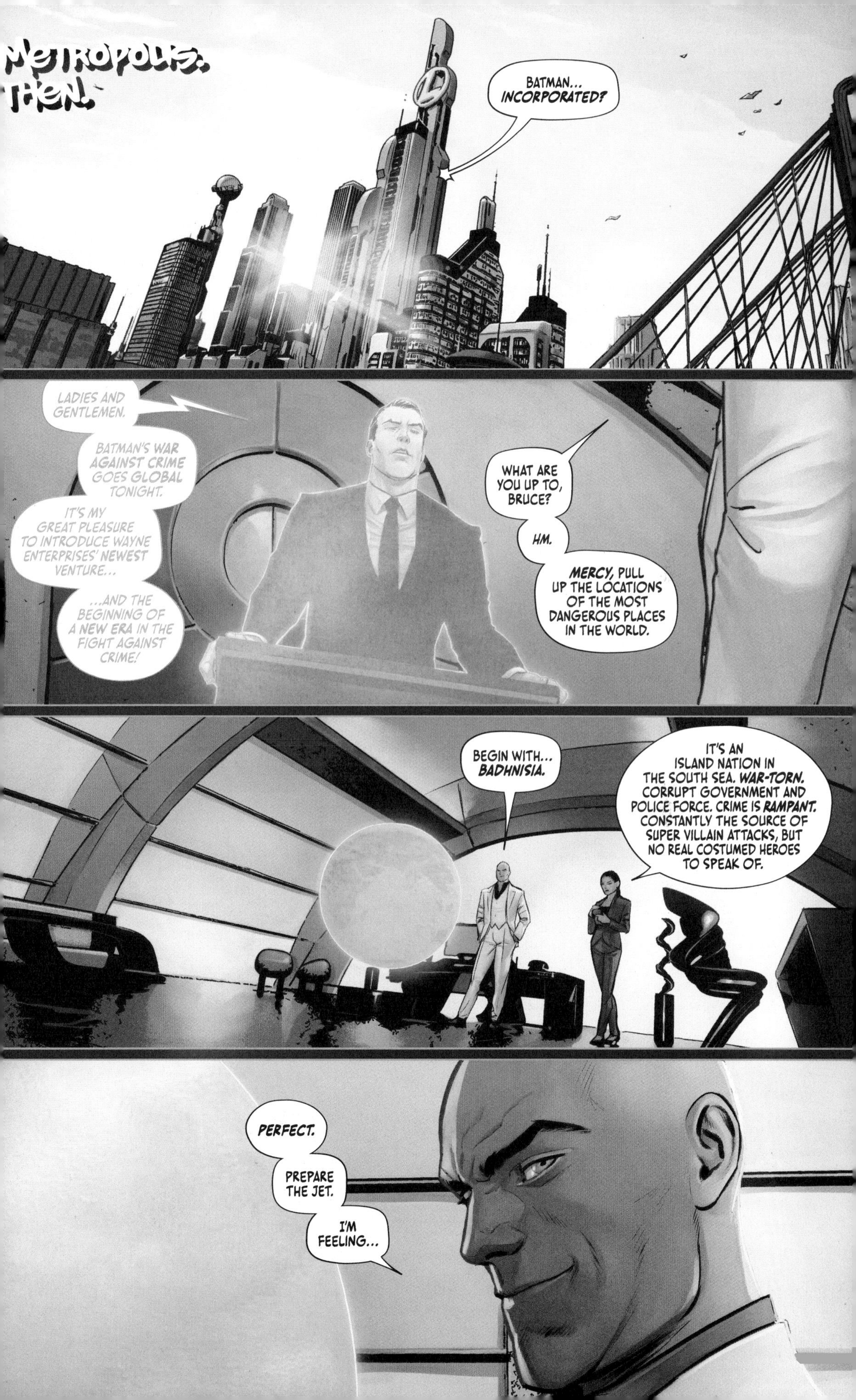

METROPOLIS. THEN!
BATMAN... INCORPORATED?
LADIES AND GENTLEMEN.
BATMAN'S WAR AGAINST CRIME GOES GLOBAL TONIGHT.
IT'S MY GREAT PLEASURE TO INTRODUCE WAYNE ENTERPRISES' NEWEST VENTURE...
...AND THE BEGINNING OF A NEW ERA IN THE FIGHT AGAINST CRIME!
WHAT ARE YOU UP TO, BRUCE?
HM.
MERCY, PULL UP THE LOCATIONS OF THE MOST DANGEROUS PLACES IN THE WORLD.
BEGIN WITH... BADHNISIA.
IT'S AN ISLAND NATION IN THE SOUTH SEA. WAR-TORN. CORRUPT GOVERNMENT AND POLICE FORCE. CRIME IS RAMPANT. CONSTANTLY THE SOURCE OF SUPER VILLAIN ATTACKS, BUT NO REAL COSTUMED HEROES TO SPEAK OF.
PERFECT.
PREPARE THE JET.
I'M FEELING...

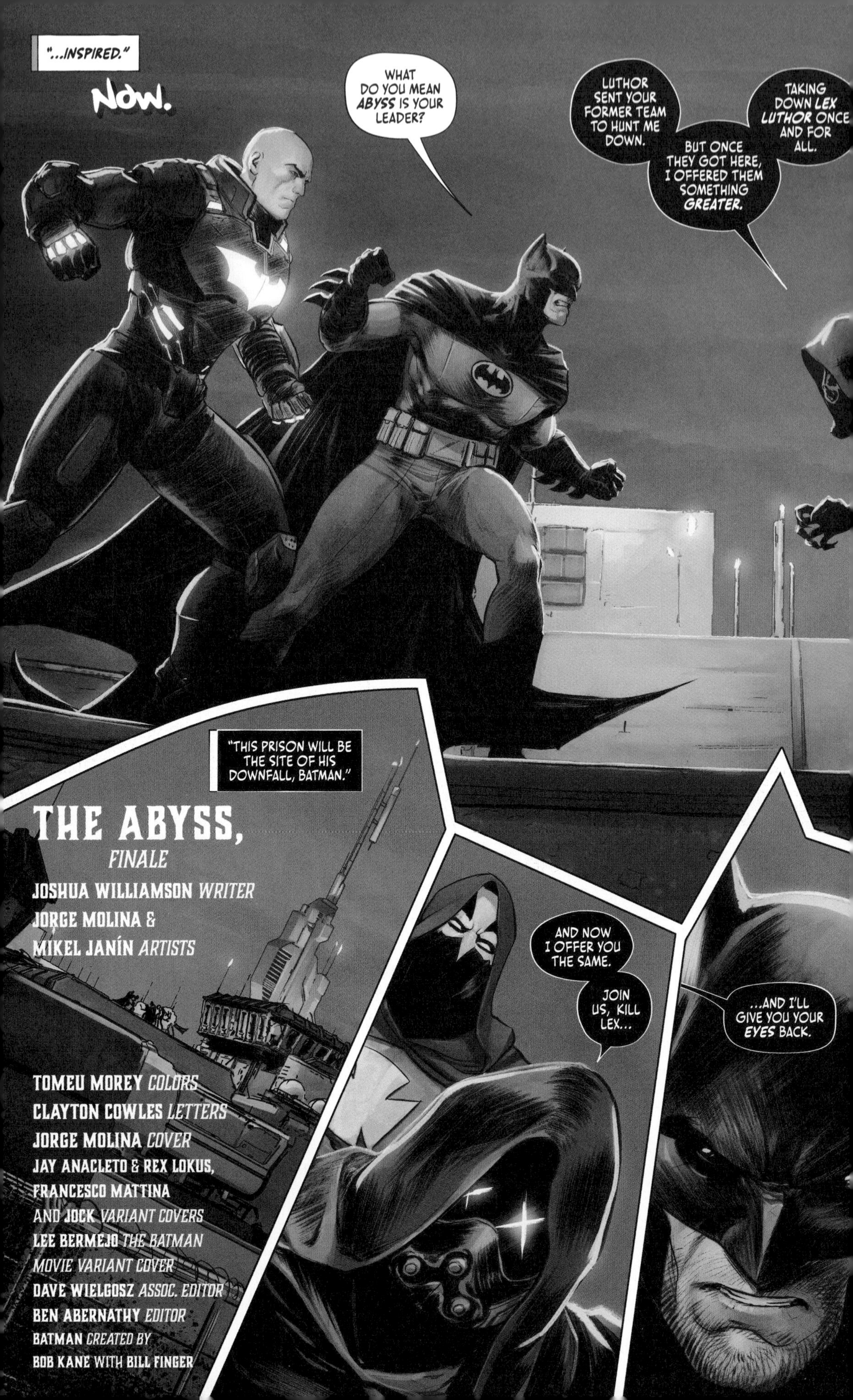
"...INSPIRED."
NOW.
WHAT DO YOU MEAN ABYSS IS YOUR LEADER?
LUTHOR SENT YOUR FORMER TEAM TO HUNT ME DOWN.
BUT ONCE THEY GOT HERE, I OFFERED THEM SOMETHING GREATER.
TAKING DOWN LEX LUTHOR ONCE AND FOR ALL.
"THIS PRISON WILL BE THE SITE OF HIS DOWNFALL, BATMAN."
THE ABYSS,
FINALE
JOSHUA WILLIAMSON WRITER
JORGE MOLINA &
MIKEL JANÍN ARTISTS
TOMEU MOREY COLORS
CLAYTON COWLES LETTERS
JORGE MOLINA COVER
JAY ANACLETO & REX LOKUS,
FRANCESCO MATTINA
AND JOCK VARIANT COVERS
LEE BERMEJO THE BATMAN
MOVIE VARIANT COVER
DAVE WIELGOSZ ASSOC. EDITOR
BEN ABERNATHY EDITOR
BATMAN CREATED BY
BOB KANE WITH BILL FINGER
AND NOW I OFFER YOU THE SAME.
JOIN US, KILL LEX...
...AND I'LL GIVE YOU YOUR EYES BACK.

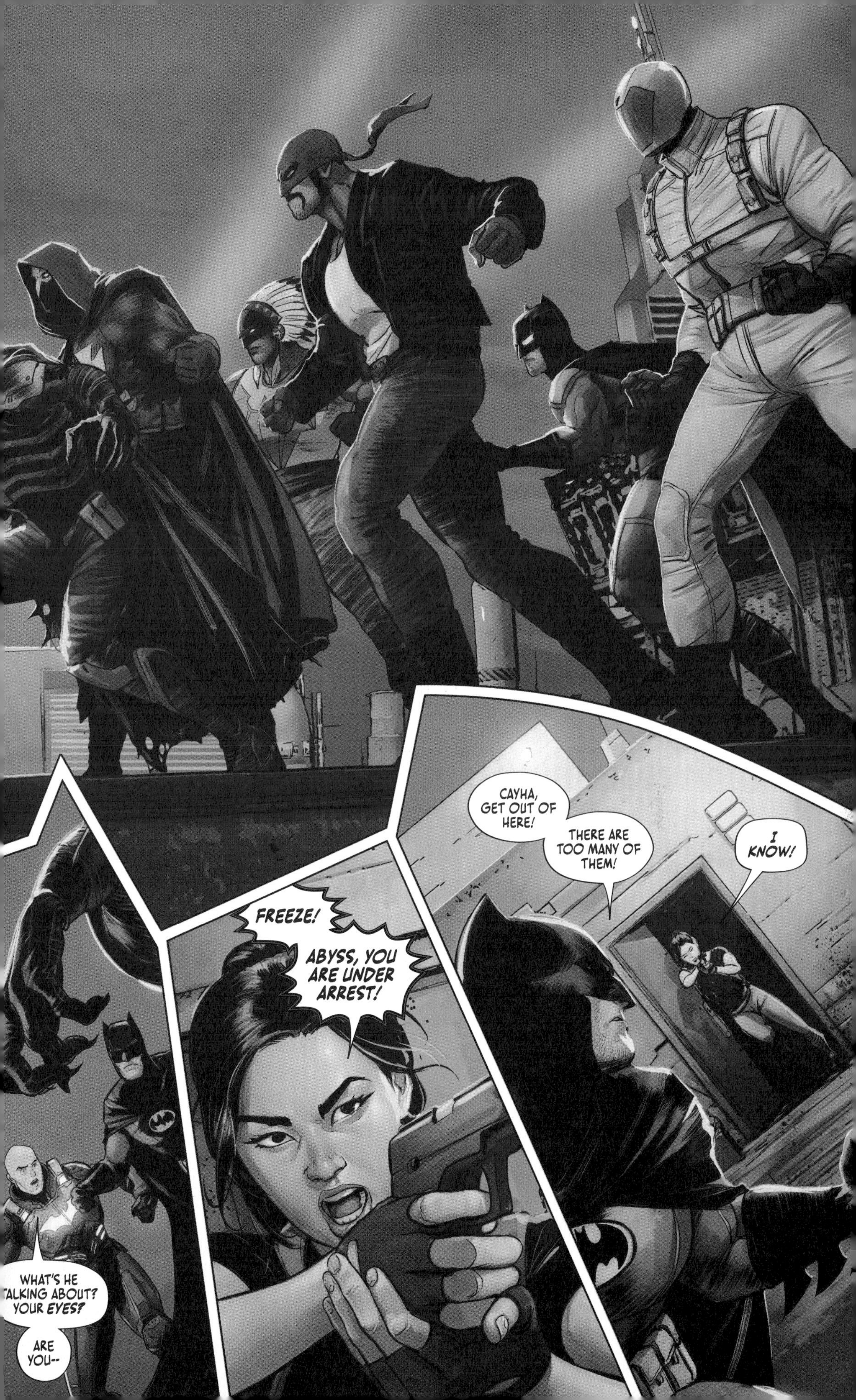

WHAT'S HE TALKING ABOUT? YOUR EYES?
ARE YOU--
FREEZE!
ABYSS, YOU ARE UNDER ARREST!
CAYHA, GET OUT OF HERE!
THERE ARE TOO MANY OF THEM!
I KNOW!

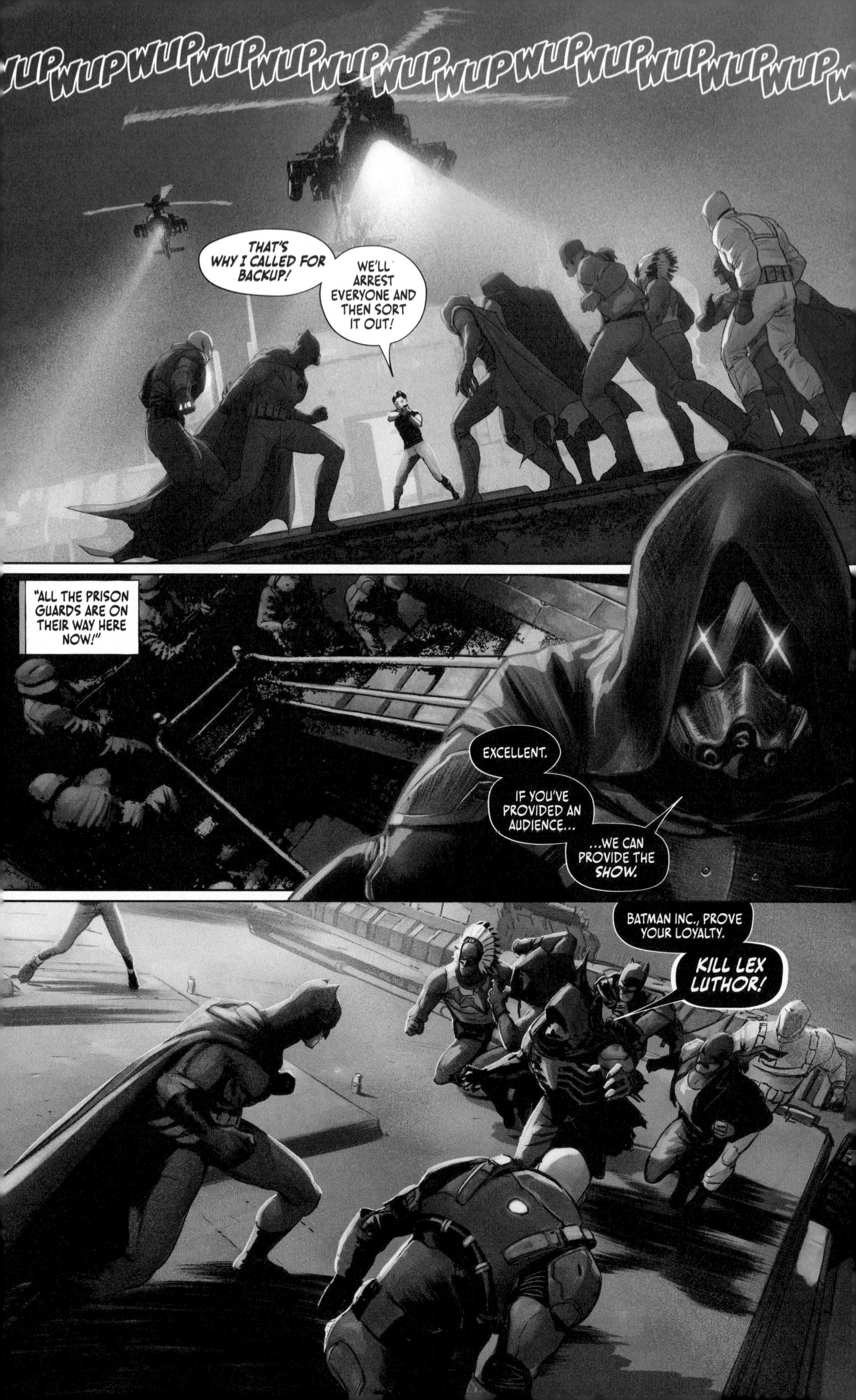
WUP WUP WUP WUP WUP WUP WUP WUP WUP WUP WUP WUP WUP W
THAT'S WHY I CALLED FOR BACKUP!
WE'LL ARREST EVERYONE AND THEN SORT IT OUT!
"ALL THE PRISON GUARDS ARE ON THEIR WAY HERE NOW!"
EXCELLENT.
IF YOU'VE PROVIDED AN AUDIENCE...
...WE CAN PROVIDE THE SHOW.
BATMAN INC., PROVE YOUR LOYALTY.
KILL LEX LUTHOR!

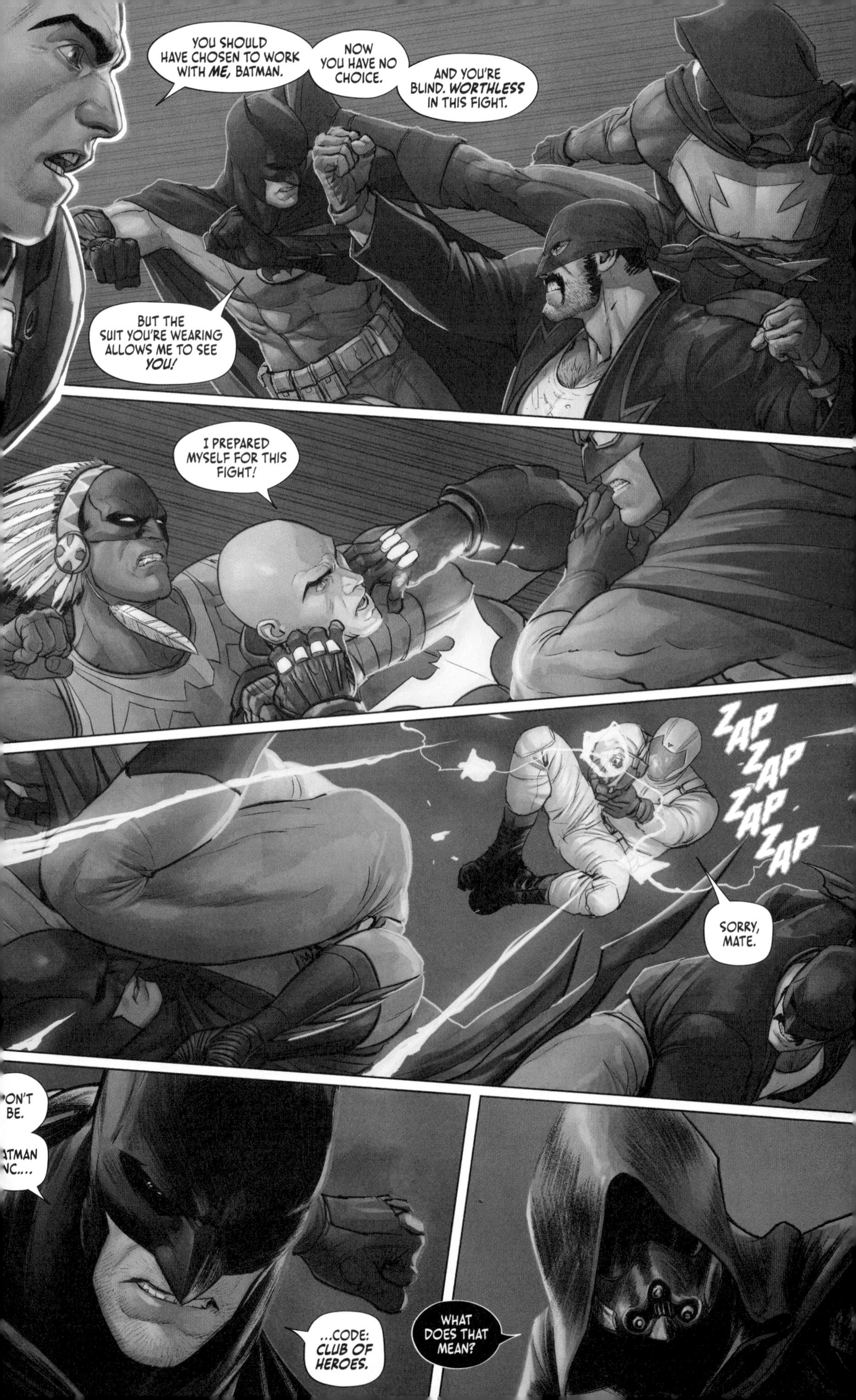
YOU SHOULD HAVE CHOSEN TO WORK WITH *ME,* BATMAN.
NOW YOU HAVE NO CHOICE.
AND YOU'RE BLIND. ***WORTHLESS*** IN THIS FIGHT.
BUT THE SUIT YOU'RE WEARING ALLOWS ME TO SEE *YOU!*
I PREPARED MYSELF FOR THIS FIGHT!
ZAP ZAP ZAP ZAP
SORRY, MATE.
ON'T BE.
ATMAN NC....
...CODE: *CLUB OF HEROES.*
WHAT DOES THAT MEAN?

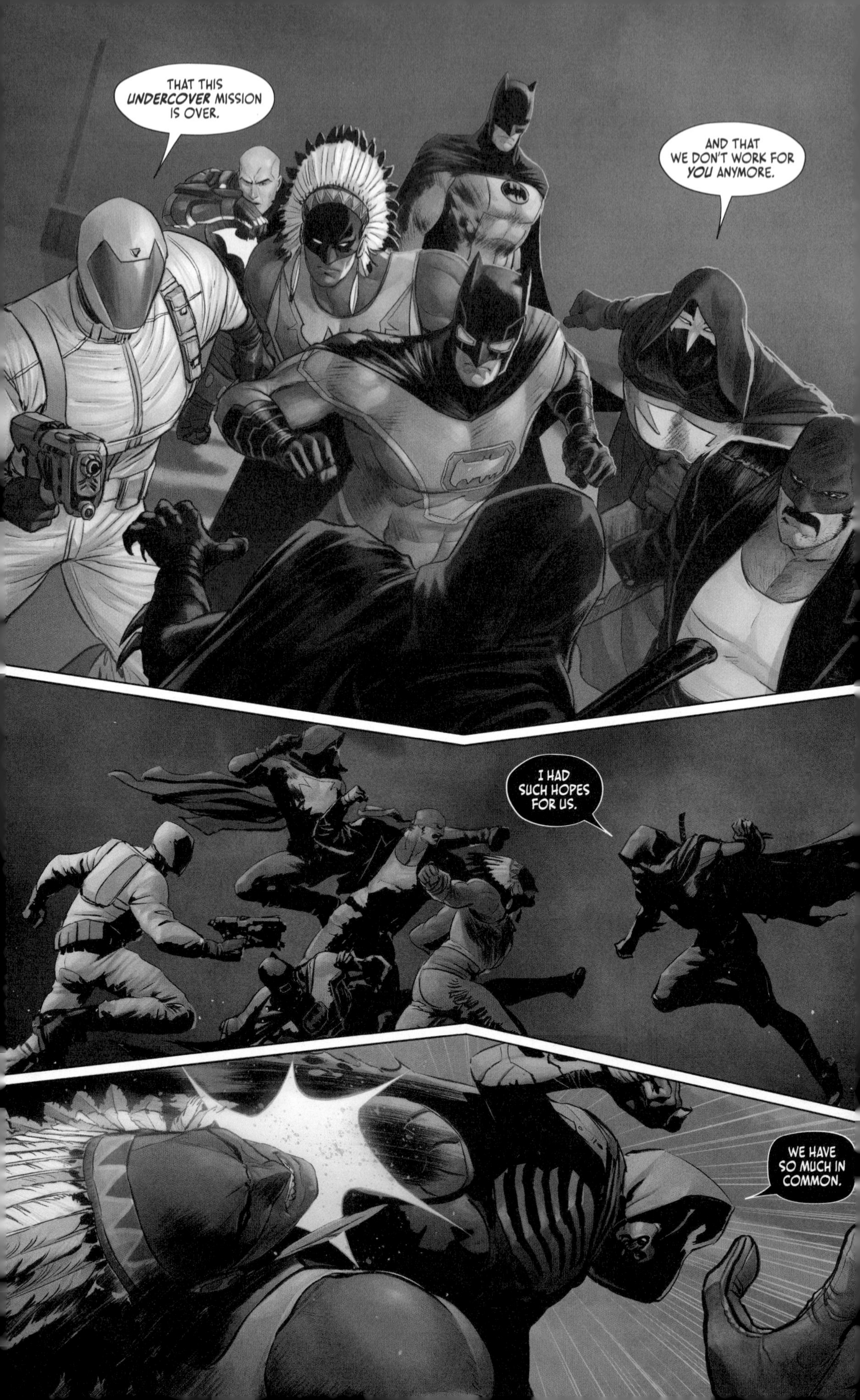
THAT THIS UNDERCOVER MISSION IS OVER.
AND THAT WE DON'T WORK FOR YOU ANYMORE.
I HAD SUCH HOPES FOR US.
WE HAVE SO MUCH IN COMMON.

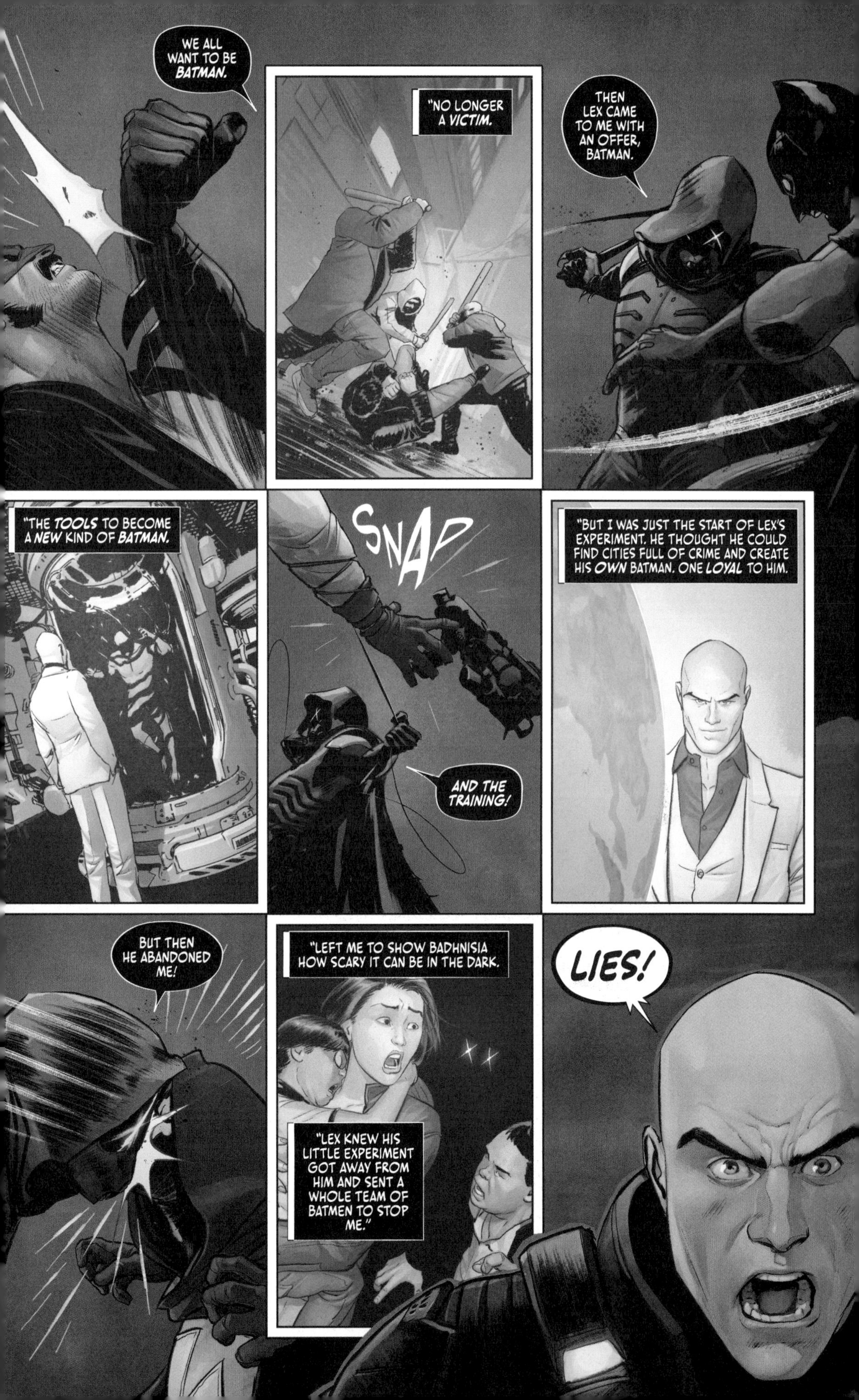
WE ALL WANT TO BE BATMAN.
"NO LONGER A VICTIM.
THEN LEX CAME TO ME WITH AN OFFER, BATMAN.
"THE TOOLS TO BECOME A NEW KIND OF BATMAN.
SNAP
AND THE TRAINING!
"BUT I WAS JUST THE START OF LEX'S EXPERIMENT. HE THOUGHT HE COULD FIND CITIES FULL OF CRIME AND CREATE HIS OWN BATMAN. ONE LOYAL TO HIM.
BUT THEN HE ABANDONED ME!
"LEFT ME TO SHOW BADHNISIA HOW SCARY IT CAN BE IN THE DARK.
"LEX KNEW HIS LITTLE EXPERIMENT GOT AWAY FROM HIM AND SENT A WHOLE TEAM OF BATMEN TO STOP ME."
LIES!

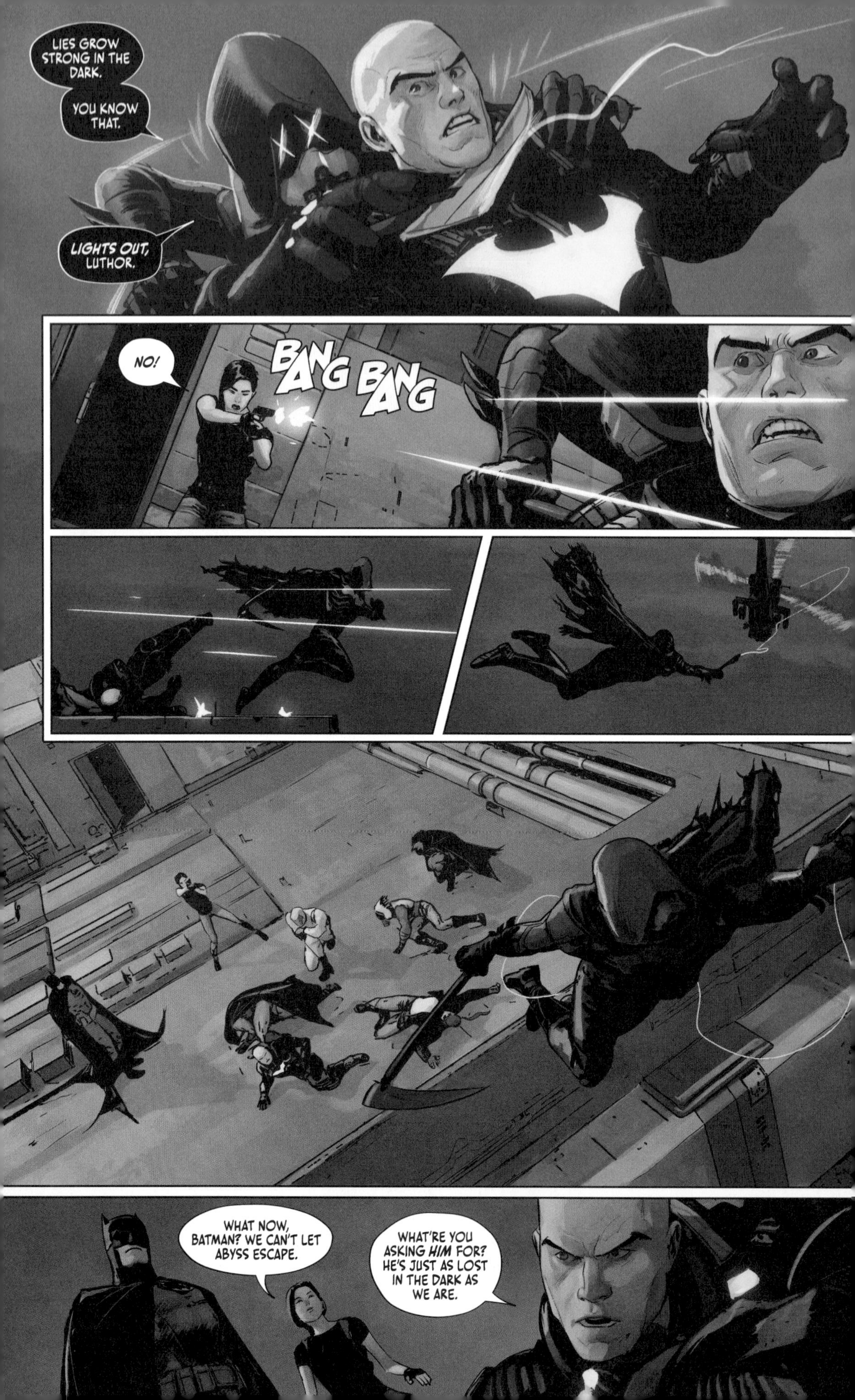
LIES GROW STRONG IN THE DARK.
YOU KNOW THAT.
LIGHTS OUT, LUTHOR.
NO!
BANG BANG
WHAT NOW, BATMAN? WE CAN'T LET ABYSS ESCAPE.
WHAT'RE YOU ASKING HIM FOR? HE'S JUST AS LOST IN THE DARK AS WE ARE.

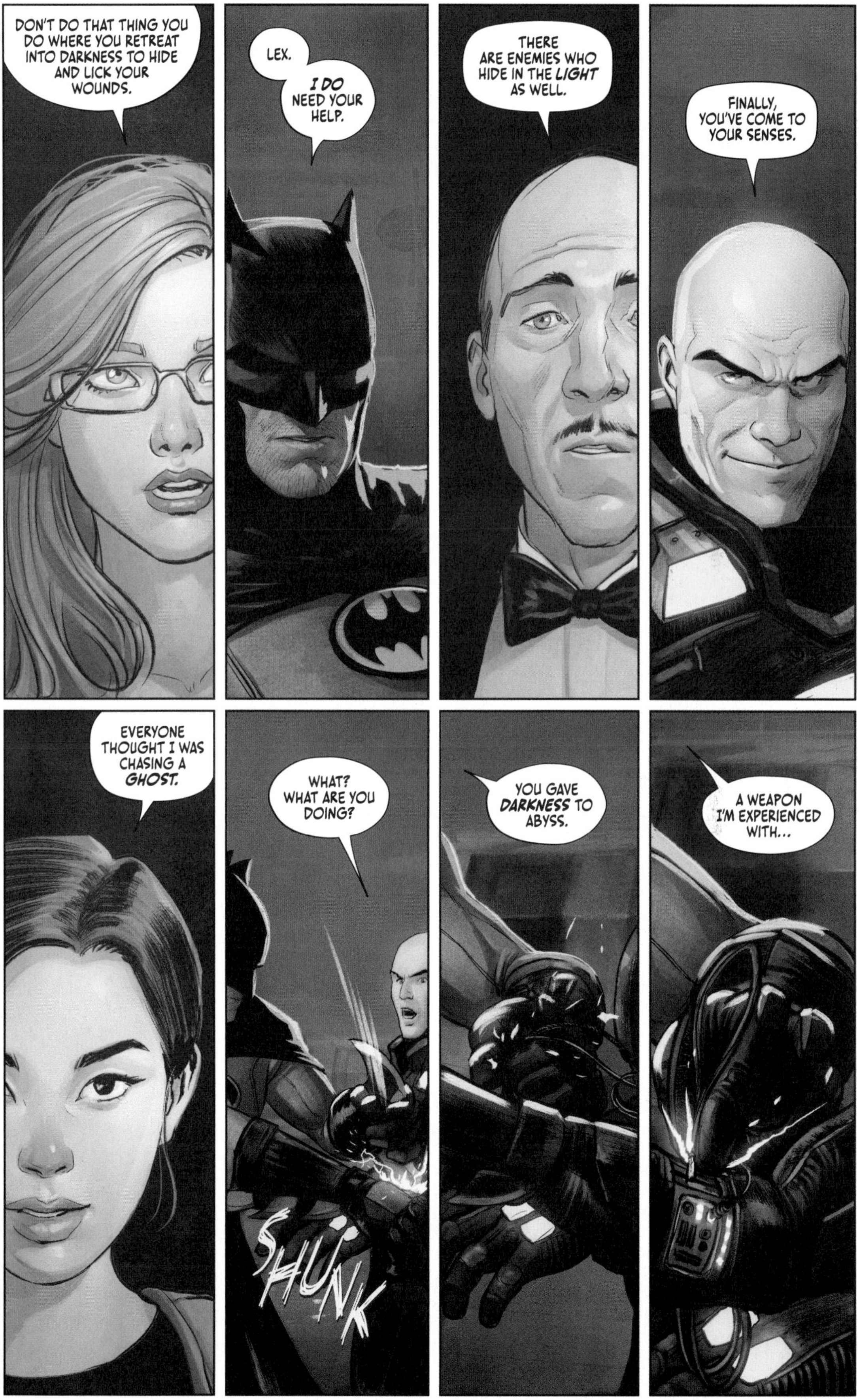
DON'T DO THAT THING YOU DO WHERE YOU RETREAT INTO DARKNESS TO HIDE AND LICK YOUR WOUNDS.
LEX.
I DO NEED YOUR HELP.
THERE ARE ENEMIES WHO HIDE IN THE *LIGHT* AS WELL.
FINALLY, YOU'VE COME TO YOUR SENSES.
EVERYONE THOUGHT I WAS CHASING A *GHOST.*
WHAT? WHAT ARE YOU DOING?
SHUNK
YOU GAVE *DARKNESS* TO ABYSS.
A WEAPON I'M EXPERIENCED WITH...

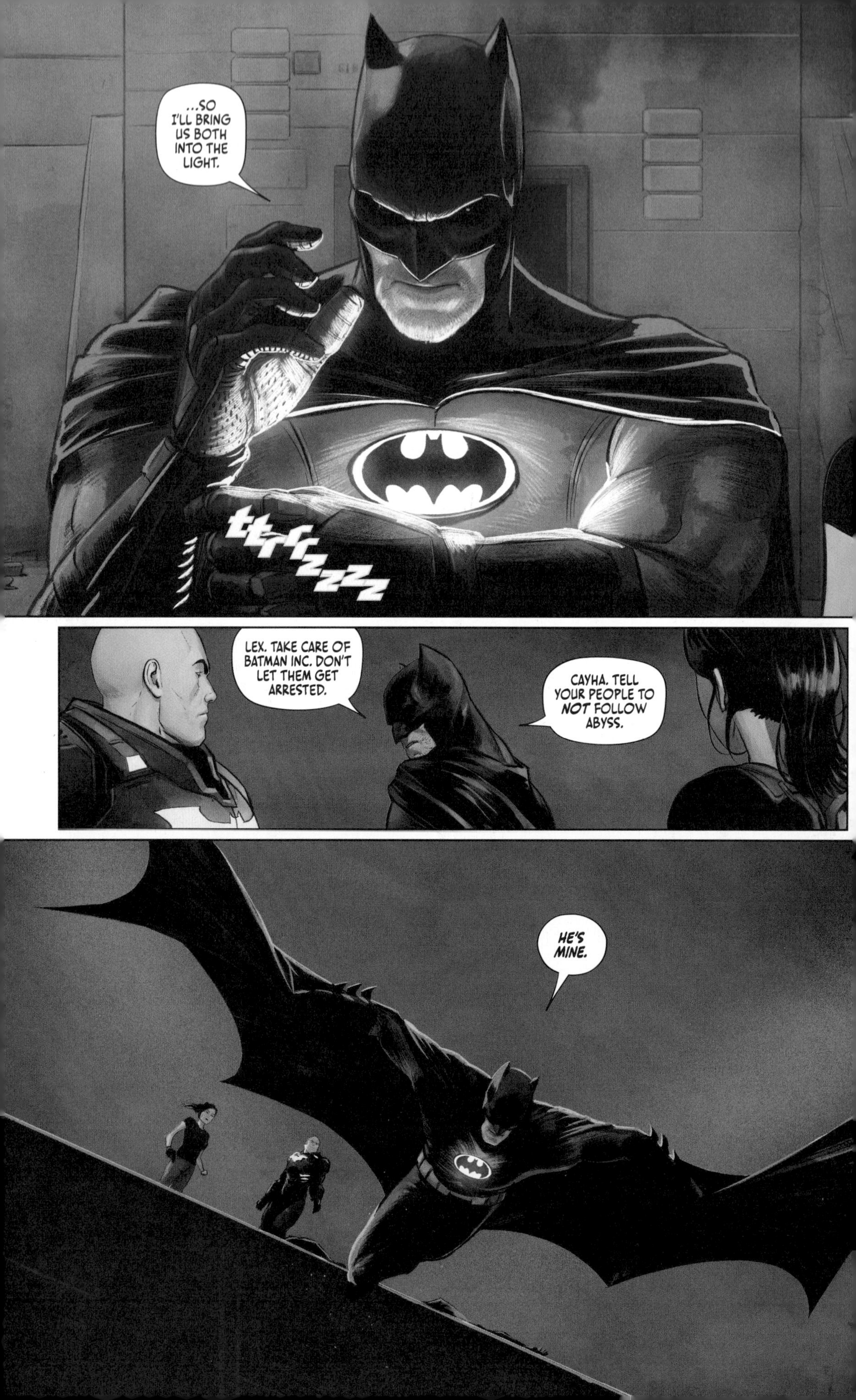
...SO I'LL BRING US BOTH INTO THE LIGHT.
tttrrzzzz
LEX. TAKE CARE OF BATMAN INC. DON'T LET THEM GET ARRESTED.
CAYHA. TELL YOUR PEOPLE TO NOT FOLLOW ABYSS.
HE'S MINE.

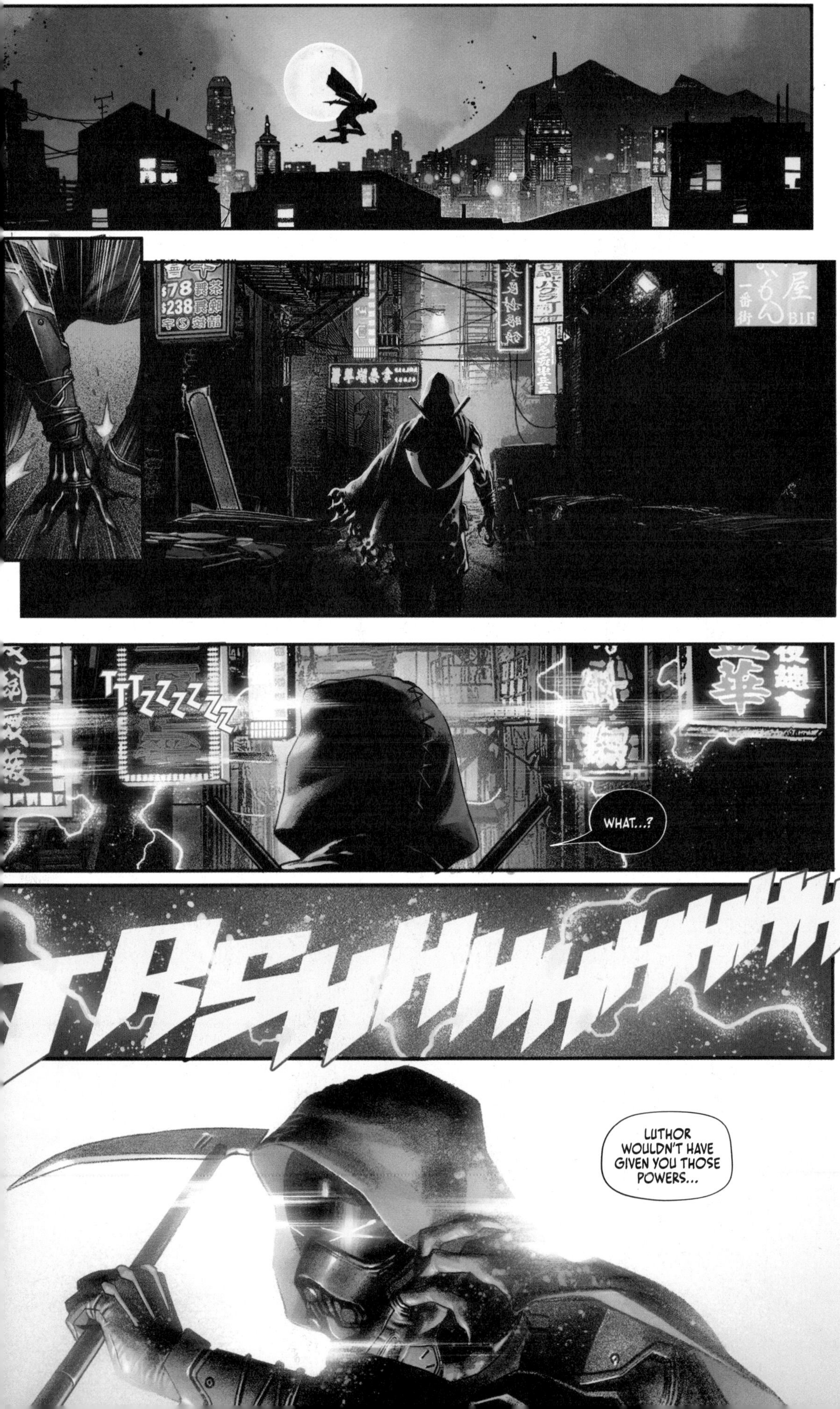

TTTZZZZZZZ
WHAT...?
TRSHHHHHHHH
LUTHOR WOULDN'T HAVE GIVEN YOU THOSE POWERS...

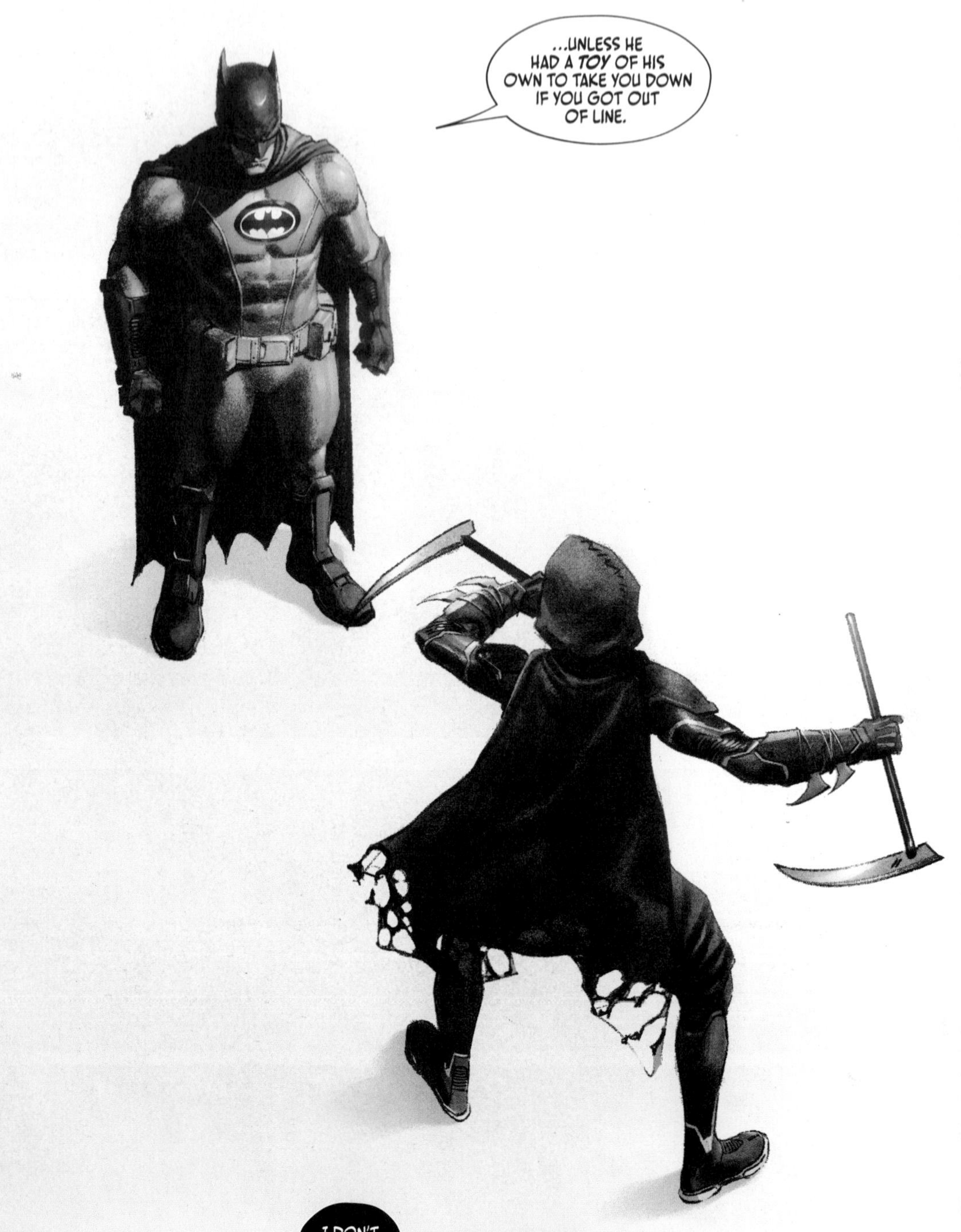
...UNLESS HE HAD A *TOY* OF HIS OWN TO TAKE YOU DOWN IF YOU GOT OUT OF LINE.

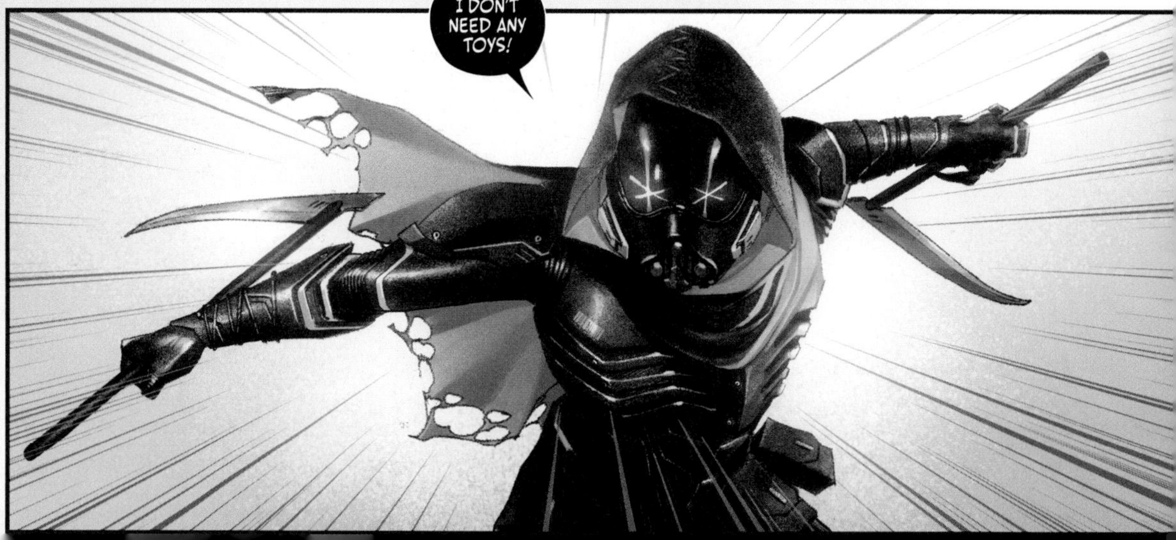
I DON'T NEED ANY TOYS!

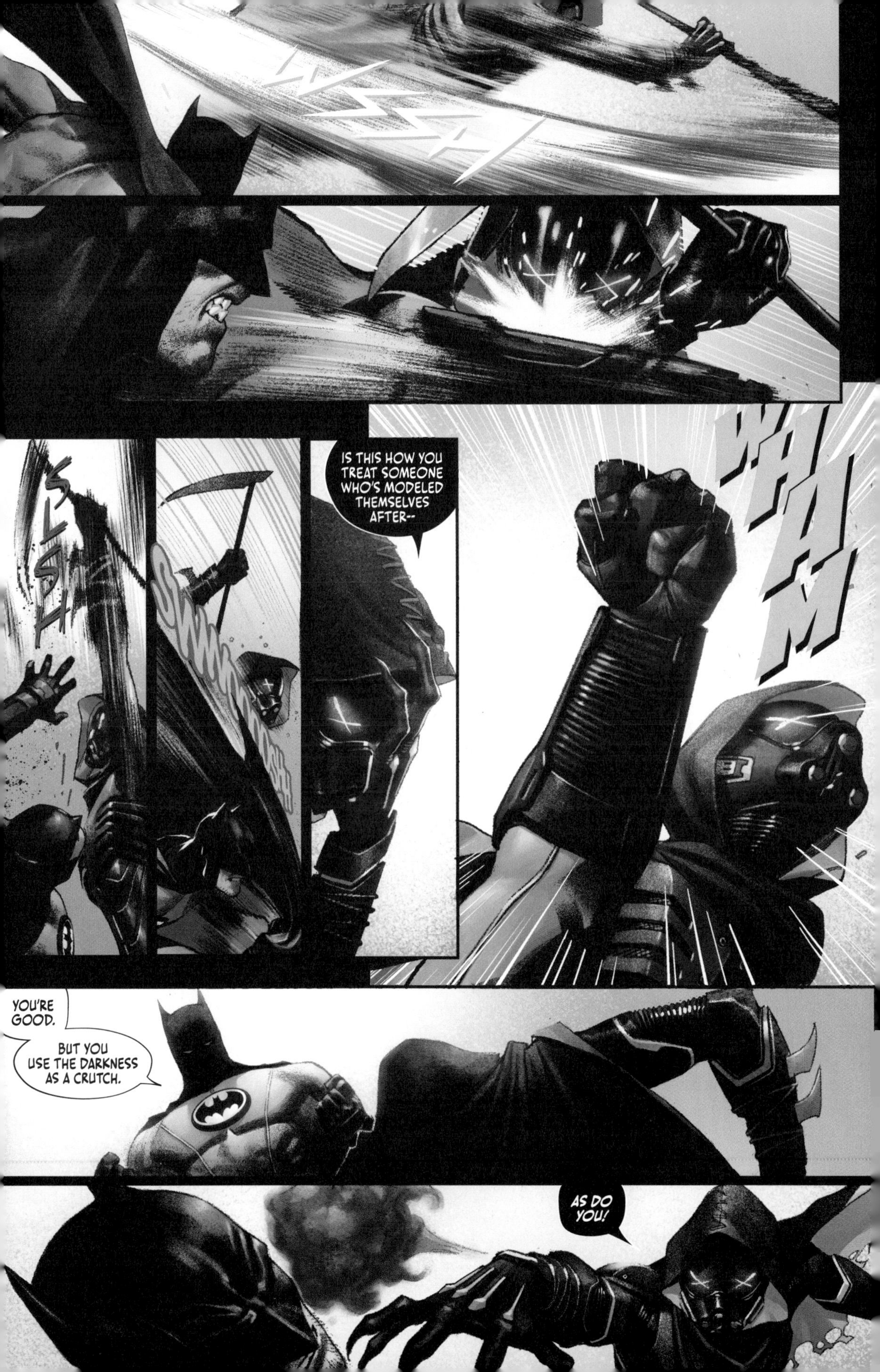

WSSH
SLSH
SWWOOSH
IS THIS HOW YOU TREAT SOMEONE WHO'S MODELED THEMSELVES AFTER--
WHAM
YOU'RE GOOD.
BUT YOU USE THE DARKNESS AS A CRUTCH.
AS DO YOU!

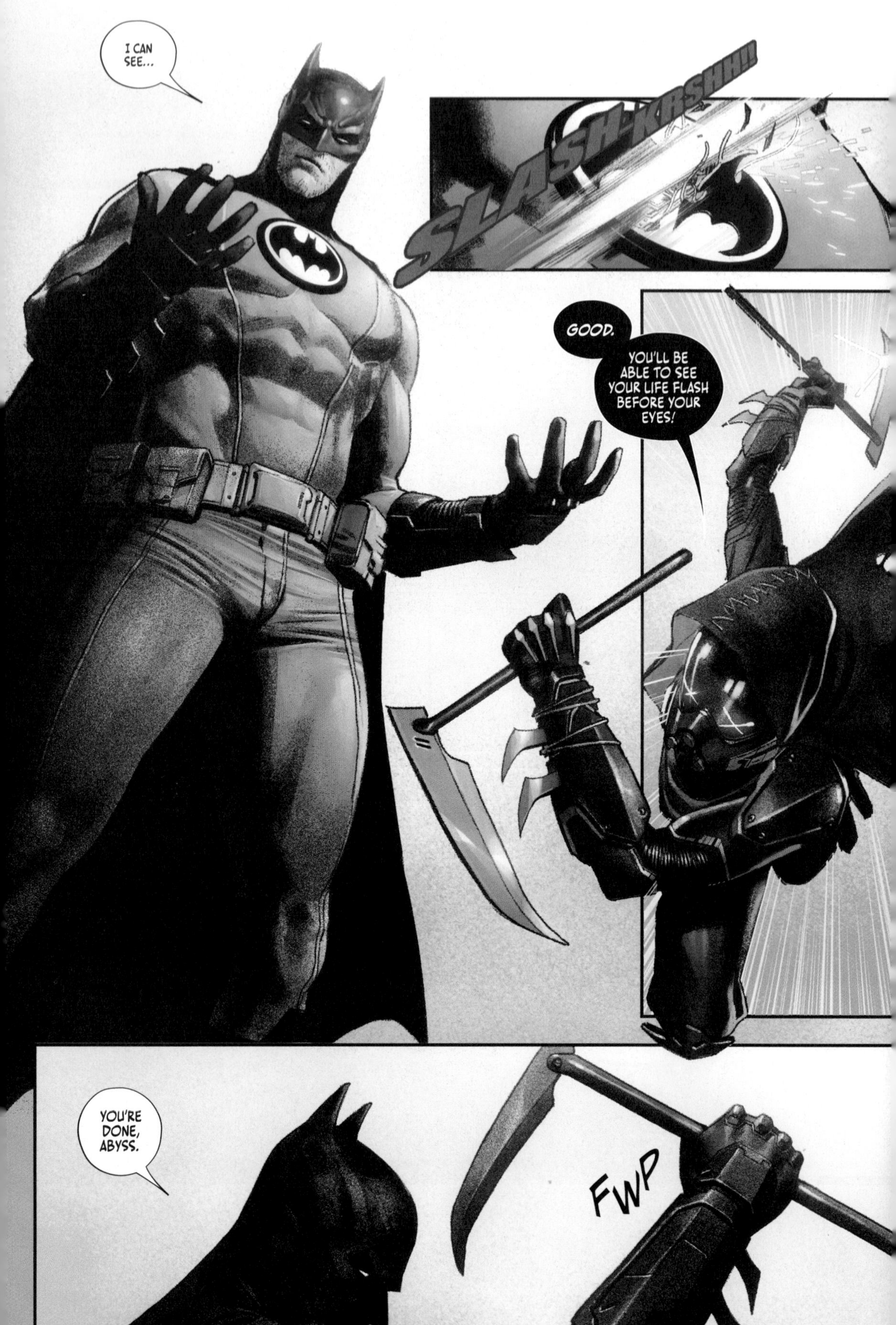
I CAN SEE...
SLASH-KRSHH!!
GOOD.
YOU'LL BE ABLE TO SEE YOUR LIFE FLASH BEFORE YOUR EYES!
YOU'RE DONE, ABYSS.
FWP

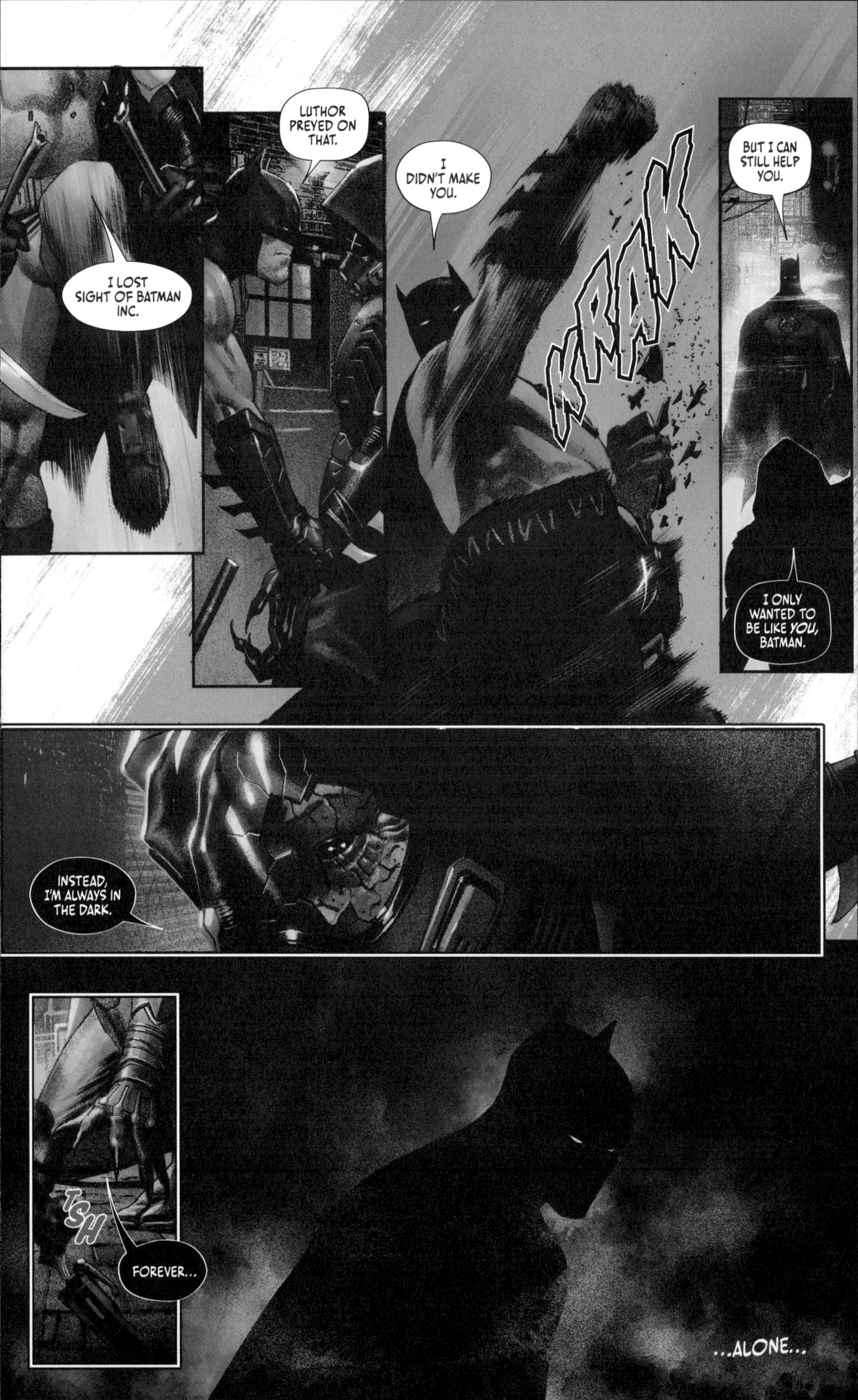
I LOST SIGHT OF BATMAN INC.
LUTHOR PREYED ON THAT.
I DIDN'T MAKE YOU.
KRAK
BUT I CAN STILL HELP YOU.
I ONLY WANTED TO BE LIKE *YOU*, BATMAN.
INSTEAD, I'M ALWAYS IN THE DARK.
TSH
FOREVER...
...ALONE...

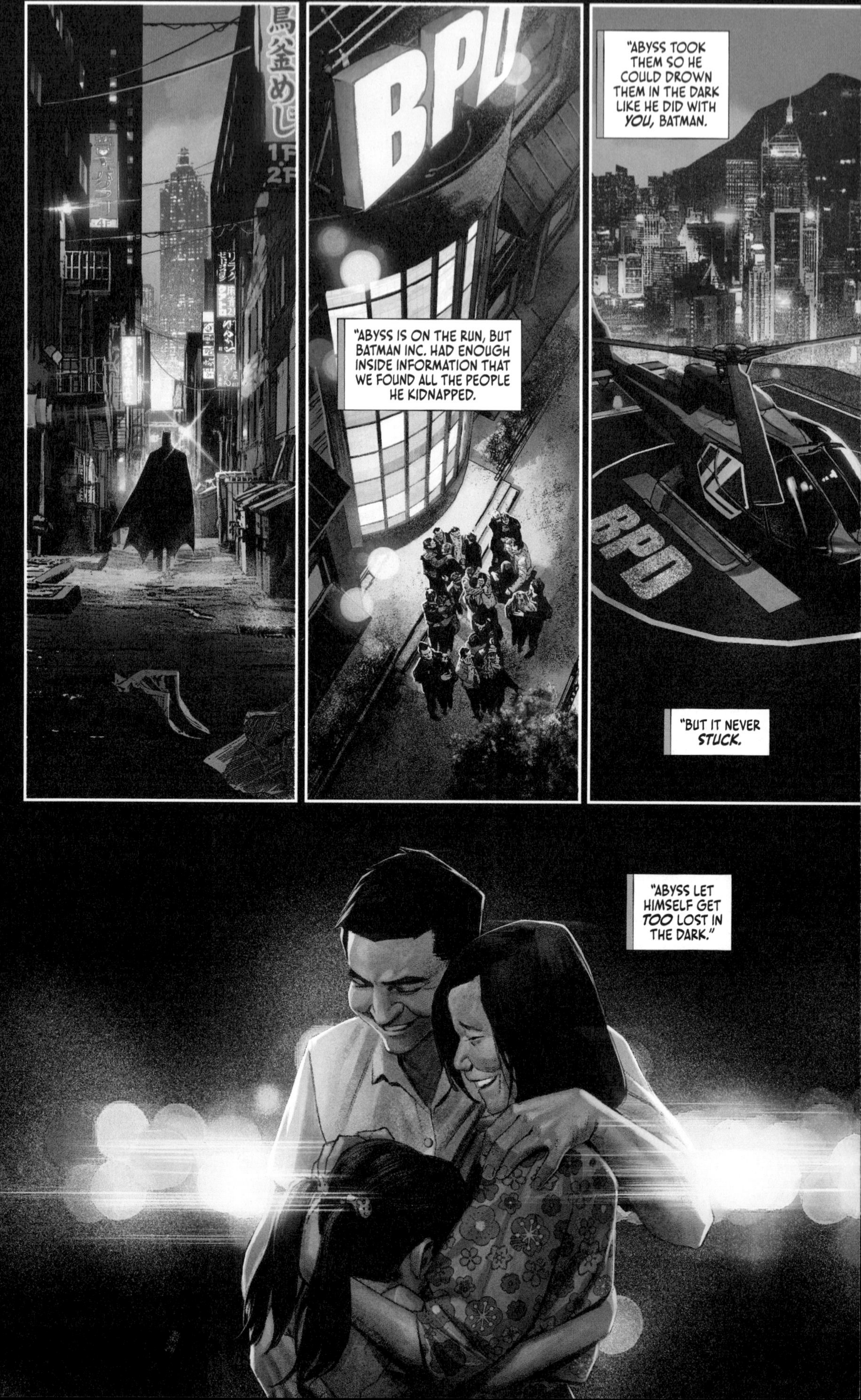
鳥釜めし
1F
2F
BPD
"ABYSS IS ON THE RUN, BUT BATMAN INC. HAD ENOUGH INSIDE INFORMATION THAT WE FOUND ALL THE PEOPLE HE KIDNAPPED.
"ABYSS TOOK THEM SO HE COULD DROWN THEM IN THE DARK LIKE HE DID WITH *YOU,* BATMAN.
BPD
"BUT IT NEVER *STUCK.*
"ABYSS LET HIMSELF GET *TOO* LOST IN THE DARK."

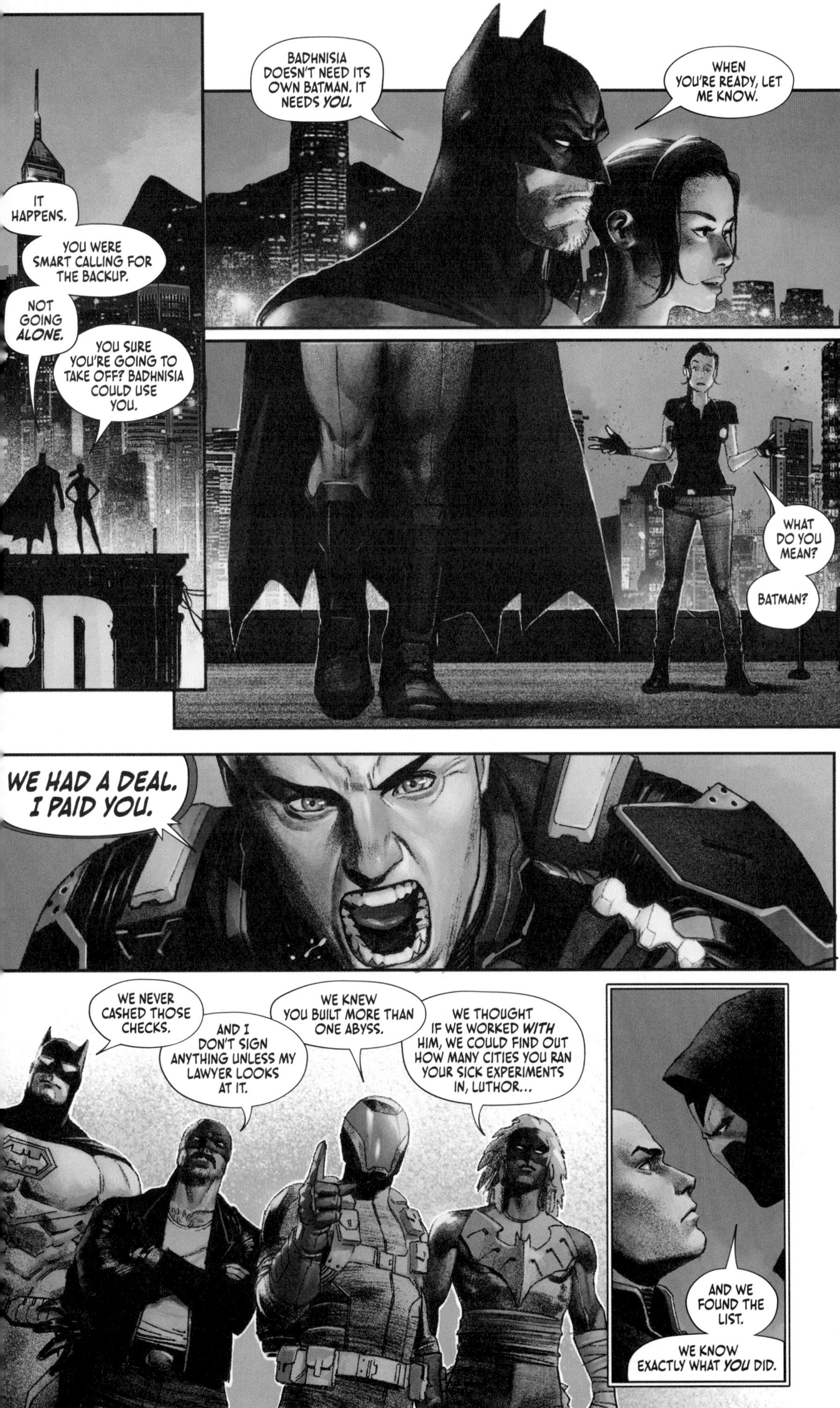
IT HAPPENS.
YOU WERE SMART CALLING FOR THE BACKUP.
NOT GOING ALONE.
YOU SURE YOU'RE GOING TO TAKE OFF? BADHNISIA COULD USE YOU.
BADHNISIA DOESN'T NEED ITS OWN BATMAN. IT NEEDS YOU.
WHEN YOU'RE READY, LET ME KNOW.
WHAT DO YOU MEAN?
BATMAN?
WE HAD A DEAL. I PAID YOU.
WE NEVER CASHED THOSE CHECKS.
AND I DON'T SIGN ANYTHING UNLESS MY LAWYER LOOKS AT IT.
WE KNEW YOU BUILT MORE THAN ONE ABYSS.
WE THOUGHT IF WE WORKED WITH HIM, WE COULD FIND OUT HOW MANY CITIES YOU RAN YOUR SICK EXPERIMENTS IN, LUTHOR...
AND WE FOUND THE LIST.
WE KNOW EXACTLY WHAT YOU DID.

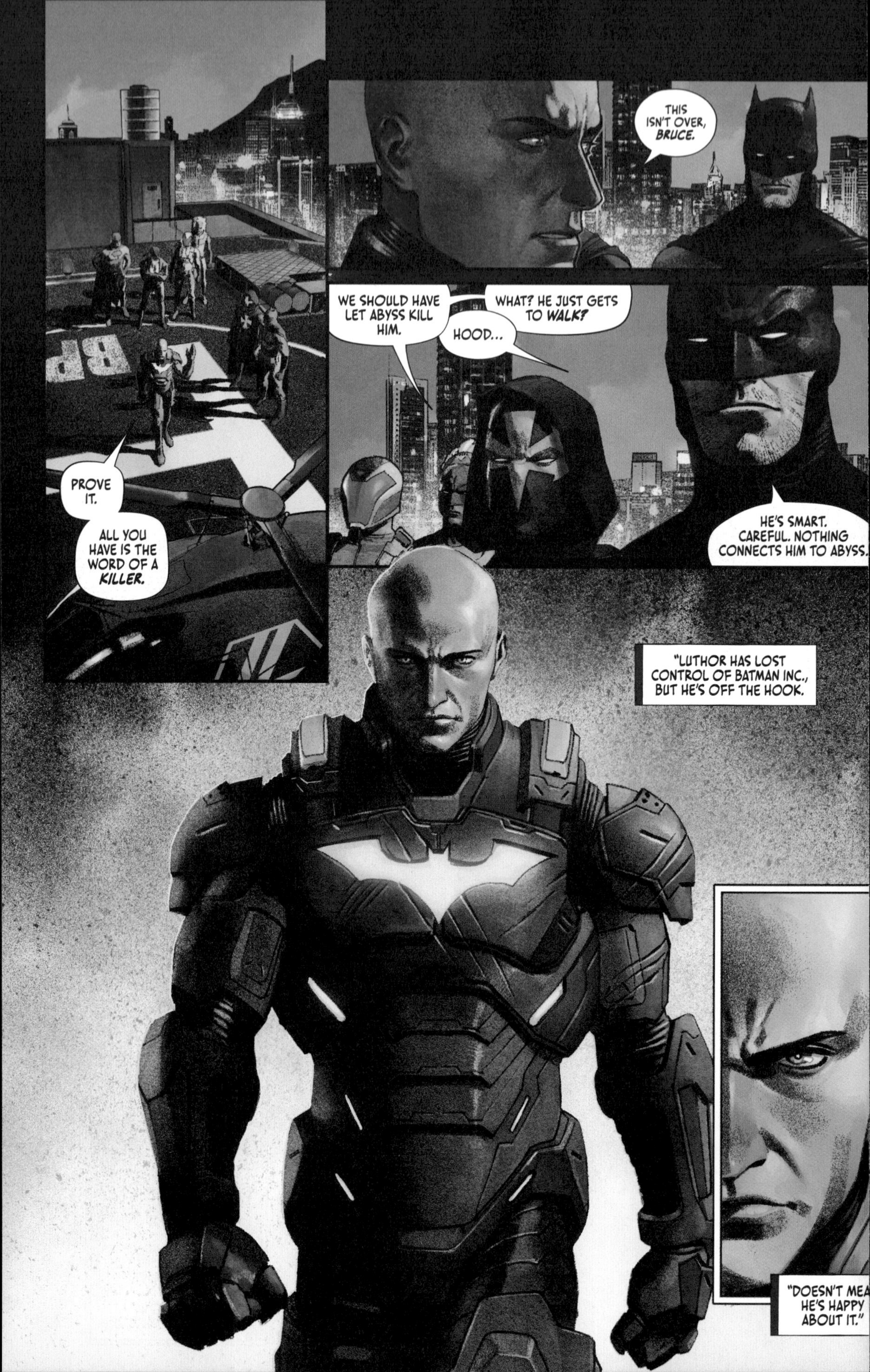

PROVE IT.
ALL YOU HAVE IS THE WORD OF A KILLER.
THIS ISN'T OVER, BRUCE.
WE SHOULD HAVE LET ABYSS KILL HIM.
WHAT? HE JUST GETS TO WALK?
HOOD...
HE'S SMART. CAREFUL. NOTHING CONNECTS HIM TO ABYSS.
"LUTHOR HAS LOST CONTROL OF BATMAN INC., BUT HE'S OFF THE HOOK.
"DOESN'T MEA
HE'S HAPPY
ABOUT IT."

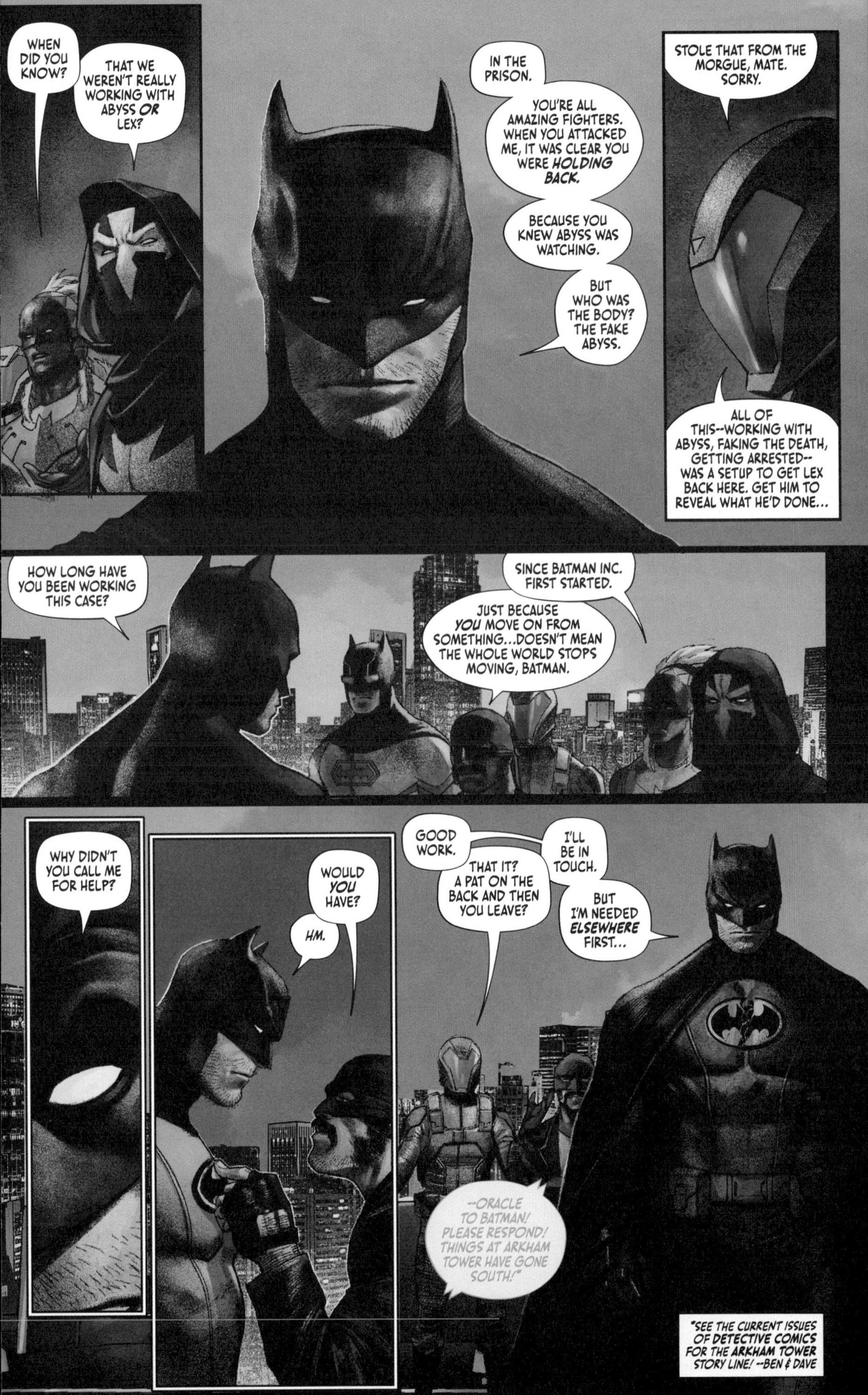

WHEN DID YOU KNOW?
THAT WE WEREN'T REALLY WORKING WITH ABYSS OR LEX?
IN THE PRISON.
YOU'RE ALL AMAZING FIGHTERS. WHEN YOU ATTACKED ME, IT WAS CLEAR YOU WERE HOLDING BACK.
BECAUSE YOU KNEW ABYSS WAS WATCHING.
BUT WHO WAS THE BODY? THE FAKE ABYSS.
STOLE THAT FROM THE MORGUE, MATE. SORRY.
ALL OF THIS--WORKING WITH ABYSS, FAKING THE DEATH, GETTING ARRESTED--WAS A SETUP TO GET LEX BACK HERE. GET HIM TO REVEAL WHAT HE'D DONE...
HOW LONG HAVE YOU BEEN WORKING THIS CASE?
SINCE BATMAN INC. FIRST STARTED.
JUST BECAUSE YOU MOVE ON FROM SOMETHING...DOESN'T MEAN THE WHOLE WORLD STOPS MOVING, BATMAN.
WHY DIDN'T YOU CALL ME FOR HELP?
WOULD YOU HAVE?
HM.
GOOD WORK.
I'LL BE IN TOUCH.
THAT IT? A PAT ON THE BACK AND THEN YOU LEAVE?
BUT I'M NEEDED ELSEWHERE FIRST...
--ORACLE TO BATMAN! PLEASE RESPOND! THINGS AT ARKHAM TOWER HAVE GONE SOUTH!*
*SEE THE CURRENT ISSUES OF DETECTIVE COMICS FOR THE ARKHAM TOWER STORY LINE! --BEN & DAVE

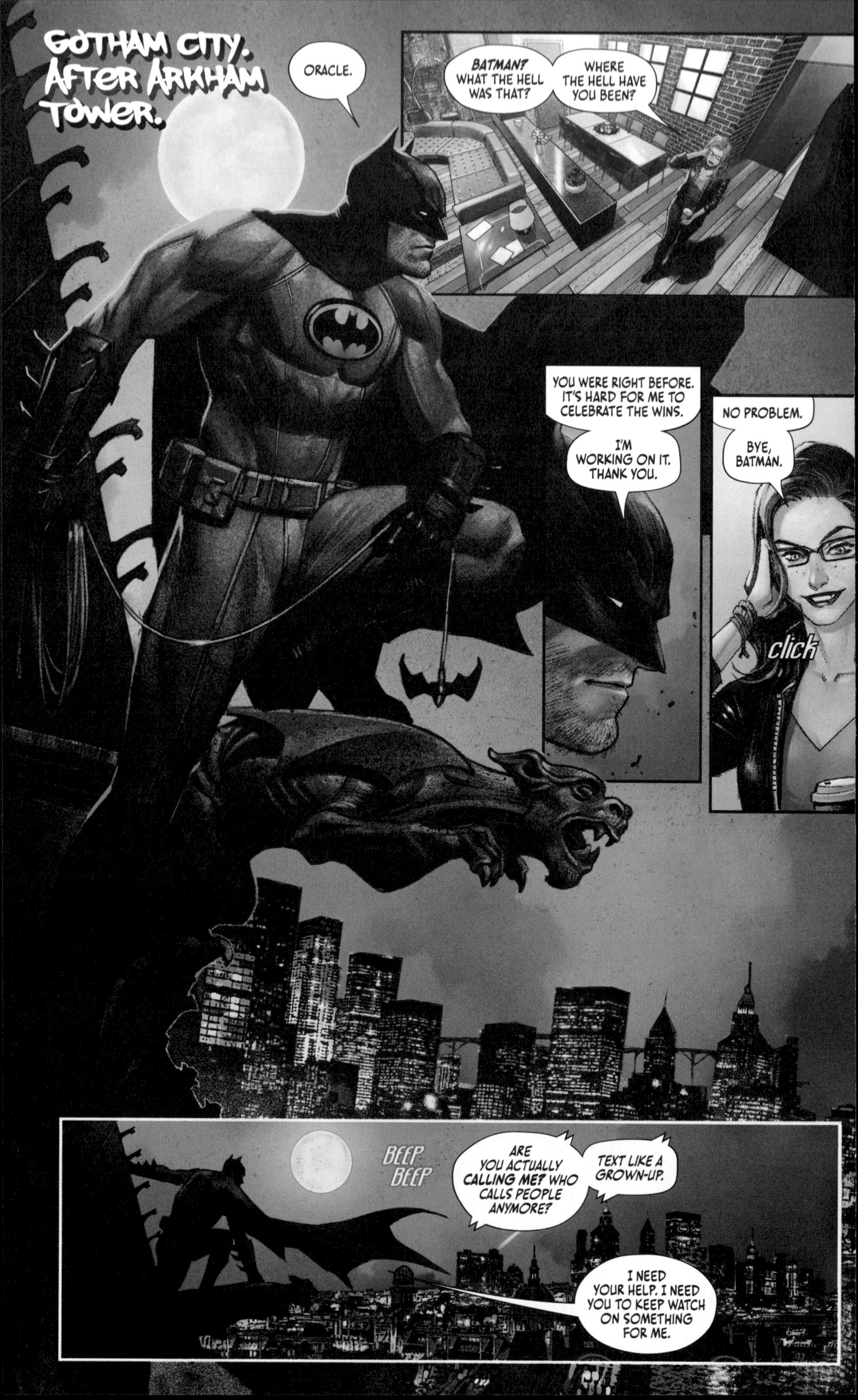
GOTHAM CITY. AFTER ARKHAM TOWER.
ORACLE.
BATMAN? WHAT THE HELL WAS THAT?
WHERE THE HELL HAVE YOU BEEN?
YOU WERE RIGHT BEFORE. IT'S HARD FOR ME TO CELEBRATE THE WINS.
I'M WORKING ON IT. THANK YOU.
NO PROBLEM.
BYE, BATMAN.
click
BEEP BEEP
ARE YOU ACTUALLY CALLING ME? WHO CALLS PEOPLE ANYMORE?
TEXT LIKE A GROWN-UP.
I NEED YOUR HELP. I NEED YOU TO KEEP WATCH ON SOMETHING FOR ME.

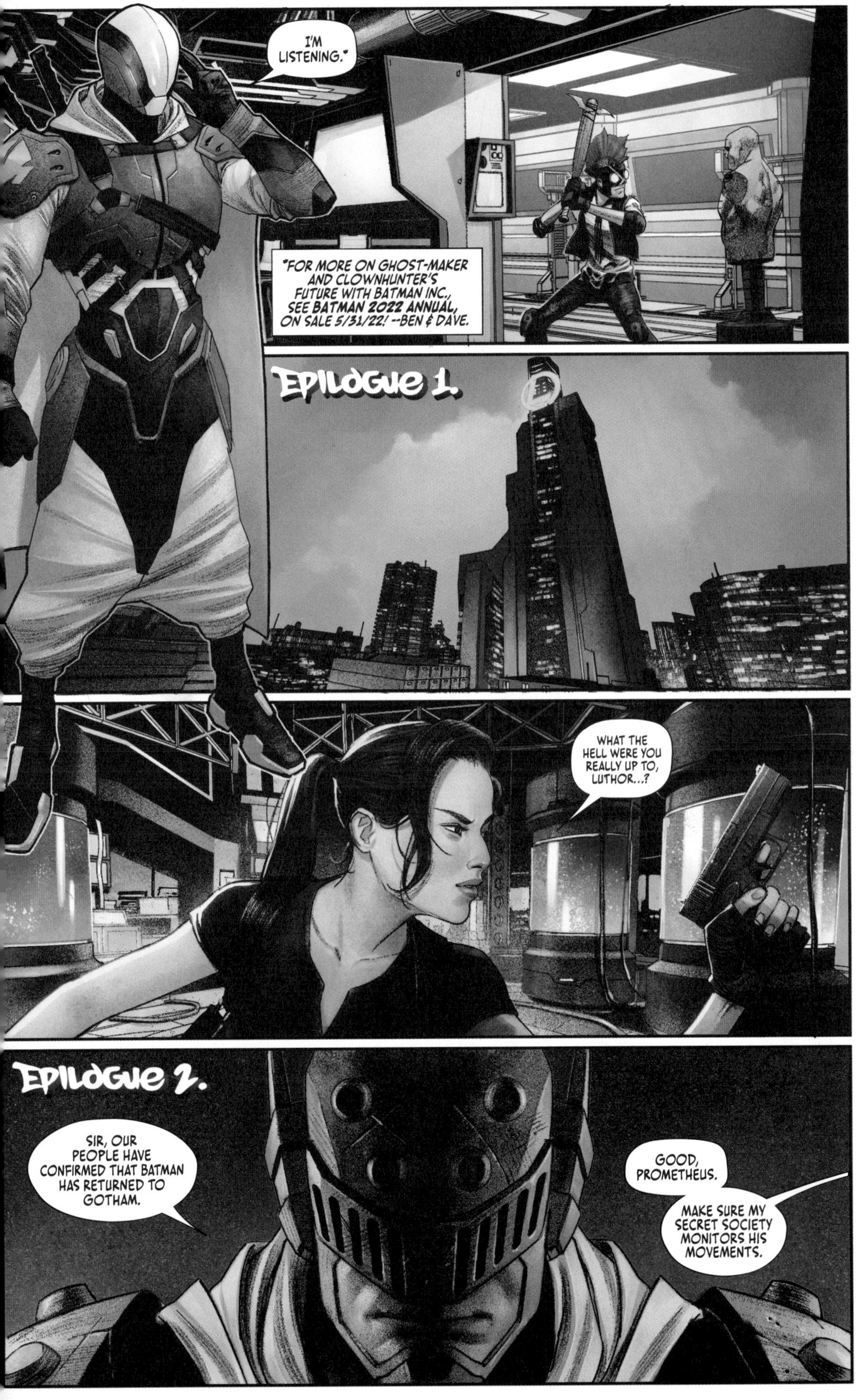

I'M LISTENING."
"FOR MORE ON GHOST-MAKER AND CLOWNHUNTER'S FUTURE WITH BATMAN INC., SEE BATMAN 2022 ANNUAL, ON SALE 5/31/22! --BEN & DAVE.
EPILOGUE 1.
WHAT THE HELL WERE YOU REALLY UP TO, LUTHOR...?
EPILOGUE 2.
SIR, OUR PEOPLE HAVE CONFIRMED THAT BATMAN HAS RETURNED TO GOTHAM.
GOOD, PROMETHEUS.
MAKE SURE MY SECRET SOCIETY MONITORS HIS MOVEMENTS.

WE NEED BATMAN DISTRACTED WHILE WE PREPARE FOR WAR.
TO BE CONTINUED IN SHADOW WAR!

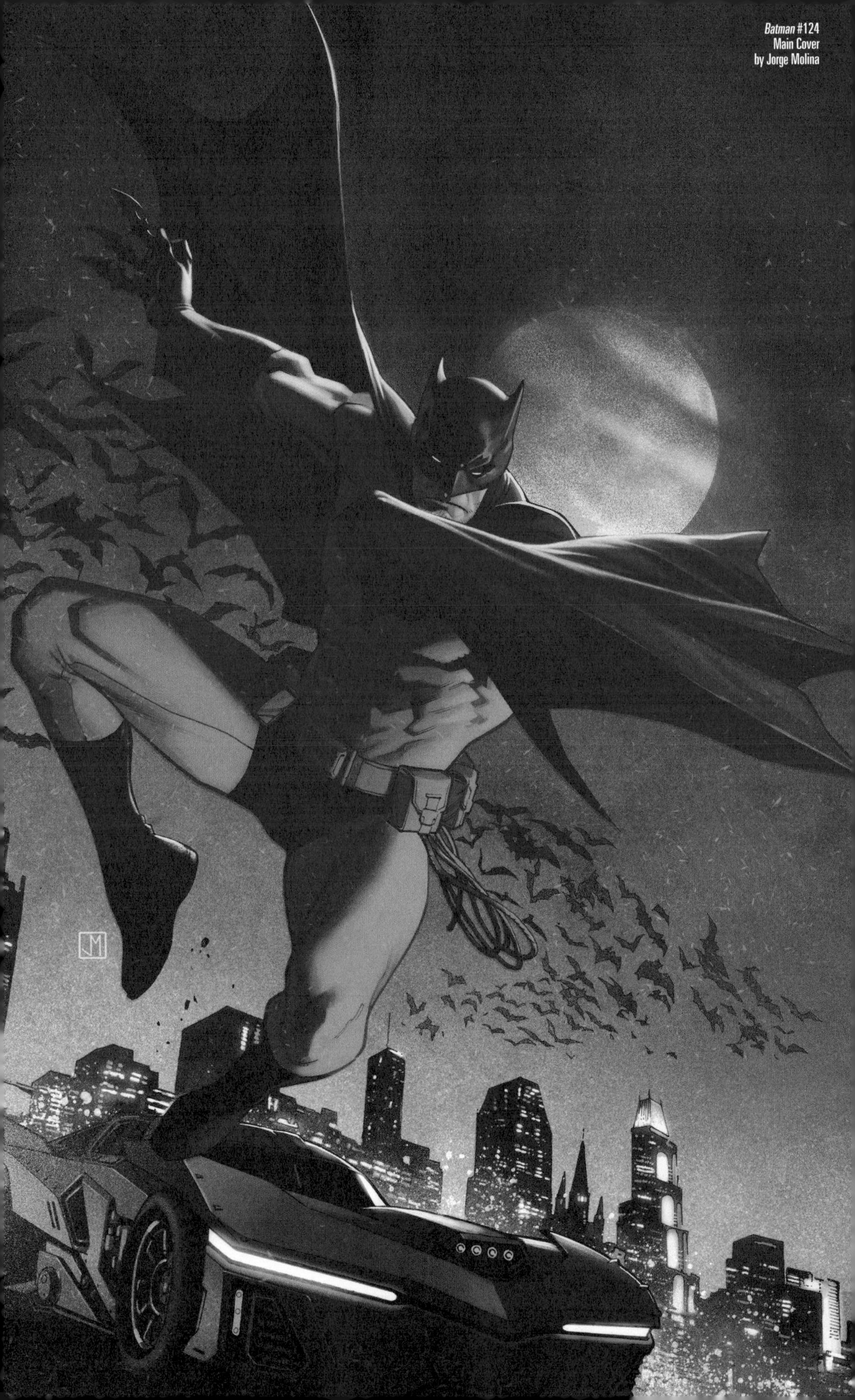

Batman #124
Main Cover
by Jorge Molina

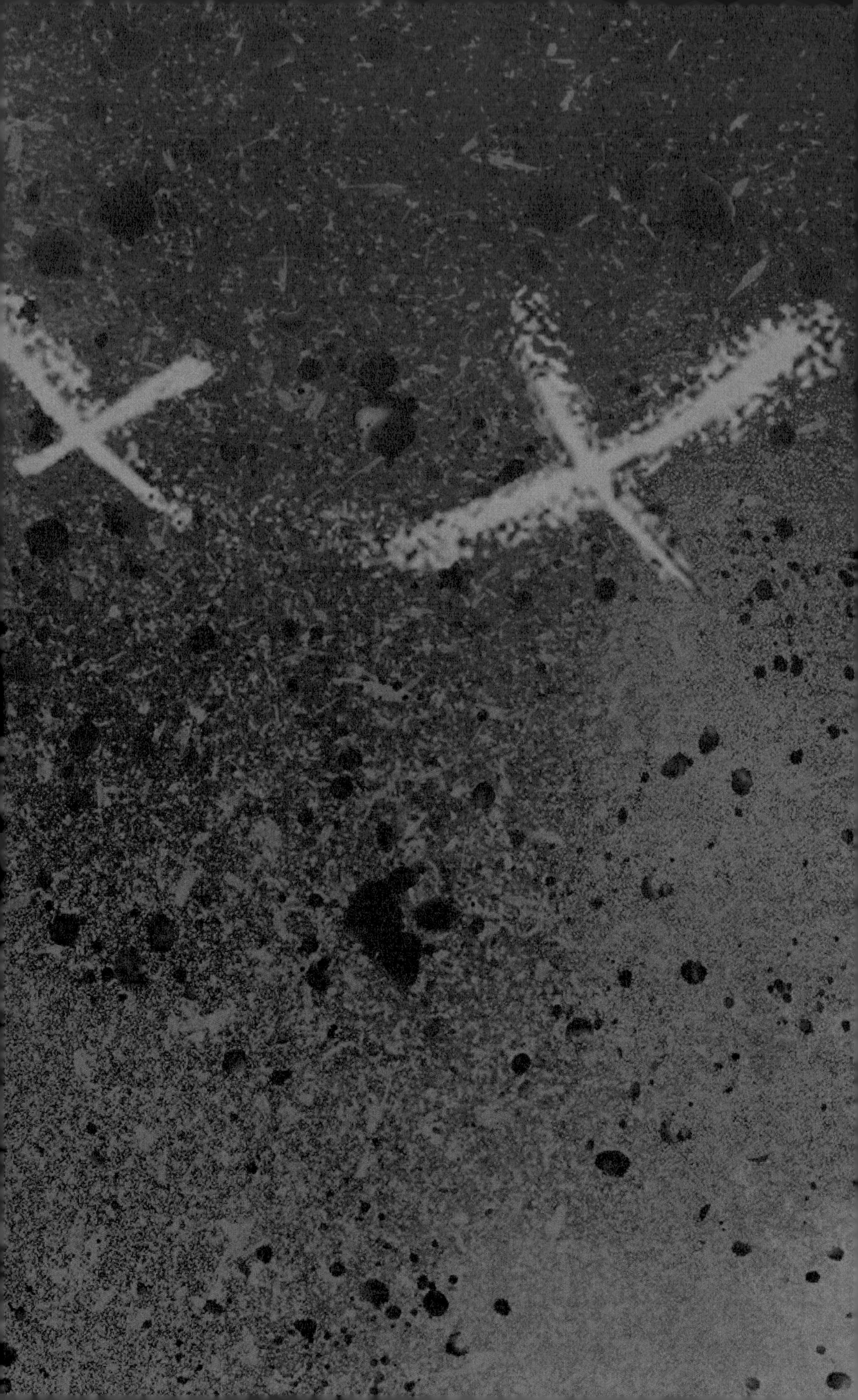

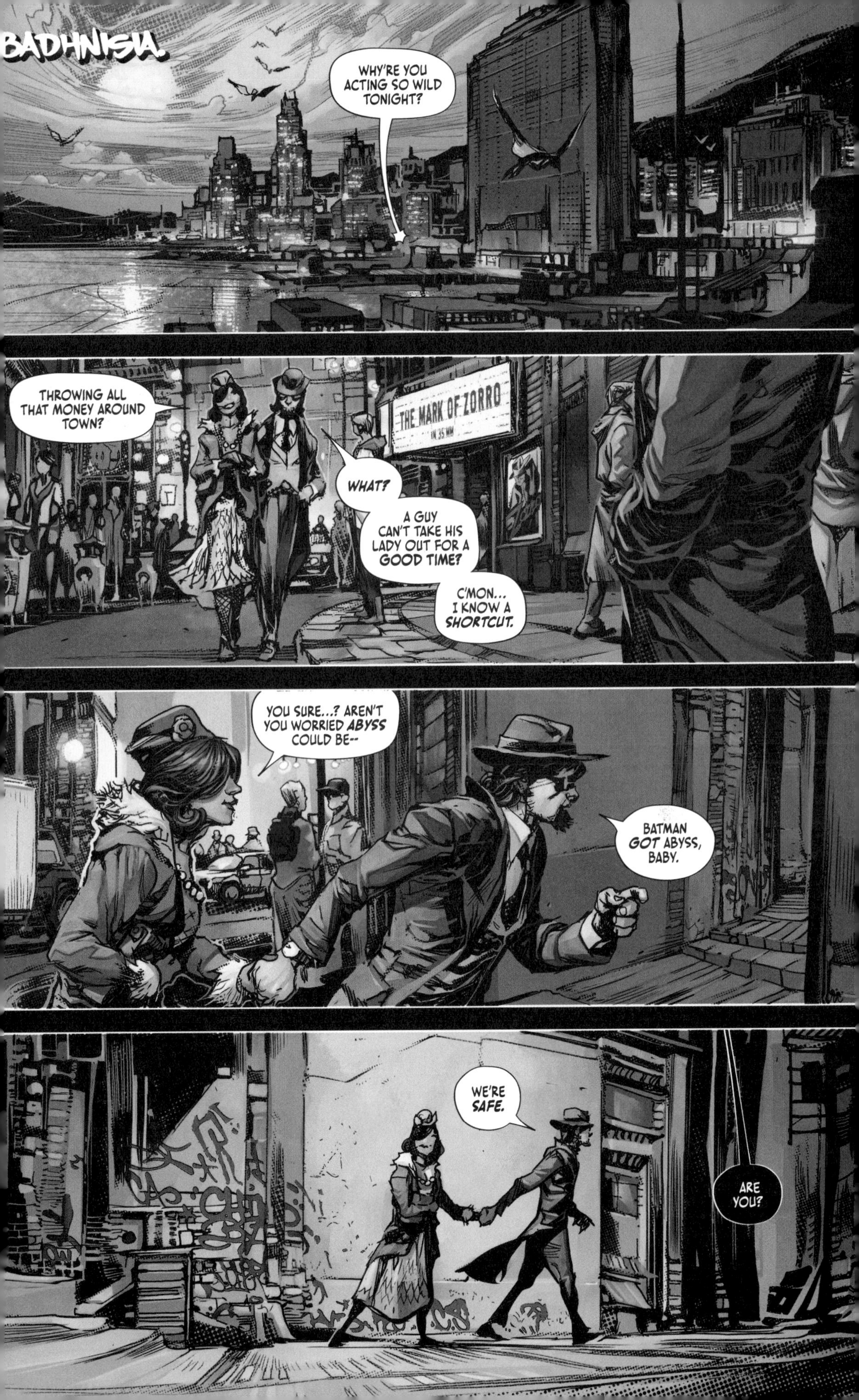
BADHNISIA.
WHY'RE YOU ACTING SO WILD TONIGHT?
THROWING ALL THAT MONEY AROUND TOWN?
THE MARK OF ZORRO
IN 35 MM
WHAT?
A GUY CAN'T TAKE HIS LADY OUT FOR A GOOD TIME?
C'MON... I KNOW A SHORTCUT.
YOU SURE...? AREN'T YOU WORRIED ABYSS COULD BE--
BATMAN GOT ABYSS, BABY.
WE'RE SAFE.
ARE YOU?

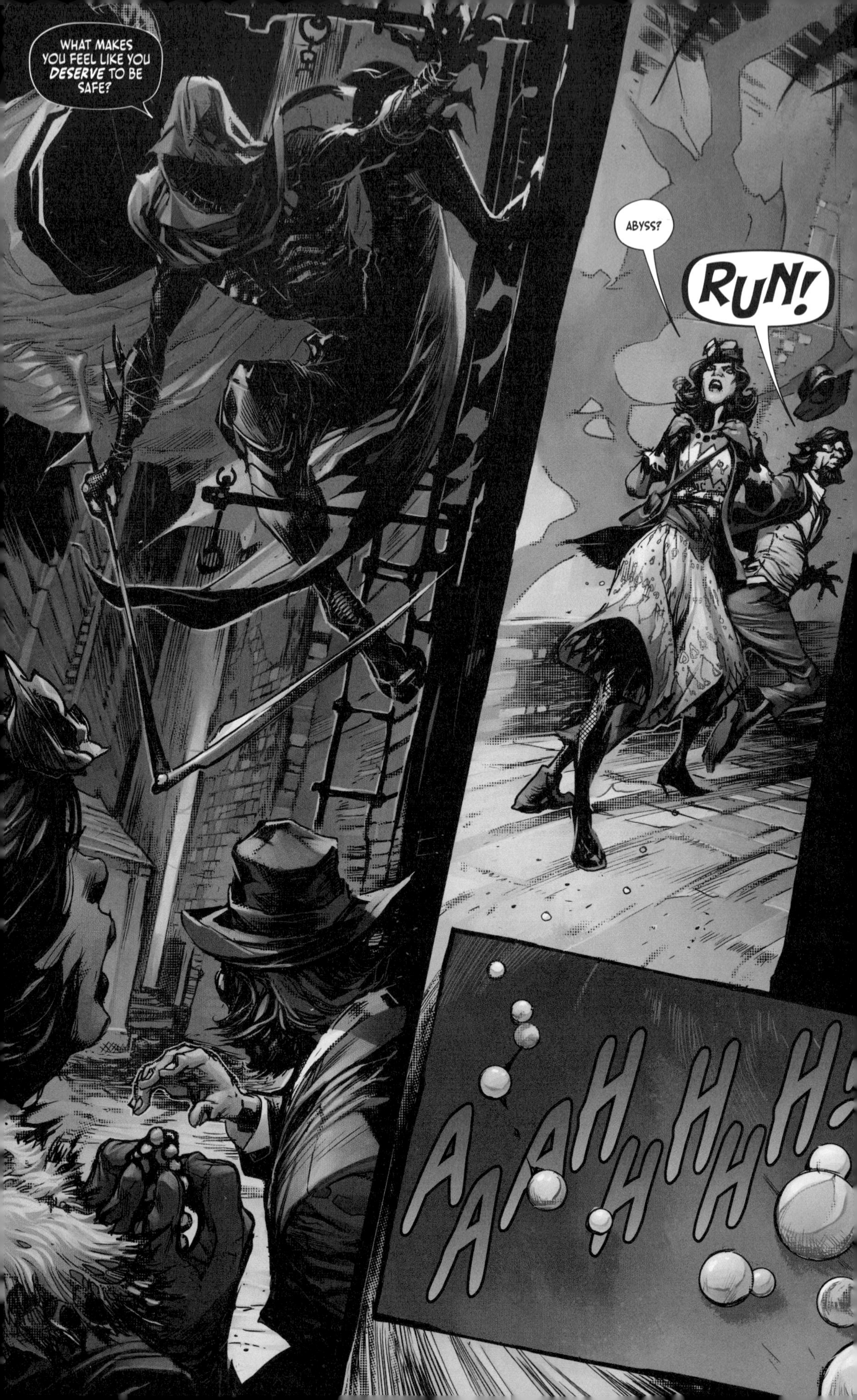
WHAT MAKES YOU FEEL LIKE YOU *DESERVE* TO BE SAFE?
ABYSS?
RUN!
AAAHHHHHH

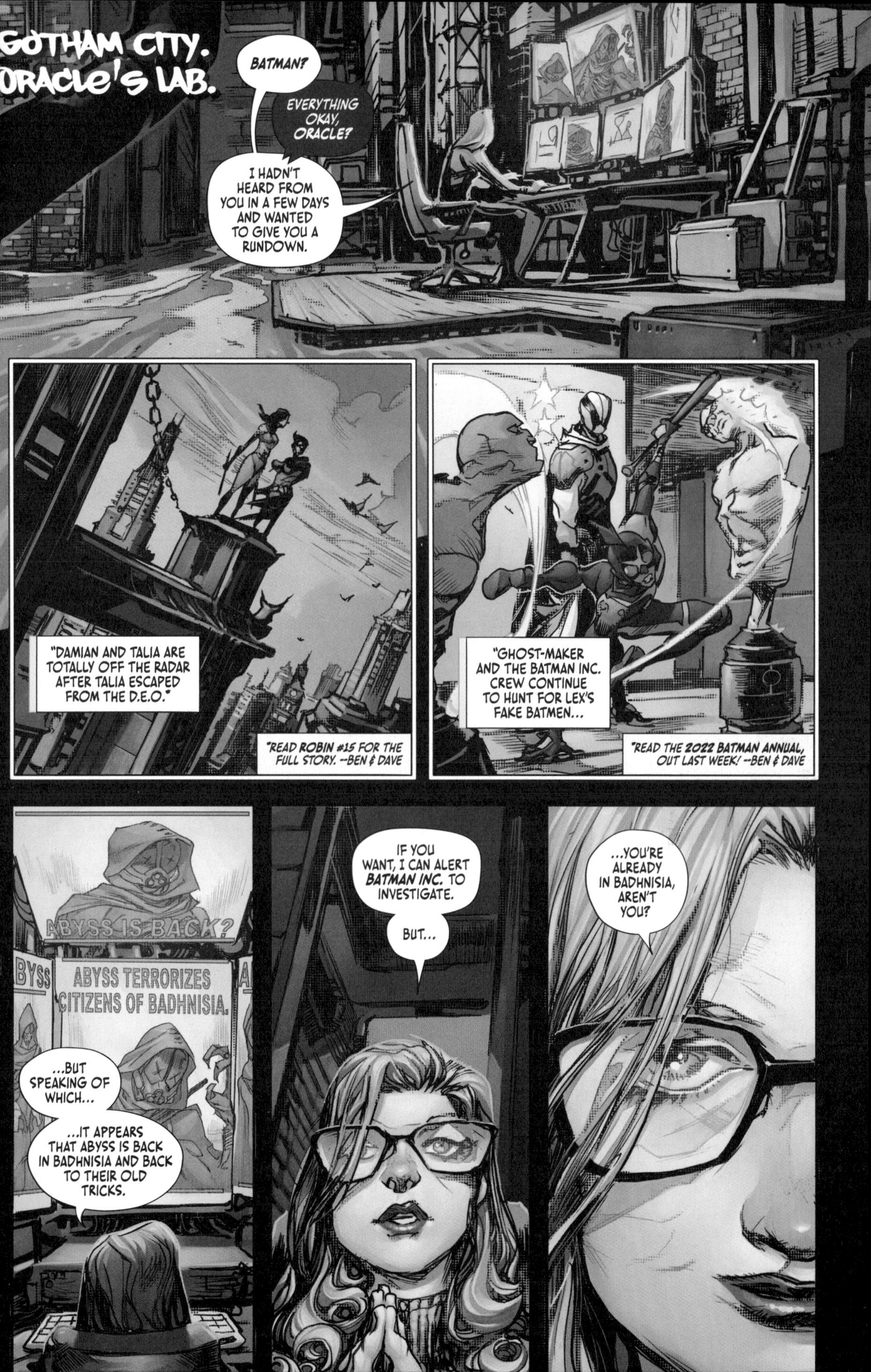
GOTHAM CITY.
ORACLE'S LAB.
BATMAN?
EVERYTHING OKAY, ORACLE?
I HADN'T HEARD FROM YOU IN A FEW DAYS AND WANTED TO GIVE YOU A RUNDOWN.
"DAMIAN AND TALIA ARE TOTALLY OFF THE RADAR AFTER TALIA ESCAPED FROM THE D.E.O."
*READ ROBIN #15 FOR THE FULL STORY. --BEN & DAVE
"GHOST-MAKER AND THE BATMAN INC. CREW CONTINUE TO HUNT FOR LEX'S FAKE BATMEN...
*READ THE 2022 BATMAN ANNUAL, OUT LAST WEEK! --BEN & DAVE
ABYSS IS BACK?
ABYSS TERRORIZES CITIZENS OF BADHNISIA.
...BUT SPEAKING OF WHICH...
...IT APPEARS THAT ABYSS IS BACK IN BADHNISIA AND BACK TO THEIR OLD TRICKS.
IF YOU WANT, I CAN ALERT BATMAN INC. TO INVESTIGATE.
BUT...
...YOU'RE ALREADY IN BADHNISIA, AREN'T YOU?

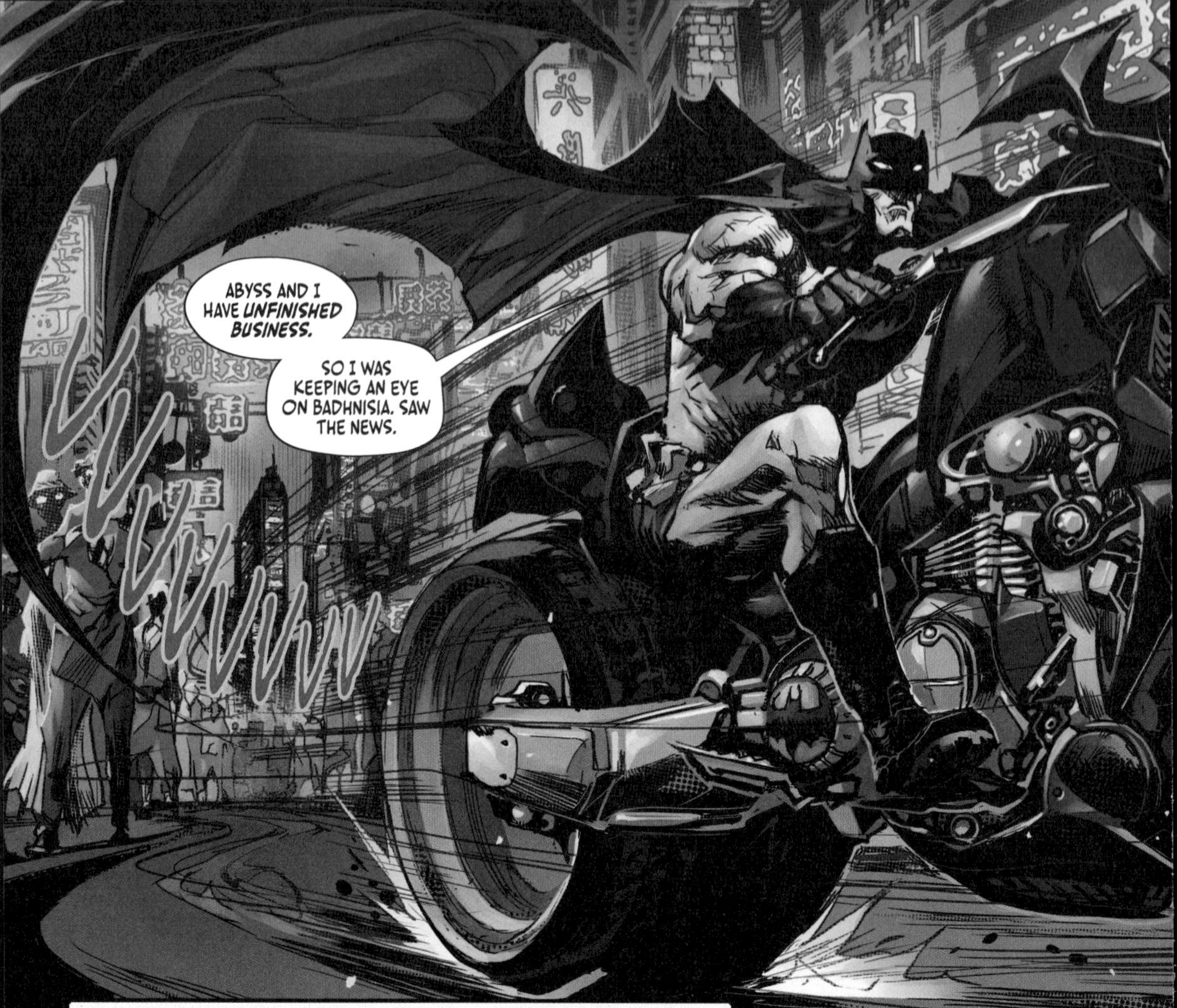
ABYSS AND I HAVE *UNFINISHED BUSINESS.*
SO I WAS KEEPING AN EYE ON BADHNISIA. SAW THE NEWS.
VVVVVVVVVV

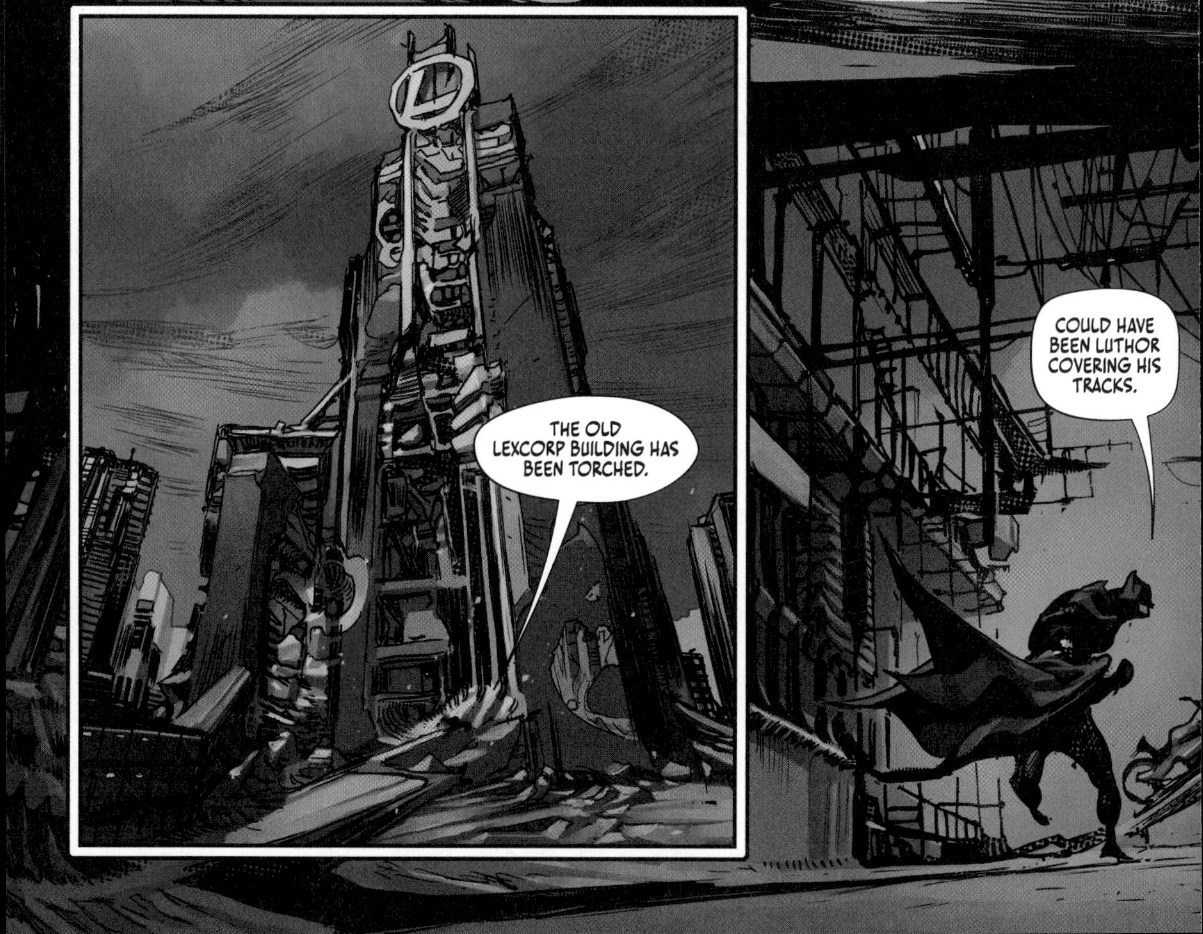
THE OLD LEXCORP BUILDING HAS BEEN TORCHED.
COULD HAVE BEEN LUTHOR COVERING HIS TRACKS.

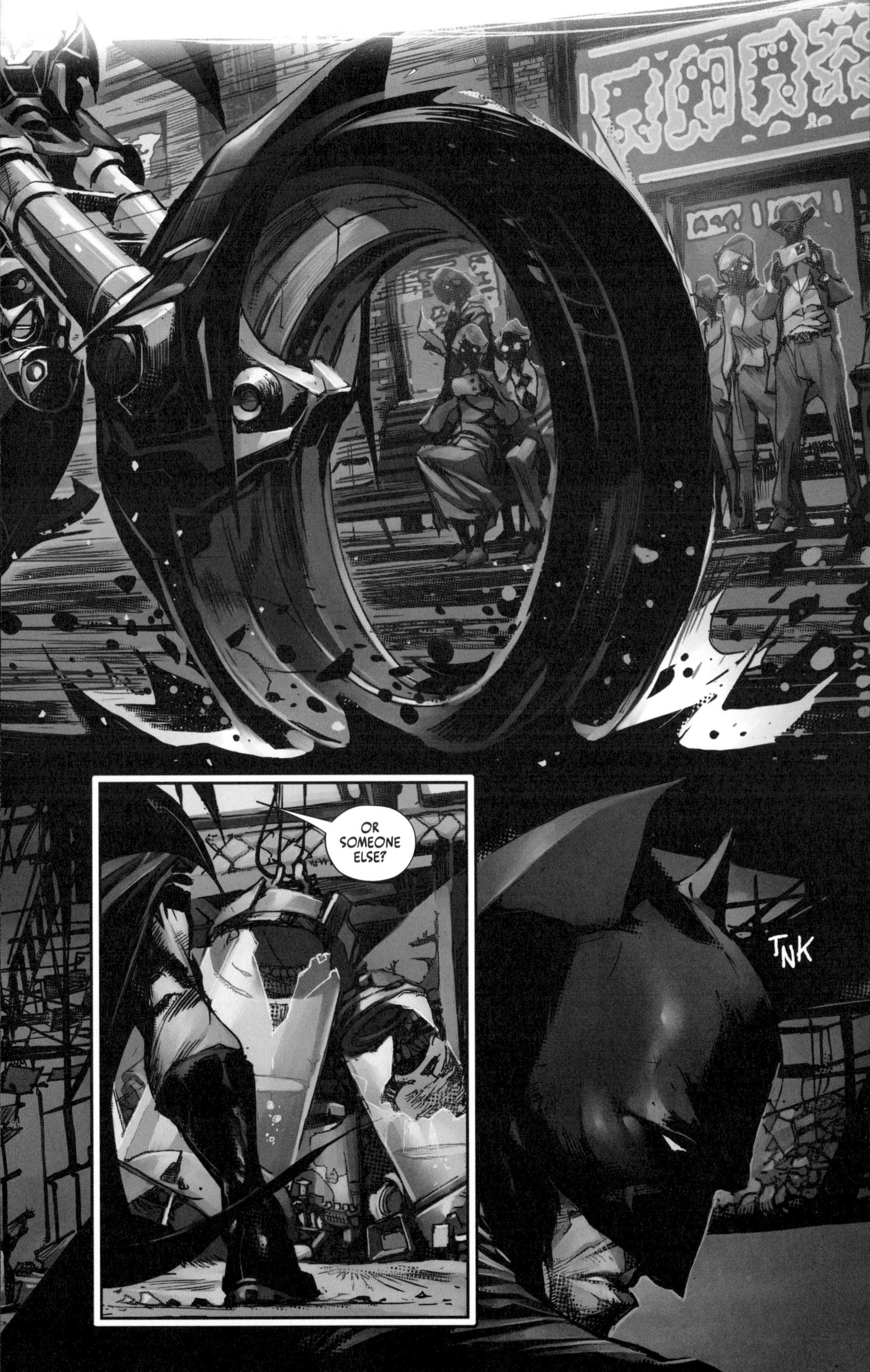
OR SOMEONE ELSE?
TNK

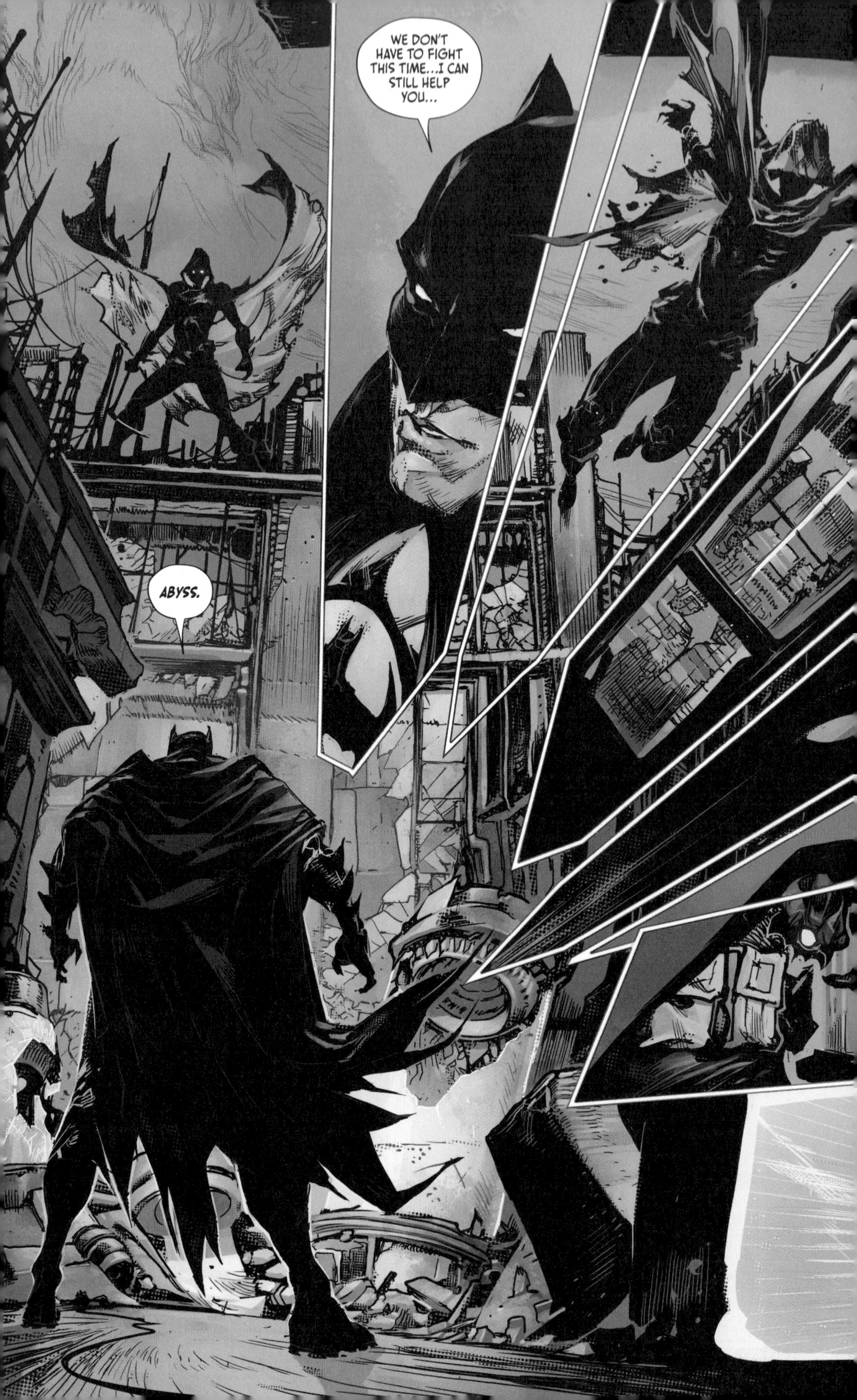
ABYSS.
WE DON'T HAVE TO FIGHT THIS TIME...I CAN STILL HELP YOU...

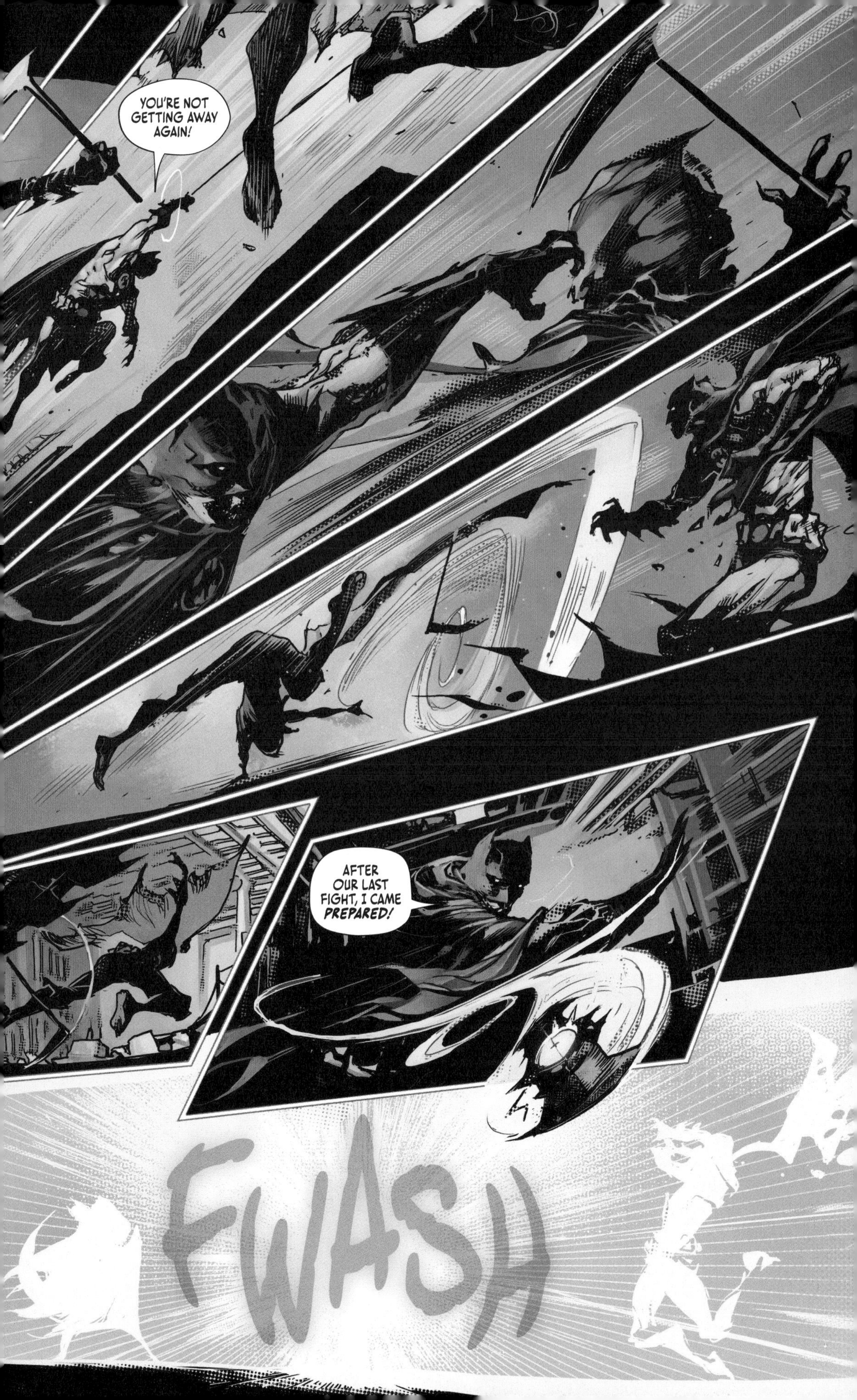
YOU'RE NOT GETTING AWAY AGAIN!
AFTER OUR LAST FIGHT, I CAME *PREPARED!*
FWASH

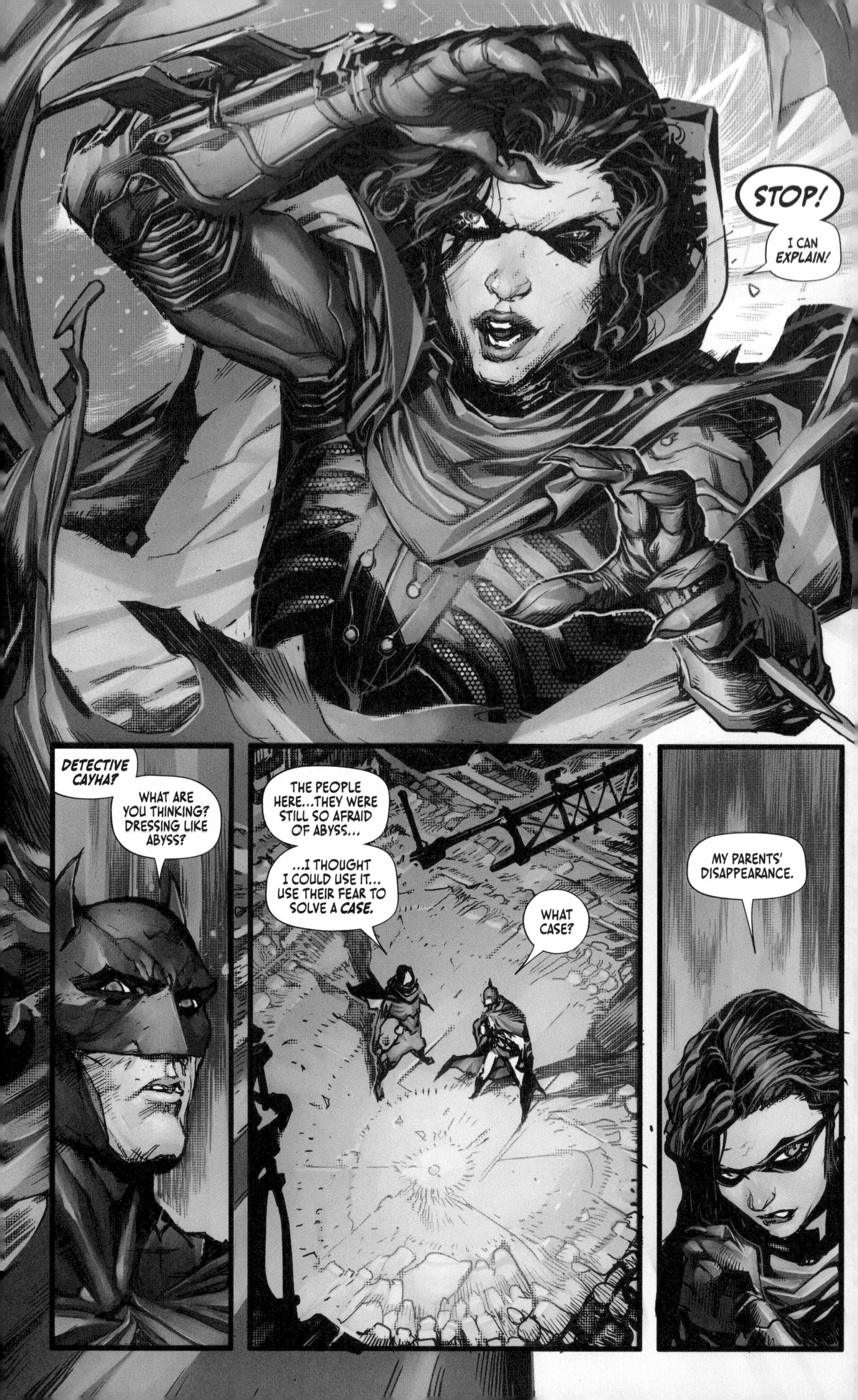
STOP!
I CAN EXPLAIN!
DETECTIVE CAYHA?
WHAT ARE YOU THINKING? DRESSING LIKE ABYSS?
THE PEOPLE HERE...THEY WERE STILL SO AFRAID OF ABYSS...
...I THOUGHT I COULD USE IT... USE THEIR FEAR TO SOLVE A CASE.
WHAT CASE?
MY PARENTS' DISAPPEARANCE.

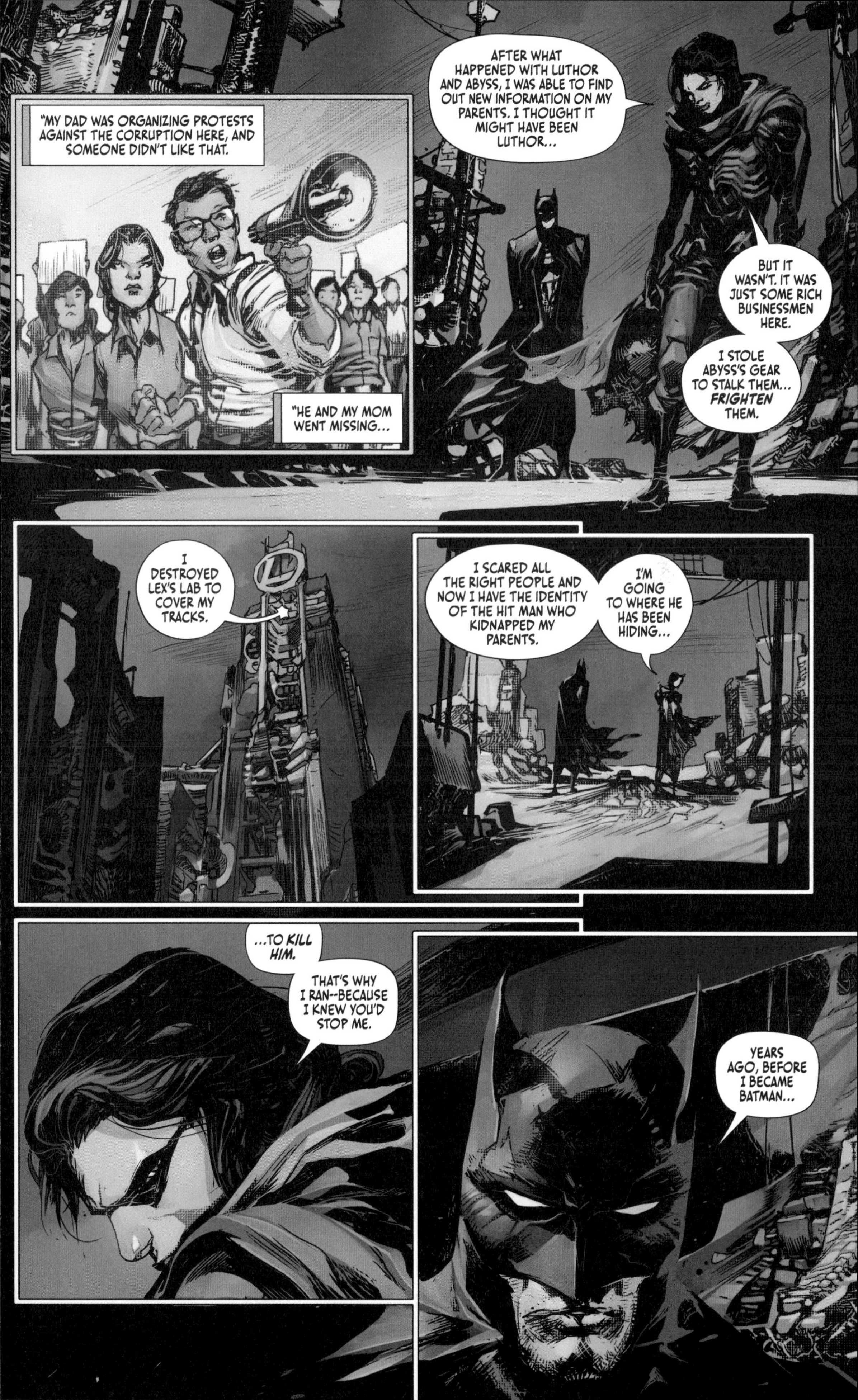
"MY DAD WAS ORGANIZING PROTESTS AGAINST THE CORRUPTION HERE, AND SOMEONE DIDN'T LIKE THAT.
"HE AND MY MOM WENT MISSING...
AFTER WHAT HAPPENED WITH LUTHOR AND ABYSS, I WAS ABLE TO FIND OUT NEW INFORMATION ON MY PARENTS. I THOUGHT IT MIGHT HAVE BEEN LUTHOR...
BUT IT WASN'T. IT WAS JUST SOME RICH BUSINESSMEN HERE.
I STOLE ABYSS'S GEAR TO STALK THEM... *FRIGHTEN* THEM.
I DESTROYED LEX'S LAB TO COVER MY TRACKS.
I SCARED ALL THE RIGHT PEOPLE AND NOW I HAVE THE IDENTITY OF THE HIT MAN WHO KIDNAPPED MY PARENTS.
I'M GOING TO WHERE HE HAS BEEN HIDING...
...TO *KILL HIM.*
THAT'S WHY I RAN--BECAUSE I KNEW YOU'D STOP ME.
YEARS AGO, BEFORE I BECAME BATMAN...

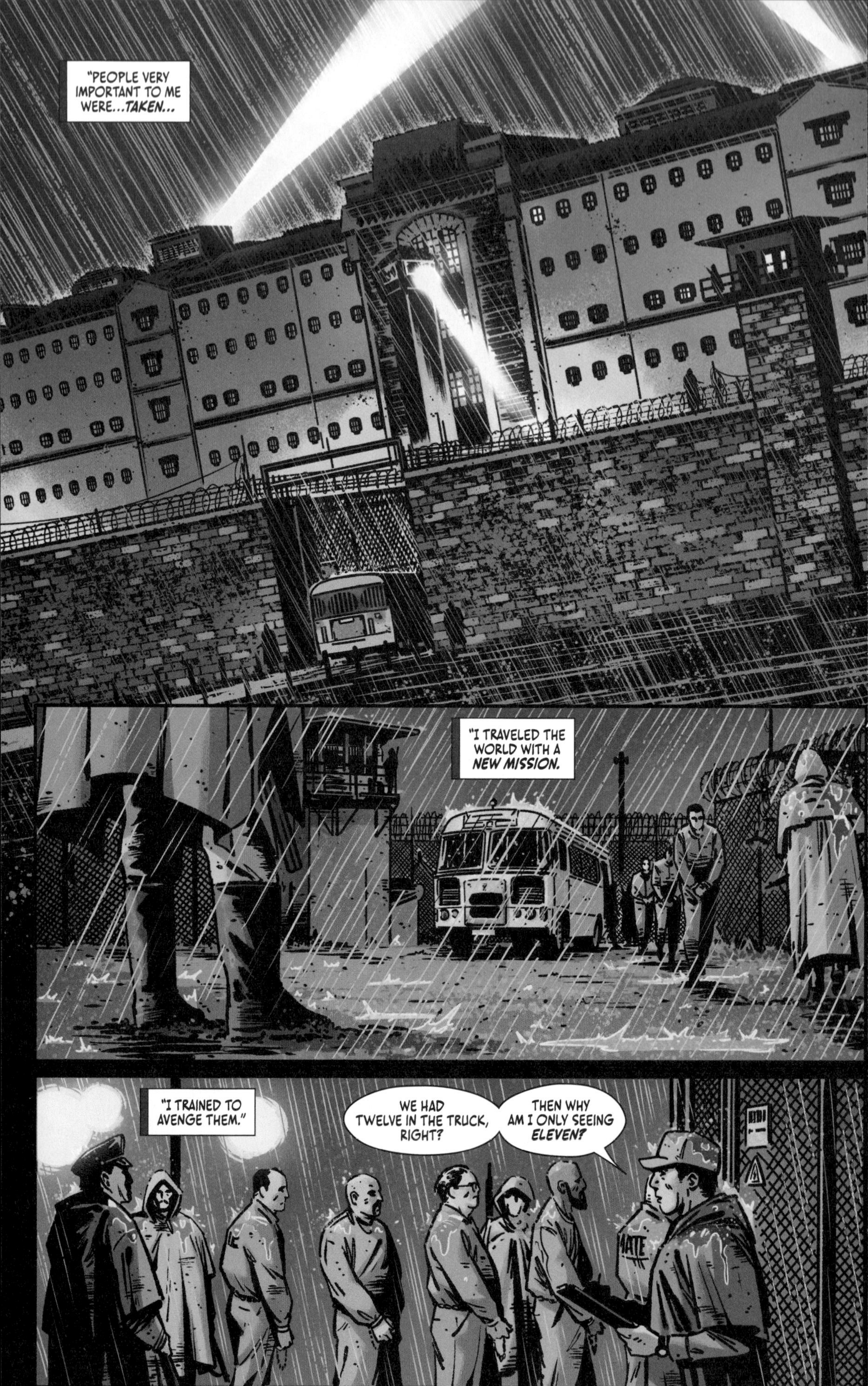
"PEOPLE VERY IMPORTANT TO ME WERE...*TAKEN...*
"I TRAVELED THE WORLD WITH A *NEW MISSION.*
"I TRAINED TO AVENGE THEM."
WE HAD TWELVE IN THE TRUCK, RIGHT?
THEN WHY AM I ONLY SEEING *ELEVEN?*

"AND THEN WHEN I RETURNED HOME..."

HEY, WHICH ONE OF YOU JOKERS STOLE MY GEAR?!

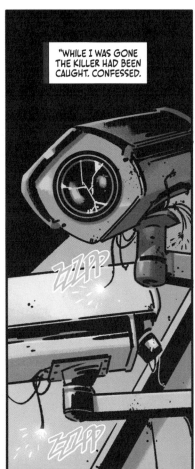

"WHILE I WAS GONE THE KILLER HAD BEEN CAUGHT. CONFESSED.

ZZZP

ZZZP

"JUSTICE HAD BEEN SERVED. BUT THAT WASN'T GOOD ENOUGH.

"IN MY TRAVELS, I HAD LEARNED TO KILL.

"I MADE A VOW TO NEVER COMMIT THAT ACT.

"BUT I NEEDED TO SEE HIM."

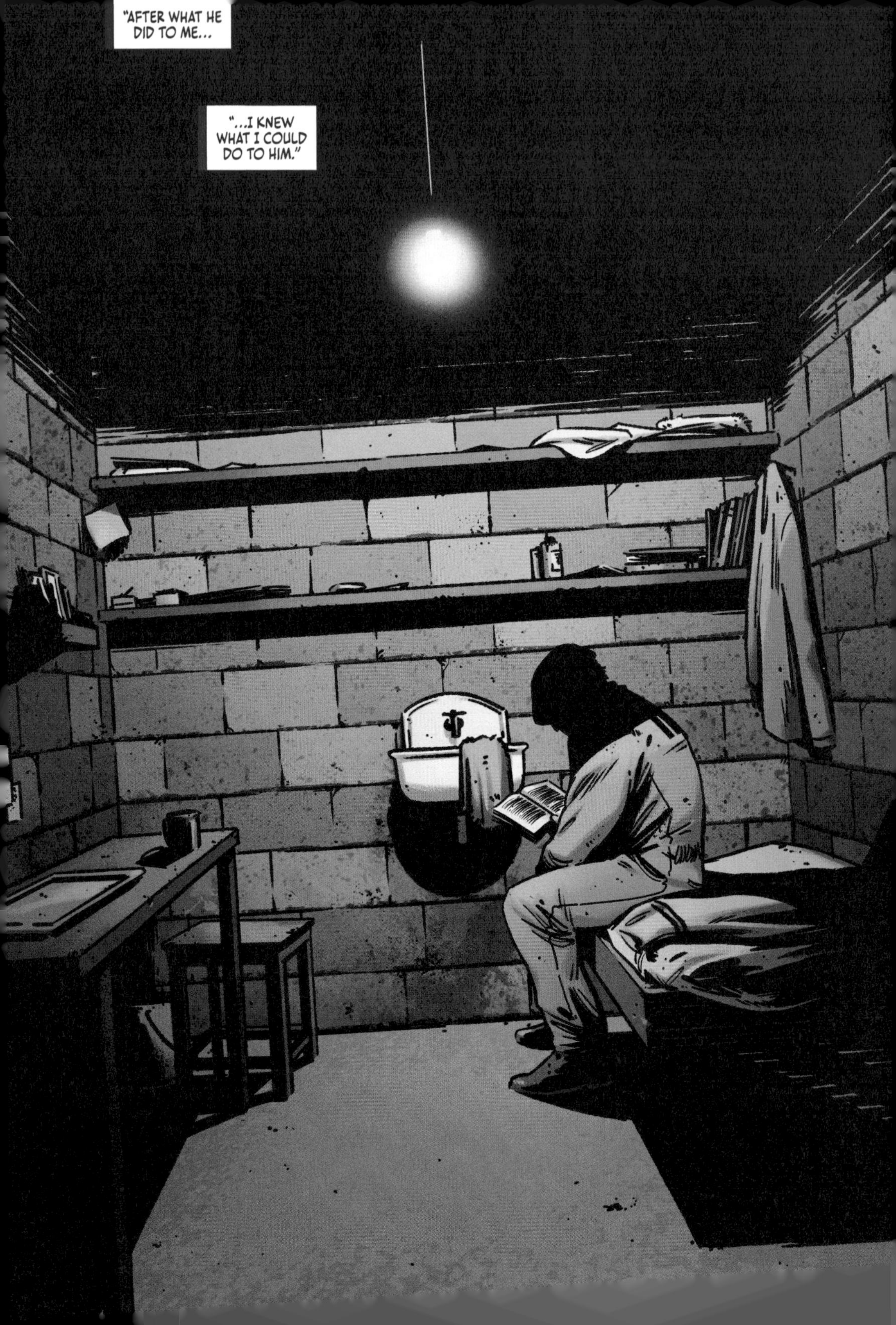
"AFTER WHAT HE DID TO ME...
"...I KNEW WHAT I COULD DO TO HIM."

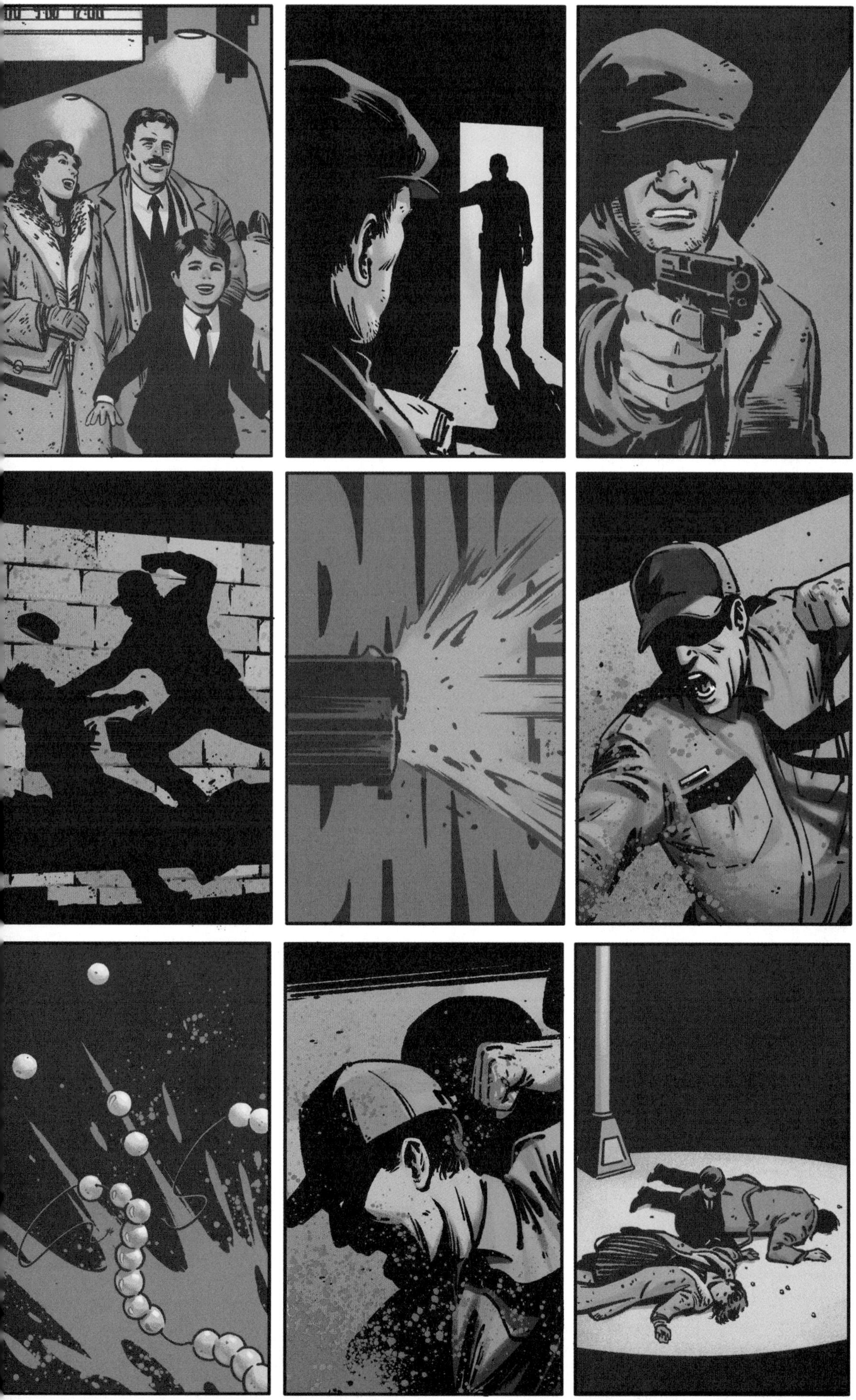

"I STARED AT HIM FOR A LONG TIME.

"CURIOUS WHAT I WOULD DO...

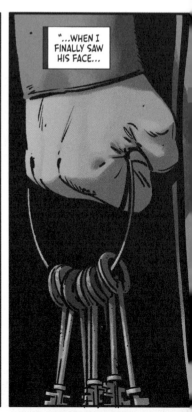

"...WHEN I FINALLY SAW HIS FACE...

"...BUT I WANTED HIM TO SEE *ME*.

"TO BE AFRAID.

"AND IN THAT MOMENT, I MADE A CHOICE..."

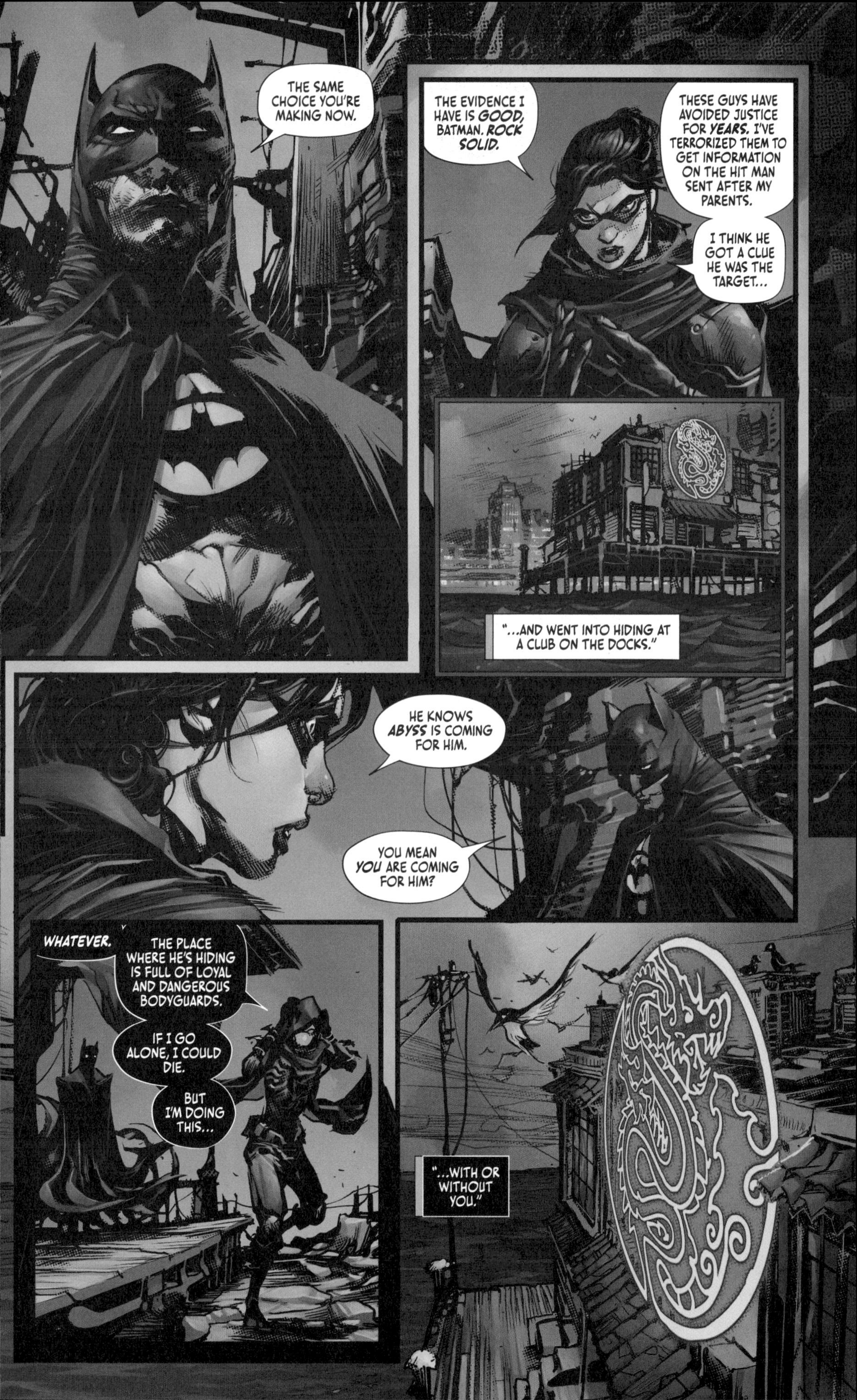
THE SAME CHOICE YOU'RE MAKING NOW.
THE EVIDENCE I HAVE IS GOOD, BATMAN. ROCK SOLID.
THESE GUYS HAVE AVOIDED JUSTICE FOR YEARS. I'VE TERRORIZED THEM TO GET INFORMATION ON THE HIT MAN SENT AFTER MY PARENTS.
I THINK HE GOT A CLUE HE WAS THE TARGET...
"...AND WENT INTO HIDING AT A CLUB ON THE DOCKS."
HE KNOWS ABYSS IS COMING FOR HIM.
YOU MEAN YOU ARE COMING FOR HIM?
WHATEVER.
THE PLACE WHERE HE'S HIDING IS FULL OF LOYAL AND DANGEROUS BODYGUARDS.
IF I GO ALONE, I COULD DIE.
BUT I'M DOING THIS...
"...WITH OR WITHOUT YOU."

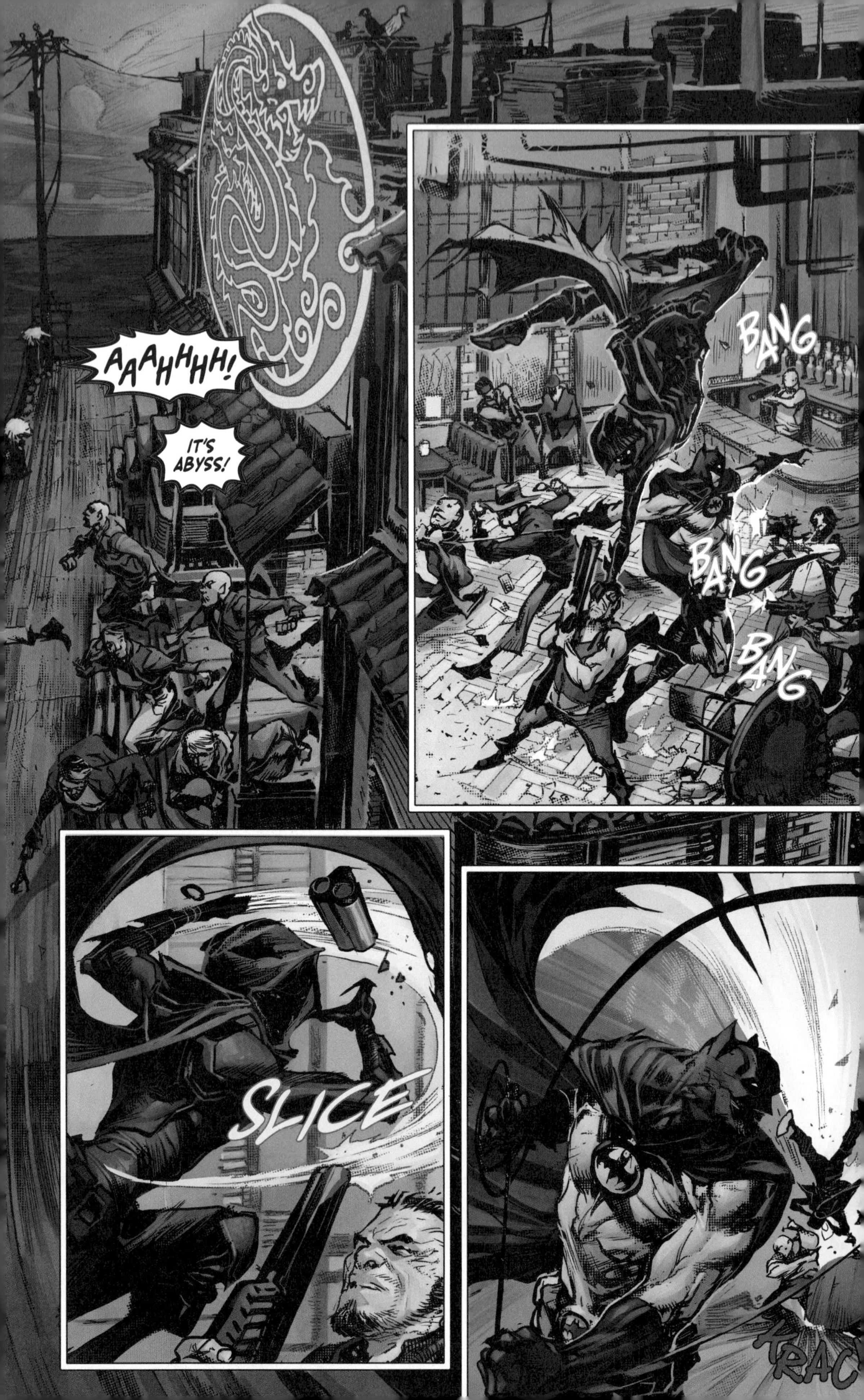
AAAHHHH!
IT'S ABYSS!
BANG
BANG
BANG
SLICE
TRAC

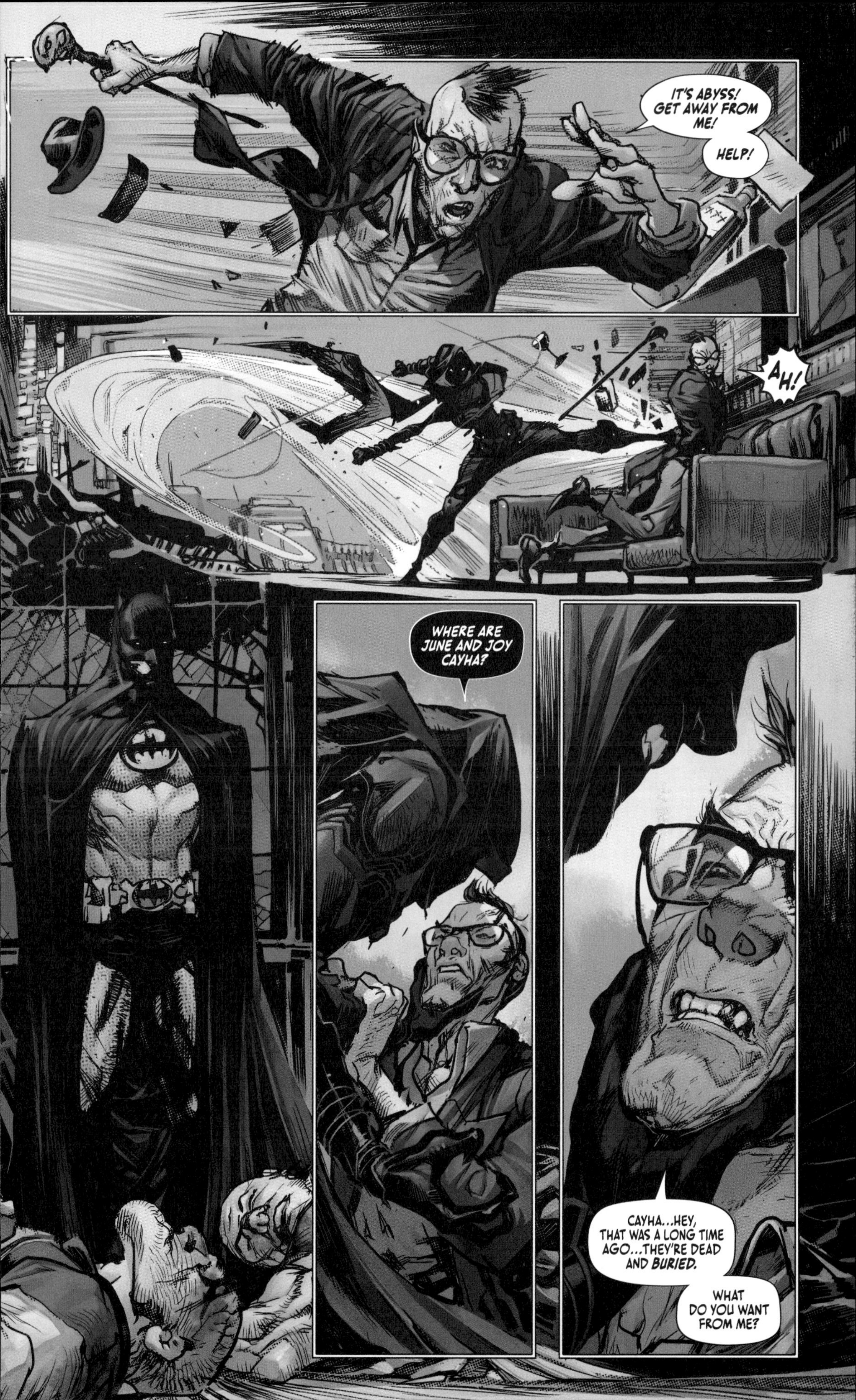

IT'S ABYSS! GET AWAY FROM ME!
HELP!
AH!
WHERE ARE JUNE AND JOY CAYHA?
CAYHA...HEY, THAT WAS A LONG TIME AGO...THEY'RE DEAD AND BURIED.
WHAT DO YOU WANT FROM ME?

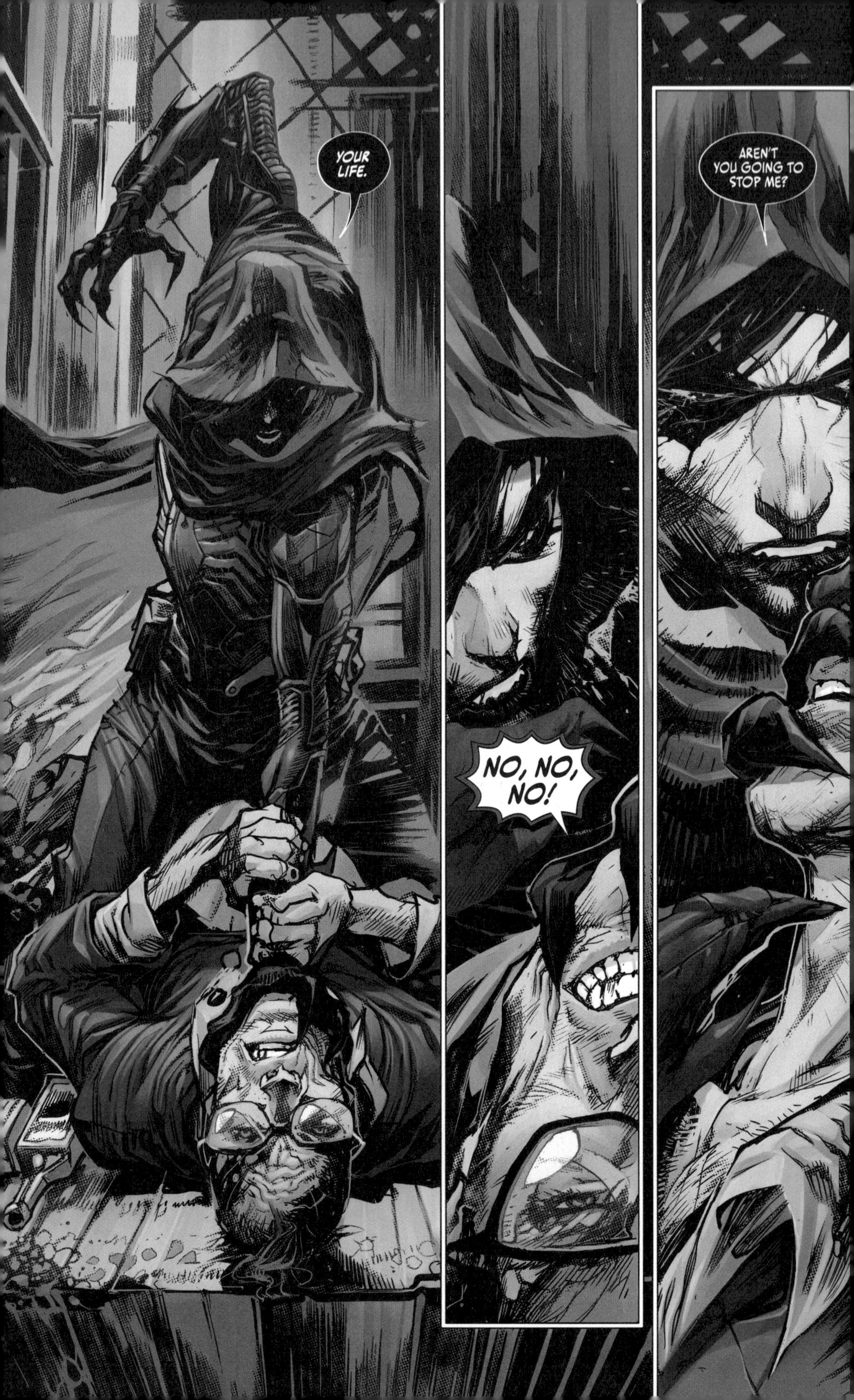
YOUR LIFE.
NO, NO, NO!
AREN'T YOU GOING TO STOP ME?

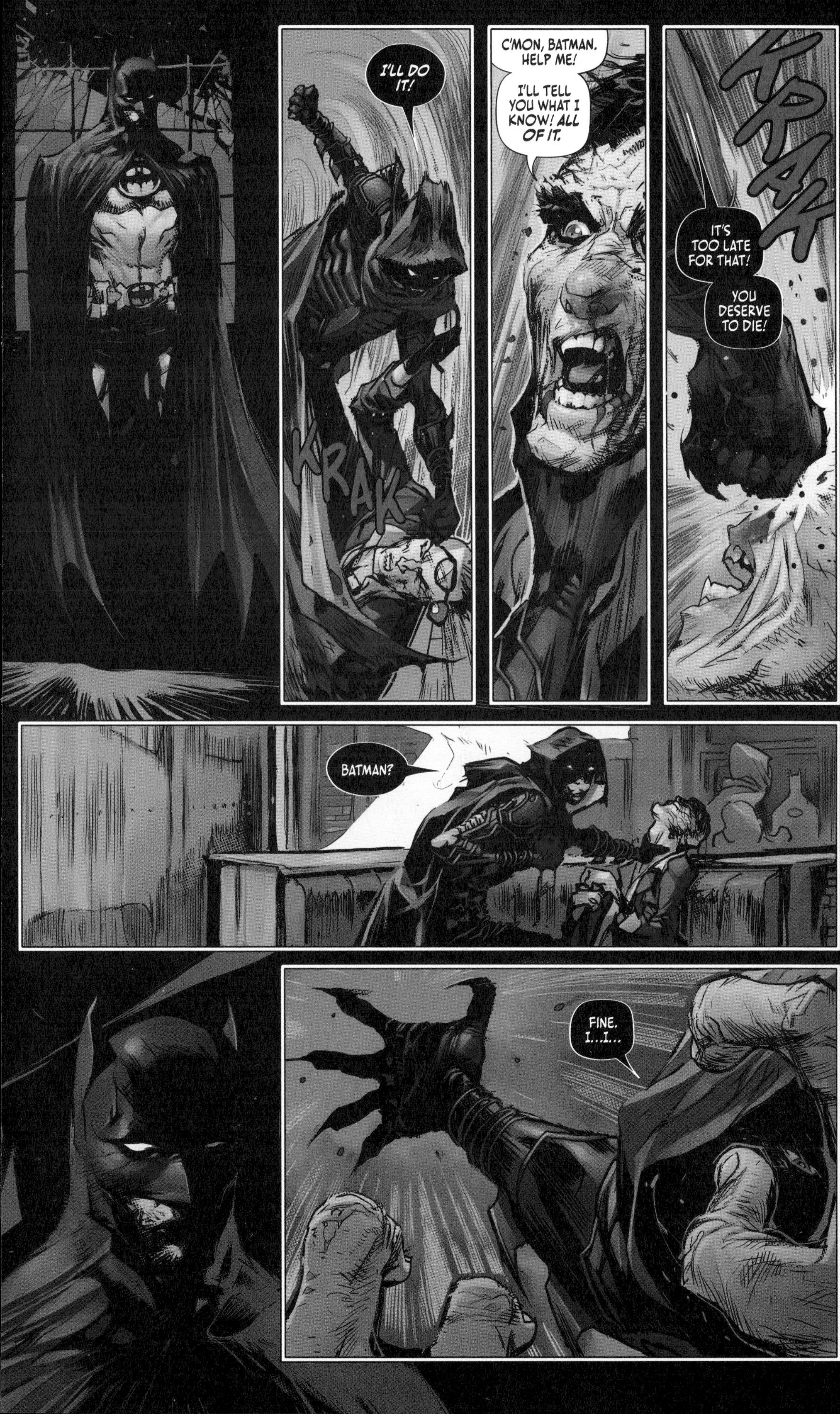
I'LL DO IT!
KRAK
C'MON, BATMAN. HELP ME!
I'LL TELL YOU WHAT I KNOW! ALL OF IT.
KRAK
IT'S TOO LATE FOR THAT!
YOU DESERVE TO DIE!
BATMAN?
FINE. I...I...

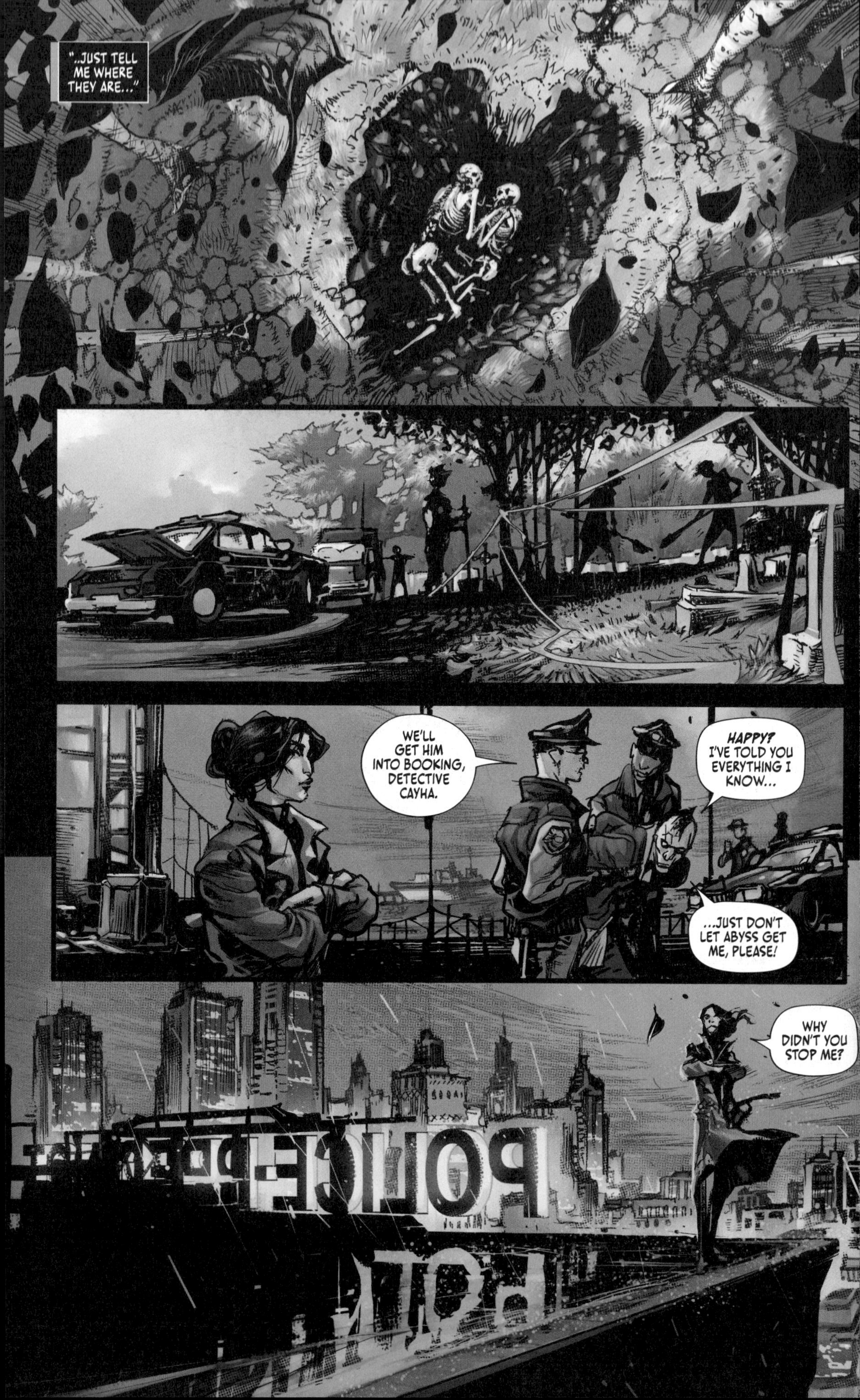
"..JUST TELL ME WHERE THEY ARE..."
WE'LL GET HIM INTO BOOKING, DETECTIVE CAYHA.
HAPPY? I'VE TOLD YOU EVERYTHING I KNOW...
...JUST DON'T LET ABYSS GET ME, PLEASE!
WHY DIDN'T YOU STOP ME?

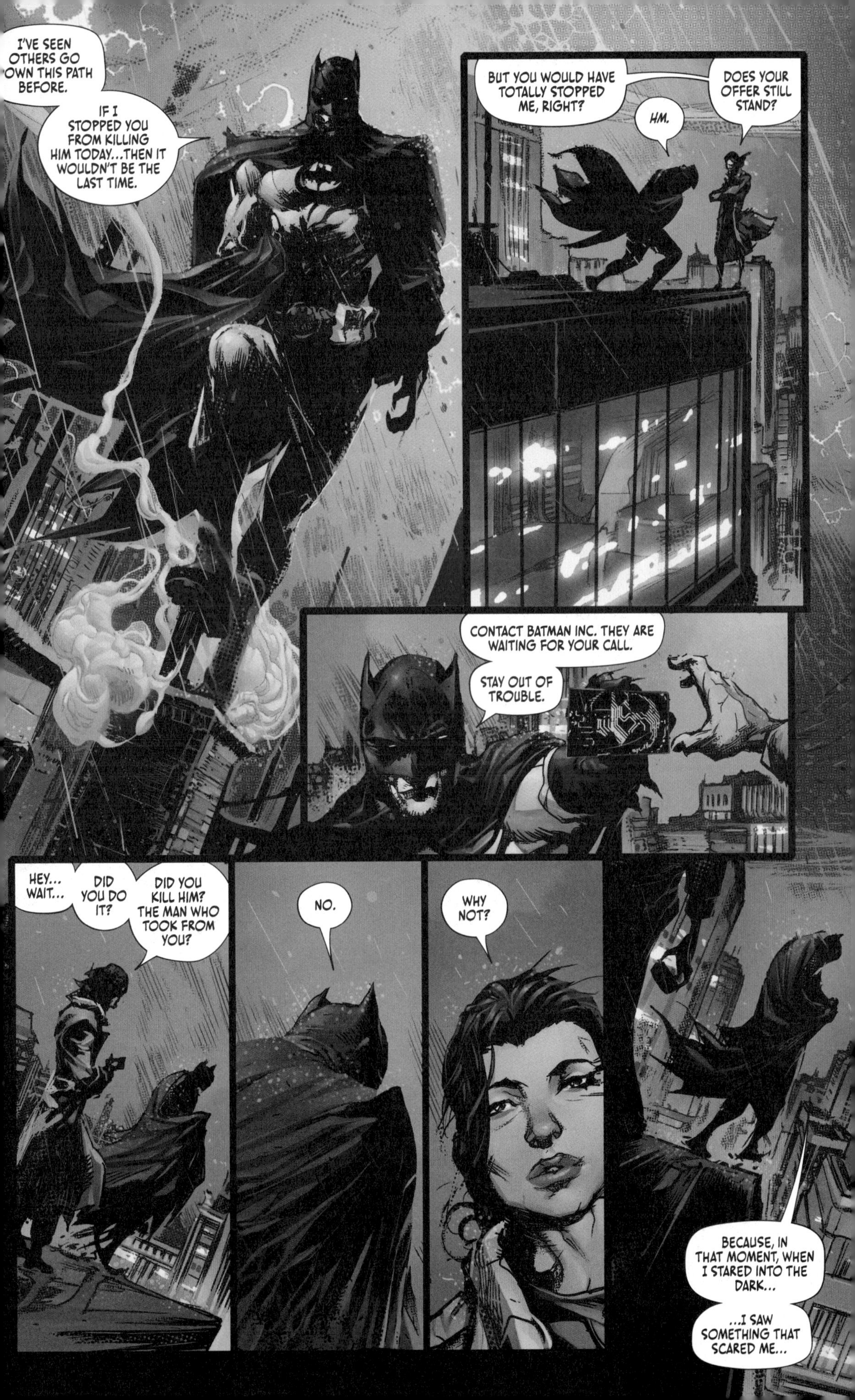
I'VE SEEN OTHERS GO OWN THIS PATH BEFORE.
IF I STOPPED YOU FROM KILLING HIM TODAY...THEN IT WOULDN'T BE THE LAST TIME.
BUT YOU WOULD HAVE TOTALLY STOPPED ME, RIGHT?
HM.
DOES YOUR OFFER STILL STAND?
CONTACT BATMAN INC. THEY ARE WAITING FOR YOUR CALL.
STAY OUT OF TROUBLE.
HEY... WAIT...
DID YOU DO IT?
DID YOU KILL HIM? THE MAN WHO TOOK FROM YOU?
NO.
WHY NOT?
BECAUSE, IN THAT MOMENT, WHEN I STARED INTO THE DARK...
...I SAW SOMETHING THAT SCARED ME...

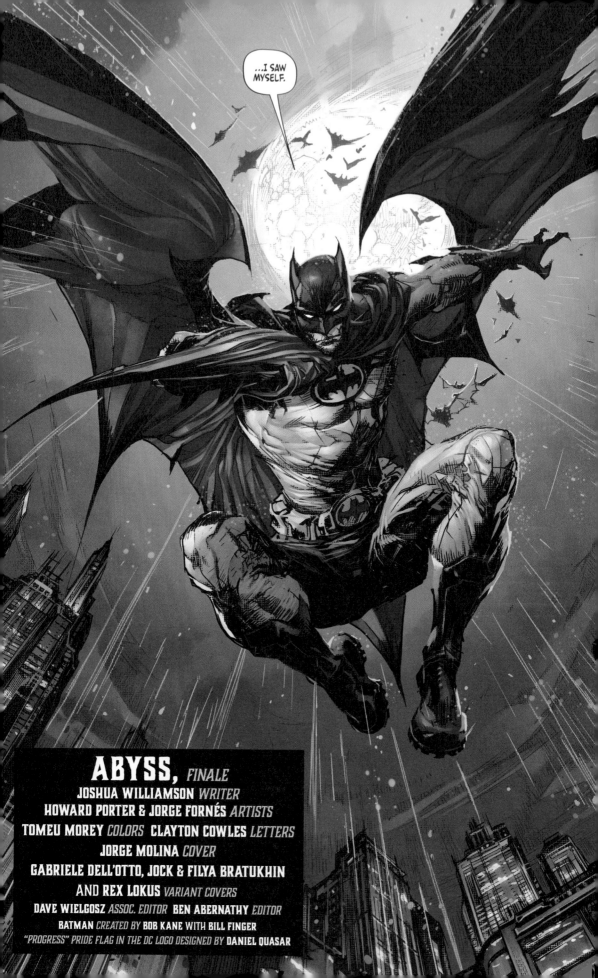

ABYSS, *FINALE*

JOSHUA WILLIAMSON *WRITER*

HOWARD PORTER & JORGE FORNÉS *ARTISTS*

TOMEU MOREY *COLORS* **CLAYTON COWLES** *LETTERS*

JORGE MOLINA *COVER*

GABRIELE DELL'OTTO, JOCK & FILYA BRATUKHIN

AND REX LOKUS *VARIANT COVERS*

DAVE WIELGOSZ *ASSOC. EDITOR* **BEN ABERNATHY** *EDITOR*

BATMAN *CREATED BY* **BOB KANE** WITH **BILL FINGER**

"PROGRESS" PRIDE FLAG IN THE DC LOGO DESIGNED BY **DANIEL QUASAR**

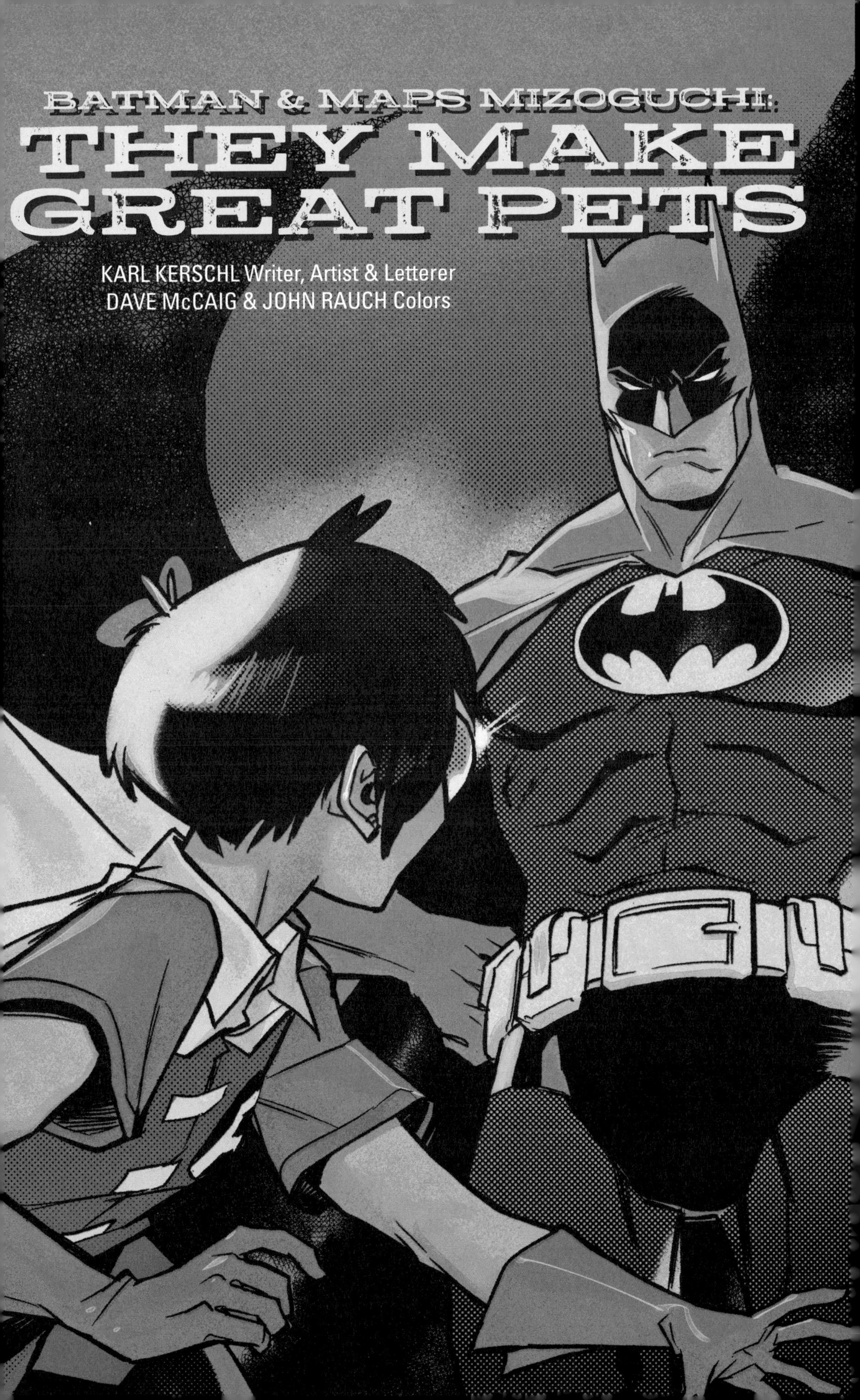
BATMAN & MAPS MIZOGUCHI:
THEY MAKE GREAT PETS
KARL KERSCHL Writer, Artist & Letterer
DAVE McCAIG & JOHN RAUCH Colors

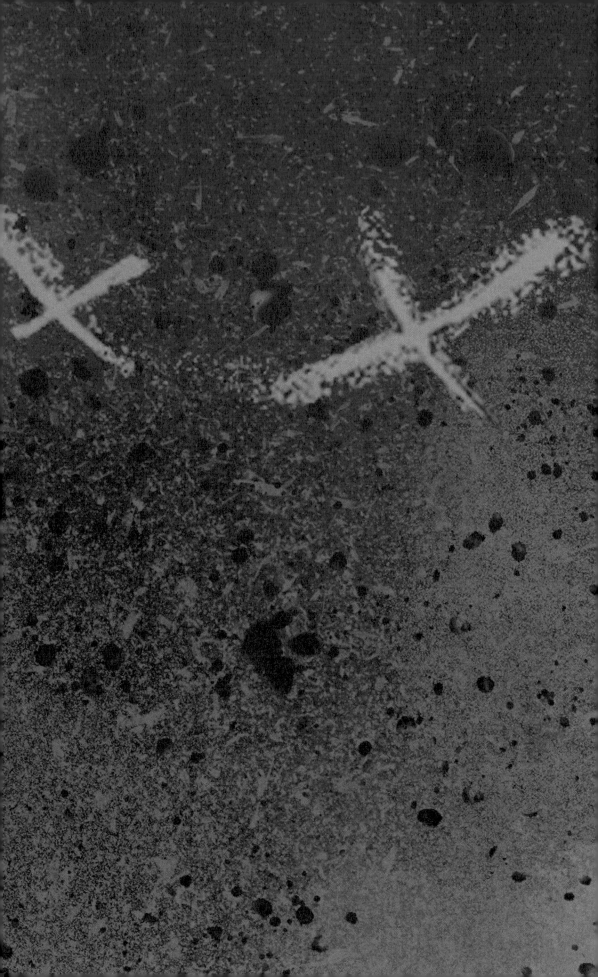

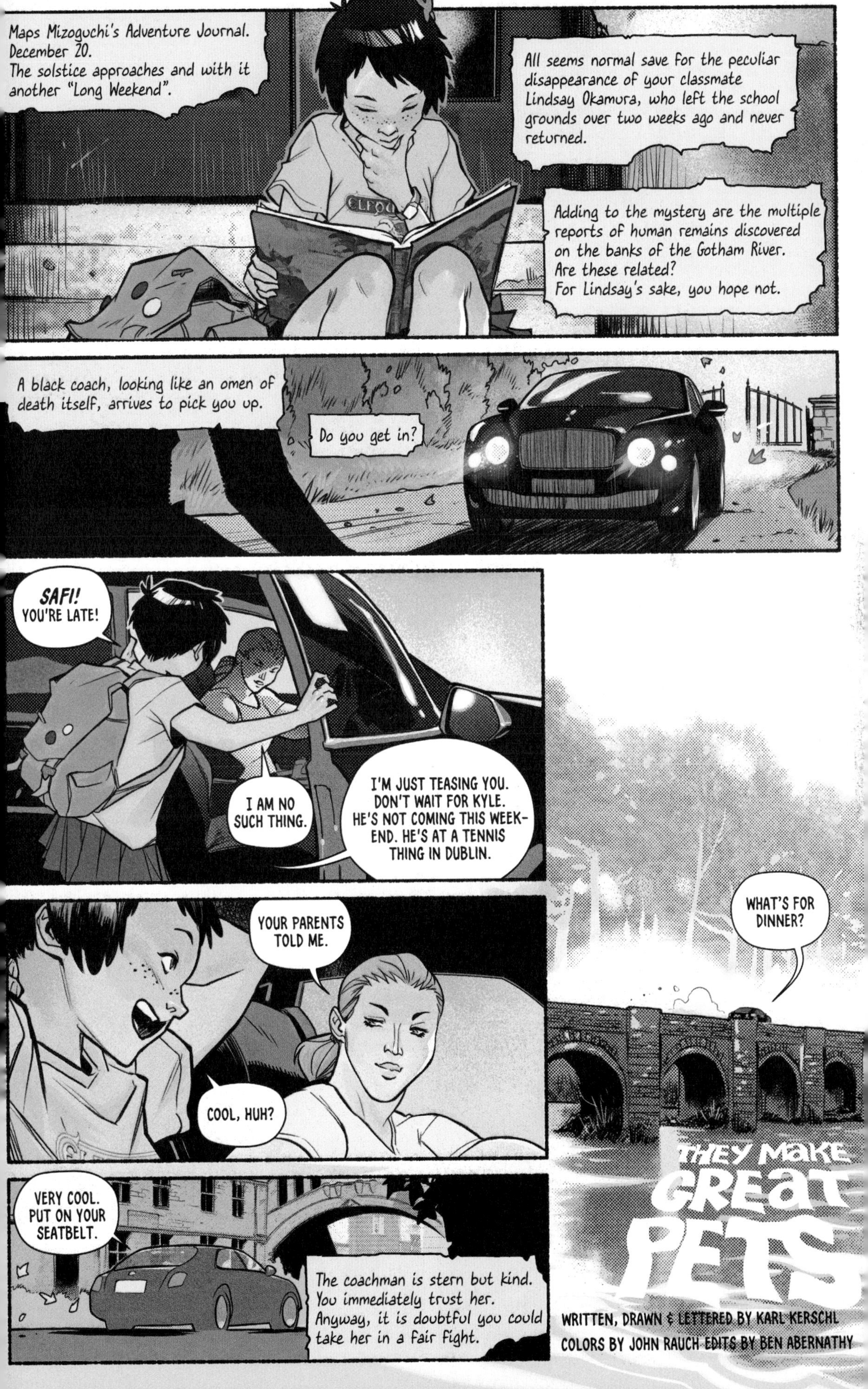

Maps Mizoguchi's Adventure Journal. December 20. The solstice approaches and with it another "Long Weekend".
All seems normal save for the peculiar disappearance of your classmate Lindsay Okamura, who left the school grounds over two weeks ago and never returned.
Adding to the mystery are the multiple reports of human remains discovered on the banks of the Gotham River. Are these related? For Lindsay's sake, you hope not.
A black coach, looking like an omen of death itself, arrives to pick you up.
Do you get in?
SAFI! YOU'RE LATE!
I AM NO SUCH THING.
I'M JUST TEASING YOU. DON'T WAIT FOR KYLE. HE'S NOT COMING THIS WEEK-END. HE'S AT A TENNIS THING IN DUBLIN.
YOUR PARENTS TOLD ME.
COOL, HUH?
VERY COOL. PUT ON YOUR SEATBELT.
The coachman is stern but kind. You immediately trust her. Anyway, it is doubtful you could take her in a fair fight.
WHAT'S FOR DINNER?
THEY MAKE GREAT PETS
WRITTEN, DRAWN & LETTERED BY KARL KERSCHL
COLORS BY JOHN RAUCH EDITS BY BEN ABERNATHY

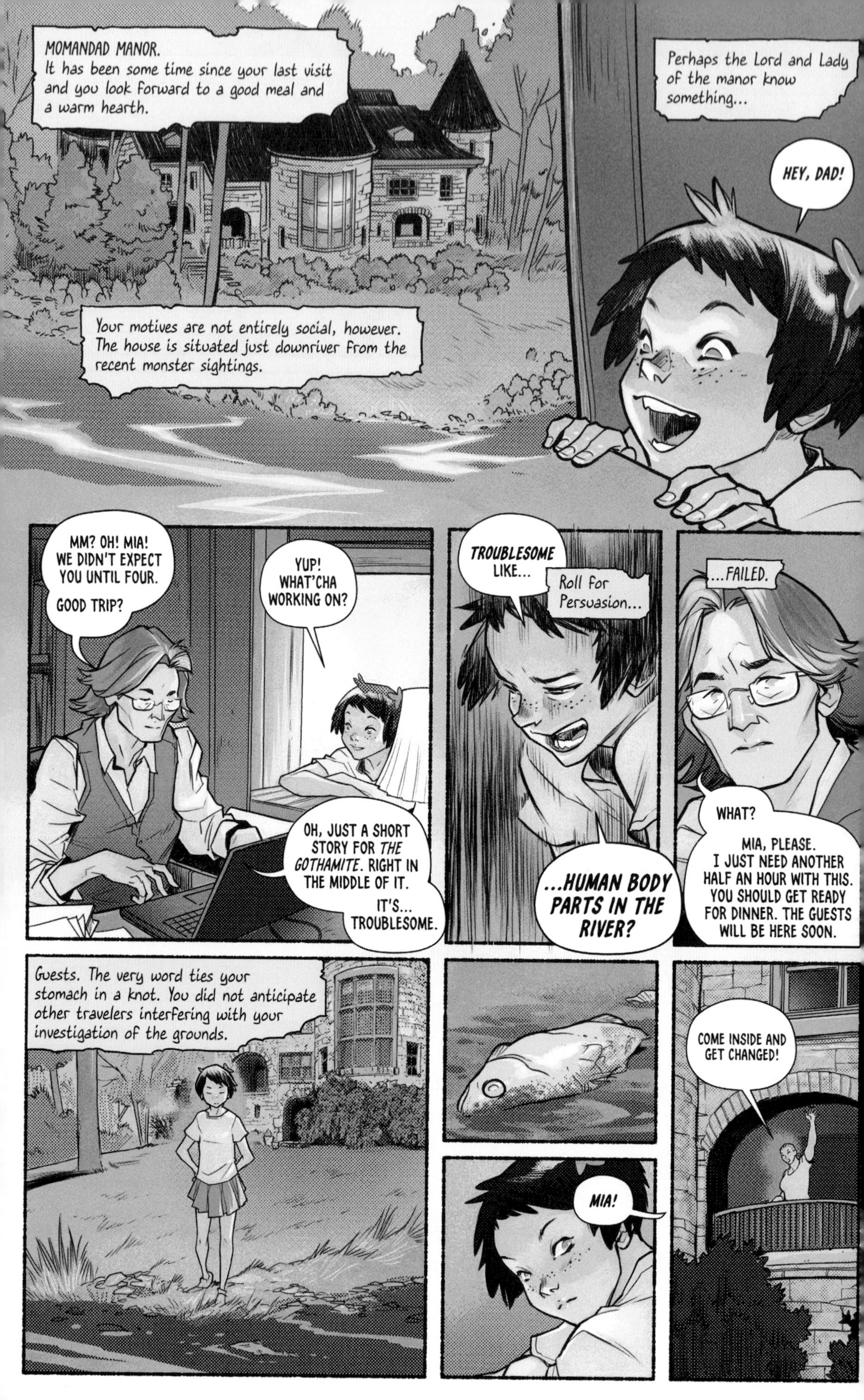
MOMANDAD MANOR.
It has been some time since your last visit and you look forward to a good meal and a warm hearth.
Your motives are not entirely social, however. The house is situated just downriver from the recent monster sightings.
Perhaps the Lord and Lady of the manor know something...
HEY, DAD!
MM? OH! MIA! WE DIDN'T EXPECT YOU UNTIL FOUR.
GOOD TRIP?
YUP! WHAT'CHA WORKING ON?
OH, JUST A SHORT STORY FOR THE GOTHAMITE. RIGHT IN THE MIDDLE OF IT.
IT'S... TROUBLESOME.
TROUBLESOME LIKE...
Roll for Persuasion...
...HUMAN BODY PARTS IN THE RIVER?
...FAILED.
WHAT?
MIA, PLEASE. I JUST NEED ANOTHER HALF AN HOUR WITH THIS. YOU SHOULD GET READY FOR DINNER. THE GUESTS WILL BE HERE SOON.
Guests. The very word ties your stomach in a knot. You did not anticipate other travelers interfering with your investigation of the grounds.
MIA!
COME INSIDE AND GET CHANGED!

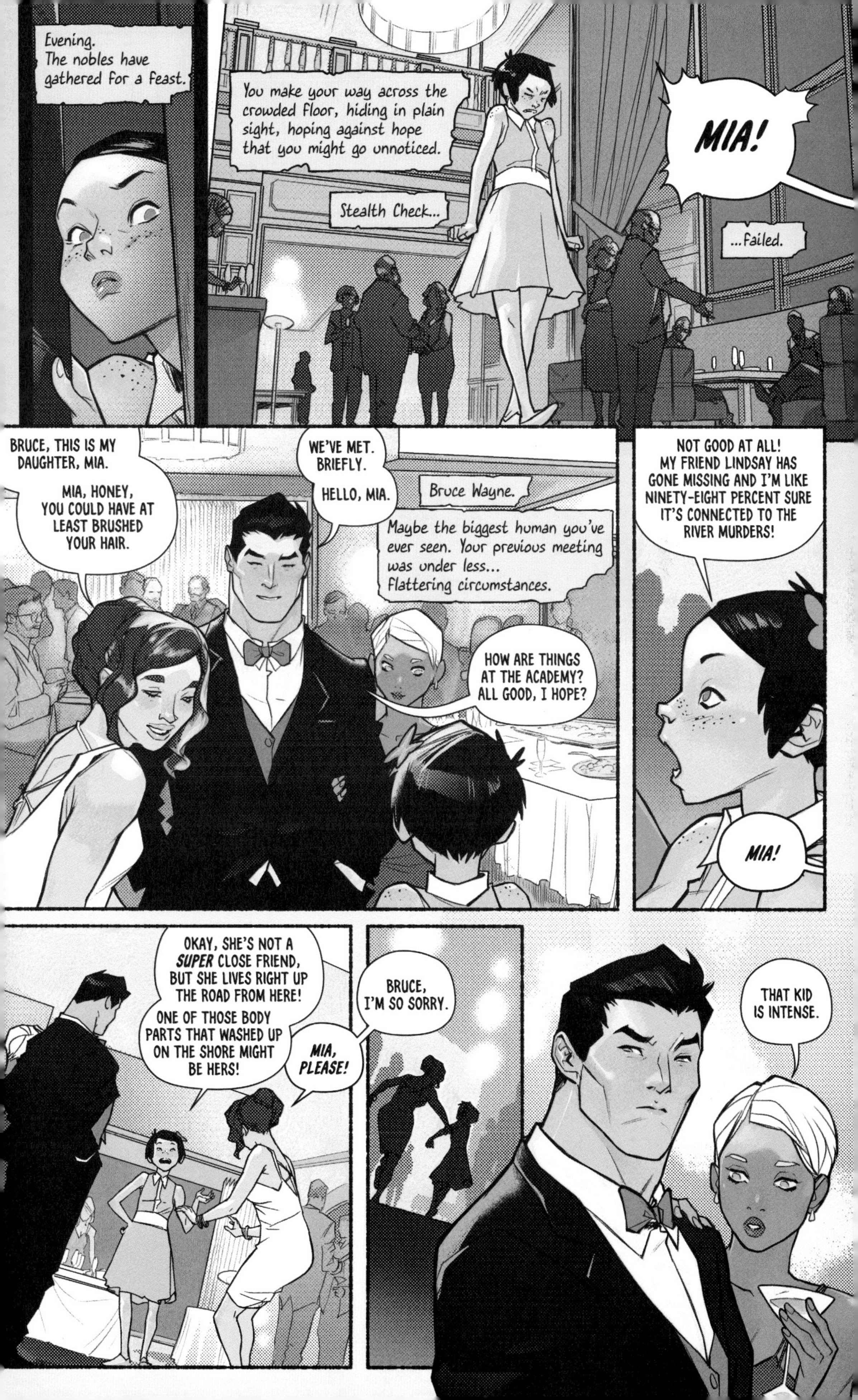

Evening.
The nobles have gathered for a feast.
You make your way across the crowded floor, hiding in plain sight, hoping against hope that you might go unnoticed.
Stealth Check...
MIA!
...Failed.
BRUCE, THIS IS MY DAUGHTER, MIA.
MIA, HONEY, YOU COULD HAVE AT LEAST BRUSHED YOUR HAIR.
WE'VE MET. BRIEFLY.
HELLO, MIA.
Bruce Wayne.
Maybe the biggest human you've ever seen. Your previous meeting was under less... Flattering circumstances.
HOW ARE THINGS AT THE ACADEMY? ALL GOOD, I HOPE?
NOT GOOD AT ALL! MY FRIEND LINDSAY HAS GONE MISSING AND I'M LIKE NINETY-EIGHT PERCENT SURE IT'S CONNECTED TO THE RIVER MURDERS!
MIA!
OKAY, SHE'S NOT A *SUPER* CLOSE FRIEND, BUT SHE LIVES RIGHT UP THE ROAD FROM HERE!
ONE OF THOSE BODY PARTS THAT WASHED UP ON THE SHORE MIGHT BE HERS!
MIA, PLEASE!
BRUCE, I'M SO SORRY.
THAT KID IS INTENSE.

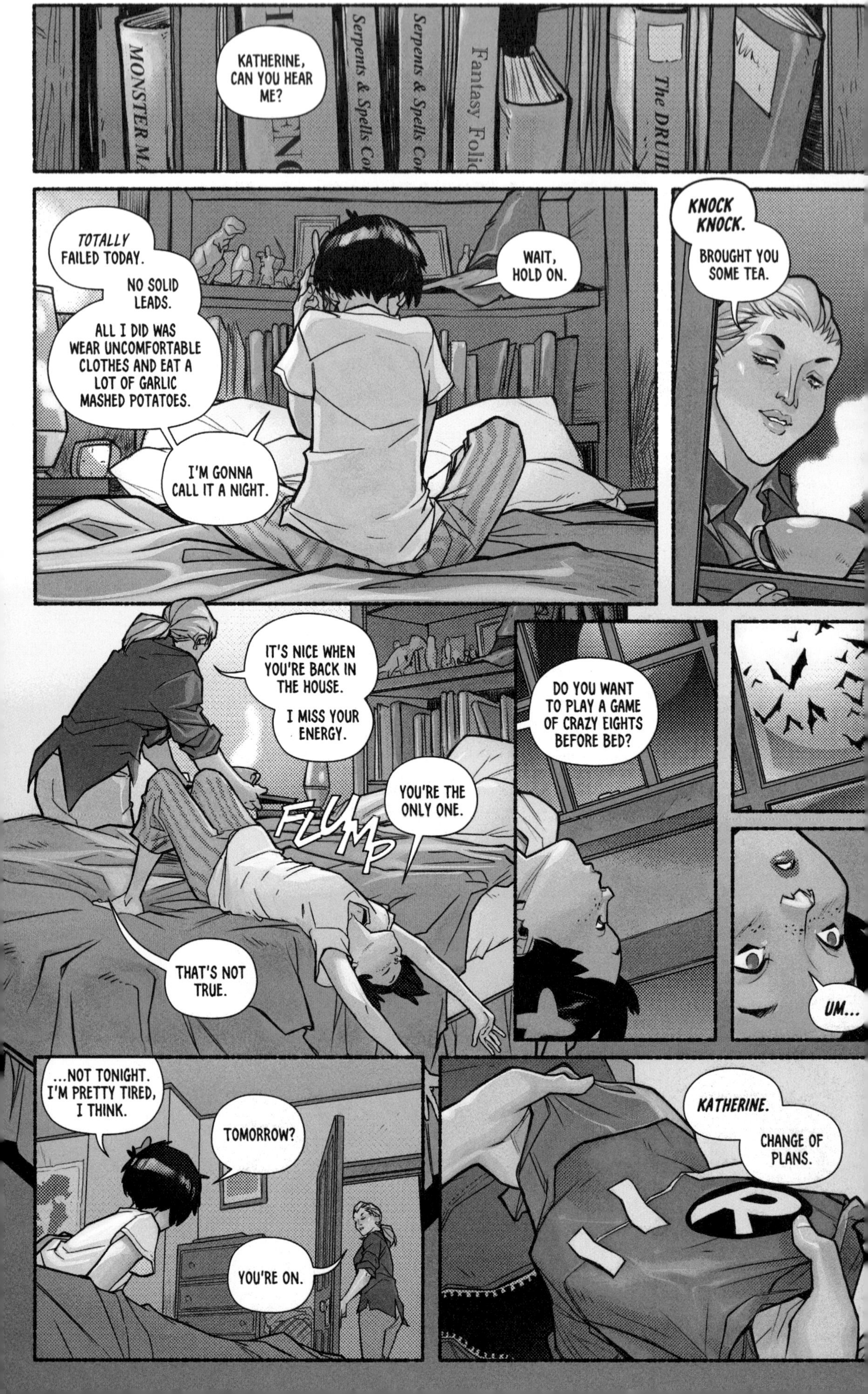
MONSTER MA
Serpents & Spells Co
Serpents & Spells Co
Fantasy Folio
The DRUI
KATHERINE, CAN YOU HEAR ME?
TOTALLY FAILED TODAY.
NO SOLID LEADS.
ALL I DID WAS WEAR UNCOMFORTABLE CLOTHES AND EAT A LOT OF GARLIC MASHED POTATOES.
WAIT, HOLD ON.
I'M GONNA CALL IT A NIGHT.
KNOCK KNOCK.
BROUGHT YOU SOME TEA.
IT'S NICE WHEN YOU'RE BACK IN THE HOUSE.
I MISS YOUR ENERGY.
FLUMP
YOU'RE THE ONLY ONE.
THAT'S NOT TRUE.
DO YOU WANT TO PLAY A GAME OF CRAZY EIGHTS BEFORE BED?
UM...
...NOT TONIGHT. I'M PRETTY TIRED, I THINK.
TOMORROW?
YOU'RE ON.
KATHERINE.
CHANGE OF PLANS.

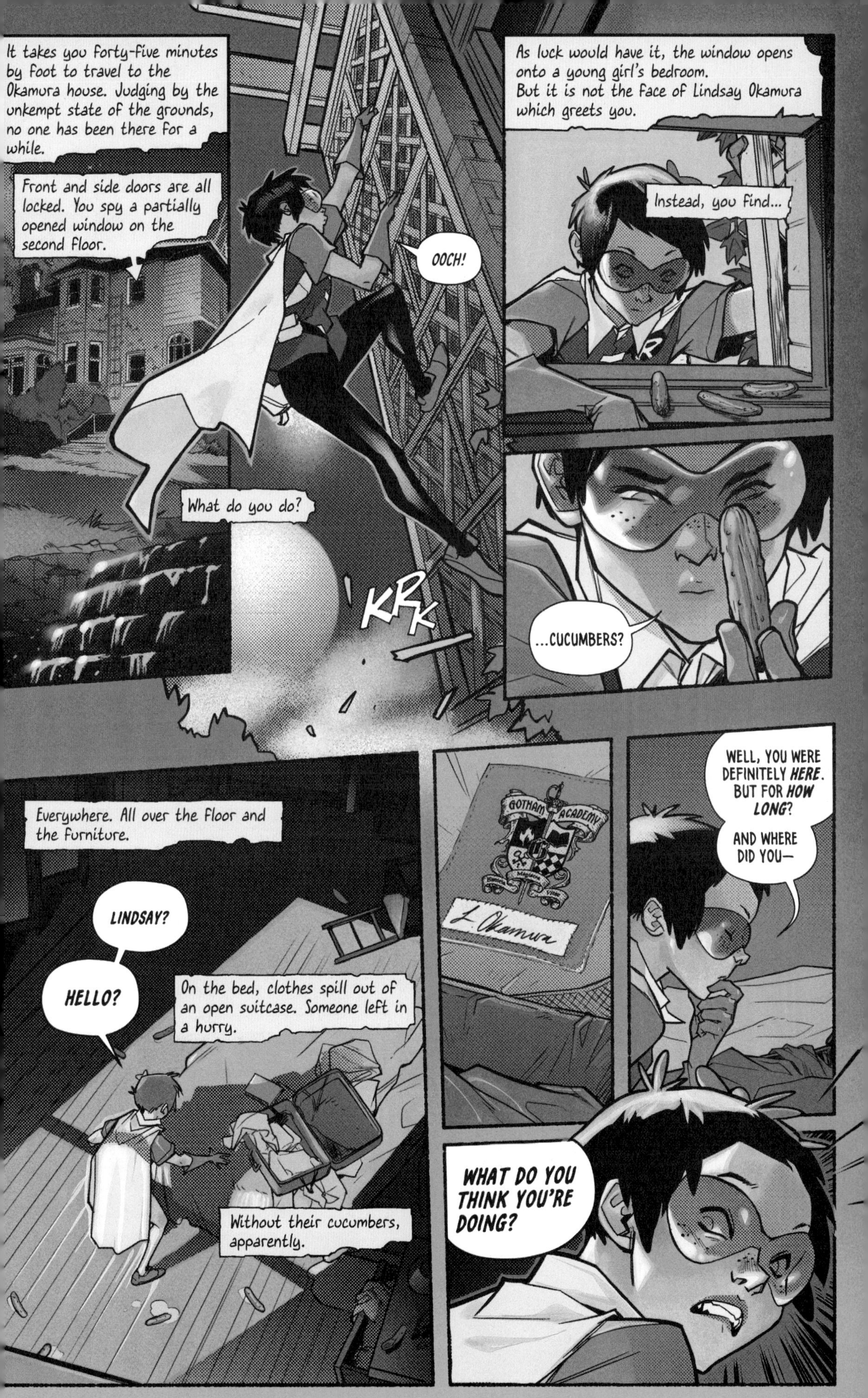
It takes you forty-five minutes by foot to travel to the Okamura house. Judging by the unkempt state of the grounds, no one has been there for a while.
Front and side doors are all locked. You spy a partially opened window on the second floor.
OOCH!
What do you do?
KRK
As luck would have it, the window opens onto a young girl's bedroom.
But it is not the face of Lindsay Okamura which greets you.
Instead, you find...
...CUCUMBERS?
Everywhere. All over the floor and the furniture.
LINDSAY?
HELLO?
On the bed, clothes spill out of an open suitcase. Someone left in a hurry.
Without their cucumbers, apparently.
GOTHAM ACADEMY
L. Okamura
WELL, YOU WERE DEFINITELY HERE. BUT FOR HOW LONG?
AND WHERE DID YOU—
WHAT DO YOU THINK YOU'RE DOING?

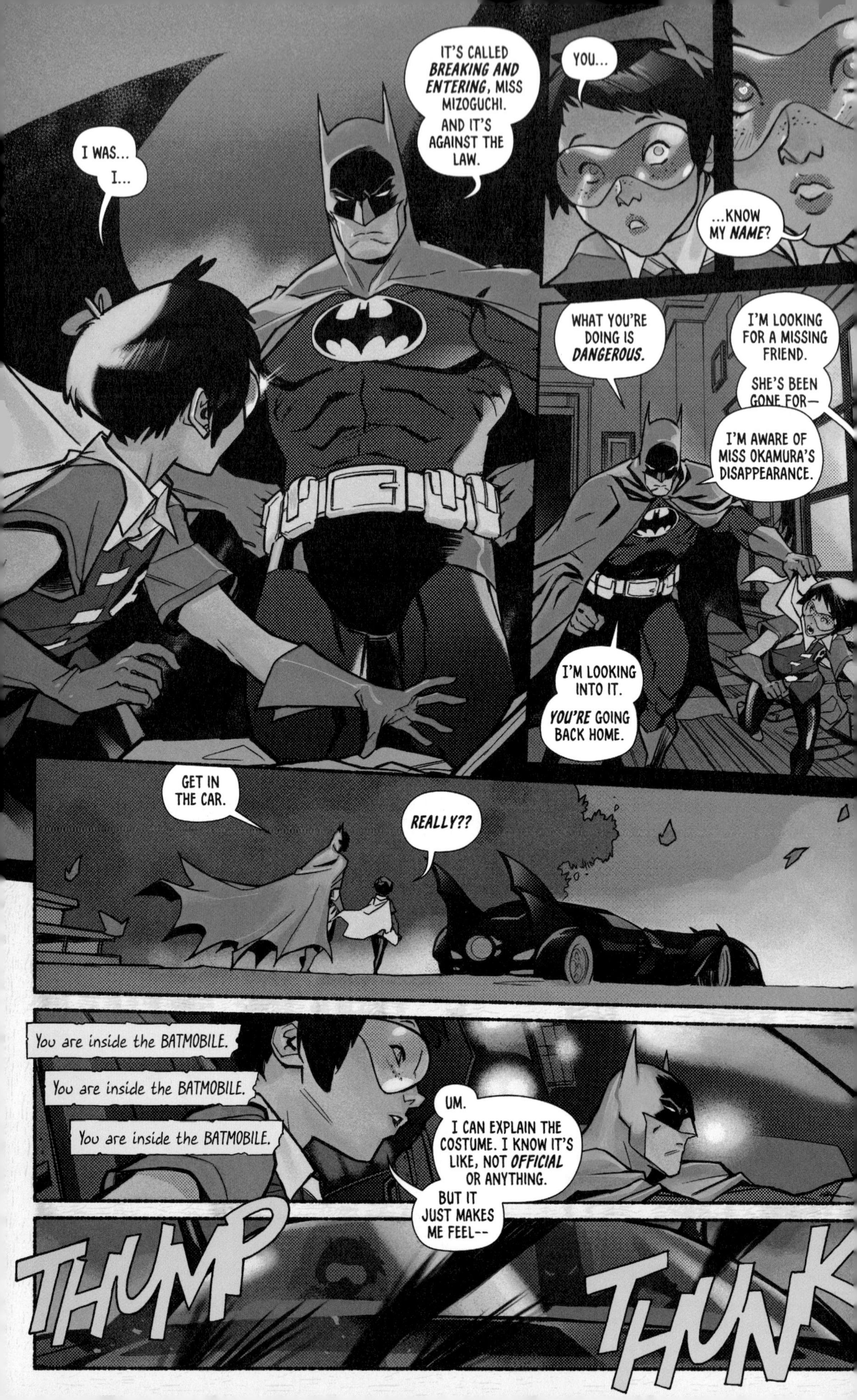

I WAS... I...
IT'S CALLED BREAKING AND ENTERING, MISS MIZOGUCHI.
AND IT'S AGAINST THE LAW.
YOU...
...KNOW MY NAME?
WHAT YOU'RE DOING IS DANGEROUS.
I'M LOOKING FOR A MISSING FRIEND.
SHE'S BEEN GONE FOR—
I'M AWARE OF MISS OKAMURA'S DISAPPEARANCE.
I'M LOOKING INTO IT.
YOU'RE GOING BACK HOME.
GET IN THE CAR.
REALLY??
You are inside the BATMOBILE.
You are inside the BATMOBILE.
You are inside the BATMOBILE.
UM.
I CAN EXPLAIN THE COSTUME. I KNOW IT'S LIKE, NOT OFFICIAL OR ANYTHING.
BUT IT JUST MAKES ME FEEL--
THUMP
THUNK

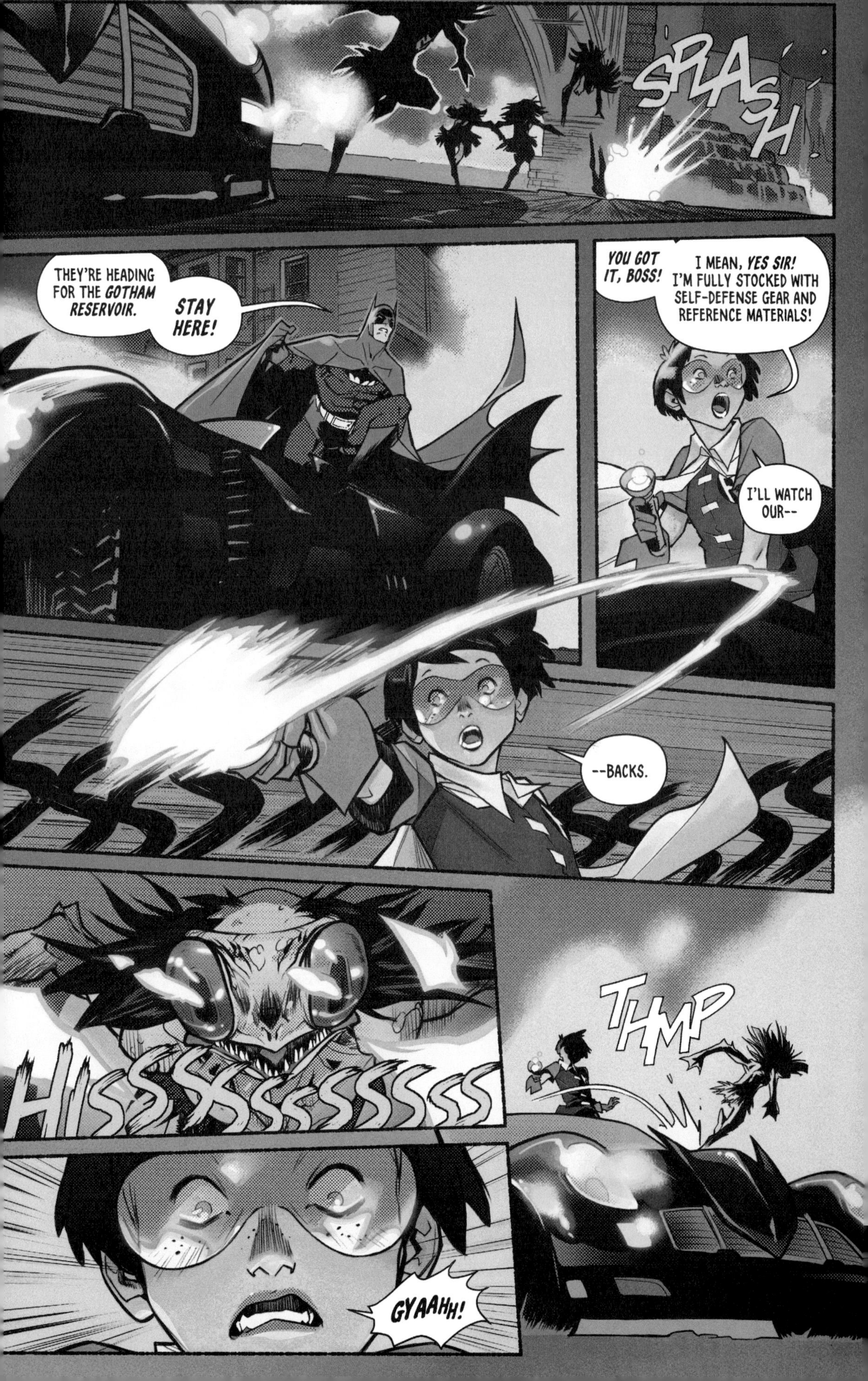
SPLASH
THEY'RE HEADING FOR THE *GOTHAM RESERVOIR.*
STAY HERE!
YOU GOT IT, BOSS!
I MEAN, *YES SIR!* I'M FULLY STOCKED WITH SELF-DEFENSE GEAR AND REFERENCE MATERIALS!
I'LL WATCH OUR--
--BACKS.
HISSSSSSSSSSS
THMP
GYAAHH!

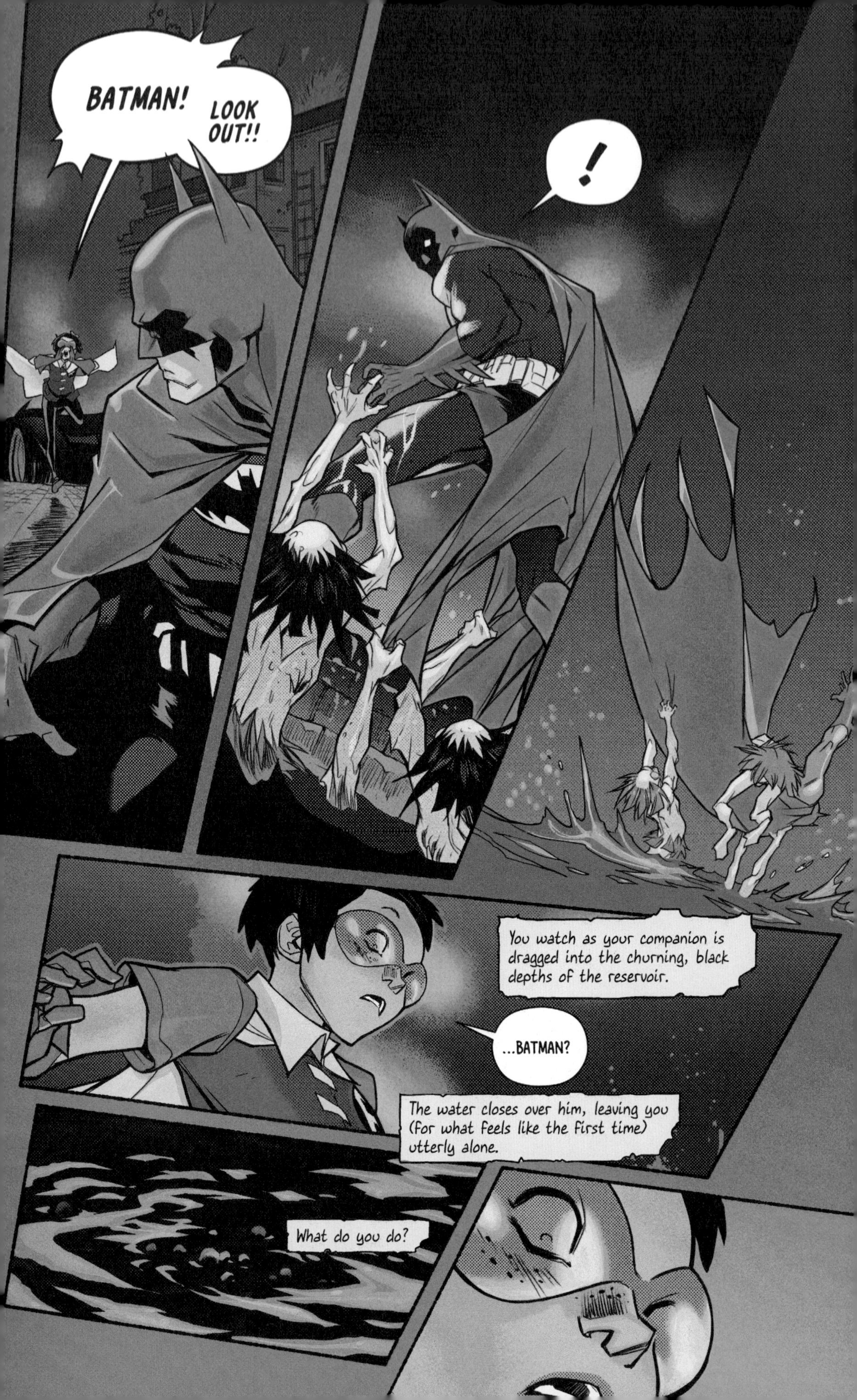
BATMAN! LOOK OUT!!
!
You watch as your companion is dragged into the churning, black depths of the reservoir.
...BATMAN?
The water closes over him, leaving you (for what feels like the first time) utterly alone.
What do you do?

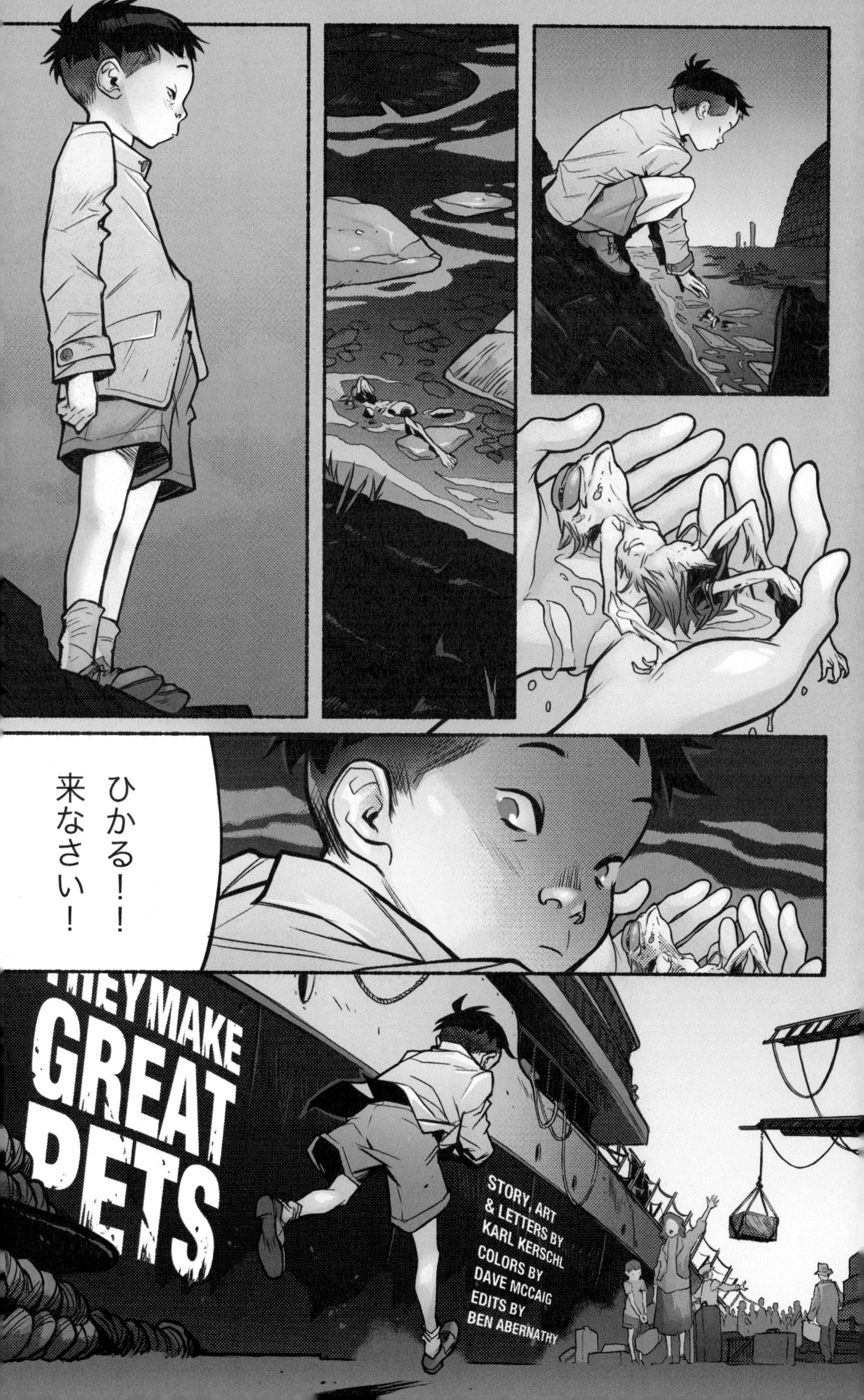

ひかる！！
来なさい！
THEY MAKE
GREAT
PETS
STORY, ART
& LETTERS BY
KARL KERSCHL
COLORS BY
DAVE MCCAIG
EDITS BY
BEN ABERNATHY

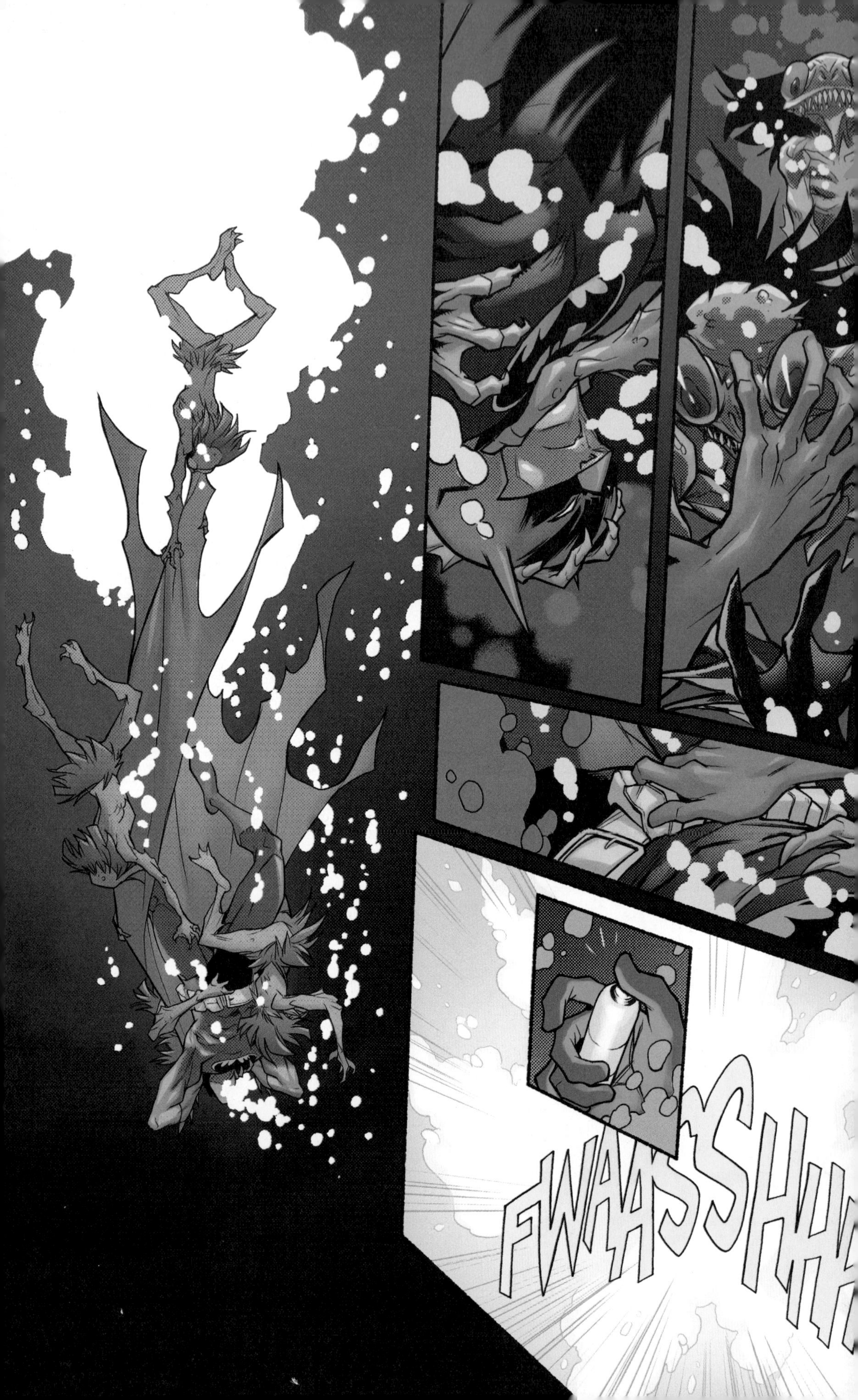
FWAASSHH

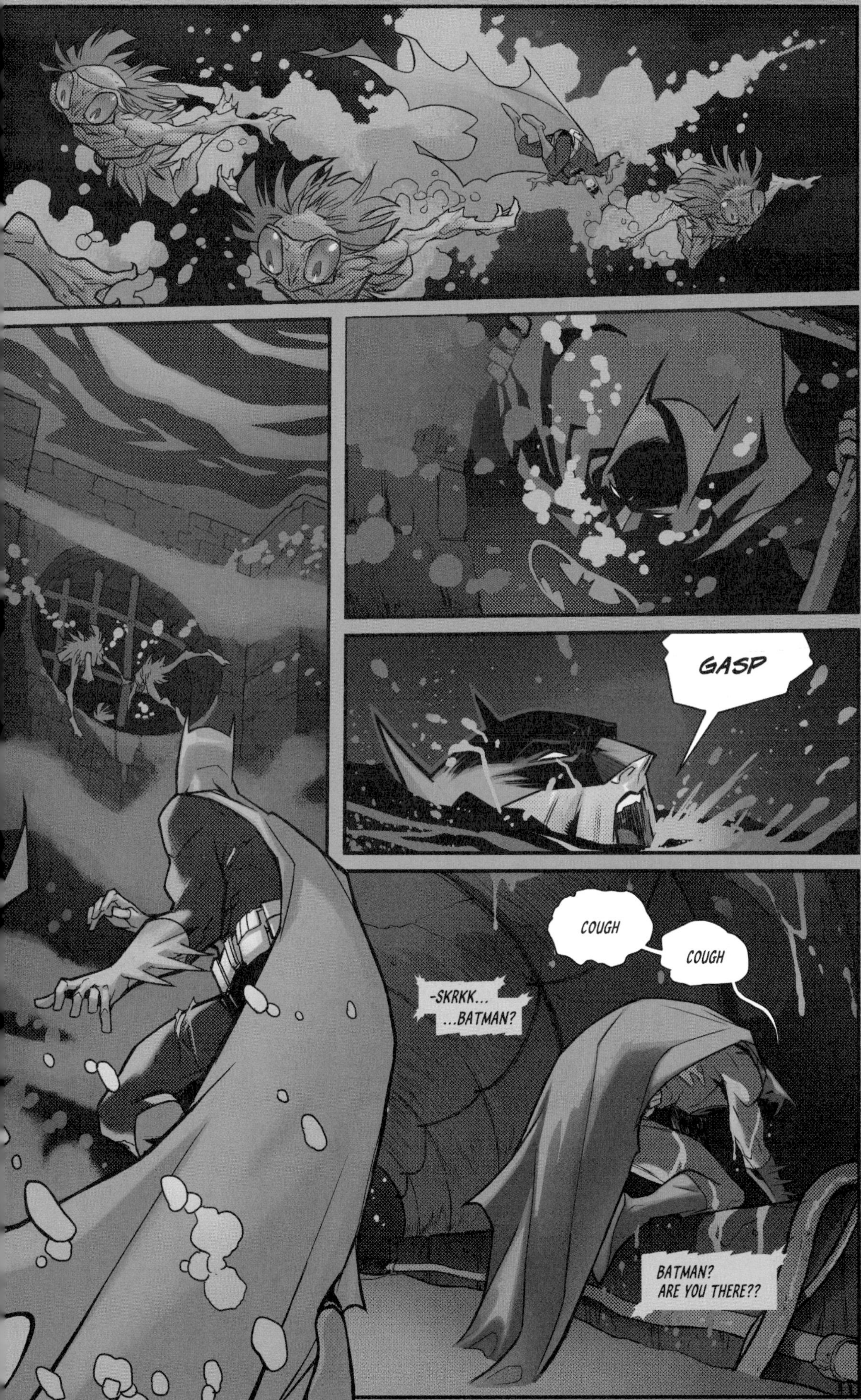
GASP
COUGH
COUGH
-SKRKK...
...BATMAN?
BATMAN?
ARE YOU THERE??

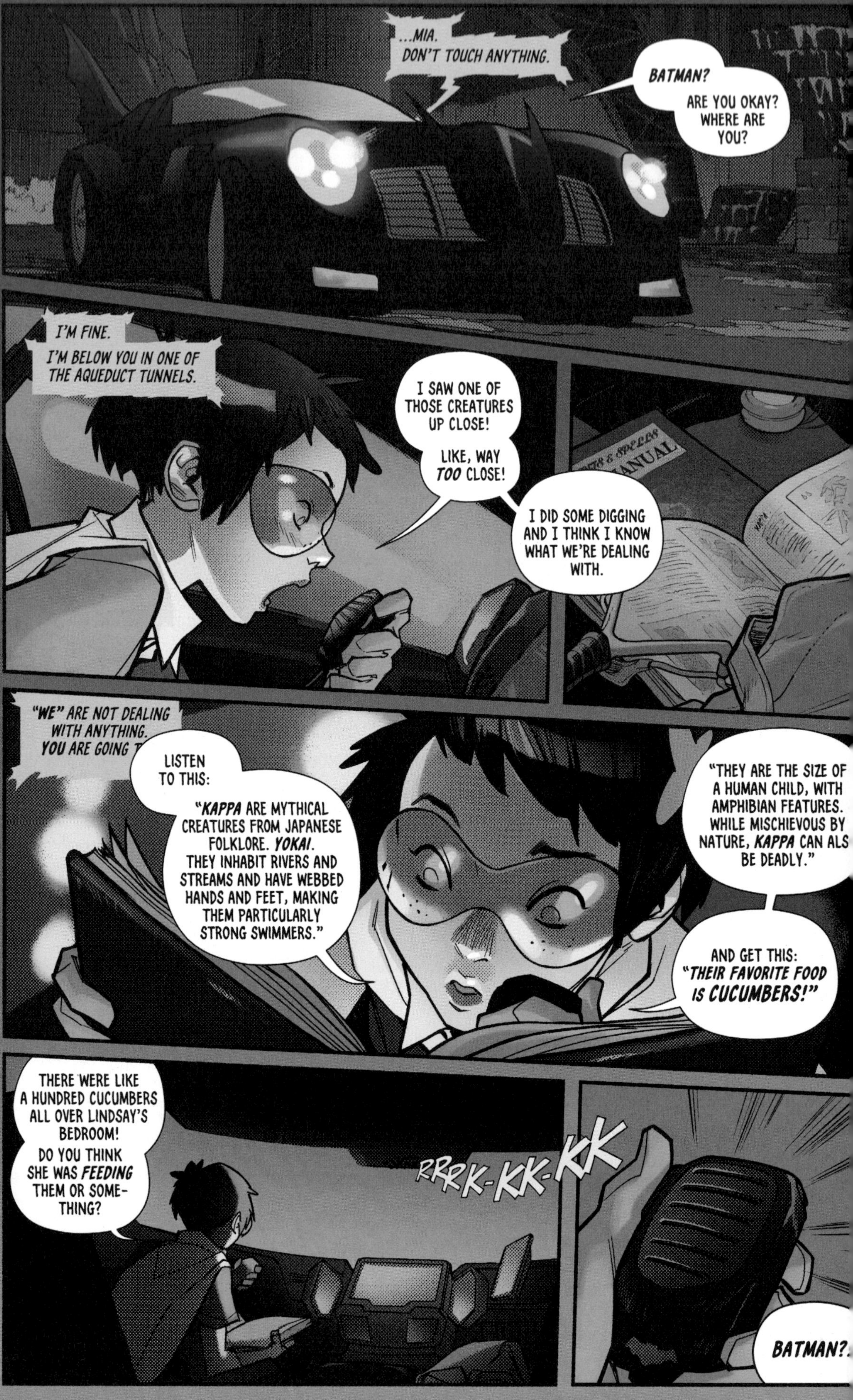
...MIA.
DON'T TOUCH ANYTHING.
BATMAN?
ARE YOU OKAY? WHERE ARE YOU?
I'M FINE.
I'M BELOW YOU IN ONE OF THE AQUEDUCT TUNNELS.
I SAW ONE OF THOSE CREATURES UP CLOSE!
LIKE, WAY *TOO* CLOSE!
I DID SOME DIGGING AND I THINK I KNOW WHAT WE'RE DEALING WITH.
"*WE*" ARE NOT DEALING WITH ANYTHING. *YOU* ARE GOING T
LISTEN TO THIS:
"*KAPPA* ARE MYTHICAL CREATURES FROM JAPANESE FOLKLORE. *YOKAI*. THEY INHABIT RIVERS AND STREAMS AND HAVE WEBBED HANDS AND FEET, MAKING THEM PARTICULARLY STRONG SWIMMERS."
"THEY ARE THE SIZE OF A HUMAN CHILD, WITH AMPHIBIAN FEATURES. WHILE MISCHIEVOUS BY NATURE, *KAPPA* CAN ALS BE DEADLY."
AND GET THIS: "*THEIR FAVORITE FOOD IS CUCUMBERS!*"
THERE WERE LIKE A HUNDRED CUCUMBERS ALL OVER LINDSAY'S BEDROOM!
DO YOU THINK SHE WAS *FEEDING* THEM OR SOME-THING?
RRRK-KK-KK
BATMAN?.

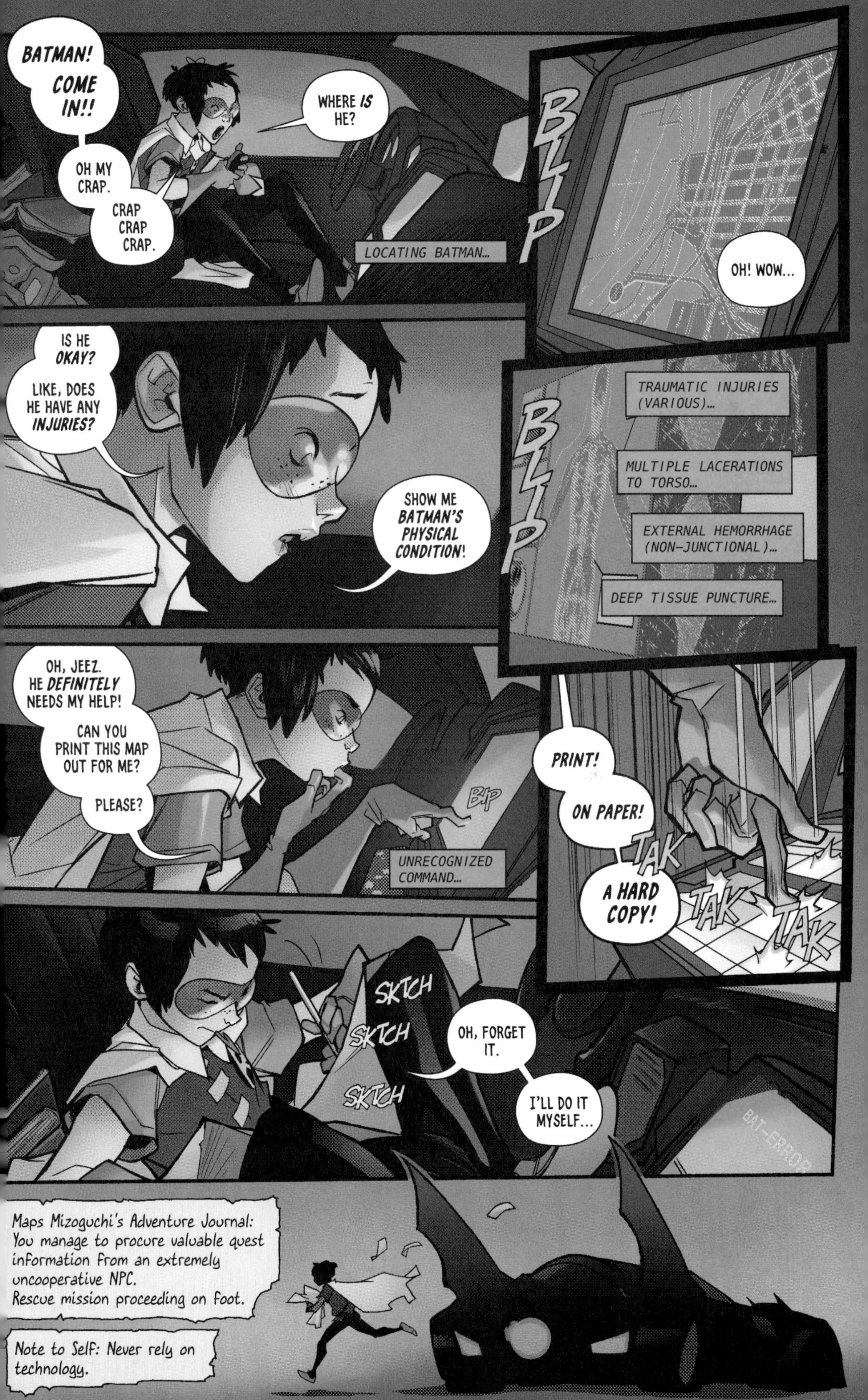
BATMAN! COME IN!!
WHERE IS HE?
OH MY CRAP.
CRAP CRAP CRAP.
LOCATING BATMAN...
BLIP
OH! WOW...
IS HE OKAY?
LIKE, DOES HE HAVE ANY INJURIES?
SHOW ME BATMAN'S PHYSICAL CONDITION!
BLIP
TRAUMATIC INJURIES (VARIOUS)...
MULTIPLE LACERATIONS TO TORSO...
EXTERNAL HEMORRHAGE (NON-JUNCTIONAL)...
DEEP TISSUE PUNCTURE...
OH, JEEZ. HE DEFINITELY NEEDS MY HELP!
CAN YOU PRINT THIS MAP OUT FOR ME?
PLEASE?
BIP
UNRECOGNIZED COMMAND...
PRINT!
ON PAPER!
A HARD COPY!
TAK
TAK
TAK
SKTCH
SKTCH
SKTCH
OH, FORGET IT.
I'LL DO IT MYSELF...
BAT-ERROR
Maps Mizoguchi's Adventure Journal: You manage to procure valuable quest information from an extremely uncooperative NPC. Rescue mission proceeding on foot.
Note to Self: Never rely on technology.

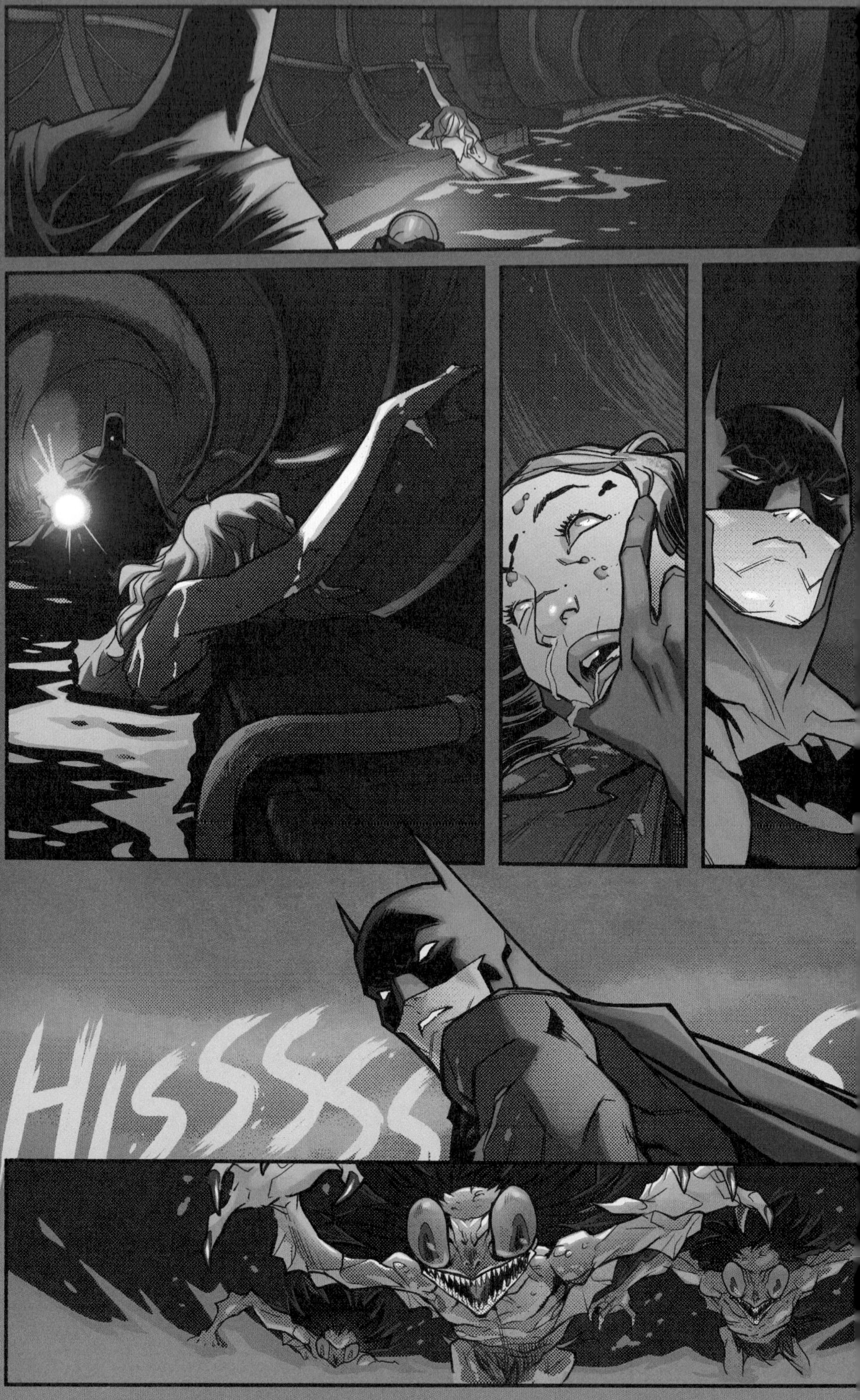
HISSSS

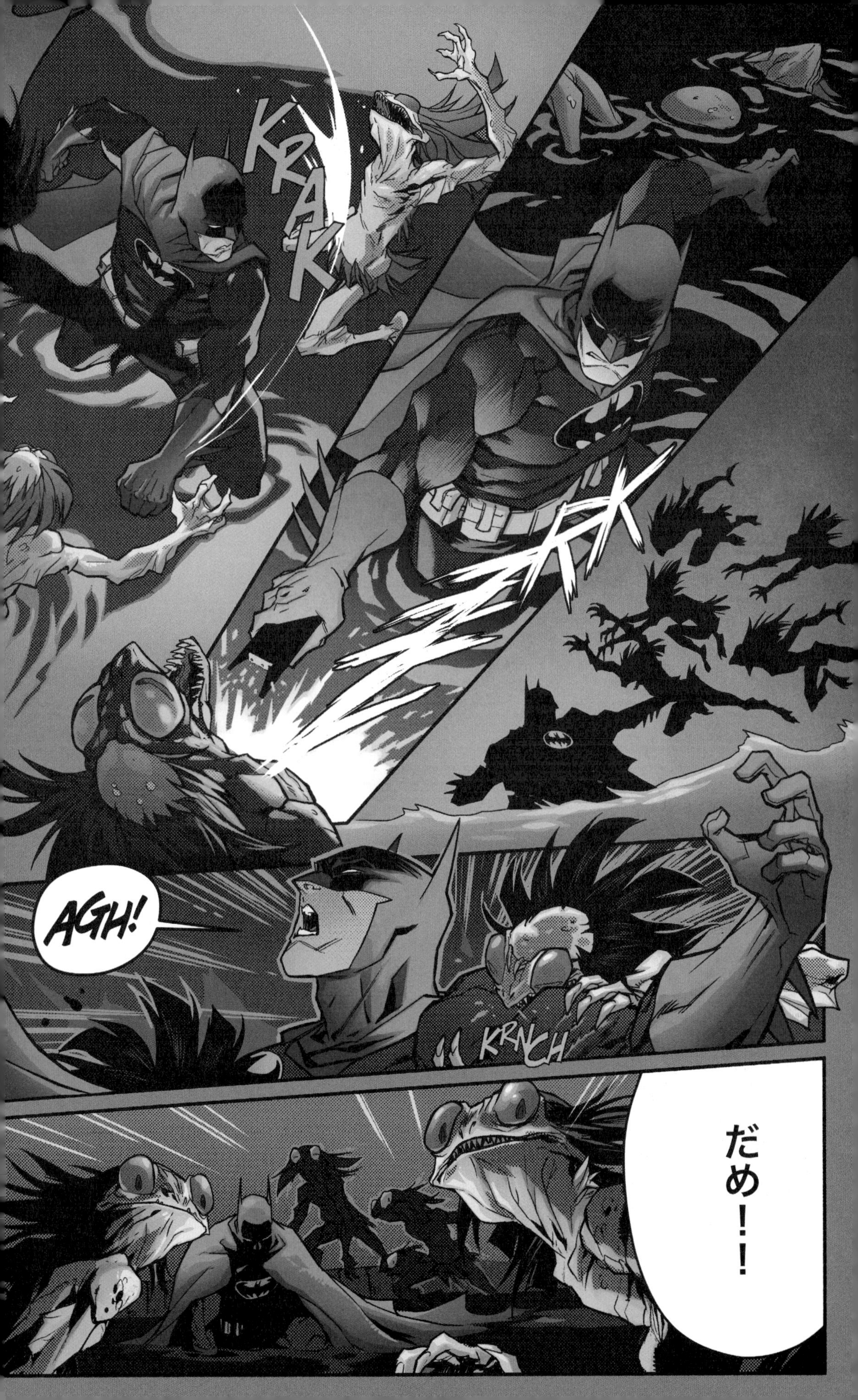

KRAK
AGH!
KRNCH
だめ!!

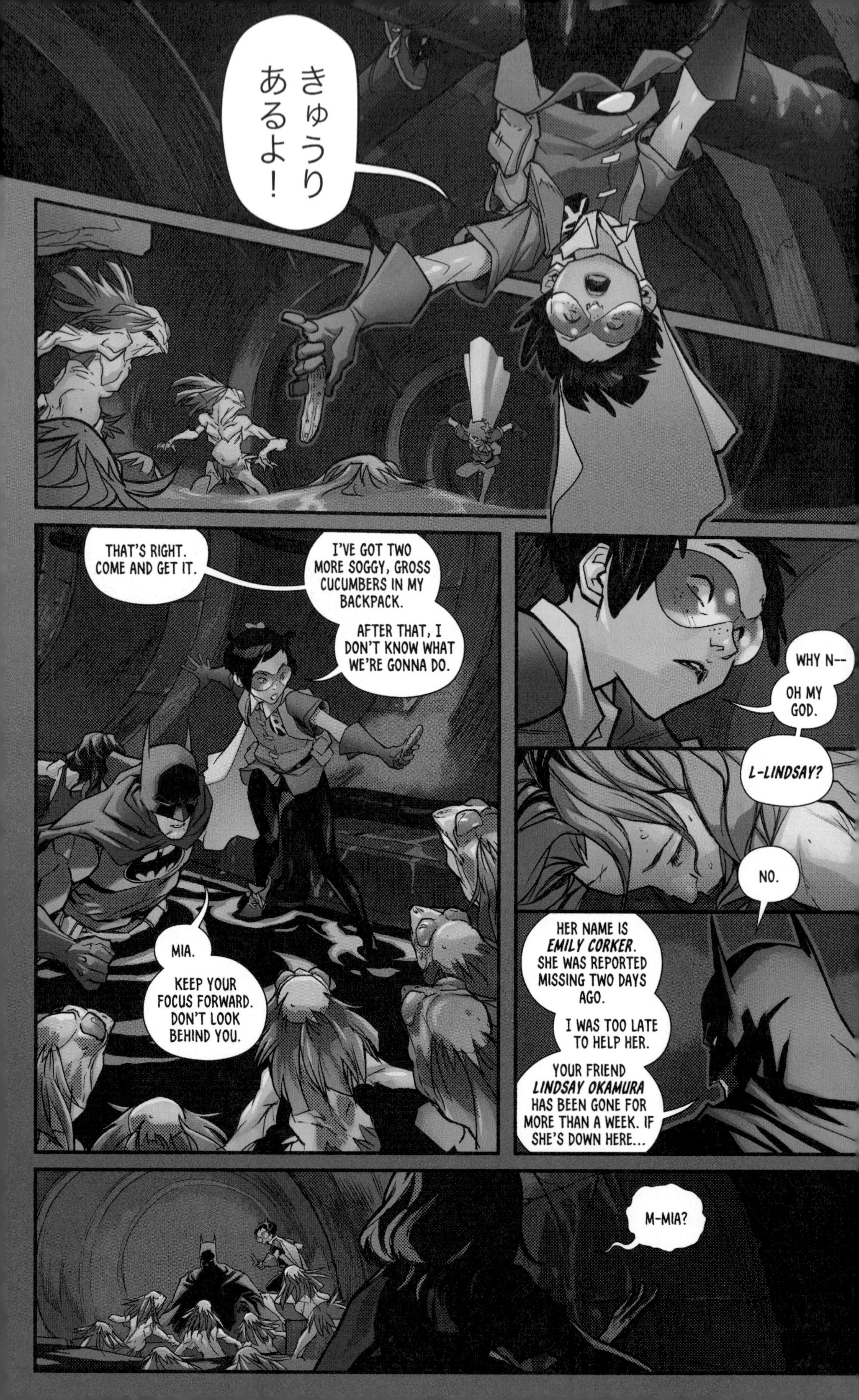
きゅうり
あるよ！
THAT'S RIGHT. COME AND GET IT.
I'VE GOT TWO MORE SOGGY, GROSS CUCUMBERS IN MY BACKPACK.
AFTER THAT, I DON'T KNOW WHAT WE'RE GONNA DO.
MIA.
KEEP YOUR FOCUS FORWARD. DON'T LOOK BEHIND YOU.
WHY N--
OH MY GOD.
L-LINDSAY?
NO.
HER NAME IS EMILY CORKER. SHE WAS REPORTED MISSING TWO DAYS AGO.
I WAS TOO LATE TO HELP HER.
YOUR FRIEND LINDSAY OKAMURA HAS BEEN GONE FOR MORE THAN A WEEK. IF SHE'S DOWN HERE...
M-MIA?

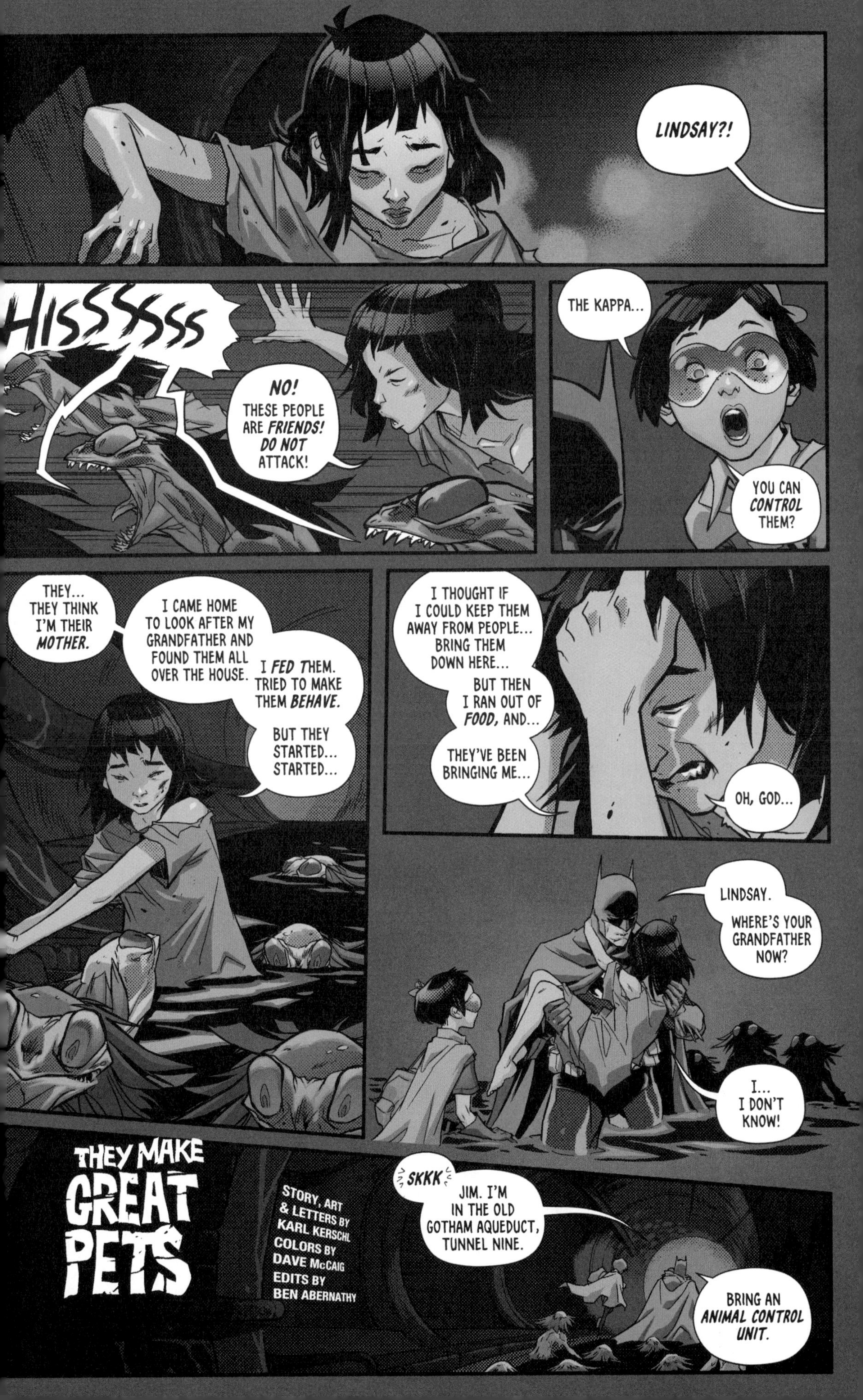
LINDSAY?!
HISSSSSS
NO! THESE PEOPLE ARE FRIENDS! DO NOT ATTACK!
THE KAPPA...
YOU CAN CONTROL THEM?
THEY... THEY THINK I'M THEIR MOTHER.
I CAME HOME TO LOOK AFTER MY GRANDFATHER AND FOUND THEM ALL OVER THE HOUSE.
I FED THEM. TRIED TO MAKE THEM BEHAVE.
BUT THEY STARTED... STARTED...
I THOUGHT IF I COULD KEEP THEM AWAY FROM PEOPLE... BRING THEM DOWN HERE...
BUT THEN I RAN OUT OF FOOD, AND...
THEY'VE BEEN BRINGING ME...
OH, GOD...
LINDSAY.
WHERE'S YOUR GRANDFATHER NOW?
I... I DON'T KNOW!
THEY MAKE GREAT PETS
STORY, ART & LETTERS BY KARL KERSCHL
COLORS BY DAVE McCAIG
EDITS BY BEN ABERNATHY
SKKK
JIM. I'M IN THE OLD GOTHAM AQUEDUCT, TUNNEL NINE.
BRING AN ANIMAL CONTROL UNIT.

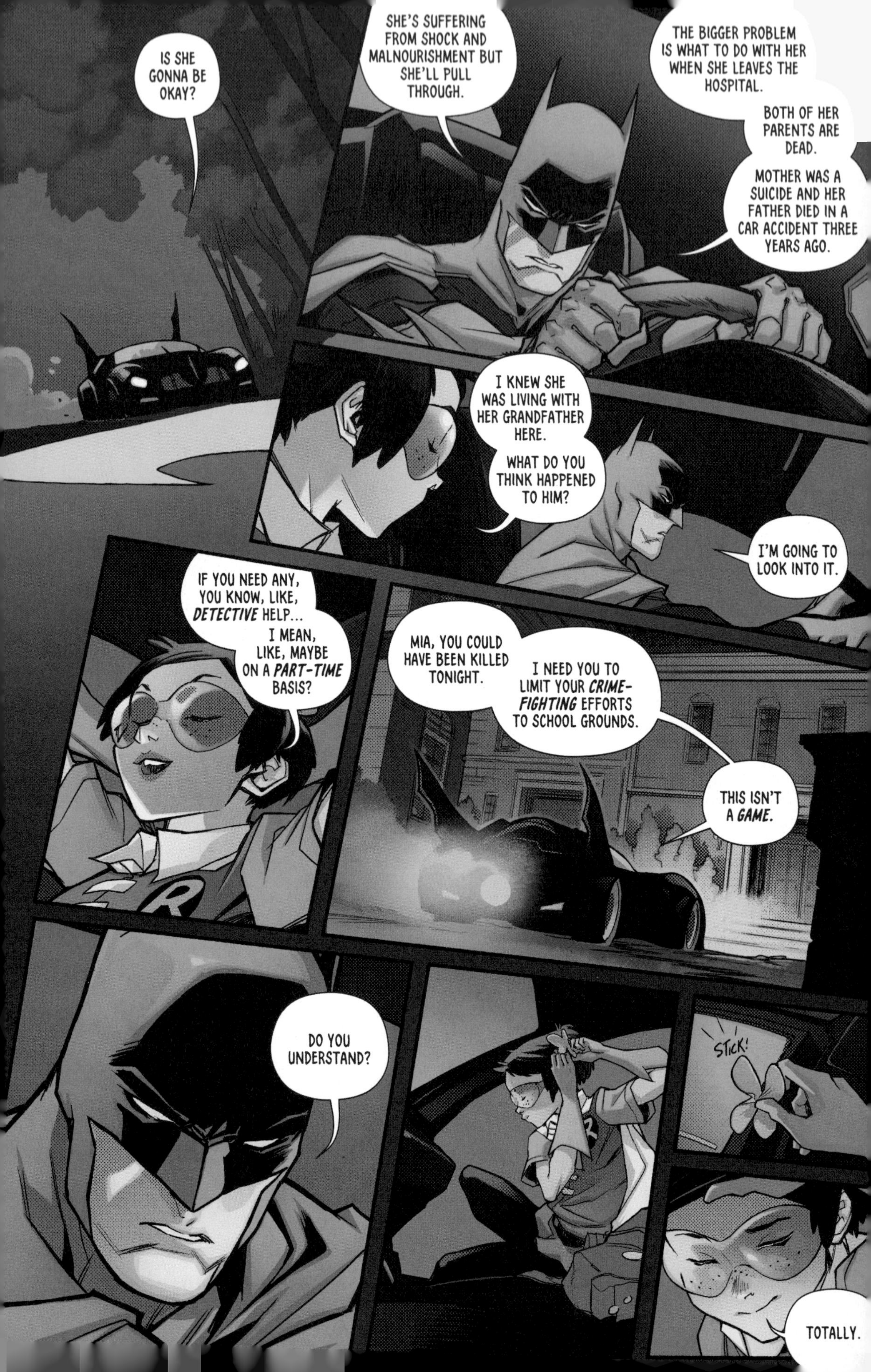
IS SHE GONNA BE OKAY?
SHE'S SUFFERING FROM SHOCK AND MALNOURISHMENT BUT SHE'LL PULL THROUGH.
THE BIGGER PROBLEM IS WHAT TO DO WITH HER WHEN SHE LEAVES THE HOSPITAL.
BOTH OF HER PARENTS ARE DEAD.
MOTHER WAS A SUICIDE AND HER FATHER DIED IN A CAR ACCIDENT THREE YEARS AGO.
I KNEW SHE WAS LIVING WITH HER GRANDFATHER HERE.
WHAT DO YOU THINK HAPPENED TO HIM?
I'M GOING TO LOOK INTO IT.
IF YOU NEED ANY, YOU KNOW, LIKE, DETECTIVE HELP...
I MEAN, LIKE, MAYBE ON A PART-TIME BASIS?
MIA, YOU COULD HAVE BEEN KILLED TONIGHT.
I NEED YOU TO LIMIT YOUR CRIME-FIGHTING EFFORTS TO SCHOOL GROUNDS.
THIS ISN'T A GAME.
DO YOU UNDERSTAND?
STICK!
TOTALLY.

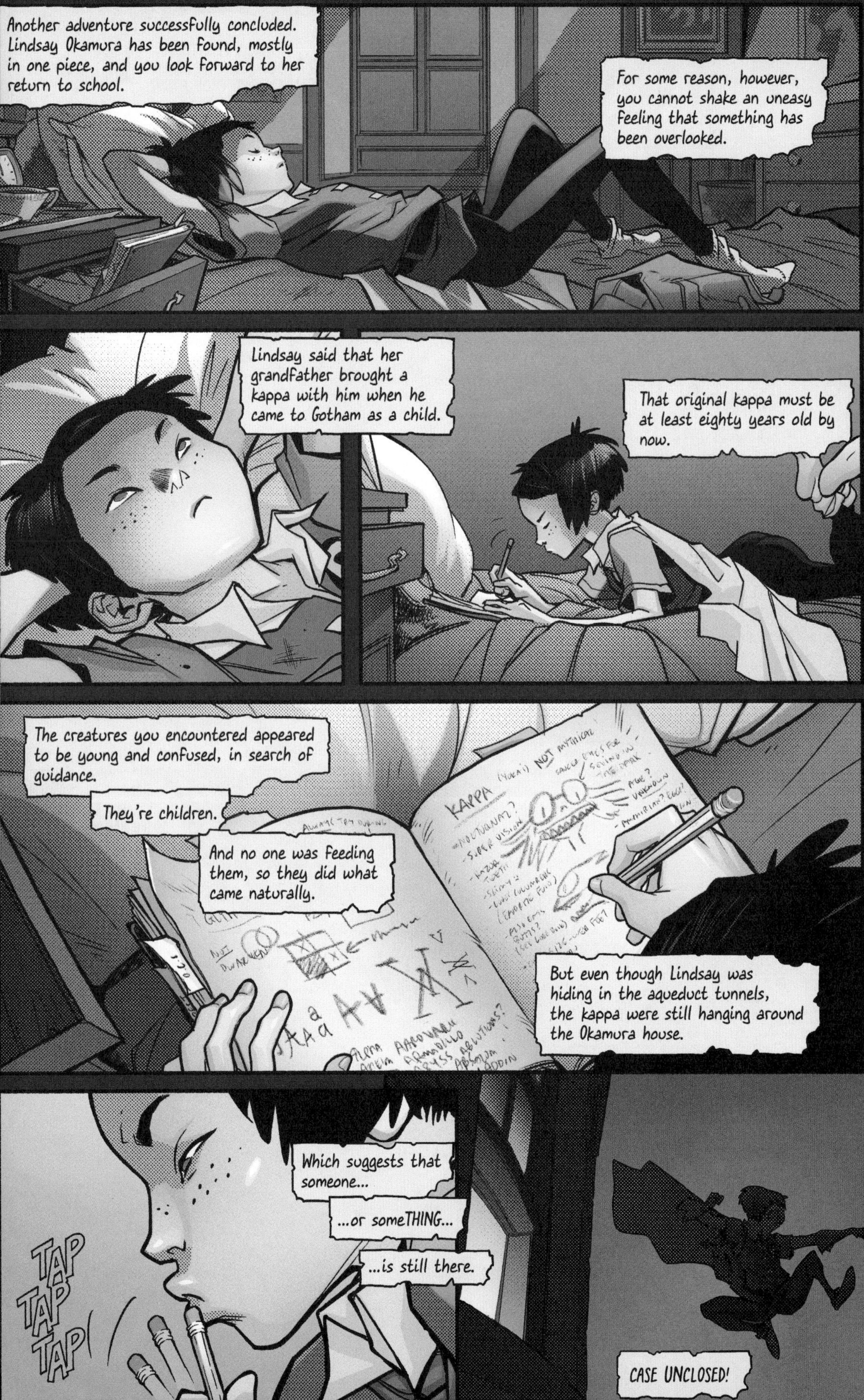
Another adventure successfully concluded. Lindsay Okamura has been found, mostly in one piece, and you look forward to her return to school.
For some reason, however, you cannot shake an uneasy feeling that something has been overlooked.
Lindsay said that her grandfather brought a kappa with him when he came to Gotham as a child.
That original kappa must be at least eighty years old by now.
The creatures you encountered appeared to be young and confused, in search of guidance.
They're children.
And no one was feeding them, so they did what came naturally.
KAPPA
But even though Lindsay was hiding in the aqueduct tunnels, the kappa were still hanging around the Okamura house.
Which suggests that someone...
...or someTHING...
...is still there.
TAP TAP TAP
CASE UNCLOSED!

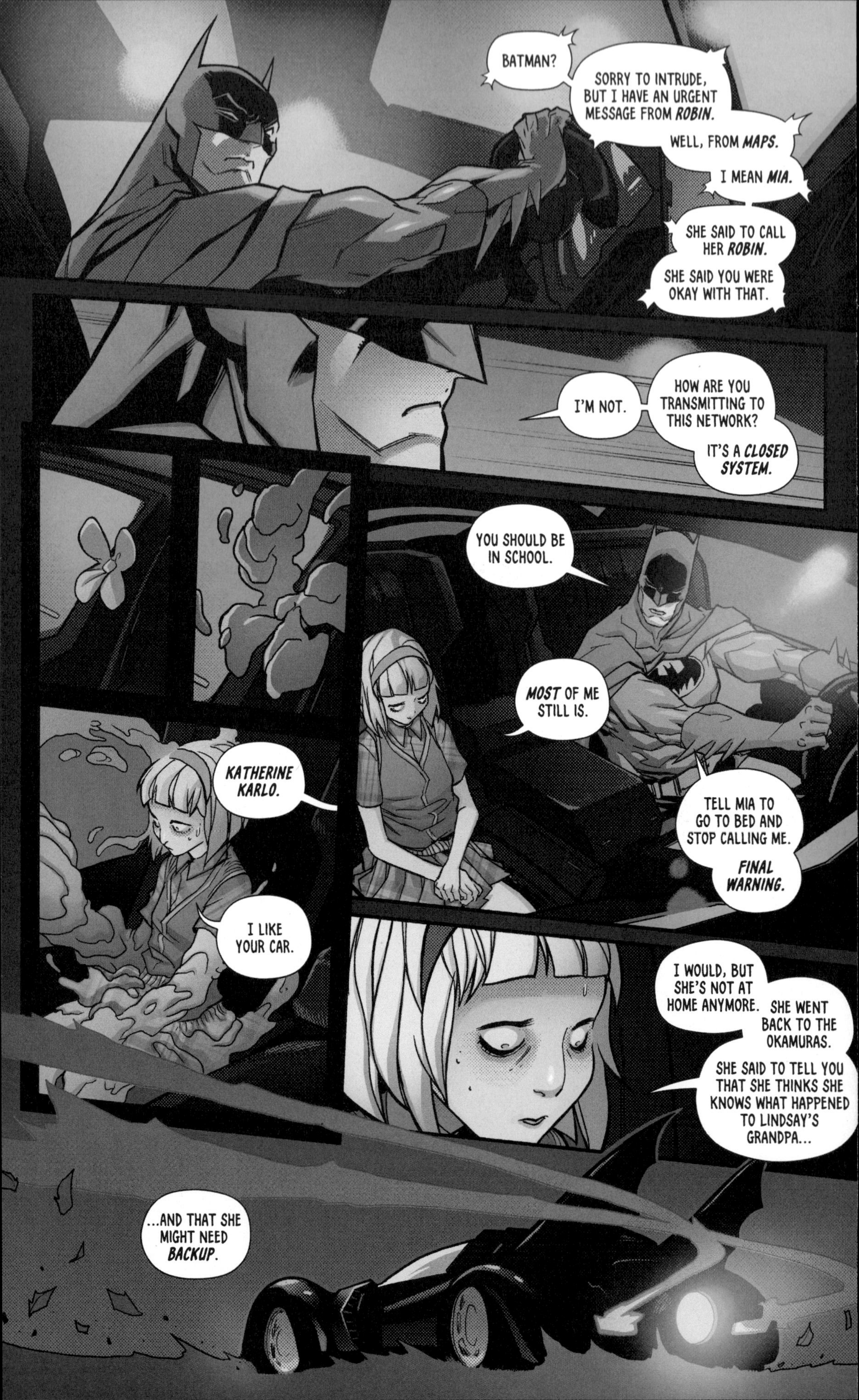

BATMAN?
SORRY TO INTRUDE, BUT I HAVE AN URGENT MESSAGE FROM *ROBIN*.
WELL, FROM *MAPS*.
I MEAN *MIA*.
SHE SAID TO CALL HER *ROBIN*.
SHE SAID YOU WERE OKAY WITH THAT.
I'M NOT.
HOW ARE YOU TRANSMITTING TO THIS NETWORK?
IT'S A *CLOSED SYSTEM*.
YOU SHOULD BE IN SCHOOL.
MOST OF ME STILL IS.
TELL MIA TO GO TO BED AND STOP CALLING ME.
FINAL WARNING.
KATHERINE KARLO.
I LIKE YOUR CAR.
I WOULD, BUT SHE'S NOT AT HOME ANYMORE.
SHE WENT BACK TO THE OKAMURAS.
SHE SAID TO TELL YOU THAT SHE THINKS SHE KNOWS WHAT HAPPENED TO LINDSAY'S GRANDPA...
...AND THAT SHE MIGHT NEED *BACKUP*.

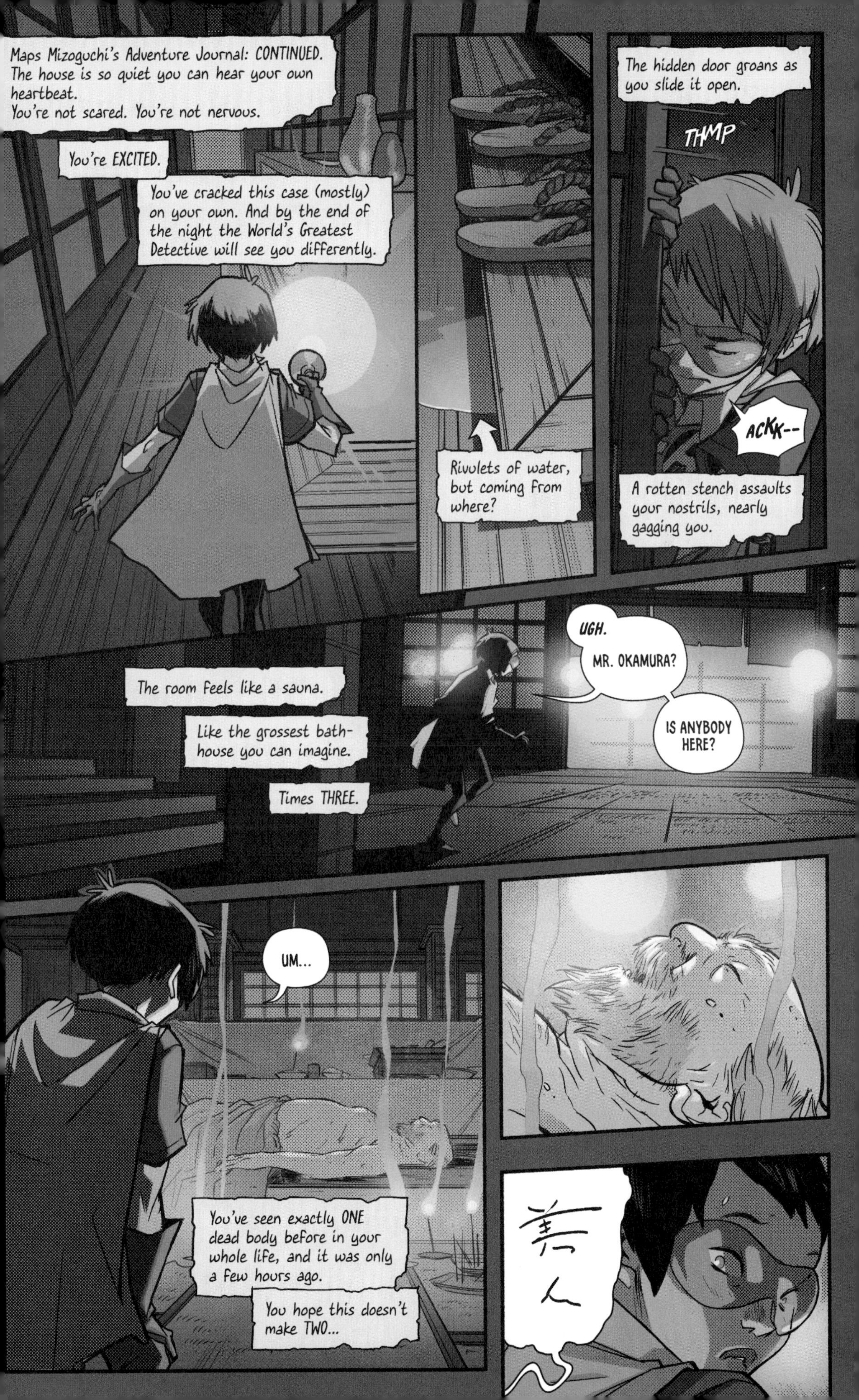
Maps Mizoguchi's Adventure Journal: CONTINUED.
The house is so quiet you can hear your own heartbeat.
You're not scared. You're not nervous.
You're EXCITED.
You've cracked this case (mostly) on your own. And by the end of the night the World's Greatest Detective will see you differently.
Rivulets of water, but coming from where?
The hidden door groans as you slide it open.
THMP
ACKK--
A rotten stench assaults your nostrils, nearly gagging you.
The room feels like a sauna.
Like the grossest bath-house you can imagine.
Times THREE.
UGH.
MR. OKAMURA?
IS ANYBODY HERE?
UM...
You've seen exactly ONE dead body before in your whole life, and it was only a few hours ago.
You hope this doesn't make TWO...

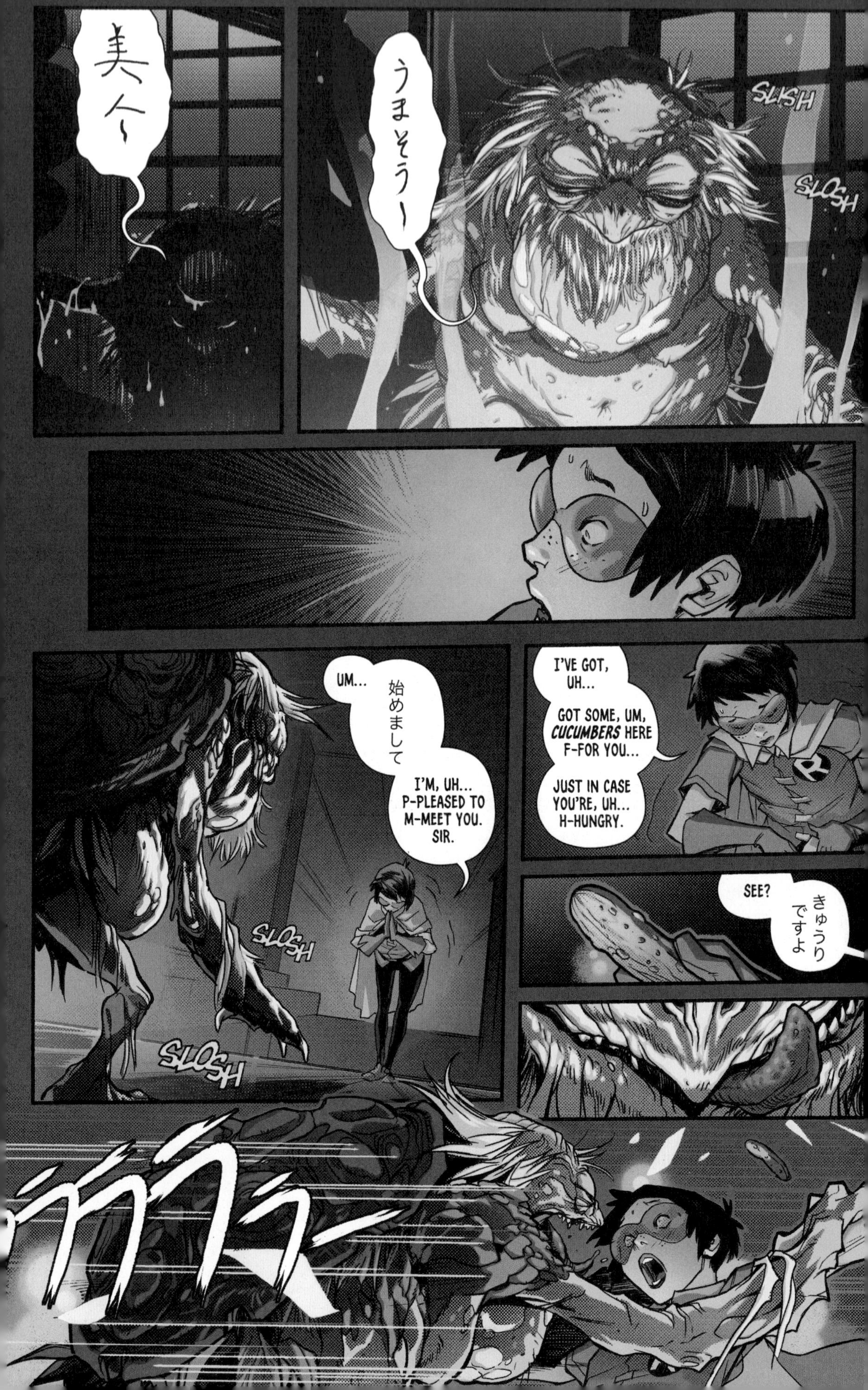
美人〜
うまそう〜
SLISH
SLOSH
UM...
始めまして
I'M, UH...
P-PLEASED TO
M-MEET YOU.
SIR.
SLOSH
SLOSH
I'VE GOT,
UH...
GOT SOME, UM,
CUCUMBERS HERE
F-FOR YOU...
JUST IN CASE
YOU'RE, UH...
H-HUNGRY.
SEE?
きゅうり
ですよ

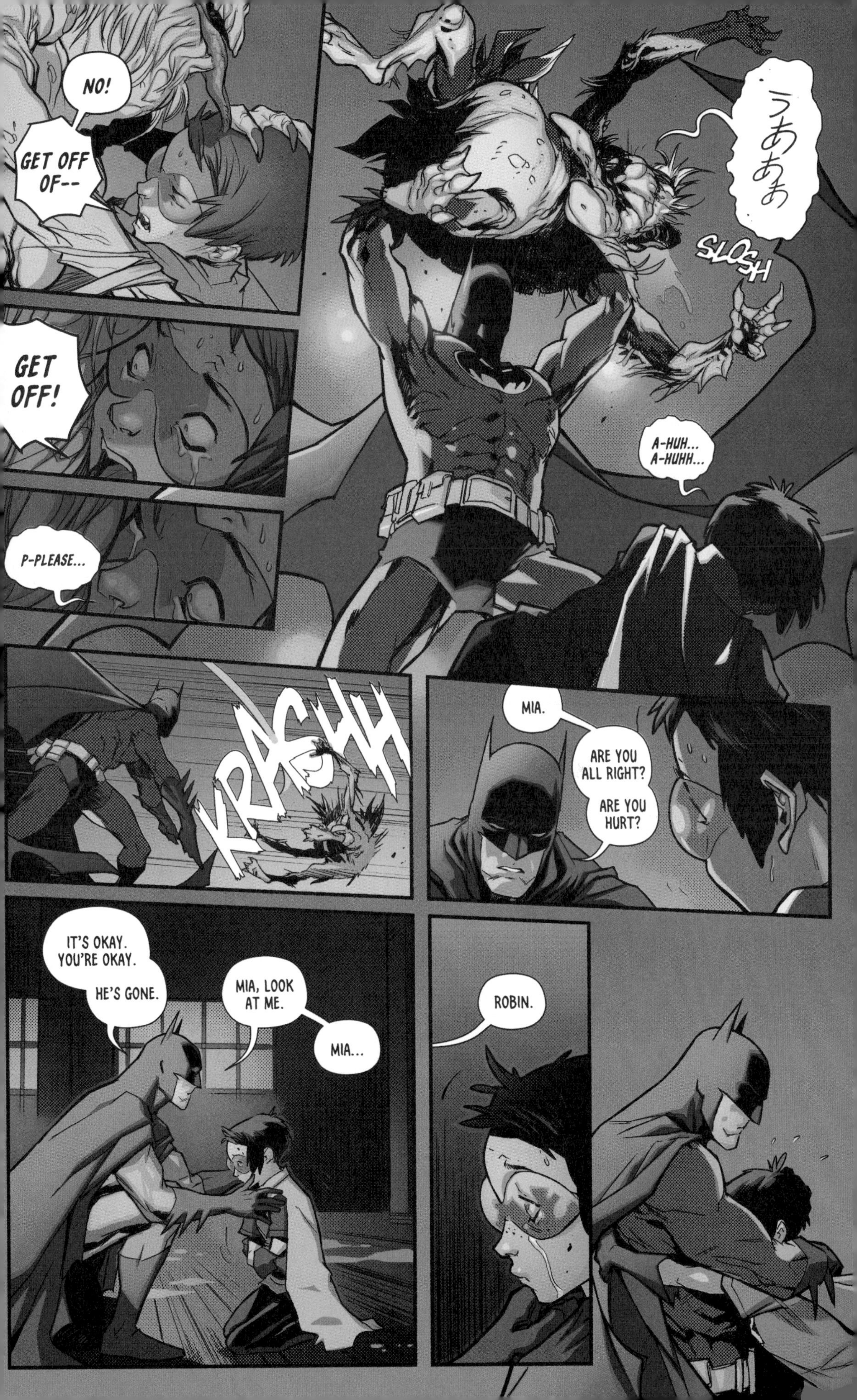
NO!
GET OFF OF--
うあああ
SLOSH
GET OFF!
A-HUH... A-HUHH...
P-PLEASE...
KRASHH
MIA.
ARE YOU ALL RIGHT?
ARE YOU HURT?
IT'S OKAY. YOU'RE OKAY.
HE'S GONE.
MIA, LOOK AT ME.
MIA...
ROBIN.

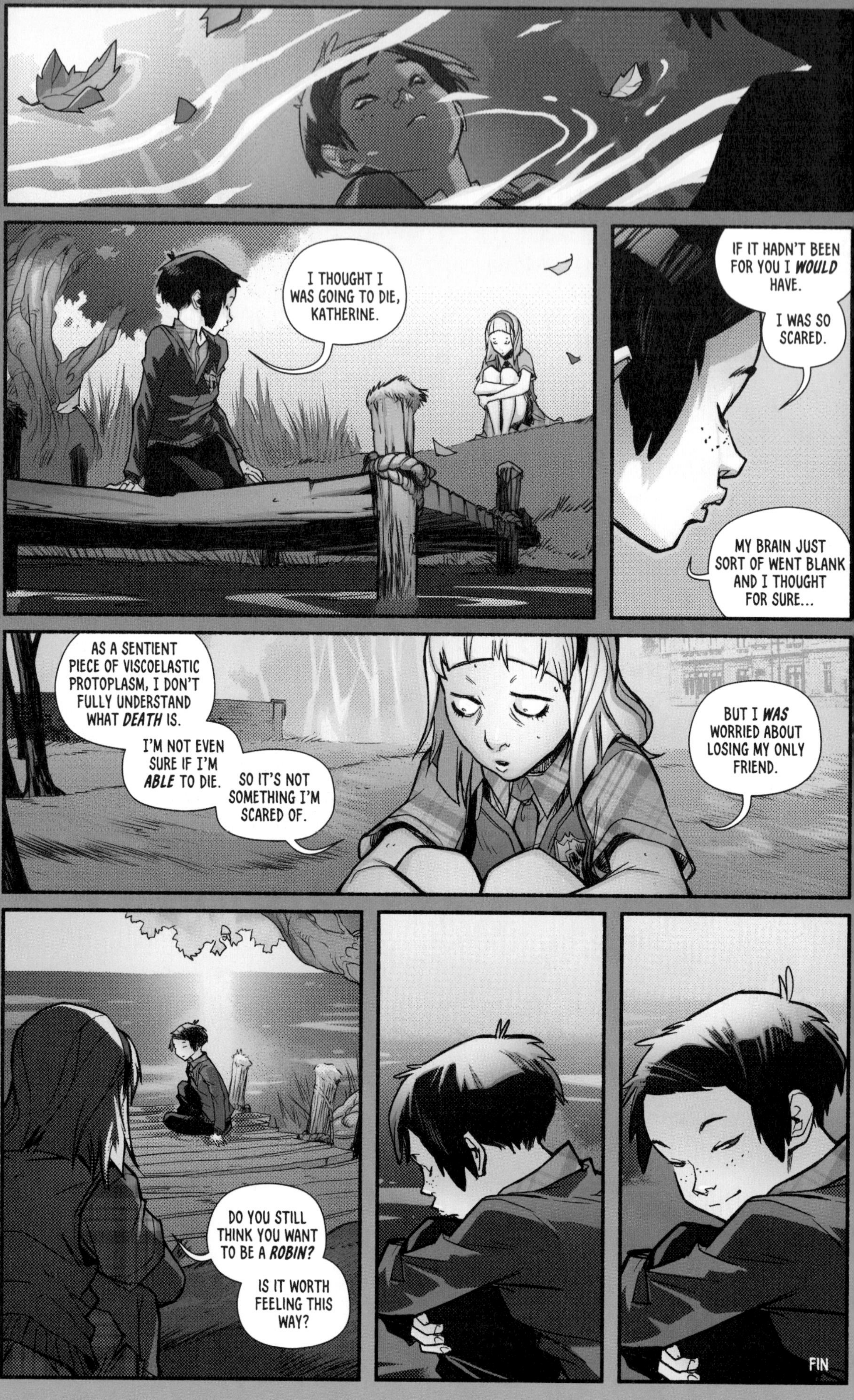
I THOUGHT I WAS GOING TO DIE, KATHERINE.
IF IT HADN'T BEEN FOR YOU I *WOULD* HAVE.
I WAS SO SCARED.
MY BRAIN JUST SORT OF WENT BLANK AND I THOUGHT FOR SURE...
AS A SENTIENT PIECE OF VISCOELASTIC PROTOPLASM, I DON'T FULLY UNDERSTAND WHAT *DEATH* IS.
I'M NOT EVEN SURE IF I'M *ABLE* TO DIE.
SO IT'S NOT SOMETHING I'M SCARED OF.
BUT I *WAS* WORRIED ABOUT LOSING MY ONLY FRIEND.
DO YOU STILL THINK YOU WANT TO BE A *ROBIN?*
IS IT WORTH FEELING THIS WAY?
FIN

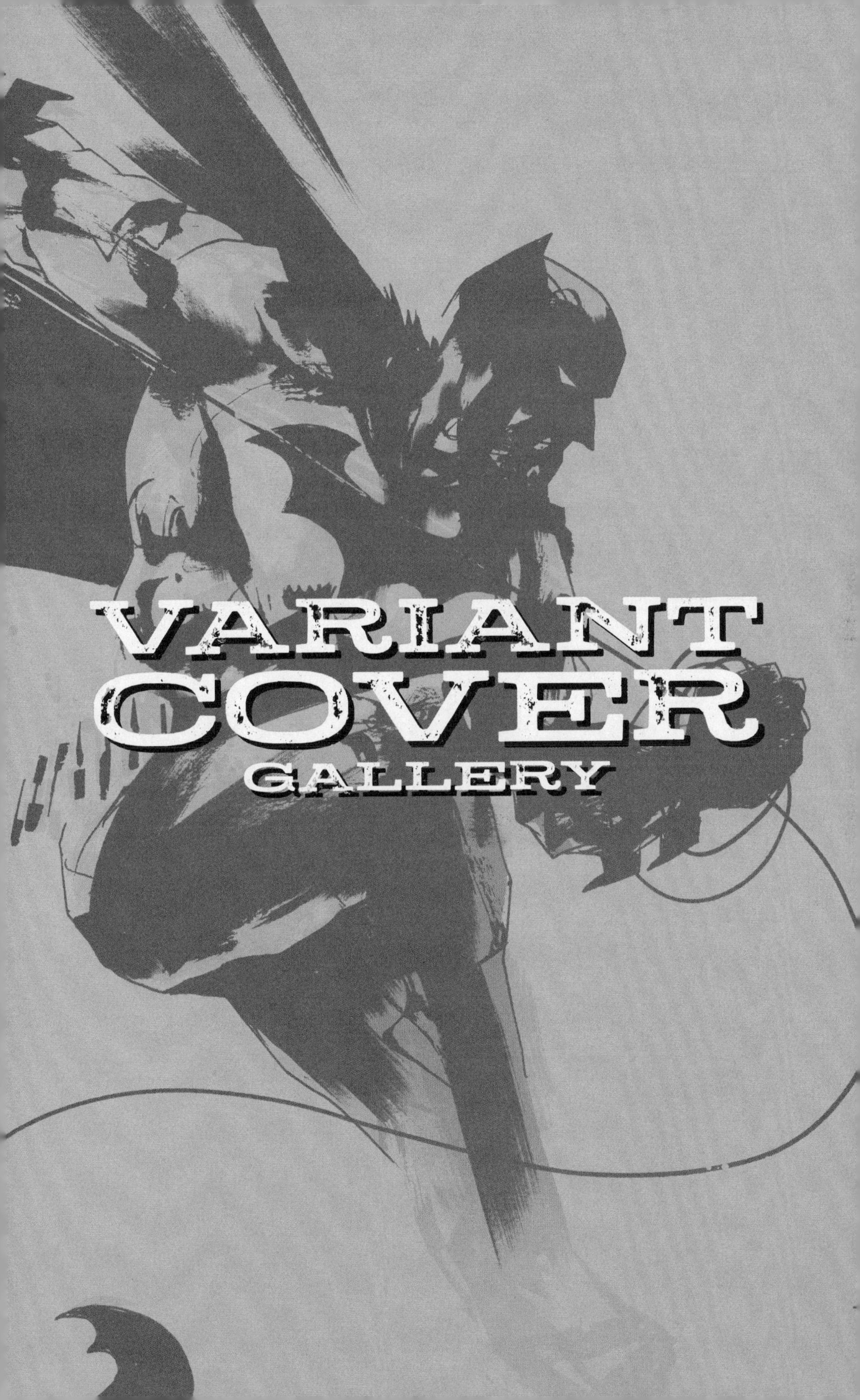

VARIANT COVER GALLERY

Batman #118 Variant Cover by Francesco Mattina

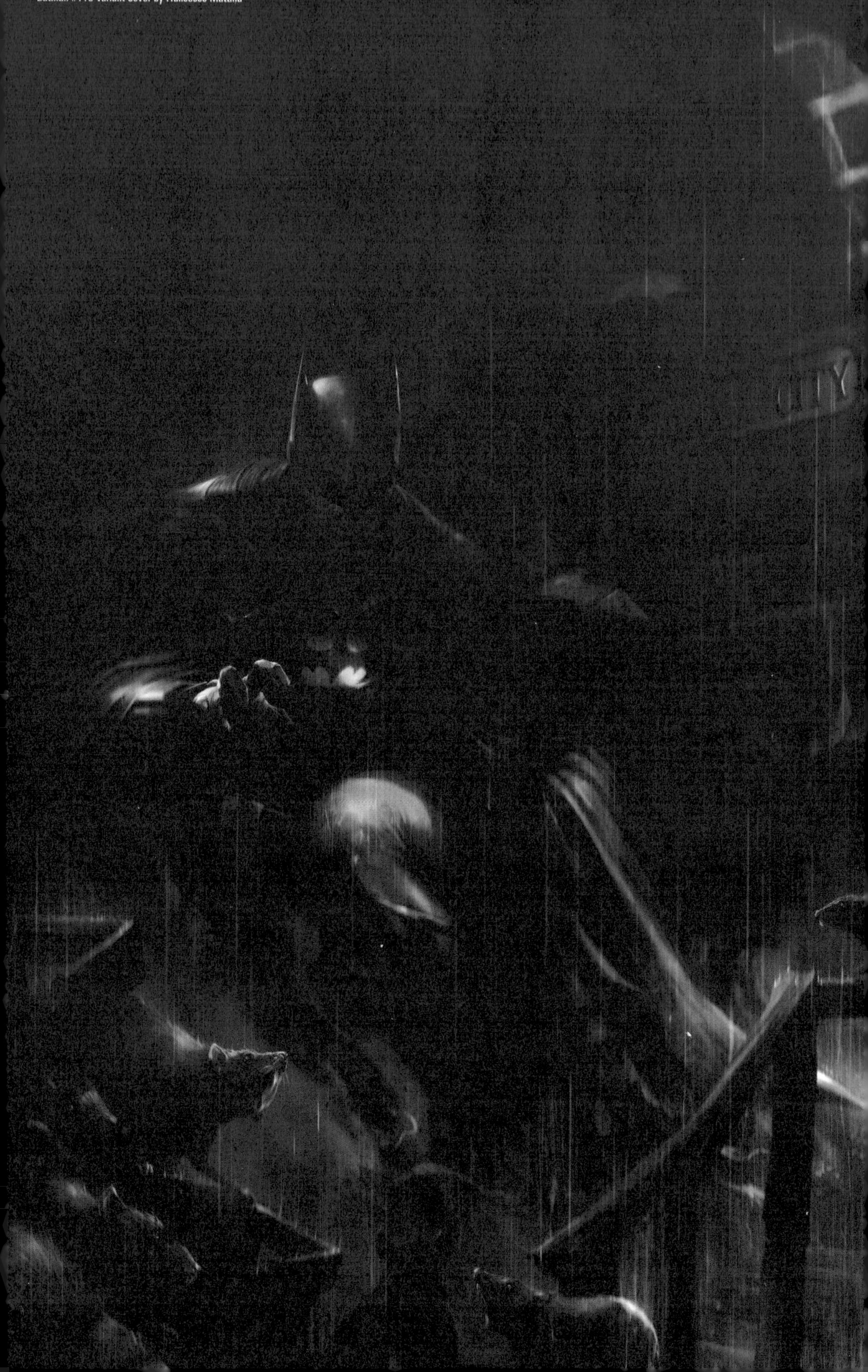

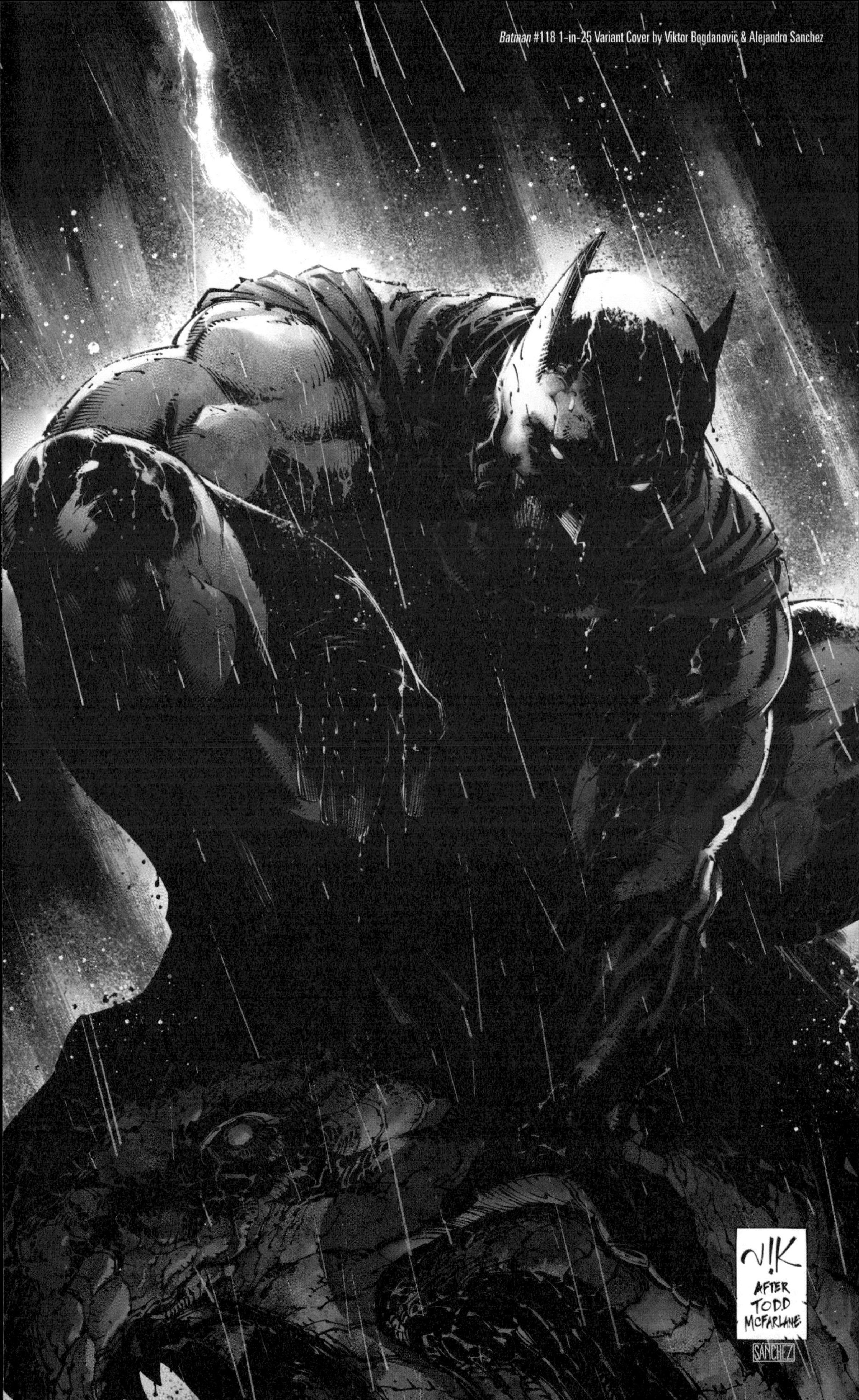
V!K
AFTER TODD McFARLANE
SÁNCHEZ
Batman #118 1-in-25 Variant Cover by Viktor Bogdanovic & Alejandro Sanchez

Batman #118 1-in-50 Variant Cover by Jock

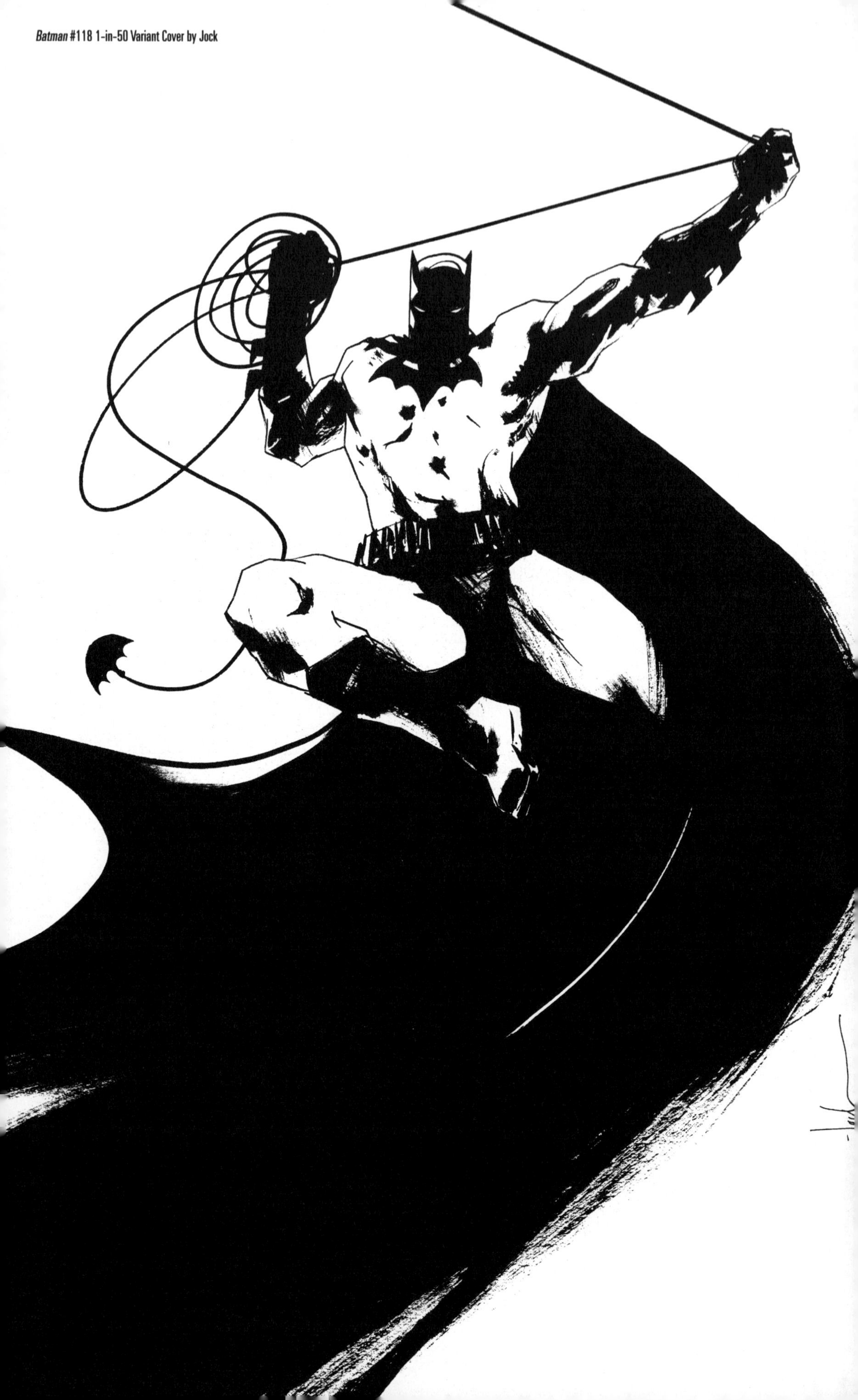

Batman #119 Variant Cover by Francesco Mattina

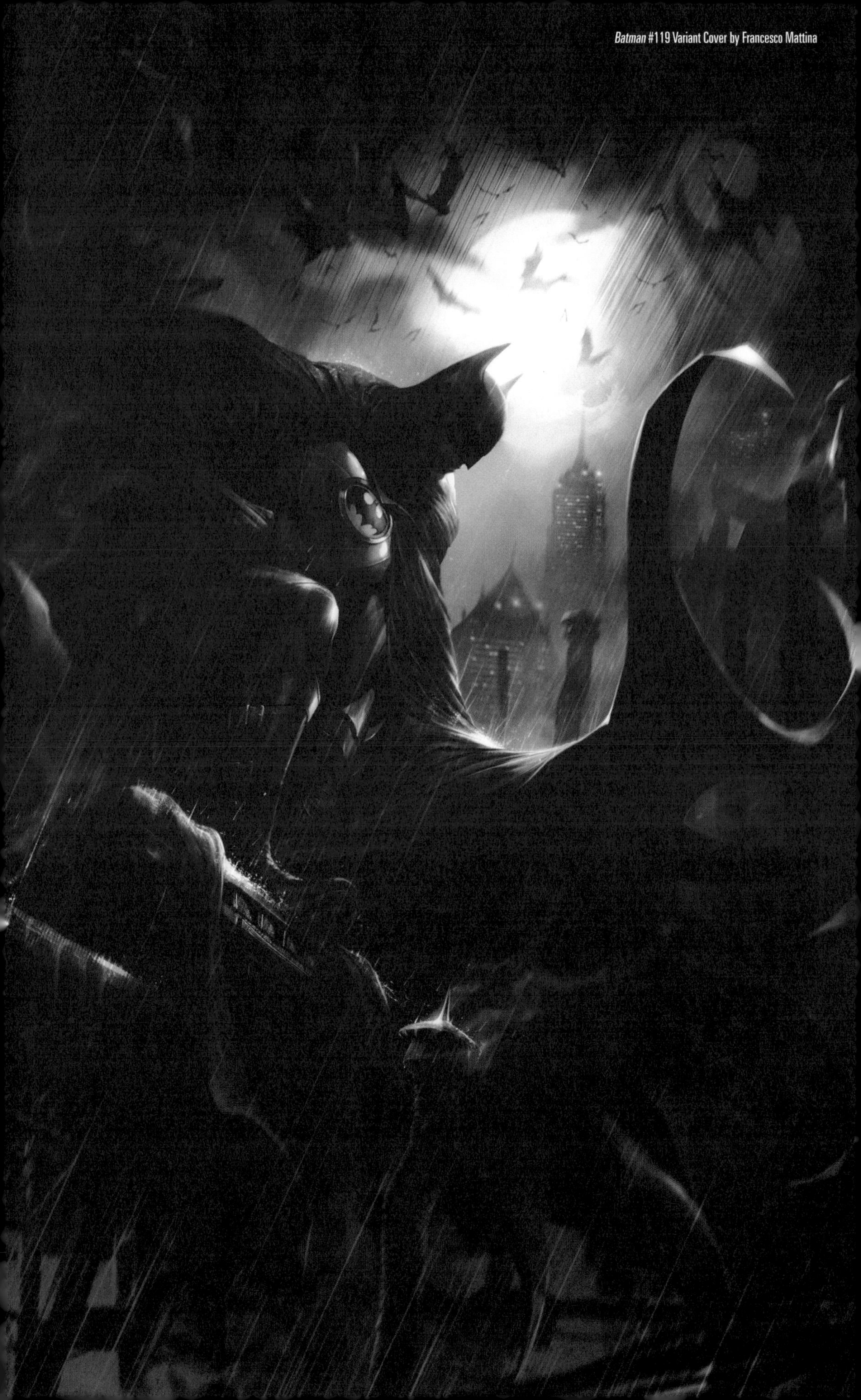

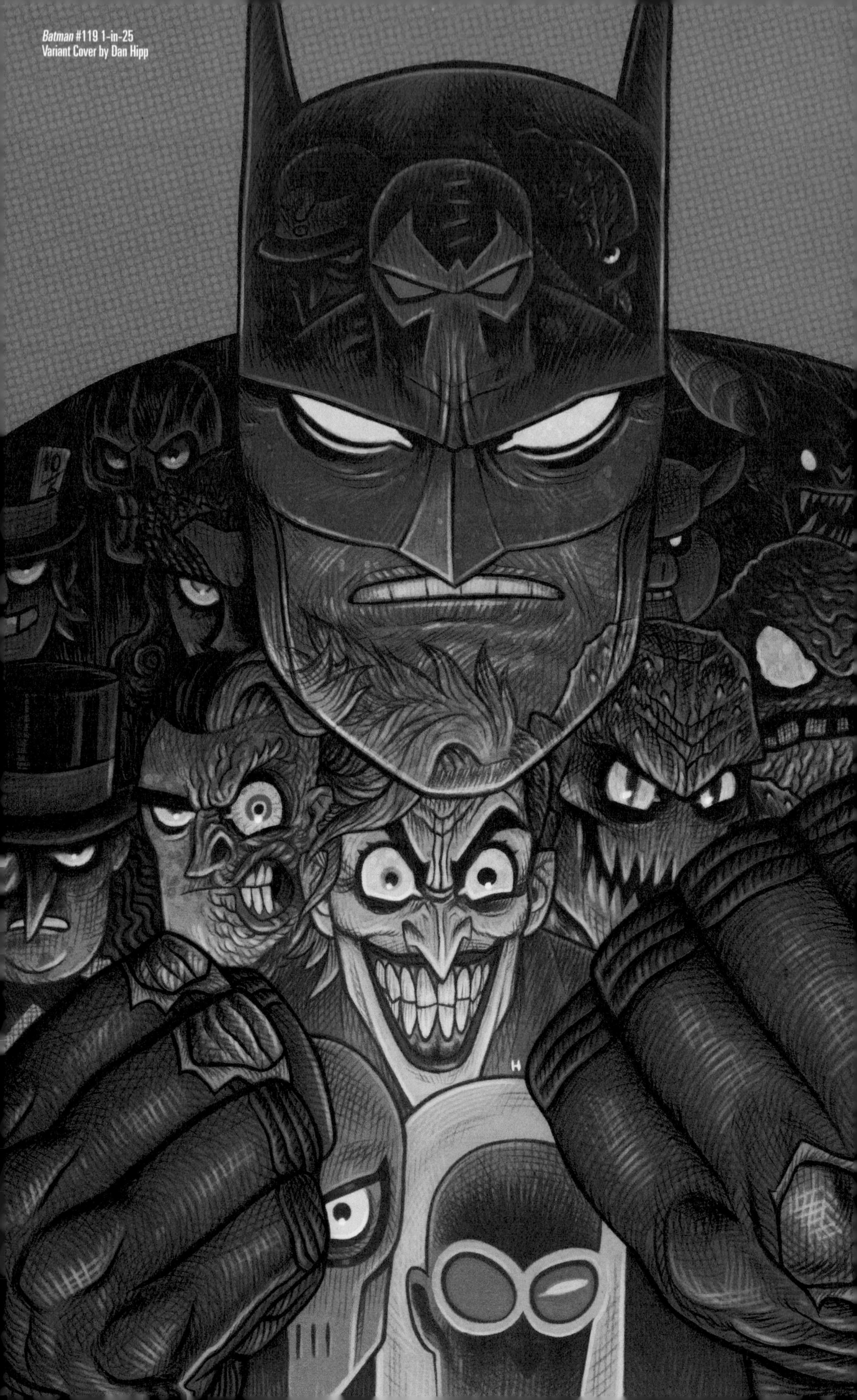

Batman #119 1-in-25
Variant Cover by Dan Hipp

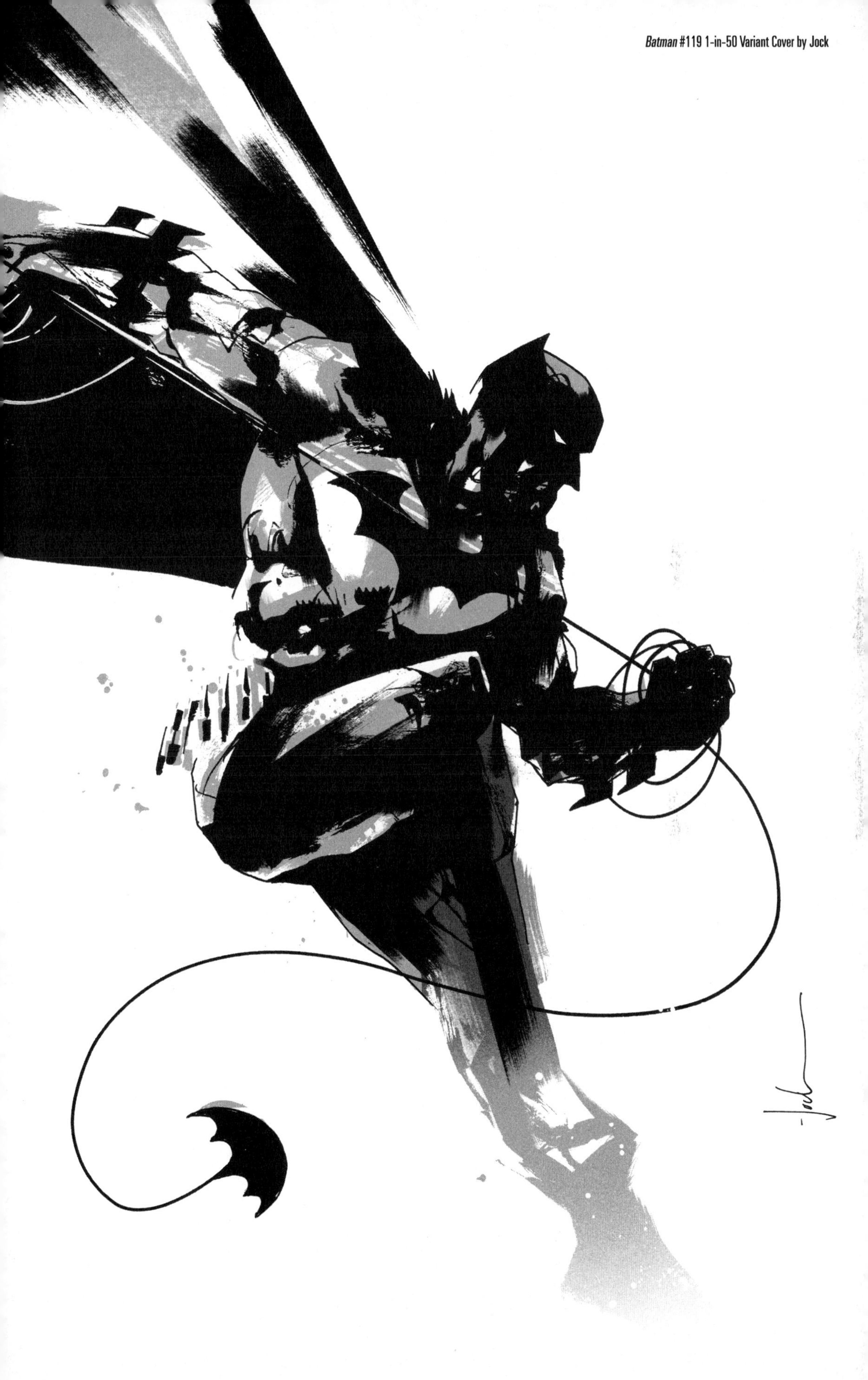

Batman #119 1-in-50 Variant Cover by Jock

Batman #120 Variant Cover by Francesco Mattina

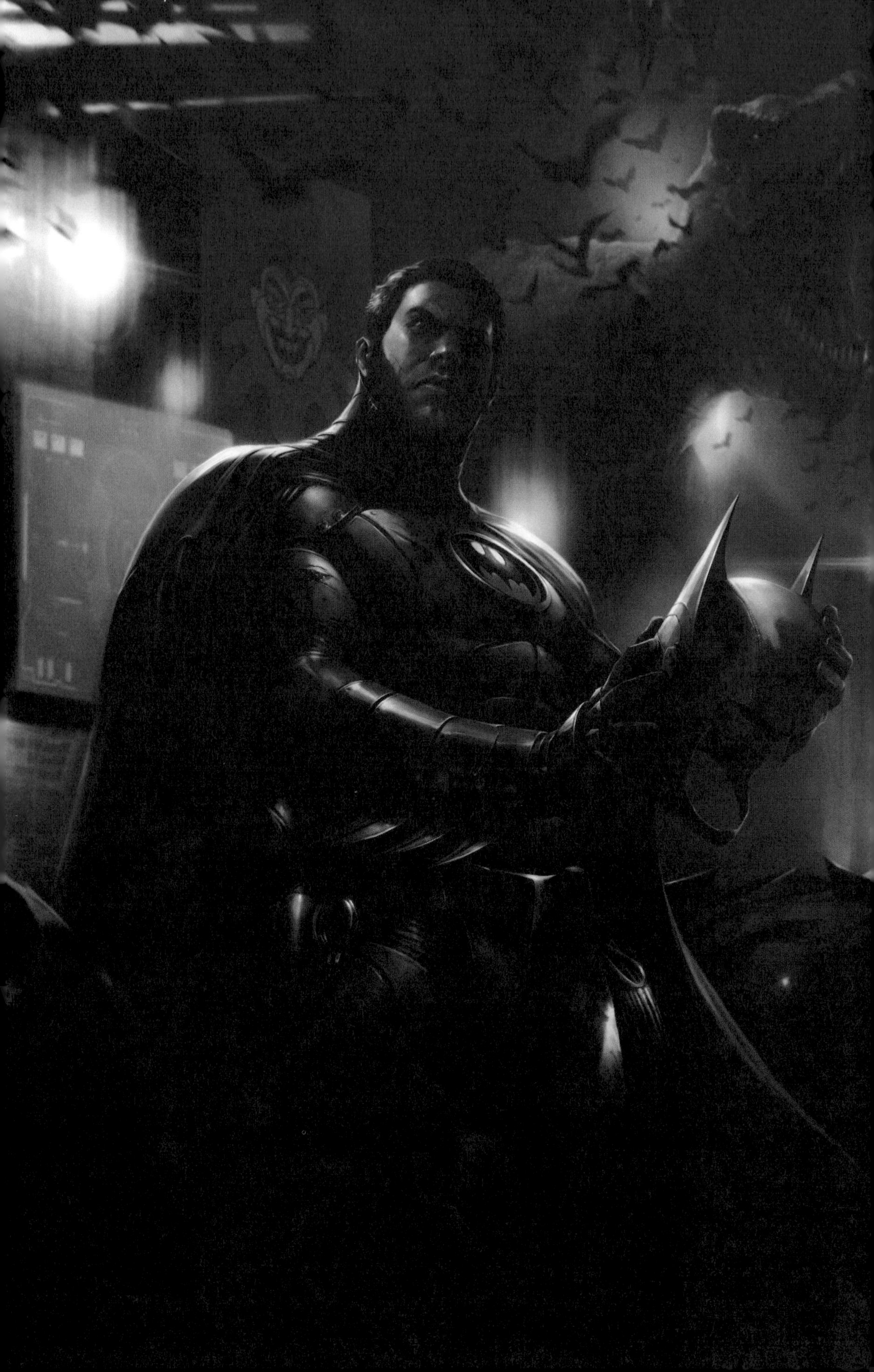

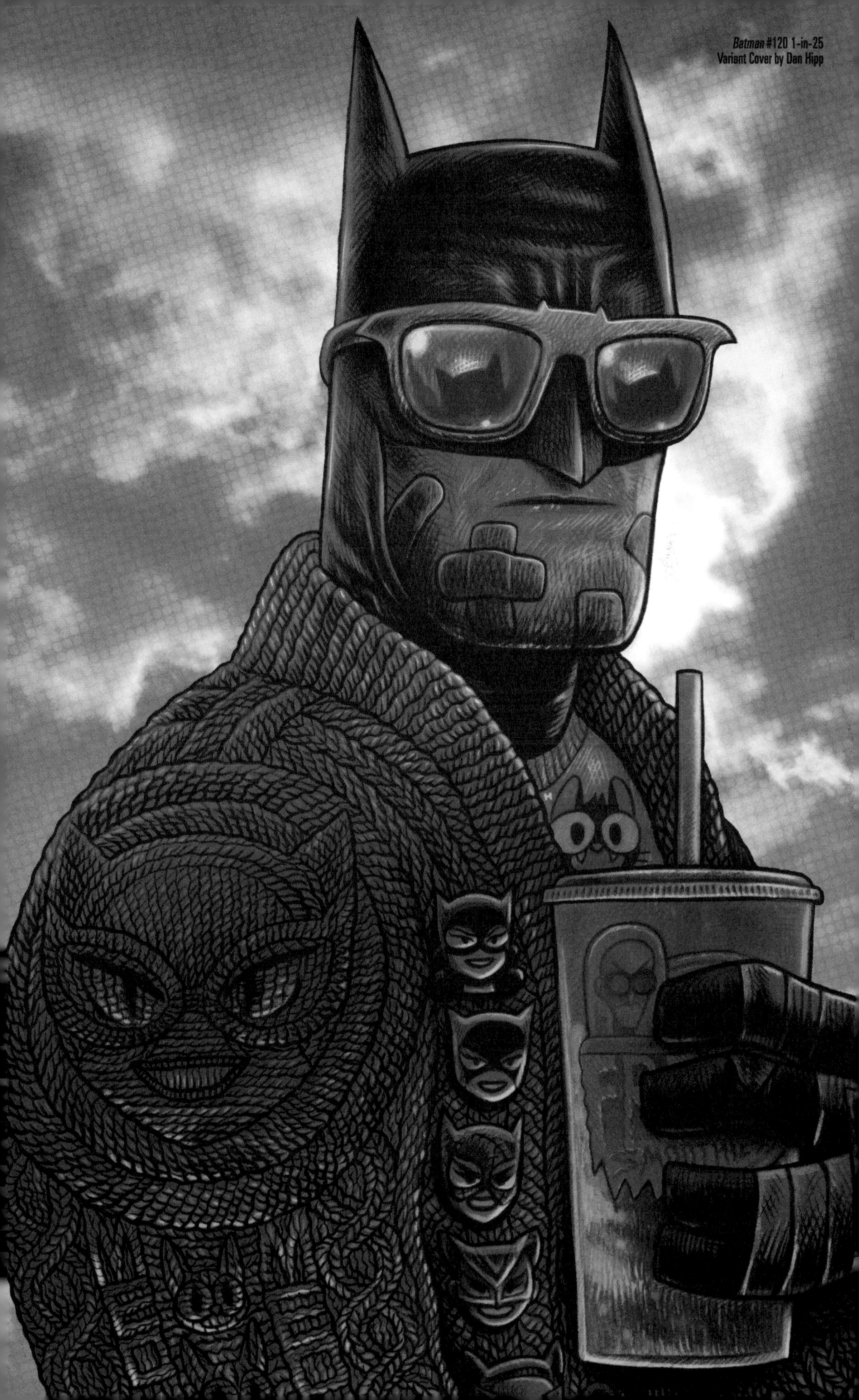

Batman #120 1-in-25
Variant Cover by Dan Hipp

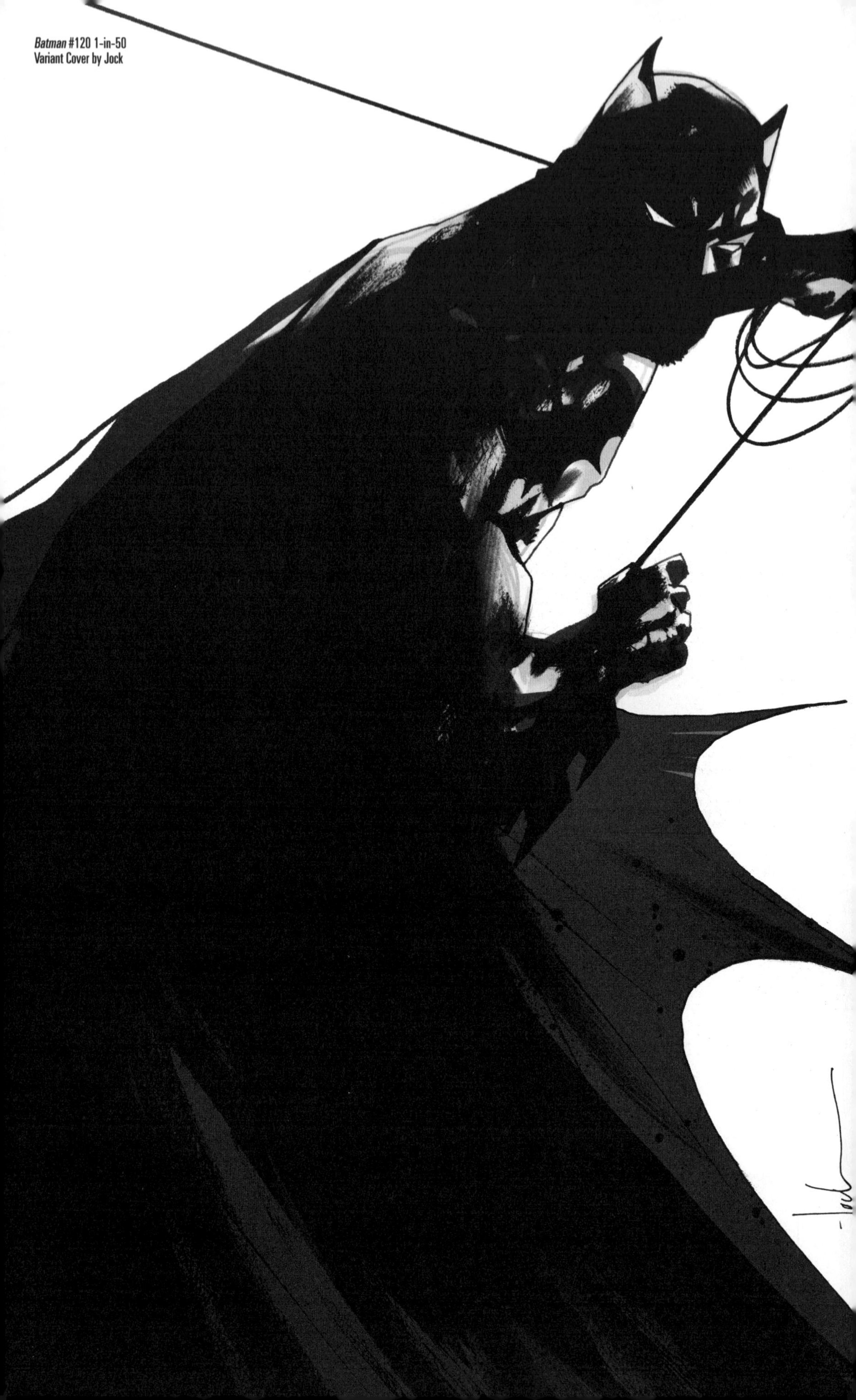

Batman #120 1-in-50
Variant Cover by Jock

Batman #121 Variant Cover by Francesco Mattina

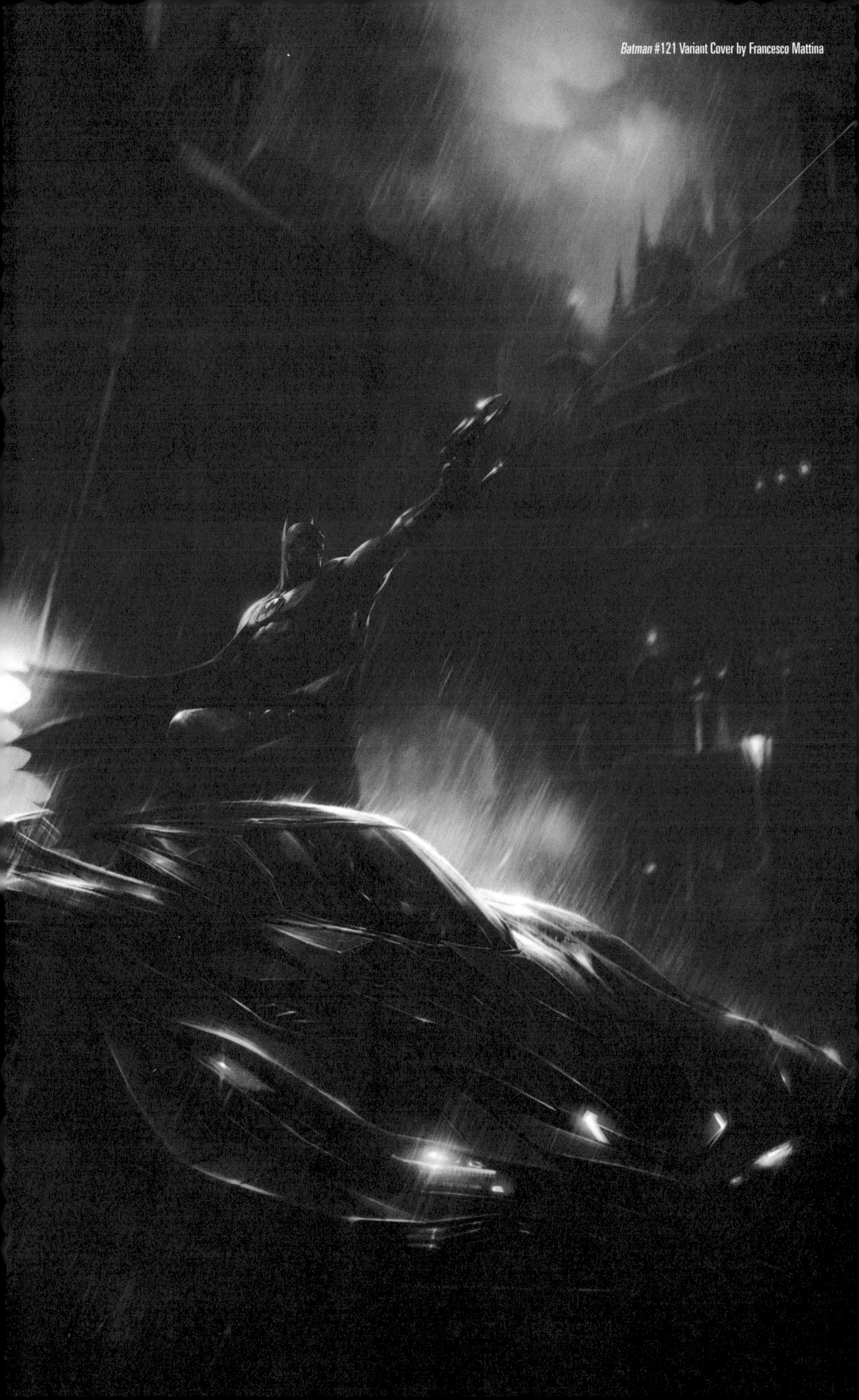

Batman #121 Variant Cover by Jay Anacleto & Rex Lokus

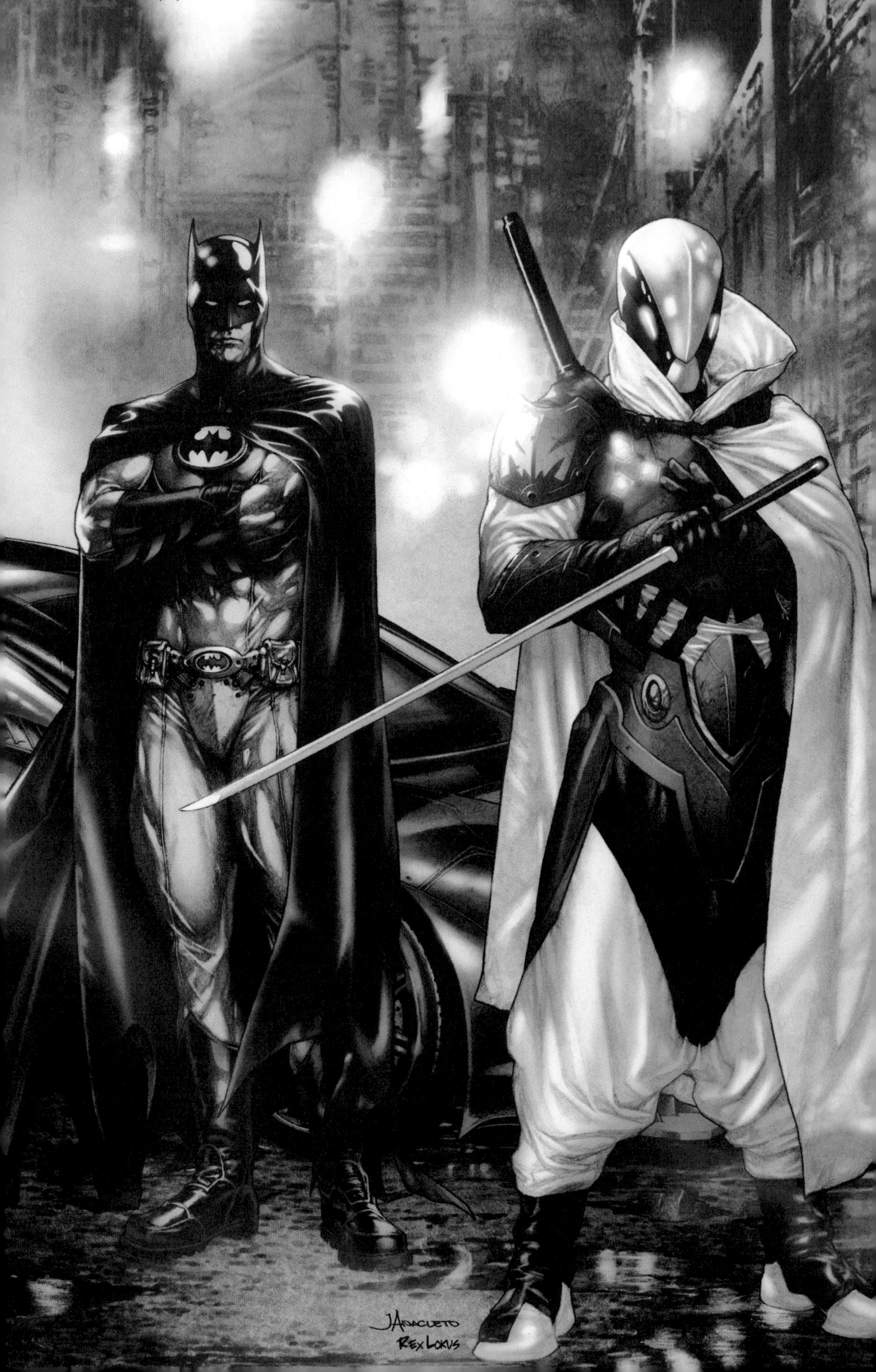
JAnacleto
Rex Lokus

Batman #121 1-in-50 Variant Cover by Jock

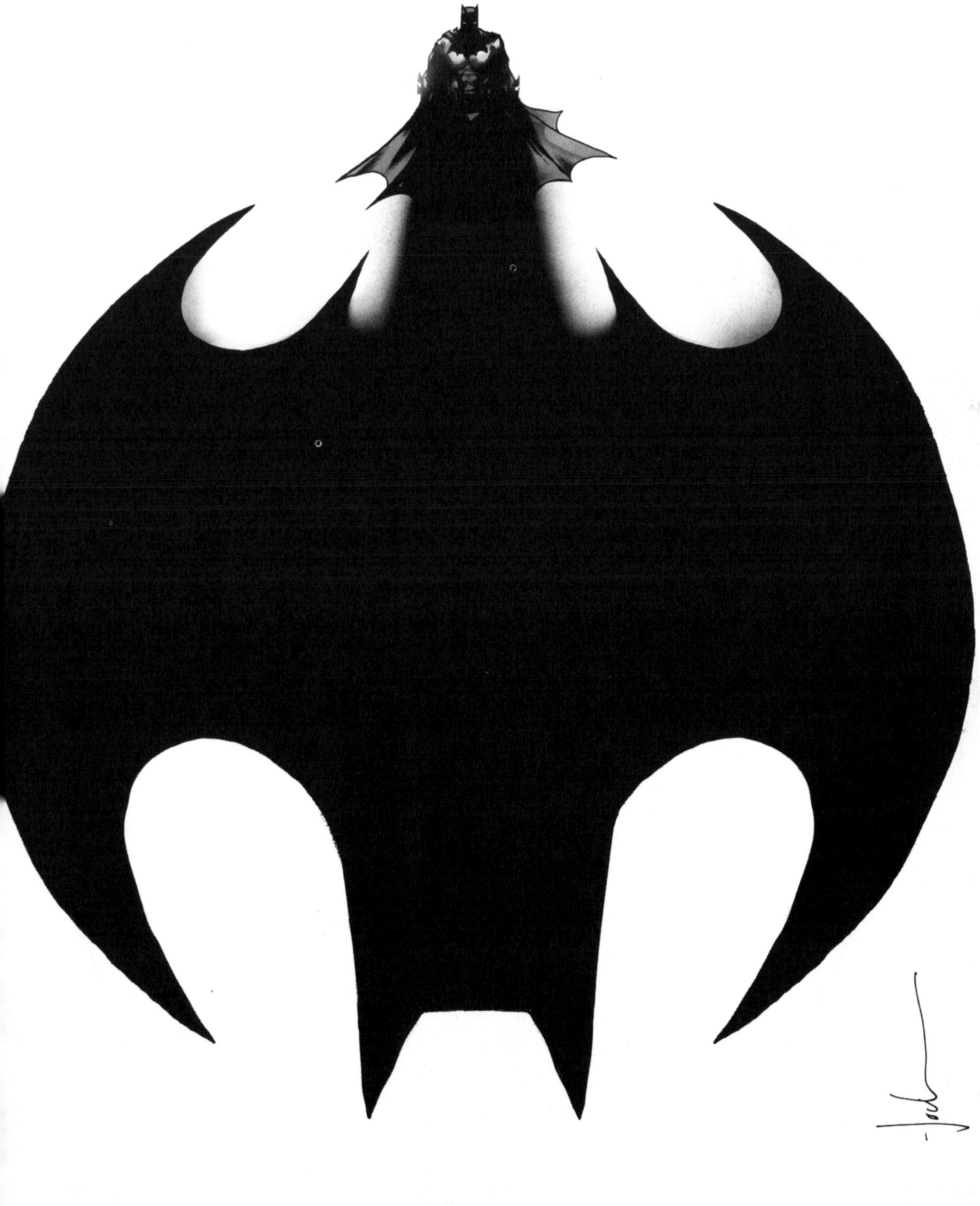

Batman #124 Variant Cover by Gabriele Dell'Otto

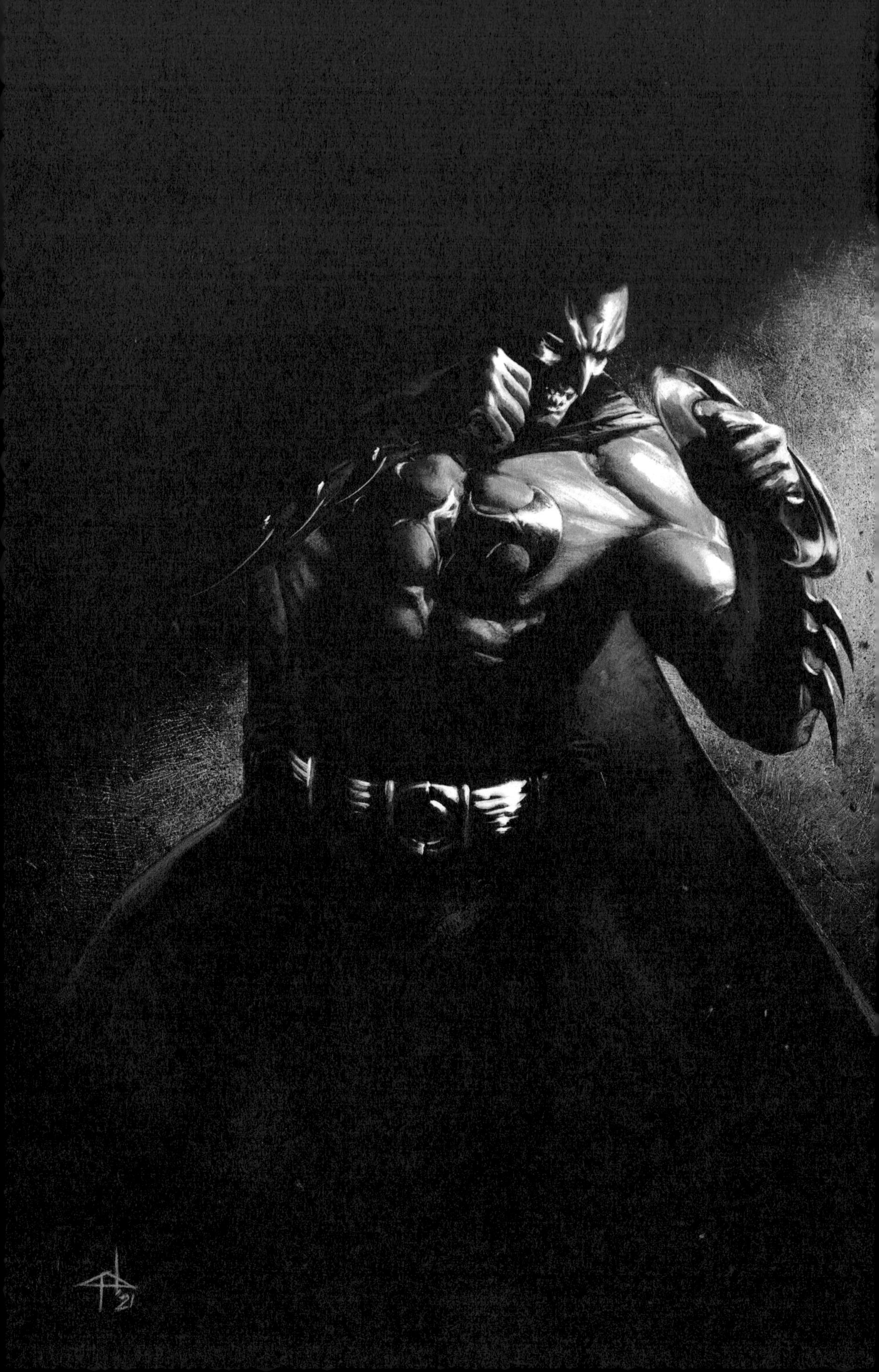

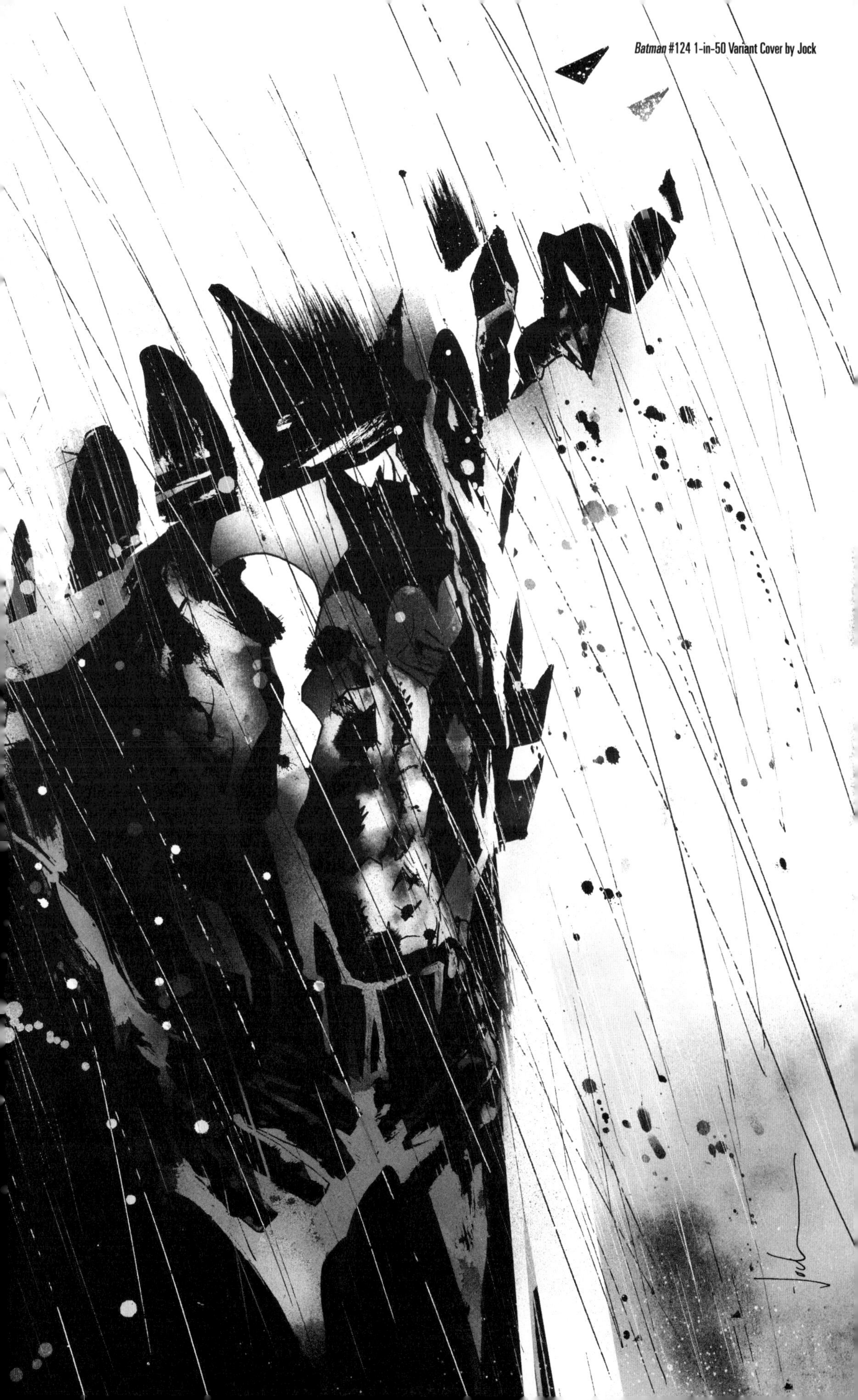

Batman #124 1-in-50 Variant Cover by Jock

BATMAN
VOL. 1: I AM GOTHAM
TOM KING
DAVID FINCH

VOL.1 I AM GOTHAM
TOM KING • DAVID FINCH

**BATMAN: VOL. 2
I AM SUICIDE**

**BATMAN: VOL. 3:
I AM BANE**

Get more DC graphic novels wherever comics and books are sold!

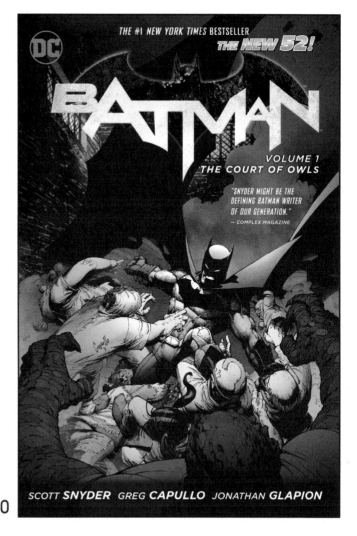

"[Writer Scott Snyder] pulls from the oldest aspects of the Batman myth, combines it with sinister-comic elements from the series' best period, and gives the whole thing terrific forward-spin."
– ENTERTAINMENT WEEKLY

START AT THE BEGINNING!

BATMAN
VOL. 1: THE COURT OF OWLS
SCOTT SNYDER with GREG CAPULLO

BATMAN VOL. 2:
THE CITY OF OWLS

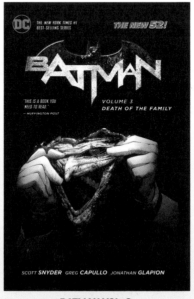

BATMAN VOL. 3:
DEATH OF THE FAMILY

READ THE ENTIRE EPIC!

BATMAN VOL. 4:
ZERO YEAR – SECRET CITY

BATMAN VOL. 5:
ZERO YEAR – DARK CITY

BATMAN VOL. 6:
GRAVEYARD SHIFT

BATMAN VOL. 7:
ENDGAME

BATMAN VOL. 8:
SUPERHEAVY

BATMAN VOL. 9:
BLOOM

BATMAN VOL. 10:
EPILOGUE

"This is the work of two men at the top
of their games."
–THE NEW YORK TIMES

"Where nightmares and reality collide."
–THE WASHINGTON POST

"The Batman of your wildest nightmares."
–POLYGON

DARK NIGHTS:
METAL
SCOTT SNYDER
GREG CAPULLO

**DARK DAYS:
THE ROAD TO METAL**

**DARK NIGHTS: METAL:
DARK KNIGHTS RISING**

**DARK NIGHTS: METAL:
THE RESISTANCE**

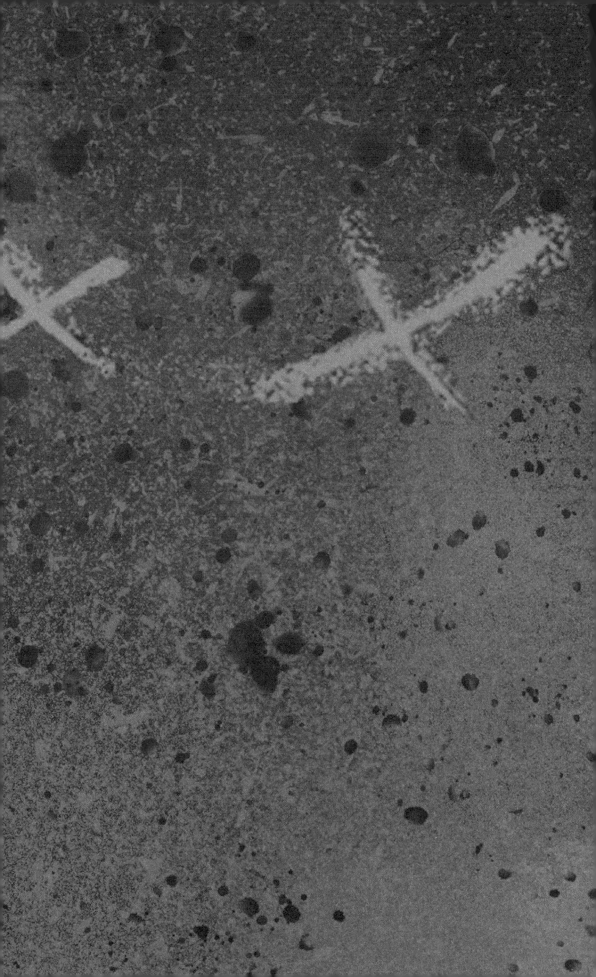

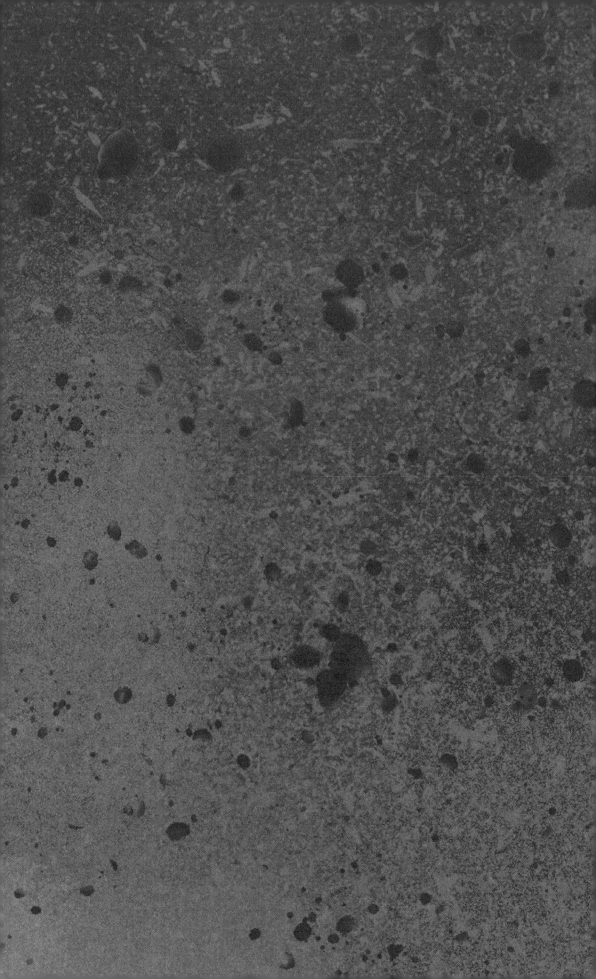